Skill Development for International Competitiveness

Skill Development for International Competitiveness

Edited by

Martin Godfrey

*Former Fellow of the Institute of Development Studies,
University of Sussex, UK*

Edward Elgar
Cheltenham, UK • Brookfield, US

Published by
Edward Elgar Publishing Limited
8 Lansdown Place
Cheltenham
Glos GL50 2HU
UK

Edward Elgar Publishing Company
Old Post Road
Brookfield
Vermont 05036
US

A catalogue record for this book is available from the British Library

Library of Congress Cataloguing in Publication Data
Skill development for international competitiveness / edited by Martin
    Godfrey
        Includes index.
        1. Labor supply—Effect of education on.   2. Labor supply—Effect
of education on—Case studies.   3. Economic development—Effect of
education on.   4. International division of labor.   I. Godfrey,
Martin.
    HD5707.S538   1997
    331'.11'422—dc21   96–48953
                                                                                          CIP

ISBN 1 85898 551 X

Typeset by Manton Typesetters, 5–7 Eastfield Road, Louth, Lincolnshire LN11 7AJ, UK
Printed and bound in Great Britain by Biddles Limited, Guildford and King's Lynn

Contents

PART IV STRUCTURAL ADJUSTMENT

PART V THE VIEW FROM THE ENTERPRISE

Figures

Tables

Contributors

Jere R. Behrman is the William R. Kenan, Jr., Professor of Economics at the University of Pennsylvania, Philadelphia, USA

Kersti Berge is a former Research Officer at the Institute of Development Studies at the University of Sussex, UK, now a Research Student at the Finance and Trade Policy Research Centre, Queen Elizabeth House, Oxford, UK.

Robert Cassen is Professor of the Economics of Development at the International Development Centre, Queen Elizabeth House, and Fellow of St. Antony's College, Oxford University, UK.

Cheah Hock Beng is a former graduate student at the Institute of Development Studies, now a Senior Lecturer in the School of Economics and Management, University College, University of New South Wales, Australia.

Chris Edwards is a Senior Lecturer in the School of Development Studies, University of East Anglia, Norwich, UK.

Martin Godfrey is a former Fellow of the Institute of Development Studies at the University of Sussex, UK, now working as a freelance researcher/ consultant.

John Humphrey is a Fellow of the Institute of Development Studies at the University of Sussex, UK.

Sanjaya Lall is the Sir John Bremridge Director of the Centre for Asian Economy, Politics and Society (Asian Centre) at the London School of Economics and Political Science, UK.

Robert E.B. Lucas is a Professor of Economics at Boston University, USA

George Mavrotas is a Lecturer in Economics at Keble College, Oxford University, and University Lecturer in Development Economics at the School of Economic Studies, University of Manchester, UK.

Lucy P. Nichols is a former graduate student at the Institute of Development Studies at the University of Sussex, UK, now working as a private development consultant, primarily for the Inter-American Development Bank and the World Bank.

Ganeshan Wignaraja is a Senior Economics Officer in the Economic Affairs Division of the Commonwealth Secretariat, London, UK.

Adrian Wood is a Fellow of the Institute of Development Studies at the University of Sussex, UK.

Foreword

This book had its origin in a workshop held at the Institute of Development Studies at the University of Sussex in March 1994, at which the possibility of a research project on this topic was explored. Early drafts of what eventually became Chapters 2, 3, 5, 9 and 10 were discussed by Christopher Colclough, Christopher Dougherty, Raphie Kaplinsky, Walter McMahon and Nicholas Oulton, in addition to the chapter authors. In the event, the 1990s being what they are, research funding was not obtained, but it was decided to press ahead with the production of a collection of papers on the topic, and invitations were sent to the authors of the remaining chapters to fill gaps in coverage. Those who have contributed to the preparation of this book include: Penny Admiraal, who organized the workshop; Tracie Gunn and Glenis Morrison, who liaised between a wandering editor and chapter authors; Adrian Wood and Christopher Colclough, successive research managers for programme II at IDS, who encouraged its development; Katherine Henry, who has managed the search for a publisher and the subsequent preparations for publication; and Marion Huxley who reshaped the manuscripts to the appropriate format. Many have commented on individual chapters and are acknowledged therein. As always, the blame for any shortcomings attaches to none of these but to the chapter authors and, of course, the editor.

Introduction

Martin Godfrey

What skill development strategies should developing economies follow to meet the challenges in and from international market places in the twenty-first century? This question is relevant for economies of various kinds – those which have already achieved the status of newly industrialising country (NIC) and are trying to raise the technology- and skill-intensity of their manufacturing sectors; those which are striving to join the next generation of NICs; and those which are merely struggling for survival and rehabilitation. Some have suggested that economies in all these circumstances should adopt an 'activist' human resource development policy, going beyond what would occur as a result of the normal combination of public provision and private decisions. In particular, it is often argued that the success in international markets of the East Asian NICs has been due to the deliberate adoption of such human-resource-led development strategies, and that other countries seeking to change the basis of their comparative advantage from cheap labour or natural resources to technology and skill should follow their example. The chapters in this book approach this question from two angles. (1) How does skill development affect a country's international competitiveness? (2) What should a government do to develop a country's skills?

HOW DOES SKILL DEVELOPMENT AFFECT A COUNTRY'S INTERNATIONAL COMPETITIVENESS?

The first question is addressed within two broad theoretical frameworks, growth models and international trade theory.

Growth Theory

Behrman, in Chapter 1, shows how current discussions of endogenous growth can be traced back to the neoclassical *growth models* of forty years ago. The 'new neoclassical growth models' have added the concepts of increasing returns, externalities and public goods, and have thus revolutionized the models' predictions. If human resource development gives rise to external benefits (implying that social gains exceed private gains); if there are increasing returns to the use of more skilled workers in certain sectors (in the sense that marginal costs decline as output and such employment increase); or if knowledge (in the production and dissemination of which human resources are critical) is a public good, the use of which by one individual does not reduce its use by others: in all these cases, an activist human resource development policy could be justified.

For instance, Romer's assumptions, that new knowledge is produced with diminishing returns, that there is a positive externality in knowledge production, that there are increasing returns in production of consumer goods (which is a function of the stock of knowledge and of other inputs), and that the marginal productivity of the stock of knowledge increases rather than diminishes as that stock grows, ensure that there is no necessary tendency towards convergence of different countries' levels of output per head (Romer 1986, 1989, 1993, 1994). More important for our purposes, these assumptions open up the possibility of boundless growth of knowledge and of output per head, with no necessary tendency for the rate of return on capital to fall as its stock increases, and they give a central role to skills in the development process. As Behrman notes, this suggests 'that active policy to favour human resource investment may have a social payoff because of the externalities and increasing returns associated with such investments'.

Similarly, Lucas (1988, 1990, 1993) adds to the neoclassical model the assumptions that a worker's productivity is affected not only by his/her own skill level but also by the average level of human capital in his/her country, and that rates of learning by doing vary between sectors. This is consistent with differences in levels of income and rates of growth between countries, and suggests the possibility of changing a country's comparative advantage by deliberately fostering sectors in which learning-by-doing externalities are relatively large. These and similar models, discussed by Behrman, give powerful theoretical backing to those who argue for an activist human resource development policy. However, they have been subject to very limited systematic empirical testing.

Trade Theory

The second framework within which this question is addressed is that of *international trade theory*. As Lewis pointed out in 1954, the law of comparative costs predicts that 'those countries which have inadequate agricultural resources in relation to their populations (e.g. India, Japan, Egypt, Great Britain, Jamaica) must live by importing agricultural products and exporting manufactures; metal manufactures if they have the coal and ores (India, Great

Britain) and light manufactures if they have not (Japan, Egypt, Jamaica)'. (1954: pp. 180.

Wood (1994, and with Berge in Chapter 2) takes this further, using a Heckscher–Ohlin framework, in which the factors of production are simply human resources and natural resources. He divides the labour force into three skill categories: (1) those with no (or almost no) schooling (labelled NO-ED); (2) those with a basic general education – complete primary or lower secondary – but no more (BAS-ED); and (3) those with substantial post-basic education and training – professional and technical workers with advanced qualifications, experienced managers, and manual craftsmen who have been through an apprenticeship or other extended training (SKILD). A country's comparative advantage as between manufactures and primary products is determined by its relative endowments of skill and land. Within manufacturing its comparative advantage is determined by its relative supplies of SKILD and BAS-ED labour. Thus, as a country transforms its labour force from one that consists mainly of NO-EDs to one that consists mainly of SKILD workers, it moves both from primary exports to manufactures and from labour-intensive to skill-intensive manufactures.

Godfrey, in Chapter 3, uses a related framework, derived from Lewis (1954), in which a rise in the real product wage of unskilled labour (BAS-ED in Wood's terms) and a narrowing of wage differentials between more- and less-qualified workers (between SKILD and BAS-ED) are necessary conditions for the transition from cheap-labour-based to skill-based competitiveness in manufacturing.

Evidence on Countries

Theoretical frameworks are one thing, empirical backing quite another. In an earlier review of evidence, Behrman (1990) examines several country case studies and cross-country analyses. He argues that studies emphasizing the role of human resources in changing Korean comparative advantage are 'primarily speculative' (p. 68), that the experience of the Philippines, Sri Lanka and Kerala (good human resources but relatively poor economic performance) are 'troublesome for those who advocate the advantages of human-resource-led development' (p. 69), that human resource development appears to follow rather than lead economic development in Thailand (p. 71), and that 'cross-country aggregate estimates often indicate weak or no impact of human resources on growth, and provide little robust evidence on externalities, public-good characteristics and increasing returns to scale' (p. 90).

In the last few years many more empirical investigations of the role of human capital formation in economic growth have been carried out. One of the most widely quoted, discussed by Cassen and Mavrotas in Chapter 5, is the World Bank's study of the East Asian miracle (World Bank 1993). Its cross-economy regressions for 113 economies (pp. 48–51) find that an increase of 10 percentage points in the primary or secondary school enrolment rates would increase the rate of growth in income per head by 0.3 percentage points. A simple 'accounting-for-growth' exercise shows that, except for Hong Kong (44 per cent), 60 per cent or more of the actual 1960–85 real per-capita growth rate in eight high-performing Asian economies (the others being Indonesia, Japan, Korea, Malaysia, Taiwan, Singapore and Thailand) is predicted by a model including investment, human capital (measured by both primary enrolment and secondary enrolment), population growth, and income relative to the US as independent variables. Primary school enrolment is by far the largest single contributor to this group of economies' predicted growth rates, accounting for between 58 per cent (Japan) and 87 per cent (Thailand) of predicted growth. Physical investment comes second (between 35 and 49 per cent), followed by secondary enrolment.

Cheah's case study of Singapore, in Chapter 4, is consistent both with the growth models and with these econometric results. He shows how the government set out to change the country's comparative advantage. The Economic Restructuring Strategy, adopted in 1979, included measures to increase the skills of the labour force. 'The number of years of schooling was to be increased and its quality improved, technical and higher education expanded, and various programmes to upgrade the skills of the workforce mounted with the support of the Skills Development Fund, financed by a tax on employers. As a result, the number of people in the workforce with tertiary-level qualifications increased at an annual average rate of 10 per cent between 1983 and 1993, while the number with only lower-primary or no qualifications declined in absolute terms. By now not only are almost all junior and middle-level supervisory posts held by nationals: so are a significant proportion of senior executive and managerial positions, even in wholly foreign-owned subsidiaries of large multinational corporations. Cheah comments that progress could have been even more impressive, had not an elitist bias against expanding tertiary education previously been sustained for too long. His overall verdict is that 'Singapore's experience demonstrates that competitiveness can be created, and not just be endowed. More specifically, this experience shows that a government can successfully promote competitiveness through skills development ... [which] has played an important part in facilitating a technological catching-up process in Singapore'. Between 1970 and 1991 human-capital-intensive and technology-intensive products (the other categories being agriculture-, mineral- and unskilled-labour-intensive) rose from 14 per cent to 54 per cent of the total value of Singapore's exports (Chapter 4, Table 4.10).

Evidence on Firms

The theme that countries can reshape their own comparative advantage is taken up by Cassen and Mavrotas (in Chapter 5) who review a number of studies of the impact of education and training on firms' ability to adopt new technology and to make other productivity advances. For instance, Japan's ability to introduce robotics and microelectronics in industry is attributed to its educational improvements of the 1970s and 1980s. They emphasize the changing character of manufacturing production and trade, which puts a premium on information and other skills for marketing, design and quality control.

This is pursued in more detail by Humphrey, in Chapter 9. He identifies three new developments in the organization of work which have implications for skill requirements: the spread of flexible automation, the reemergence of small-scale flexible production and the development of Japanese-inspired organization of work. Automation, in which routine, repetitive tasks are increasingly performed by robots and other automated machinery, shifts the balance of work towards skilled problem solvers. Flexible specialization, in contrast, requires broad skills, with production workers able to shift rapidly from one job to another. Japanese just-in-time (JIT) and total-quality-management (TQM) methods increase the range of tasks to be performed by production workers (including quality control and maintenance as well as production), who also become involved in the process of improvement on the shop floor. This implies a need for a systematic and continuous acquisition of knowledge through on-the-job learning. In some versions, as he puts it, 'training of production workers becomes a determinant of the production process rather than vice versa' and 'training requirements are defined by what workers might come to need to know in the future'.

Although these developments are more important in industrialized countries, Humphrey points out that Japanese-style methods are being used in a number of developing countries, particularly in Latin America, and that skill deficiencies are a serious problem for firms wanting to restructure in this way. Such firms complain about workers' aptitudes, basic educational standards and skills: workers have difficulty in taking responsibility and initiatives, and lack the qualities which a basic education might be expected to provide, such as the ability to concentrate, to learn new skills and to read and write, a capacity for abstraction, and verbal skills. Although these weaknesses have not prevented firms from adopting JIT and TQM methods, they raise the costs of such reorganization and increase the danger that firms will adapt their organization of work to fit the characteristics of a badly-educated labour force.

Evidence on Trade

Within the second framework for analysis of skill development for international competitiveness, that of international trade theory, the expectation that the composition of trade depends on human resources is strongly confirmed by some of the evidence in Wood (1994). In one of his submodels, the ratio of a country's exports of manufactures to its exports of primary products is determined simply by the ratio of its skill per worker (average years of schooling) to its land per worker (total land area divided by adult population). This hypothesis is consistent with cross-section data from 114 countries. It yields a scatter diagram (of export composition against ratio of human to natural resources) close to a straight line, and explains a surprisingly high proportion of variance. A second submodel, postulating that the skill composition of a country's manufactured exports depends on its ratio of SKILD to BAS-ED labour, does not work so well. The results suggest that the relationship exists, but the fit is poor, which could be due to problems in measuring both the dependent and the independent variables.

When the model is extended, in Chapter 2 of this book (by Berge and Wood), to distinguish between female and male workers (the hypothesis being that *female* education is important for exporting manufactures), measurement problems again arise. Cross-country collinearity between the overall level of education and the relative educational position of women makes it difficult to isolate the effect of the latter on either the manufactured-to-primary export ratio or the skill composition of manufactured exports. When demand-side influences on the labour market are controlled for, a comparative advantage in manufactured goods for countries which have more educated females does emerge, but the results are surprisingly weak, given previous case-study evidence that educated female workers comprise most of the workforce in labour-intensive manufacturing for export. The new statistical results thus raise some doubts about the underlying assumption of female intensity of manufactured exports: this may vary across countries and may be less than case studies (mainly of export-processing zones) suggest. The authors recommend, therefore, that future research should focus on evidence at a level intermediate between micro case studies and cross-country regressions, and in particular on country studies.

Evidence on Adjustment

One such country study is Nichols's econometric analysis of Costa Rica, in Chapter 8. She hypothesizes that a country's capacity to adjust structurally, expanding production of tradables relative to non-tradables, of exportables relative to import substitutes, and of non-traditional relative to traditional exports, varies directly with the quality of human resources. Better-educated workers provide the flexibility needed to switch production between sectors and branches, and so to restore external balance through innovation, retraining and relocation. Supply elasticities are higher, and workers have a greater capacity to learn and innovate. This favours the expansion not only of more competitive branches of manufacturing but also of exotic agriculture and services such as tourism. She tests the hypothesis against national household survey data between 1980 and 1989, and finds that the sectors that expanded their employment most in that period had a higher proportion of well-educated workers than did those which contracted or expanded less. This result holds up even when differences between sectors in average hourly earnings and in trade status (traditional exportable, non-traditional exportable, importable and non-traded) are controlled for. Thus this study supports the conclusions of Chapter 4 (Cheah on Singapore) and Chapter 5 (the literature review by Cassen and Mavrotas) on the importance of skills in adapting technology, and of Chapter 9 (Humphrey on Latin America) on the importance of skills in adapting to new process and product requirements. An unexpected result of Nichols's study is that female education is negatively associated with sectoral expansion. In this case, the problem is not econometric (as it was in that of Berge and Wood) but institutional: two of the four sectors into which female workers are clustered are social services, which has high average educational levels but contracted, and personal services, which has low average educational levels but expanded.

The hypothesis tested in Costa Rica also receives powerful backing in Chapter 10, by Lall and Wignaraja, on Ghana. They show what happens in an economy that attempts to adjust structurally *without* having built an adequate skill base. They describe industry's weak supply response to the usual 'get-prices-right' structural adjustment programme, and attribute it to the low level of technological capability of Ghanaian enterprises. In contrast to the neoclassical approach to adjustment (which assumes efficient markets and freely-available technology, costlessly and instantly absorbed) their technological-capabilities approach emphasizes that an economy's competitiveness depends on how individual firms manage the process of technological and managerial development. They find that, since adjustment started in 1983, competition from imports has curbed manufacturing growth and led to a big fall in employment. The adverse impact has been strongest in the most modern large-scale sector. Indeed, only enterprises with 'natural' protection survive. Manufacturing export growth has been disappointing, with no diversification or entry of new firms. The necessary managerial and technical skills are lacking: the typical locally-owned firm has an entrepreneur with little education, a poorly-skilled workforce, and no way of raising its technological capabilities. In this situation, 'rapid liberalization, unaccompanied by supply-side measures to develop skills, capabilities and technical support, have led to significant and costly deindustrialization'.

In contrast to Ghana, and as discussed by Godfrey in Chapter 3, Indonesia has emerged as a successful exporter of labour-intensive manufactured goods in recent years, and the question now arises as to whether it is ready for the transition to skill-based competitiveness. 'The experience of Korea, from 1982 to 1988, and Singapore, from 1986 to 1990, suggests that this transition involves, alongside expansion in the number of wage employees, sustained growth in value added per employee, followed, with a lag, by increases in wages. Indonesia is showing some symptoms consistent with a move into this phase, but most observers doubt that such a shortage of unskilled labour is imminent. In any case, as in Ghana, there are skill constraints. The supply of better-educated labour has been increasing and earnings differentials between the more and the less qualified have narrowed, but Indonesia is still in the category of countries with relatively low senior secondary and tertiary enrolment levels. Moreover, there are doubts (raised by assessments of schools and views of international employers) as to whether the quality, as well as the quantity, of its educated labour and of its management is yet sufficient to sustain an early transition.

Limitations of the Evidence

Behrman, in Chapter 1, cautions against putting too much faith in empirical research results of the kind described in the previous few pages. He distinguishes association between human resources and various outcomes from *causation*, about which 'we know surprisingly little'. He bases his scepticism partly on the inadequacy of the analytical frameworks used in much empirical research, partly on estimation problems (such as omitted variables, simultaneity, selectivity bias and measurement errors), and partly on difficulties with data. The latter are particularly acute in cross-country comparisons, especially of training and skill levels. Even in the case of investment in schooling, as Behrman points out, the use of enrolment rates as proxies ignores cross-country differences, in definitions of both numerator and denominator, in starting ages and durations, and in quality. In all these circumstances, it is not surprising that disputes over interpretation of results abound. Cassen and Mavrotas, for instance, in Chapter 5 of this book, refer to a comparative study of three countries with outward-oriented strategies (Korea, Thailand and Malaysia) and three countries with inward-oriented strategies (Nigeria, Egypt and Tunisia). The authors of the study (Adams, Goldfarb and Kelly 1992) argue that outward orientation encouraged more efficient human capital development, in the sense that levels of private-sector vocational education and training were higher and that the internal and external efficiency of public-sector vocational education and training more closely matched that of the private sector. But, as Cassen and Mavrotas point out, anyone who has read Berge and Wood might assume that causation was in the opposite direction.

Behrman is right to emphasize the need for improvements in the analysis of the impact of skills on international competitiveness and development, based on better analytical frameworks, better data and better estimation techniques. But the complexity of the issues and the limits of statistical testing make it unlikely that the search for clear-cut results will ever succeed. Behrman judged in 1990 (p. 90) that empirical studies in support of an activist human resource development policy did not 'satisfy the Anglo-Saxon legal definition for a conviction in a criminal case of making the case "beyond a reasonable doubt", though some may argue that they satisfy the criteria for a civil case of creating a presumption "more likely than not" in favour of the case'. Maybe, in the nature of things, this is the best that can be hoped for. Meanwhile, research results, reported in this book and elsewhere, are at least consistent with the view that skill development is a necessary condition for transition from primary exports to manufactures and from labour-intensive to skill-intensive manufacturing. The experience of the East Asian economies, Wood's cross-country regressions, and the accumulation of country case studies, including those just discussed on Singapore, Costa Rica, Ghana and Indonesia, suggest that such a transition is likely to run into trouble unless an adequate basis of skills is laid. With the backing of the new growth models and international trade theory framework, this may be enough to convince some government advisers of the advantages of an activist policy.

However, they should also bear in mind the evidence that, while skill development is a necessary condition for this transition, it is not a sufficient condition. Lucas, in Chapter 7, emphasizes the need for training policy decisions to be coordinated with financial reforms and trade and industrial policy. In Chapter 4, Cheah shows how the economic restructuring strategy of the government of Singapore encompassed not only education and training, but also policies on wages, industrial relations, the import of foreign labour and promotion of foreign investment The emergence of Indonesia, also, as a competitive labour-intensive manufacturer, as Chapter 3 shows, has been due to its programme of deregulation and institutional reform, a relatively orthodox fiscal policy, and, within manufacturing, increasing productivity combined with real devaluation and wage restraint. These, together with the development of adequate skills, are preconditions for transition to skill-based competitiveness. This is underlined by the unsatisfactory economic performance of the Philippines, in spite of the fact that it is in the highest category of senior secondary school and tertiary education enrolment ratios and receives the highest rating from international businessmen for the availability and quality of its managerial labour. As Godfrey comments in Chapter 3, '[t]he

Philippines, thus, is an example of an economy with all the educational preconditions for transition to skill-based competitiveness, but without the necessary combination of wage, productivity and exchange-rate conditions. The sad conclusion is that skill-based competitiveness requires competitiveness as well as skill'.

WHAT SHOULD A GOVERNMENT DO TO DEVELOP A COUNTRY'S SKILLS?

The general principle on which this question should be addressed is well stated by Behrman in Chapter 1, building on his discussion of Becker's marginalist analysis, production functions, conditional demand functions, Mincer-type earnings functions, hedonic wage functions, and efficiency in the production of human resources. '[I]n thinking about policy changes from an efficiency perspective', he argues, 'priority should be given to identifying market failures and to considering whether they can be remedied at a reasonable marginal social cost by improving markets or by other means'. This means that policies have to be justified by 'evidence that social returns are greater than private returns and that there are high social returns to offsetting the difference'.

Most of the empirical work equates skill development with general education. For instance, Berge and Wood (Chapter 2), Nichols (Chapter 8) and the World Bank East Asian study, largely for reasons of data availability, all use years of schooling as a proxy for human resources. Most of the discussion of externalities and market failure, however, focuses on training, and the chapters in this book are no exception.

Improving Markets

Cassen and Mavrotas (Chapter 5) and Edwards (Chapter 6) discuss the reasons for market failure and its effect on skill development. They begin with Becker's distinction between general (or transferable) and specific skills. General skills command an equal return in other firms; skills specific to a particular firm, on the other hand, are not marketable outside. Becker argues that the acquisition of general skills will be financed by the employee, either by acceptance of a lower wage during training or by payment of fees and other training costs, in return for a higher wage later on. The acquisition of specific skills, on the other hand, will be financed by employers, who will recoup the cost later by paying trained workers less than their marginal product, secure in the knowledge that these workers cannot obtain a higher price for their skills elsewhere. The implication is that training can be left to the market, without any need for state intervention.

Cassen and Mavrotas, in the appendix to their chapter, summarize the criticisms that have been made of the three assumptions underlying this distinction between general and specific skills and of the conclusions based on it: that there is no uncertainty as to the value of future returns to training, no limitations on the possibility of borrowing to finance the development of one's own skills, and no turnover of workers who have received specific training financed by their employer. If these assumptions do not apply, then, as Edwards shows, the market fails and the level of training is socially suboptimal. Employees (or the unemployed) do not know which are the most profitable skills to acquire, and, even if they did, could not find anyone to lend them the money to finance their acquisition. Employers who spend money on training their workforce, see all, except a small category of truly specific, non-transferable skilled workers, poached by other employers who do no training. So individuals refuse to sacrifice now in order to gain later, and employers take the 'free-rider' route, hoping that other employers will develop a pool of skills that they can tap.

The minimalist response to this dilemma is to try, as Behrman puts it, to improve the market. This, explored particularly by Lucas in Chapter 7, would involve the provision of more information about the market for qualified workers and about the content of and returns to different types of training, and the development of institutions to finance individual skill acquisition without insistence on immediate collateral and to make loans to enterprises to develop training programmes. The provision of information would need to extend to standardization and certification of programmes and qualifications, so that their meaning is understood in the market. Lucas also suggests a need to address other factors affecting the market for skills, particularly regulation of wages and layoffs. Minimum wage regulations have two effects on the market for skills: they compress differentials between the more and the less skilled, thus reducing the incentive to acquire skills, and they prevent employers from recouping the cost of training by paying lower 'trainee' wages, thus reducing the incentive to impart skills. Employment security regulations favour training of an existing workforce, but, as Lucas points out, they can also, in the context of structural adjustment, discourage hiring and training of workers in new skills.

Such improvements would make the market work better, but it is not clear that they would eliminate most market failures. In these times of rapid changes in technology and trade, risk and uncertainty have never been higher. Information can be provided, but cannot be relied on. As for loans, Lucas emphasizes the high risk of default by both individual borrowers and small enterprises (which is why private financiers avoid this type of lending). A programme of unsecured training loans would require substantial subsidies. Labour-market deregulation is politically difficult in many countries, and its impact on training has yet to be empirically tested. Intervention to internalize externalities is still likely to be needed.

Improving Government Intervention

Edwards explores various models that have been used for this purpose: the state training model, under which the government both pays for and runs training centres for industry; what he calls the voluntarist model, whereby employers train, but the finance is provided by government; and a levy-grant system, where all employers pay for training through a payroll levy or tax, and those employers who actually train are reimbursed through grants. Other dimensions of various training models, besides who pays and who provides, include: timing (pre-career, in-service or during unemployment); location (school, training centre or place of work); and, if in place of work, mode (on or off the job).[1]

Edwards describes the systems actually used in various countries, and shows how they are variably successful in providing incentives to individuals and employers. Germany's 'corporatist' or dual system, combining on-the-job training in the place of work with attendance at vocational school, gives young employees an assurance that their qualifications will pay off, and employers the chance to obtain the skilled workers they need for high-value-added production, and to pay them very low wages during their apprenticeship. Japan's 'company' model provides on-the-job, state-certificated training in both transferable and specific skills in the context of lifetime employment. Both these systems successfully deal with the incentives problem and are tempting to imitators, but both, Edwards argues, rely on institutional structures that are difficult to copy. In Germany, these include strong collective pressures in favour of training and a general willingness on the part of companies to take a long-term view. In Japan the success of the training system depends on a major market imperfection – lifetime employment and low interfirm mobility of labour – which few countries would be able to imitate even if they wanted to.

Probably the most widely-adopted model, state direction, is the weakest, as far as impact on incentives is concerned. Exemplified in Edwards's chapter by Sri Lanka and pre-1993 Malaysia, such a system tends to be essentially supply driven. Poorly motivated students, usually pre-career or unemployed, are trained in out-of-date specializations, usually in workshops which are far from industrial reality, and subsequently fail to attract job offers from employers. Cassen and Mavrotas give examples of the cost-ineffectiveness of vocational schools and of low rates of return to institutional training. Training of the unemployed is, as emphasized also by Lucas, particularly problematic (and particularly during recessions), and persists in many countries primarily for political reasons, despite evidence of its low impact in relation to cost. Such systems can be brought closer to reality by involving employers in planning and management, but incentive problems remain unless they are also involved in finance.

The way out of the incentives dilemma, Edwards argues, given the difficulty of copying the institutionally-specific systems of Germany and Japan, and the inherent problems of the fully-state-financed models, is the levy-grant system. The most successful example of this is probably Singapore, and the new Malaysian scheme looks promising. Humphrey also describes the positive role of the levy-financed training agency, SENAI, in Brazil. In other places it has worked less well and is often written off as a model for developing countries. However, Edwards argues convincingly, on the particular basis of British experience, that the system has not been given a chance. Its weaknesses in many cases reflect the particular form that it has taken. In Britain it seems to have been abandoned just as the quality of training was improving and a training culture was being created. In order to create this culture, stability is needed: a levy-grant system, once set up, must be given a chance to work.

The emphasis on incentives is echoed by Humphrey, who shows how the introduction of just-in-time (JIT) and total quality management (TQM) encouraged three Brazilian firms to make big investments in training, even though there was little assurance that they would capture the benefits of such training. He explains this willingness by: the pressures from trade liberalization to improve competitive performance; the immediate productivity gains to be reaped from training; the increased risk of losses from disruption of production as a result of *not* training; the way in which JIT/TQM reveals training needs over time; and the opportunities given to change both occupational and reward structures in the interests of reducing labour turnover. In effect, institutions are being moved in a Japanese direction. However, Humphrey emphasizes that this does not preclude a government role. Market failures will still occur, even if JIT/TQM becomes widespread. Small and medium enterprises will have particular difficulties in adapting to the changing situation, in which poaching will become more difficult because of the comprehensive nature of the training needed. Humphrey emphasizes the need for training to be linked to reorganization of companies, in order to create the conditions whereby they can benefit from training, and recognizes the potential role of levy-financed training boards, such as those of Brazil and Colombia.

Of course, many economies are starting from a much lower level. Lall and Wignaraja, as already described, emphasize the supply-side problems of manufacturing in Ghana, probably similar to those faced in many African economies. They recommend the provision of specialized training to industry, including technical extension services to small and medium enterprises. At the same time they recognize the weakness of such services as already exist, lacking the expertise and equipment to conduct technical activities (such as testing, quality assurance, troubleshooting and product design), and bureaucratic and inflexible in their approach to service provision. On the side of incentives, they recommend a more gradual process of trade liberalization, but to a strict timetable, coordinated with industrial restructuring and upgrading. They recognize the risk of government failure in this strategy: this implies a need for improvement in government capabilities, which includes but goes beyond training of civil servants. The weakness of enterprises makes it both more difficult and more urgent not only to provide training but to set up a training system which will prevent market failure from compounding the consequences of government failure.

Education and Training

While discussion of skill development policy has concentrated on training, several of the chapters in this book recognize the prior importance of education. Lucas makes the general case for educational reform and for the provision of adult education as part of retraining programmes where necessary. Humphrey, and Cassen and Mavrotas, suggest that improvement in basic education is the real priority in Latin America, and particularly in Brazil, where innovating firms are having to introduce their own programmes of adult education and basic training in literacy and numeracy: Humphrey argues that state support for these activities is desirable. Edwards suggests that the success of Japan's training system is based on its high standards of education. Significantly, children in the bottom half of the ability range, dangerously neglected by the education systems of the US and Britain, are particularly well served in Japan.

To return, finally, to Behrman's statement that skill development policies have to be justified by 'evidence that social returns are greater than private returns and that there are high social returns to offsetting … the difference', the chapters in this book at least suggest that this criterion can often be met. On the basis of a general education system that recognizes the returns to improvement in quality, particularly in basic education, a training system can be built that internalizes externalities and reduces market failures. A mechanism for this purpose that deserves reconsideration is the levy-grant system. Under such a system, if it works properly, employers determine their own training needs, which are met competitively by training providers, in plant or off plant, and financed by the sector as a whole. Those who choose not to train can continue to poach but they contribute through the levy to the training of the poached. In this way a culture of training is gradually built up and the rewards are reaped in international markets. The alternative, as several chapter authors point out, is low-skill equilibrium, and an endless prospect of competitiveness based on keeping labour cheap.

NOTE

1. See Godfrey (1994) for further discussion.

REFERENCES

Adams, A.V., R. Goldfarb and T. Kelly (1992), *How the Macroeconomic Environment Affects Human Resource Development*, WPS No. 828, Washington, DC: World Bank.

Behrman, Jere R. (1990), *Human Resource Led Development? Review of Issues and Evidence*, Geneva: ILO ARTEP.

Godfrey, Martin (1994), 'Planning for Vocational Education, Training and Employment: A Minimalist Approach', in Rashid Amjad and Peter Richards (eds), *New Approaches to Manpower Planning and Analysis*, Geneva: ILO. pp. 29–51.

Lewis, W. Arthur (1954), 'Economic Development with Unlimited Supplies of Labour', *The Manchester School of Economic and Social Studies*, **22** (2), May, 139–91.

Lucas, Robert E. (1988), 'On the Mechanics of Economic Development', *Journal of Monetary Economics*, **21**, 3–42.

Lucas, Robert E. (1990), 'Why Doesn't Capital Flow from Rich to Poor Countries?', *American Economic Review*, **80** (2), 3–42.

Lucas, Robert E. (1993), 'Making a Miracle', *Econometrica*, **61** (2), March, 251–72.

Romer, Paul M. (1986), 'Increasing Returns and Long-Run Growth', *Journal of Political Economy*, **94** (5), 1002–36.

Romer, Paul M. (1989), 'Human Capital and Growth: Theory and Evidence', Chicago, IL: University of Chicago, mimeo.

Romer, Paul M. (1993), 'Two Strategies for Economic Development: Using Ideas and Producing Ideas', *Proceedings of the World Bank Annual Conference on Development Economics 1992*, Washington, DC World Bank, 63–116.

Romer, Paul M. (1994), 'The Origins of Endogenous Growth', *Journal of Economic Perspectives*, **8** (1), Winter, 3–22.

Wood, Adrian (1994), *Skill, Land and Trade: A Simple Analytical Framework*, IDS Working Paper No. 1, February.

World Bank (1993), *The East Asian Miracle: Economic Growth and Public Policy*, New York: Oxford University Press.

PART I

Theoretical Framework

1. Simple analytical considerations for skill development for international competitiveness

Jere R. Behrman*

INTRODUCTION

Skill development and other human resources increasingly are emphasized as important in international competitiveness and economic development.[1] This heightened emphasis originates in part in applied focus on the impact of skill enhancement and other human resources on international competitiveness and development such as in recent UNDP *Human Development Reports* and World Bank *World Development Reports*, in part in the 'new economic growth' academic literature in which human resources play a critical role in productivity growth, and in part in related interpretations of empirical micro and aggregate associations between indicators of skill development and attainment of various goals including international competitiveness and development.

But, despite this intensified emphasis on skill development and other human resources, there are many lacunae in our knowledge about the details of this topic. In part these lacunae reflect limitations of much of the related applied work because of inadequate attention in many cases to the basic foundations for undertaking applied social science analysis based on behavioural data.

This chapter considers the tripartite foundations for good social science empirical analysis in the particular context of the impact of skill development and other human resources on international competitiveness and development: (1) theory, (2) data, and (3) estimation. These three dimensions of empirical social science analysis are critically interrelated. Theory provides frameworks for exploring systematically various dimensions of the impact of skill development and other human resources on international competitiveness and development, points to what data are needed for such explorations, and to some of the probable estimation issues that should be addressed. Data, of course, are essential for empirical analysis, limit the extent to which analyses can be undertaken, and shape most of the estimation problems. The estimation problems, thus, reflect implications of theory and the data that are available and, often more importantly, data that are not available – such as variables that may not be observed in the data or measured only imperfectly in the data but that may affect importantly skill development and other human resources as well as international competitiveness and other outcomes of interest.

SIMPLE ANALYTICAL FRAMEWORKS FOR THE ANALYSIS OF THE IMPACT OF SKILL DEVELOPMENT AND OTHER HUMAN RESOURCES ON INTERNATIONAL COMPETITIVENESS AND DEVELOPMENT

Good theories about the impact of skill development and other human resources on international competitiveness and development abstract the essence of complex empirical phenomena in ways that lead to testable empirical propositions about behaviour. There are a number of theories that illuminate different dimensions of the relations between skill development and international competitiveness and development. I begin with aggregate theories primarily in the 'new neoclassical growth model' style. I then turn to micro theories that underlie some dimensions of the behaviour determining investments in skill development and other human resources, the returns to those investments, and the provision of services related to such investments. Finally I consider the justification for policies related to skill development and other human resource investments.

Aggregate Models of Human Resources and Development

Aggregate growth models shape the intuition that many economists have about long-run growth, in part because of the simplicity and elegance of such models. In the past decade the so-called 'new neoclassical growth models' of Romer (1986), Lucas (1988), Azariadis and Drazen (1991), Stokey (1991), Young (1991) and others have emphasized the possibilities of diverging growth rates among countries, ongoing per-capita growth in equilibrium, and multiple equilibrium growth paths.[2] At the heart of much of this literature are investments in skills and other human resources and assumptions about externalities of human resource stocks – that is, effects that are not transferred through markets, returns to scale to human resources, or learning-by-doing that increases productivity differentially by product (that is, a lot for 'high-tech products' but not much for traditional manufacturing such as textiles).[3] This literature has provided a set of more systematic frameworks that appears more consistent with some of the important stylized facts about growth than the neoclassical models, that has provided a better aggregate rationale for interest in human resources among analysts with an applied bent, and that has renewed interest in the aggregate relations between human resources and development among more academic economists.

Romer on 'Increasing Returns and Long-Run Growth'

Romer (1986) develops an equilibrium growth model of endogenous technological change in which long-run growth is driven primarily by the accumulation of knowledge. The critical assumptions of this model are: (1) New knowledge is produced with diminishing returns.[4] (2) There is a positive externality in the production of knowledge because knowledge is assumed not to be perfectly patented or kept secret.[5] (3) Production of consumption goods as a function of the stock of knowledge and of other inputs has increasing returns,[6] and the stock of knowledge may have an increasing marginal product in such use. The third assumption is key. In contrast to models that posit that capital has diminishing marginal productivity in the earlier growth literature, in this model knowledge grows without bound. Even if all other inputs are fixed, it is not optimal to stop at some steady state in which knowledge is constant. Per-capita output can grow without bound, the rate of investment and the rate of return on capital stock may increase with increased capital stock, and the level of per-capita product need not converge across countries. These results are substantially different from those in the earlier growth model literature. They point both to the possibility of a central role for skills and other human resources in the development process and to the possibility that active policy to favour human resource investment may have a social payoff because of the externalities and increasing returns associated with such investments. In the absence of such policies, the equilibrium growth path is suboptimal because of the externalities and increasing returns to scale.

Lucas 'On the Mechanics of Economic Development'

Lucas emphasizes that the Solow (1956) neoclassical model is not a useful theory of economic development for two reasons. (1) The apparent inability to account for the considerable real-world diversity in growth experiences. (2) The 'strong and counterfactual prediction that international trade should include rapid movement toward equality in capital–labor ratios and factor prices'. Lucas's first adaptation is to add human capital with externalities (that is, the average level of human capital affects a worker's productivity in addition to the effect of his or her own human capital) so that persistent differences across countries in per-capita income levels can be maintained. Lucas's second adaptation considers human capital to have only external effects. With this assumption, with many commodities (each with different learning-by-doing) and with international trade, producers do not take learning possibilities into account, but only maximize their returns according to immediate comparative advantage, which can result in very different paths of human capital accumulation through learning-by-doing. Such a model is consistent with very different levels and rates of growth of production across countries, as well as with sudden jumps in production patterns and in growth rates in response to small changes in world prices. This formulation suggests the possibilities of policies to encourage more socially optimal human resource development by focusing more on those sectors in which such externalities are relatively large.

Azariadis and Drazen on 'Threshold Externalities in Economic Development'

Azariadis and Drazen (1991) attempt to model the variations in growth experience by augmenting the Diamond (1965) overlapping-generations neoclassical growth model through adding technological externalities with a threshold property that permits returns to scale to change very rapidly and therefore for there to be multiple, locally-stable, balanced-growth equilibrium paths. As a result of such threshold externalities, countries with higher human capital investment relative to their per-capita incomes can experience periods of high sustained growth. This framework again may imply high payoffs in growth to human resource investments at higher levels than would result from private decisions alone not only because of the positive growth externalities, but because private decisions may lead to a lower equilibrium growth path than is possible.

Stokey on 'Human Capital, Product Quality, and Growth'

Stokey (1991) develops a growth model based on human capital accumulation and a continuum of products indexed by quality that she claims is consistent with the East Asian experience of rapid growth in per-capita income, rapid growth in trade, rapid growth in education, and rapid change in the composition of output. She argues that such a model must contain heterogeneous goods and labour. Without the former, there is no motivation for trade. Without the latter, comparative advantage must depend on natural resource endowments or capital immobility – neither of which seems to provide an adequate explanation of the East Asian experiences with rapidly changing output composition. In her model, human capital investments have a positive external effect on the human capital of later cohorts, so average human capital tends to grow over time. Products contain characteristics, with higher-quality products having more characteristics. Labour is the only factor of production. Labour with more human capital produces higher-quality products and units of labour with different human capital are not substitutable. She demonstrates the existence of a stable (stationary) growth path on which there is a competitive equilibrium in which human capital and the quality of consumption goods grow at a common, constant rate.[7] If there is a unique equilibrium growth path, she shows that a lower discount rate, a higher intertemporal elasticity of substitution in consumption, and less-severe diminishing returns to investment in education all lead to a stationary growth path with higher investment and growth. Finally, she considers a two-country model in which there is a large developed country following a stationary growth path and a small open developing country. She shows that individuals in the small open economy invest *less* heavily in human capital with international trade than they would with autarky. She notes, however, that it does *not* necessarily follow that the developing country is made worse off by free trade since the faster productivity growth in the developed economy may cause the terms of trade of the developing country to improve more than enough to offset its own slower rate of technical progress due to its slower change towards production of higher-quality products and slower increase in human capital.

Young on 'Learning by Doing and the Dynamic Effects of International Trade'

Young (1991) presents a model in which learning-by-doing, though bounded for each product, exhibits spillovers across goods. He explores the interaction between two countries distinguished by initial knowledge levels. At any given time, learning-by-doing will have been exhausted in a subset of products (because it is bounded for each product), but will continue in the remainder. Under fairly weak assumptions regarding preferences and technology, aggregate growth is unbounded. Over time growth involves changes in product composition, with both the quantity and the variety of goods consumed increasing. If there is no international diffusion of knowledge, the effect of international trade depends on whether static comparative advantage leads an economy to specialize in goods with mostly exhausted learning-by-doing or in goods with learning-by-doing still proceeding. International trade decelerates the technical progress and growth in the former and accelerates technical progress and growth in the latter. However, even in an economy for which international trade slows technical progress, consumers might experience improved intertemporal welfare because technological progress abroad can improve real consumption at home. Thus, if there is bounded learning-by-doing with intracountry (but not intercountry) positive spillovers, slight initial knowledge differences under perfect competition may lead to ever-increasing divergence in per-capita product (though if the static gains from trade are sufficient consumer welfare in the country with initially-low knowl-

edge may improve). He explicitly acknowledges that the impact of international trade on growth might be much different if it affects research and
development or human capital or if there are international spillovers in learning-by-doing. From the point of view of the present book his model points to
the importance of human resource investments (or R&D or international
spillovers of learning-by-doing) in developing countries to offset the pressures for divergence from bounded learning-by-doing with only intracountry
spillovers.

Wood on 'Skill, Land and Trade: A Simple Analytical Framework'
Wood (1994) develops a 'minimal model of the relationship between human
resources and foreign trade in developing countries' to attempt to bridge the
gap between those working on human resources and those working on foreign trade. Similar to Stokey (and Young with regard to products), he posits
that heterogeneous labour and products are critical to understanding skill
development and international competitiveness and development. He identifies three skill categories – no skills or education, basic education, and skilled
– to represent a country's skills endowments (fixed at any point of time). He
posits that manufacturing is more skill-intensive in production than the primary sector, and that within manufacturing there may be a range of skill
intensities. He then develops simple two-factor Heckscher–Ohlin models –
with 'skills' (human resources) and 'land' (natural resources) being given (in
the short run) non-traded factors – to explore the determinants of countries'
comparative advantages. The higher the given skill levels relative to land per
capita, the more likely that domestic relative factor prices favour skill-intensive manufacturing over land-intensive primary production and, within manufacturing, more-skill-intensive products. The impact of trade policies that
favour one sector (or subsector), depends on the relative factor endowments
of skills and land. Trade policy obviously can either increase or reduce skills,
depending on whether they facilitate or reduce skill investments including
learning-by-doing through working with new technologies that are embodied
in imported intermediate and capital goods. This model does not incorporate
explicitly some of the concerns of the 'new growth models' such as externalities of skill and other human resource stocks, divergence in equilibrium
growth paths or multiple equilibria. Instead it explicitly is very simple, building on a strong tradition in economics (with strengths and weakness that
Wood addresses), which makes its implications relatively transparent and
therefore accessible to a wide audience. By linking to an older tradition, it
facilitates understanding for such an audience of concerns such as in the
Stokey model regarding foreign-sector policies, learning-by-doing, skill development, and international competitiveness and development.

Micro Frameworks for the Analysis of the Impact of Skills and Other Human Resource Investments on International Competitiveness and Development

Aggregate theories (see the previous subsection) help motivate interest in the impact of skills and other human resources on international competitiveness and development and, in particular, the role of externalities, scale economies, product composition and the skill composition of the labour force. Some of the more recent aggregate models explicitly incorporate important dimensions of foreign trade. But these aggregate approaches do not provide much explicit guidance for analysis of behaviour at the micro level at which skill and other human resource investments are made. Micro theories provide frameworks for analysis at these levels. In this subsection I summarize briefly some of these micro analytical frameworks – those related to behaviour determining investments in skills and other human resources, the returns to those investments including those related to international competitiveness, and the provision of services related to human resource investments.

Becker's Woytinsky lecture on the determinants of skill and other human resource investments

Households (and individuals therein) are major proximate demanders for skill and other human resource investments, given predetermined assets, human resource production functions, and current and expected prices for inputs used in human resource investments and for outcomes of the production processes. These demands reflect the equating of expected marginal benefits and marginal costs (both in present discounted terms) for human resource investments in a given individual as in Becker's (1967) Woytinsky lecture (Figure 1.1A). The marginal benefit curve is downward sloping because of diminishing returns to human resource investments since individuals have given endowments (genetic and environmental)[8] and since, to the extent that human resource investments take time (such as schooling and training), greater investments imply greater lags in obtaining the returns and a shorter post-investment period in which to reap the returns from the investment. The marginal cost may increase with human resource investments because of the increasing opportunity costs of more time devoted to such investments (especially for schooling and training) and because of the increasing marginal costs of borrowing on financial markets. The equilibrium human resource investment for this individual is H^*, where the two curves intersect, with both the marginal benefit and the marginal cost equal to r^*. This equilibrium human resource investment is associated with an equilibrium rate of return, i^*, that equates the present discounted value of expected marginal benefits with the present discounted value of expected marginal costs.

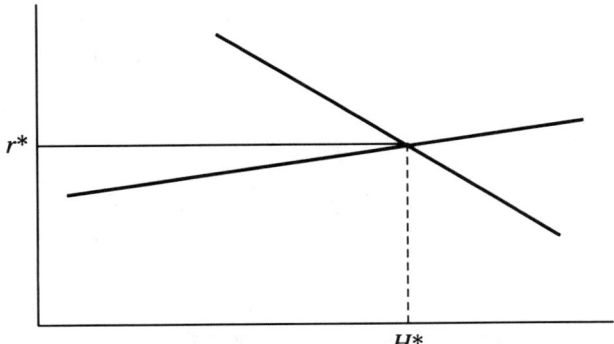

A   *Initial equilibrium*

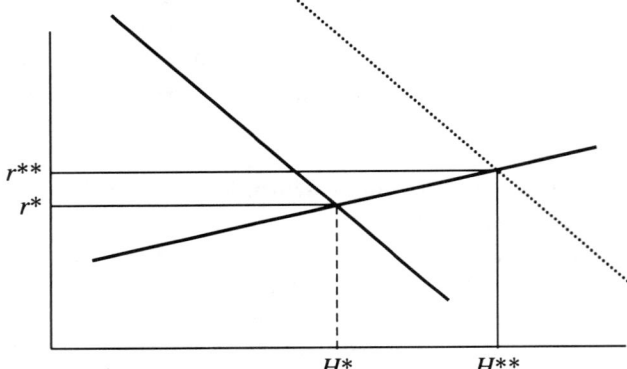

B   *Equilibrium with higher marginal benefits (dotted line)*

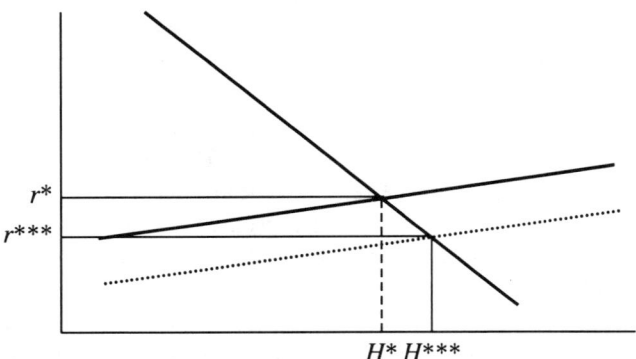

C   *Equilibrium with lower marginal costs (dotted line)*

Figure 1.1   Marginal benefits and marginal costs determining human resource investments (H)

If the marginal benefit curve were higher for every level of human resource investment as for the dotted line in Figure 1.1B, all else equal, the equilibrium human resource investment ($H**$) and the equilibrium marginal benefit ($r**$) would both be greater. The marginal benefit curve may be higher for one of two otherwise identical individuals because one individual:[9] (1) has greater endowments that are rewarded in schooling, training and labour markets;[10] (2) has lower time preference and thus greater present discounted value of the same post-investment resource stream; (3) has better health and a longer expected life due to complementary investments, so that the post-investment period in which that individual reaps the returns to the investment is greater and therefore the expected returns are greater; (4) has human resource investment options of higher quality so that the private marginal benefits for a given level of investment are higher, and the equilibrium investments are greater;[11] (5) has greater marginal benefits to a given level of such investments because of labour market discrimination that favours that individual because of gender, race, language, family, village or ethnic group; (6) has returns to human resources investments that are obtained more by the investor or the relevant decision maker (for example, if there is gender specialization in providing old-age support); (7) has greater marginal benefits to a given level of such investments because of greater externalities from the human resource investments of others in the same labour market; (8) has greater marginal benefits to a given level of investment because of being in a more dynamic economy (which may relate to expectations regarding the extent of integration into the international economy); or (9) lives in a more stable economy so that the discount rate for future returns is lower. Some of these possibilities tie directly into the aggregate models of the previous subsection.

If the marginal cost is lower for human resource investment (that is, the dotted line in Figure 1.1C), *ceteris paribus*, the equilibrium human resource investment ($H***$) is greater, with the marginal benefit ($r***$) at the higher investment level lower. The marginal cost might be lower for reasons illuminated by comparing two otherwise identical individuals except that one individual: (1) has lower-cost access to educational and health services because of closer proximity to such services or lower user charges; (2) has fewer opportunity costs for time used for such investments; (3) is from a household with greater access to credit because of greater wealth or status or better connections; (4) faces lower utility costs of such investments because of cultural norms that favour some activities associated with such investments more for some individuals than for others (for example, if it is not desirable that girls intermingle with males outside of the family, the preference costs of schooling are lower for boys than for girls); (5) has lower (marginal utility) costs of going to school or undertaking formal training than have other individuals because of greater powers of concentration, more innate ability or more persistence. [12]

This simple framework systematizes three critical points for identifying what is the impact of skill development and other human resource investments.[13] (1) Human resource investments are associated with a number of individual, family and community characteristics. To identify the impact of human resource investments on international competitiveness (or other outcomes), it is important to control for these other characteristics (see later subsection on omitted variable bias). (2) Empirically observed returns to human resource investments are for given expectations regarding the macroeconomic, market, policy and regulatory environment, including importantly the extent of integration into the international economy. (3) The marginal benefits of human resource investments in a particular individual may differ depending upon the point of view from which they are evaluated: (i) there may be externalities such as those emphasized in the 'new neoclassical growth models' (see earlier subsection on aggregate models) so that the social returns differ from the private returns; (ii) there may be a difference between who makes the investment decision (for example, parents versus the individual her/himself) and in whom the investment is made (for example, children) which may result in gender differentials in incentives for investments in children given traditional gender roles such as those in old-age care for parents; (iii) Some forms of human capital investment may have general returns and others may have returns only in specific enterprises, with incentives for the individual to make the investment greater the more the returns are general.

Evaluating the impact of skills and other human resource investments
Two natural ways of evaluating impacts of skills and other human resources are to estimate (i) production functions and (ii) conditional demand functions – conditional on human resources. I briefly describe these two alternatives, then turn to (iii) Mincer-type earnings functions and (iv) hedonic price indices – two alternatives to which appeal often is made in empirical studies. Finally I turn to (v) skill development and learning from experience.

Production functions   The impact of a vector of human resources ($\underline{H}$) – together with vectors of other capital inputs ($\underline{K}$), variable inputs ($\underline{F}$), technology ($\underline{T}$), and stochastic factors ($\underline{U}$) – on a vector of outputs of interest ($\underline{O}$) can be represented by a set of production functions:

$$\underline{O} = f(\underline{H}, \underline{K}, \underline{F}, \underline{T}, \underline{U}). \tag{1.1}$$

The first derivatives with respect to $\underline{H}$ gives marginal impacts of increasing human resources, given all other production inputs. Generally these first derivatives depend upon all other inputs – for example, the marginal productivity of workers with high-school education of given qualities depends on the physical capital and technology with which the workers work. With good estimates of appropriate production functions, impacts of human resources could be evaluated with considerable confidence. Good production function estimates are difficult to obtain, however, because of unobserved inputs (for example, inherent ability, motivation) and simultaneous determination of outputs with inputs (see later subsection on simultaneity bias). Phenomena such as learning-by-doing (emphasized in the earlier subsection on aggregate models) are also difficult to capture empirically with information usually available.

Conditional demand functions   If vectors of outcomes and inputs are chosen by maximizing some objective function given resource endowments ($\underline{R}$), a matrix of output and input prices over time ($\underline{P}$) and a matrix of stochastic shocks over time ($\underline{U}$), these choices can be represented in a set of demand relations for all the outcomes and all of inputs ($\underline{Z}$):[14]

$$\underline{Z} = g\,(\underline{P}, \underline{R}, \underline{U}). \tag{1.2}$$

Adjustment processes are incorporated into these relations. If the human resources of interest are among the predetermined resources in R, direct estimation of relation (1.2) gives their impact on the outputs. For example, the schooling of adult family members might be a predetermined resource in the estimation of such a relation for family firm net profits. A necessary condition to obtain unbiased estimates of schooling impact is that there are no unobserved right-side variables with which schooling is correlated.

But in many cases interest is in the impact of a human resource that is determined simultaneously with some outcome. For example, training may be determined simultaneously with labour productivity. In such cases, it is not clear how interesting are estimates that can be obtained from relations that have the form of conditional demand functions within a one-period framework. Consider the following two linear demand relations for productivity (Q_P) and training (Q_T) as dependent on two prices (P_1, P_2), predetermined resources (R), and stochastic terms (U_P, U_T):

$$Q_P = a_{11}P_1 + a_{12}P_2 + a_{13}R + U_P \tag{1.3}$$

$$Q_T = a_{21}P_1 + a_{22}P_2 + a_{23}R + U_T. \tag{1.4}$$

These relations imply:

$$Q_P = a_{31}Q_T + a_{32}P_2 + a_{33}R + U_{P'}. \qquad (1.5)$$

   This might appear to be a conditional demand function with which the impact of training on productivity could be explored. But the coefficient of training is merely the ratio of the effect of the price that has been eliminated in relation (1.3) relative to the effect of that price in relation (1.4) (that is, $a_{31} = a_{11}/a_{21}$) Thus the coefficient of training in relation (1.5) does *not* reveal anything interesting about the training effect on productivity, but only the relative price effects (for P_1) in the two demand relations. With multiple periods the question can be asked, how does previous training affect current productivity, and a conditional demand function can obtain the estimated impact of that past training on current productivity. But the past training must be predetermined in the statistical sense to obtain unbiased estimates of the effect of training on current productivity — which means, it must be independent of the disturbance term in the relation estimated. That may be a strong requirement if, for example, unobserved ability affects productivity and also training to date.

Mincer-type earnings functions   The most common relation for estimating private rates of return to time spent in school in terms of wages is from

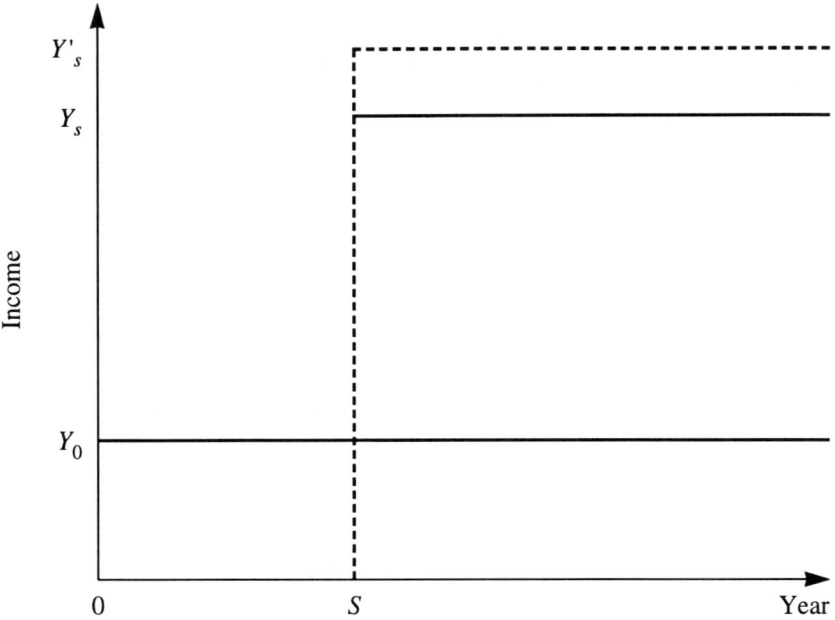

Figure 1.2   Mincerian choice between schooling levels

Mincer (1974). Figure 1.2 illustrates the basic story in the simplest case in which once one finishes school (training) and starts to work, earnings depend only on the years of schooling (training). The vertical axis measures earnings obtained with different schooling: Y_0 with zero years of schooling and Y_S with S years of schooling, but with the earnings stream starting S years later due to time spent in school. In equilibrium, the present discounted values of the earnings from the two options are equated, which implies:

$$\ln Y_S = \ln Y_0 + rS, \tag{1.6}$$

where r is the private rate of return to time spent in school in this equilibrium semilog earnings function. There are numerous estimates of (1.6) that purport to measure private rates of return to schooling (for example, Psacharopoulos 1994). How does (1.6) relate to the production function for earnings in (1.1)? Implicitly (1.6) assumes that the first derivative of that production function with respect to schooling is independent of all other inputs (for example, ability, motivation, other inputs, technology). Thus, strong assumptions are placed on the production technology, such that ability and motivation have impact on earnings only through schooling.

Hedonic wage functions   An alternative interpretation of (1.6) is as a hedonic wage function in which the coefficients are the market valuations of attributes. Estimation issues remain, however, if any of these attributes reflect choices (for example, schooling, training).

Schooling, training and learning   Education through schooling or training may enable one to deal better with uncertainty by improving one's abilities to learn, which is likely to be particularly important in dynamic environments in which there are technological innovations and new market opportunities (Schultz 1975). These notions are formalized in target-input models in which individuals choose allocations of resources or inputs knowing the production technology only up to a stochastic 'target' for the input use level (see Rosenzweig 1995 for details and references). In each production period, priors regarding optimal input use are updated based on past experience. Education can affect the production-cum-learning process by: (1) Increasing the precision of initial information because of access to more information sources.[15] In this case experience and formal education are substitutes – alternative ways to increase precision of priors. Therefore returns to formal education are high only with new options, and decline with more experience with any given technology. (2) Enabling individuals to gain more information from each use of a technology – the more educated may learn faster and decode information acquired through experience more effectively. If this is the only effect, at low levels of experience, education and experience are complements rather than substitutes so that returns to education at least initially increase with experience with a given new technology. While this approach is stated in terms of new technology, similar possibilities exist with stochastic terms and learning relating to markets as well as to technology. This role may be critical for entrants into a new market, whether they be young people searching for good matches in the labour market or entrepreneurs entering new international product or input markets.

Supply considerations for production of human resources

Important components of the marginal cost curves in Figure 1.1 are the private marginal prices paid by users of human-resource-related services such as schools and training programmes. The higher these prices, *ceteris paribus*, the higher these curves and the less are equilibrium human resource investments. The private marginal prices for human-resource-related services, in turn, reflect the public marginal financial cost[16] minus net marginal subsidies.

The production of human-resource-related services can be viewed similarly to the production of other sectors. Schools and training programmes are institutions that use certain inputs (for example, time of students, time of teachers, textbooks and other materials) to produce products (for example, greater cognitive achievement, improved skills).[17] How well – and how much – such products are produced relates to various dimensions of economic efficiency, just as in other productive institutions in society. School and training authorities can do best by using the resources that they employ fully and well in an engineering sense and by ensuring: (i) *allocative efficiency* in distributing inputs (for example, materials and teachers' services) among outputs (for example, learning literacy versus numeracy), (ii) *input choice efficiency* so that the marginal product value of various inputs equals their social opportunity costs in other uses, and (iii) *output compositional efficiency* regarding the right output combination given the relative incremental values or prices that society places on the outputs. [18] However, empirical estimates suggest that human-capital-investment-related services often are not produced very efficiently (for example, Behrman 1995b, 1996b; Hanushek 1995). Frequently institutions for providing these services do not appear to facilitate very great responsiveness in production to pressures for efficiencies. Whether or not skill development is important in international competitiveness, there may be considerable gains possible from the more efficient production of skills.

Justification for Policies Related to Skill and Other Human Resource Investments

Basic economic goals of developing economies often are characterized as (1) increasing the command over resources of members of those economies and (2) achieving an appropriate distribution of the command over resources.[19] Human resources in general and better skills in particular may be effective means for attaining both of these goals as well as the goal of the enrichment of human resources in themselves. The nature of human resources also may importantly affect international competitiveness. In any case human-resource-related policies often are advocated and, indeed, implemented. An important question, therefore, is what are the bases for making policy decisions related to skill development and other human resources?

An important part of the answer to that question depends on exactly what is the social objective function, what are the distributional weights in that function, and to what extent are human resources *per se* as opposed to (or in addition to) the broader command over resources in that objective function? As a citizen of the world I have some views about what these characteristics of the objective function should be. But being an economist does not give me any special wisdom on these important social and political issues. But I believe that economists do have something important to say about how resources can be used more productively to pursue the agreed-upon objectives of a society because the objectives always are pursued subject to resource constraints, so there is an advantage to using the available resources more rather than less effectively.

Such considerations, in a static world, lead to emphasis on policy interventions that are sensitive to economic efficiency (see the earlier subsection on supply considerations for production of human resources). For that reason it is useful here to discuss further six standard dimensions of efficiency. For convenience, the analysis of schooling is used as a reference point, but the implications are parallel for any productive unit, or for the economy as a whole.[20]

1. The efficient allocation, input, and output choices are interdependent. Suppose that society increases its relative value on incremental cognitive achievement for reading versus mathematics because of a perception that scientific skills will be relatively even more important in the future. If the production relations for producing increments in mathematics cognitive achievement are more intensive in the use of teachers, the demand for teachers' services increases at given input prices. If all school authorities make such a shift, the price of teachers' services relative to other schooling inputs probably will increase, to offset in part such a shift.

2. If one of the three efficiency conditions noted in the subsection on supply considerations is not satisfied, it is not necessarily better to satisfy the other two efficiency conditions. This observation is an illustration of the argument of 'the second best' that if it is not possible to attain the first-best outcome with all of the efficiency conditions satisfied, it is not *necessarily* preferable to satisfy a subset of the efficiency conditions. However, in the absence of information to the contrary regarding how one inefficiency offsets in part another, in a world with imperfect information the presumption is that removing or lessening any specific inefficiency probably is an improvement. A related point is that there is a *policy hierarchy* in which it probably is desirable to lessen or to eliminate any inefficiency by making changes that as directly as possible address the inefficiency (for example, Corden 1974). If too little schooling is occurring from a social point of view, for example, schooling expansion could be encouraged by subsidizing the production of paper since paper is used in textbooks that are used in school. But such a subsidy would add distortions and inefficiencies by encouraging too much use of paper in other uses, and therefore would be less effective from an efficiency perspective than directly subsidizing schooling.

3. If the school authority had perfect knowledge of all the relative incremental social values (prices) of inputs and outputs and of the production technology, it could issue regulations to the schools to produce the socially optimal combination of reading and mathematics and other knowledge increments by purchasing the right combination of material and teachers' services and other schooling inputs and allocating them among reading, mathematics and other learning so that production is at the right level for each output. It then could see that the regulations were followed through monitoring and impose strong sanctions for behaviour that differed from that prescribed. But in the real world, the situation is much more complex and information is quite imperfect. There are many inputs and many outputs, and the intensity efforts of some inputs (for example, students, teachers) reflect behavioural choices. Information is quite imperfect regarding the social values for incremental outputs, the nature of the production technology for the outputs of interest, and even the social values for incremental inputs since in some of the relevant markets (for example, the market for teachers) there may be substantial distortions due either to market failures (such as externalities[21]) or to policy distortions (laws and regulations on employment practices). Therefore there may be an important role for improved information on schooling, as well as for the design of institutions that induce efficient behaviour.

4. There remains the question of efficiency in the allocation of budgetary resources to the school authority versus other possible uses. Moving to

lessen such allocative efficiencies between the school authority under examination and other parts of the economy may have a high payoff in terms of efficiency, possibly (or possibly not) a higher payoff than lessening inefficiencies in the operation of the school authority.

5. Efficiency justifications for policy changes depend on there being differences between social and private incentives. The pervasiveness of imperfect and often asymmetrical information together with evidence of substantial behavioural responses to incentives suggests that there are likely to be gains from policies that increase information and from policies that create incentives for socially efficient behaviour even if information is imperfect (as it is likely always to be). Markets can play important roles in conveying information and in shaping the incentives that individuals and entities face. Market signals, however, do not always convey correctly the social scarcity values of products and activities because of market failures due to information imperfections, externalities, market power of some entities, increasing returns to scale and governmental regulations and subsidies. Therefore, in terms of the important concern about efficiency, there are likely to be gains from policies that make markets more efficient, though there are some market failures that are not likely to be addressed well with market changes alone. This means that in thinking of possible policy changes from an efficiency perspective, priority should be given to identifying market failures and to considering whether they can be remedied at a reasonable marginal social cost by improving markets or by other means. Note that this policy prescription means that the existence of high returns to skills or to other human resources does *not* necessarily mean that there is an efficiency reason for policies to subsidize human resources; what is required is evidence that social returns are greater than private returns and that there are high social returns to offsetting (perhaps partially) the difference.

6. The discussion to this point has been framed as a static choice. But there is nothing inherent in the discussion that precludes dynamic considerations. The choice between allocating resources for increasing cognitive achievement this year versus next year has the same general considerations as for the choices regarding allocating resources among various forms of learning this period (though the information problems are likely to be greater for dynamic choices).

DATA ISSUES

What we think we know about impacts of skills and other human resources on international competitiveness and development depends on available, mostly quantifiable, data. Such data permit the exploration of at least some important dimensions of analytical frameworks such as those discussed earlier. If accurate data were available on all relevant variables, we could explore very directly with substantial confidence their relevant dimensions for past and current time periods (though there might remain some questions about the applicability of the estimates for future time periods). But there are substantial data problems, including possibly key variables that are not observed and other variables that are observed only with errors, that make drawing inferences about behaviour related to human resources in many cases difficult, and point to estimation issues (see later). Some data problems are discussed in this section, both to point to areas in which better data might be collected and to lay the groundwork for discussing the estimation issues in the next section.

Micro Data

Micro data that have been used for analysis of skills and other human resources and international competitiveness and development include household and productive establishment (for example, firms, farms, schools, health clinics) censuses and surveys, and in a relatively few cases, experimental data. Because of the costs of collecting census data, survey data are more common and probably generally more cost-effective. Problems that are widespread in the available micro data sets include:

- *Missing variables* Data sets inevitably have missing variables (for example, ability, motivations, expected prices and labour-market conditions, training and learning-by-doing), which can cause unobserved variable bias if there is not control for such variables on the right side of relations (see later subsection on omitted variable bias) and preclude examination of their determinants if they are dependent variables of interest.
- *Selected samples* If samples are selected by some criteria that are systematically related to the relations being investigated, selectivity bias may result (see later subsection). Data collected from enterprise surveys, for example, generally are a random sample neither of enterprises nor of workers because small-scale and informal enterprises are less likely to be included than are large, formal-sector enterprises. Samples of individuals who use some facility, such as employment or training services, again are not likely to be random because they are selected on a form of behaviour (that is, using the facilities).
- *Selectivity regarding particular information* Even if the sample is random or the data are from a census, for investigation of certain

relations information may be available only for a selected subsample (for example, wage rates only are available for individuals who have wage-paying jobs; choices of training alternatives only for those who elect or who are selected to receive training). If estimates of relations related to skill development and international competitiveness and development, for example, are based on such samples the effects may be misunderstood if there is not control for such selectivity (see later subsection on selectivity bias).

- *Measurement errors* For the variables that are included in data sets there may be measurement errors (which may cause estimation biases, see later subsection on measurement errors) due to systematic reporting errors (for example, underreporting of income, reporting what the respondent thinks that the interviewer wants to hear rather than what occurred), limited recall capacities, lack of knowledge, or the mechanics of reporting/coding/processing the data. There also may be important measurement errors because analysts use variables that even if error free are imperfect indicators of desired concepts. Common examples of the latter are the widespread use of schooling attainment to represent schooling investments or participation in training programmes to represent training investment, with no recognition of the varying qualities of schools and of training programmes.

Micro data can be improved. (1) More concern can be given to assuring random samples. For example, if there is to be a sample of enterprises or of training institutions, the sampling frame can be established on the basis of a household census so that the appropriate sample weights for workers in the enterprise or trainees in the training institution sample are known and selectivity can be controlled. (2) More efforts can be made to measure the critical variables for the analysis of human resources and development. Examples of variables that sometimes are, but often are not, included in data collection efforts, include specific skills, cognitive achievement and ability test scores, wage rates, and community-level prices and facilities. (3) More efforts can be made to collect data in a manner that permits the control for unobserved individual, household and community characteristics. For example, adult sibling data permits control for shared childhood background, experimental data with random assignment to treatment versus control groups permits control for unobserved factors, and longitudinal data permits the control for unobserved effects that are fixed over time and for investigation of dynamics. (4) Purposively weighted samples are useful to investigate some phenomena that are important for only a small part of the population as long as the weights are known and there is a tie-in to a population sample so that selectivity can be controlled.

Of course, there are costs to improving micro data, and there always will be additional or better questions that analysts can think of after the data collection. But the potential gains from improvements such as those indicated in the previous paragraph, are substantial. And since data sets are almost public goods in the technical sense in that the true social marginal costs of being used by additional analysts are quite low relative to the fixed costs of collecting the data, the private incentives for data collection generally are far below the social gains. So, in the terms of the earlier subsection on supply considerations, there is an important efficiency argument for public subsidization of data collection and assuring widespread access to such data at true social marginal costs.

Aggregate Data

Aggregate data analysis has become increasingly common, in part because of greater recent availability of such data through international organizations and in part because of increased interest in skill and human resource development, international competitiveness and aggregate growth issues. However, data problems with aggregate data include those for micro data, plus additional difficulties. For example, a general problem is that most of the aggregate data refer to means, not to higher moments. Two countries with identical mean schooling may have very different distributions of schooling, with very different implications for assessment of their international competitiveness or development experience. Beyond this general problem with aggregate data, there are major human resource investments for which data across countries are so far from comparable that they have not been used much if at all for comparative purposes – importantly for the concern of this book, including training and adult education. There also are specific problems with the major aggregate schooling investment and stock variables that are used widely.[22]

Schooling investments
The most-used data for schooling investments are primary, secondary and tertiary enrolment rates compiled by UNESCO primarily from annual reports of Ministries of Education. These data have four principal problems that probably cause systematic overestimation of schooling investments for lower per-capita-income countries, which in turn probably biases downwards the estimated impact of schooling on other outcomes and biases downwards the estimated impact of income and other variables that are positively associated with development on schooling investments: (1) For many countries only gross enrolment rates (that is, enrolments in a school level of individuals of all ages relative to the census-estimated population for the age range thought appropriate for that school level) are available rather than net enrolment rates

in which the age range for the numerator is the same as for the denominator. For countries that have both, ratios of the two vary considerably because of considerable differences across countries in age when starting school and in grade repetition. For some research questions net enrolment is the more appropriate concept, but the countries for which such data are available are relatively few (though increasing rapidly for recent years) and tend to be more developed. (2) Different starting ages for school and different durations of schooling levels further make cross-country comparisons difficult. (3) Enrolment rates often reflect opening day enrolment rates, not regular attendance, with the difference inversely associated with development. (4) Enrolment rates address only the quantitative, not the qualitative, dimension of schooling investments. Differential schooling quality across countries at a point in time and changing schooling quality over time would seem to be important, but aggregate data are not readily available with which to make satisfactory comparisons of school quality over time or across countries. Possible quality indicators that UNESCO presents include only student/teacher ratios and central governmental expenditures on schooling. Teacher/student ratios over a broad range do not seem to be strongly related to the value added of schooling systems (Hanushek 1986, 1995; Harbison and Hanushek 1992), and the extent of schooling expenditures by other governmental levels and by private individuals varies considerably across countries and in some cases within countries over time (in addition to the problems of appropriately converting such expenditures into common terms, see Srinivasan 1994).

Schooling stocks

For many purposes, such as investigating the determinants of growth or of international competitiveness, schooling stocks are of interest (though a number of studies use enrolment rates in such contexts). There are three basic types of measures available of the stocks of schooling – adult literacy, adult schooling attainment collected directly in censuses or surveys, and adult schooling attainment series constructed from time series of census or survey-based enrolment data.

Literacy UNESCO summarizes literacy data, with which there are at least three problems: (1) The actual data on which available literacy measures are based often are sparse and dated and are selectively more available for more developed countries. UNESCO (1991: Table 1.3), for example, gives for 141 countries and territories the year of the last census or survey for literacy data. The median source was a census or survey over a decade earlier in 1980 and with 19 countries or territories (18 of which are in Africa) with no such survey in 1970 or later (and with significantly more and earlier literacy measures available for higher per-capita GDP countries than for lower per-capita countries). Estimates of relations between literacy and variables such as per-capita GDP, moreover, change substantially if 'constructed' literacy data are used instead of only actual literacy data (Behrman and Rosenzweig 1994). (2) Definitions of literacy differ across countries and over time within countries. (3) Conceptually literacy represents only one major dimension (that is, not numeracy, or more advanced knowledge) of basic schooling with little variance across the more-developed economies by conventional measures even though casual observations and enrolment rates suggest that schooling stocks may vary considerably.

Direct census- or survey-based schooling attainment   UNESCO also summarizes the distribution of the population 25 years of age and older by levels of schooling attainment. This measure, however, is limited to the relatively small number of censuses and surveys that are available with substantial variance of years across countries, similar to the problems with the literacy data. UNESCO (1991: Table 1.4) also notes additional problems of comparability across countries in definitions. Moreover, this indicator has the same problems as the school enrolment data with variations of schooling duration for different schooling levels across countries and over time, with variations in schooling quality, and with ignoring non-schooling education. The data gaps in the available adult schooling data have led researchers to construct schooling data series. Barro and Lee (1993) have constructed quinquennial time-series data from 1960 to 1985 for 110 countries using census data. These estimates are based on one or two actual observations for 44 countries and three or fewer actual observations for 82 countries; thus most of the items in this data set are estimates.

Enrolment-based schooling attainment   A third indicator of schooling stocks has been calculated by the perpetual inventory method based on time series of schooling investments (enrolment). Lau, Jamison and Louat (1991) calculated this measure for adults aged 15–64 under the assumption that the schooling capital stock was zero in 1900 (which has no important effect on the schooling stock in the post-1960 period in which they are interested), that country-specific primary and secondary school enrolments for the period before 1960 followed the same secular trends as those in the post-1960 period (generally 1960–87) so that estimates of these enrolment rates can be backcast (subject to the constraint that they be non-negative), that there is no depreciation in the stock of schooling, and that mortality and international migration for the 15–64 age range are not dependent on schooling (which assumptions are contradicted by empirical studies of adult mortality and migration). Nehru, Swanson and Dubey (1995) recently have revised the Lau et al. annual estimates of the schooling stock for adults aged 15–64 based on longer time series of enrolment rates (back to 1930 for most countries and 1900 for several), estimated repeater and dropout rates and estimated age-specific mortality rates for 85 countries for the 1960–87 period. These estimates are, of course, subject to the problems with the underlying enrolment data discussed above, which may result in schooling attainment measures being too high and measurement errors that are systematically related to economic growth. Moreover, there is limited information on grade repetition and on mortality rates (the former of which Nehru, Swanson and Dubey suggest is particularly important based on their sensitivity analysis).[23]

Though simple bivariate correlations among these measures of adult school stocks for common years and countries are fairly high (above 0.8), country/ year coverages differ substantially across the series in ways that are selective regarding economic and demographic developments (Behrman and Rosenzweig 1993). These data differences result in some different coefficient estimates for adult schooling across data series if schooling stocks are used as the right-side variables in estimates of relationships of schooling with various economic and social variables (for example, real per-capita GDP, infant mortality rates, total fertility rates, and life expectancies at birth). Thus there has been and is likely to continue to be a payoff to improving these series because the use of many (all?) of them may cause biased inferences.

ESTIMATION ISSUES[24]

Data problems mean that obtaining consistent estimates of critical parameters pertaining to relations among skill development, other human resources, international competitiveness and development is difficult indeed, both at the micro and the macro levels of aggregation. Therefore it is hard to know how to interpret many existing studies. Better data and more attention to the underlying models of behaviour in empirical work would lessen these estimation problems, though often it is difficult to deal with all of the possible problems at once and remedies for some may exacerbate others (for example, using fixed effects estimators to control for unobserved fixed effects may exacerbate measurement errors). Thus there is some art in empirical work in assessing what are likely to be the major estimation problems, and tests of robustness (including estimates from different samples) are important.

Considerable professional returns accrue to analysts who demonstrate for the first time in a particular context that weakening an assumption changes the estimates considerably. There appear to be considerably smaller private returns to repetition in the social sciences and policy analysis, though the social returns might be considerable. There exist some examples, however, in the literature, such as Rosenzweig and Schultz's (1988) study of birth production functions. There may be considerable social gains from encouraging more such studies. Yet a caveat is in order because it is not clear that continual repetition of studies that make implausible assumptions is of much value. For example, suppose that education is determined in part by family background (that is, genetics, parental education, home environment) and that family background also affects employment and wages in many contexts. Then it is not clear that estimating education–wage correlations in many contexts with many data sets without controlling for family background helps us to understand the impact of education *per se* (as opposed to education and correlated dimensions of family background) on wages. Yet at times, including the schooling–earnings literature, the very repetition of such studies for many data sets in many different contexts is interpreted by many as confirming the robustness of the interpretation that schooling has certain estimated effects.

Social scientists and policy analysts have become increasingly sensitive to estimation problems in assessing issues such as the impact of skill development on international competitiveness and development from non-experimental data, because of critical unobserved variables, simultaneity, selectivity and measurement errors. These problems may cause skills to be correlated with the disturbance term in the relation being specified to obtain estimates of the impact of skills on the measurement of international competitiveness so that simple estimators may yield biased and inconsistent estimates of the effects of skills. A number of estimation strategies therefore have been proposed and used to attempt to deal with these problems. Under certain assumptions each of these strategies eliminates the estimation problems. But in many cases the required assumptions are very restrictive. And many empirical applications of these methods are (usually implicitly) quite cavalier about what assumptions are required for a particular strategy to yield consistent estimates of the effects of education. It does not help simply to repeat, like a mantra, 'instrumental variables,' 'fixed effects,' or 'observed indicators of endowment'. In fact unthinking 'cookbook' application of some of these methods may result in worse rather than reduced inconsistencies. What is needed, but all too often is wanting, is thoughtful applications of estimation methods that are appropriate given the underlying behaviour models, such as discussed earlier, and/or better data.

For communicating better with most people, estimation methods that are as transparent as possible are desirable. This is so because greater transparency increases credibility, in part because greater transparency increases the probability that individuals can assess with understanding the analysis for themselves. A basic problem that is emphasized above is that some critical variables that may affect the behaviours that we observe related to skill development choices and the effects of those choices generally are not observed by data analysts. As a result, analysis of relations among the observed variables, without control for the unobserved variables, may be very misleading regarding the magnitude and even the sign of the impact of skills and other human resources on various outcomes. If better data changes critical usually-unobserved variables into observed variables, the analysis can be undertaken in a much more transparent manner and be more credible to a broader audience, though there still may be other estimation issues such as identifying the direction of causality given that both skill development and international competitiveness may importantly reflect behavioural choices. But data collection is costly, often more so for some of the possibly-critical usually-unobserved variables (which may be part of the reason that they usually are unobserved). Therefore, in order to obtain consistent estimates from much of the data that currently are available or that will become available fortuitously in the future because of data collection for other purposes, estimation techniques must substitute for data. But even if clever analysts can deal with the problems created by important unobserved variables in their investigation of the effects of skills on international competitiveness, they are likely to have limited success in communicating their results to a wider audience because the methods that they use are not likely to be sufficiently transparent to give their results much credibility with a broader audience.

So there is a basic tradeoff involved between obtaining consistent estimates with such data but having problems in communicating credibly what are the implications of such estimates, and using simpler methods that appear to be transparent by assuming away the missing variable problems so their results are easier to communicate and accepted as more credible, but the results may be biased and inconsistent. In terms of making scientific progress regarding our knowledge of the effects on international competitiveness of skills, I argue that it is important to obtain the best estimates possible with existing data despite the credibility/communication problem and also to continue to attempt to obtain better data that will permit more truly transparent analysis that leads to consistent estimates (not just analysis that is apparently more transparent because critical real problems are assumed away). Only by adopting such a two-pronged approach are we likely to learn more about the true effects of skills and other human resources on international competitiveness, development and other outcomes of interest. That does not mean that descriptive correlations that have not been controlled for some of the estimation problems are not of interest. But they should be presented as just that, descriptions of the data, and not interpreted to reflect the casual impact of skills and other human resources.

I now review four common estimation issues.

Omitted Variable Bias

Omitted variable bias occurs if there is a variable(s) that is correlated with an included variable and that should be included but is not included in the estimation. The bias is greater the more important is the missing variable and the more highly it is correlated with an included variable. Omitted variable bias may occur because there are not observations on variables that are thought to be important and no way to control for those variables, or because researchers choose empirical specifications that ignore important phenomena. The latter would seem less likely to occur if the empirical specification is tied closely to some plausible theoretical framework.

Possible omitted variable biases are pervasive in the empirical literature on the impact of skills and other human resources on international competitiveness and development, though most of this literature does not attempt to explore such possibilities. For example, an important implication of the framework that is presented in the earlier subsection on Becker's Woytinsky lecture is that skills and other human resource investments are associated with a number of individual, family, community and national characteristics: individual abilities, motivations, inherent robustness; family support, role models, household gender roles, connections, and genetic endowments; community role models, the quality of community health and educational services, the stock of production inputs in the community that are complementary to human resource investments in the individual; labour-market segmentation by gender, ethnic and racial groups; preferences regarding material–leisure tradeoffs. To identify the impact of human resource investments on a particular outcome, therefore, it is important to control for these other characteristics. Some studies of the impact of human resources in developing countries suggest that such controls make a considerable difference (see the surveys of micro studies in Behrman 1990a, b and c and aggregate estimates in Behrman and Rosenzweig 1993[25]).

Omitted variable bias can be lessened in a number of ways. Better data can help, with greater efforts to include *a priori* critical variables and to obtain data sets with which unobserved fixed effects can be controlled (for example, longitudinal data, experimental data and sibling data including twin data[26]). But it also is important to tie the empirical specifications more closely to the underlying behavioural models than often is done in order to lessen the probabilities of inadvertent conceptual omissions of critical variables. Of course this is potentially useful only because of the assumption that the behavioural models bear some relation to real determinants of behaviour (perhaps in an 'as if' rather than an explicit sense). But on a general level for models such as in the earlier subsection on micro frameworks that assumption seems to be supported, and exploration of the merits of specific forms of such models depends on careful links with empirical work.

Simultaneity Bias

Most of the studies on the impact of skills and other human resources on international competitiveness and development in the literature do not control for simultaneity. But casual observations, as well as behavioural models (for example, see the earlier subsection on Becker's Woytinsky lecture), suggest that a number of relevant decisions might be undertaken simultaneously. For instance, people with more motivation and ability related to labour-market success may be both schooled and trained more and have greater labour-market success. If, in such instances, there is no control for simultaneity, biased estimates may result. These biases may be in either direction (depending upon what is the nature of the underlying behaviour), but the inferences may be misleading, perhaps considerably so, if there is no control for simultaneity.

The most common control for simultaneity is to replace endogenous right-side variables with their instrumented estimates, perhaps after specification tests indicate that simultaneity is a problem. However the choice of variables used for the first-stage estimates often seems cavalier and probably inappropriate. Good instruments are (a) associated with the endogenous variable of interest and (b) independent of the disturbance term in the relation in which that endogenous variable is a right-side variable. If (b) is not satisfied, the estimates that are obtained are not consistent, so their interpretation is not clear. But obtaining instruments that satisfy (b) is difficult indeed in most contexts. Often prices and community characteristics are used for this purpose for micro studies. But if there are unobserved choice variables that enter into the relation of interest, such instruments do *not* satisfy (b), so it is hard to know how to interpret the estimates.[27] Once again, careful specification of empirical models in the light of appropriate theoretical frameworks with the possibility of unobserved variables is likely to be helpful.

Selectivity Bias

Many existing studies of the impact of skills and other human resources on international competitiveness and development do not control for sample selectivity determining such decisions as who receives wages, who attends private or vocational schools, who works in different occupations, who receives training, and which countries are included in aggregate data sets. The remedies for dealing with these possible selectivity problems, once again, are a combination of better data (see earlier section on data issues) and modelling of the behaviour that led to the selectivity in the first place (for example, whether to participate in the wage labour force). In cases in which observations on critical variables may be missing selectively, it may be possible to put bounds on the estimates without placing as much structure on the analysis as in the other procedures described above (Manski 1989).

Consider the case in which only individuals who have formal-sector jobs might have options of formal training. This means that analysis of the impact of schooling on formal training based on only those who had formal training options is based on a selected sample and the estimates cannot be generalized to the population. The estimates could be bounded by assuming first that all those who did not have formal-sector jobs would have had formal training if they had had formal-sector jobs and then that all those who did not have formal-sector jobs would not have had formal-sector training if they had had formal-sector jobs. The range of estimates under these two extreme assumptions then establishes a domain, which may or may not be relatively small, for the relation. If it is relatively small, then it may narrow debates about policy effectiveness considerably. The advantage of this procedure is that in some cases it may yield relatively small ranges of estimates despite selectivity in observations without making strong assumptions on model specification. But it does not always yield useful answers. Moreover, in some contexts it may ignore some possibly important aspects of the problems of analysing behaviour, such as the direction of causality between the two variables of interest. Nevertheless, it certainly adds another tool that could be used to analyse the impact of skills and other human resources on international competitiveness and development in the presence of estimation problems such as selectivity, and which might lead to quite informative results in some contexts. However, I am unaware of use of this procedure for the topics covered in this book.

Measurement Error

Random measurement errors in right-side variables, such as schooling or training in a wage or a productivity determination relation, cause biases towards zero in the estimated coefficients – and thus underestimates of the effects of skills and other human resources. These biases are exacerbated in estimates that control for unobserved fixed effects through differencing. Some recent estimates of the schooling impact on labour-market outcomes, for example, suggest that measurement errors can cause considerable downward biases in the estimated effects of schooling on wages in within-sibling estimates (for example, Ashenfelter and Krueger 1994; Behrman, Rosenzweig and Taubman 1994). Instrumental variables may be used to purge the noisy variables of their random components. But once again, the set of instruments for the first-stage estimates must be chosen carefully to avoid inconsistent estimates.

But not all measurement errors are random. Some may be systematic, and *may* cause biases in the opposite direction. For example, schooling is usually represented by years or grades of schooling, with no control for school quality even though school quality appears to vary greatly, and would seem to have an impact on outcomes of interest in addition to that of grades of schooling. If school quality does have an impact and higher school quality is correlated with more schooling, then the failure to control for schooling quality in estimates of the impact of schooling results in upward-biased estimates of the effect of extending years of schooling since in the statistical analysis grades of schooling represents not only the effect of grades of schooling itself, but also of schooling quality. The best remedy in such a case would seem to be to improve the data so that they better represent the desired constructs, though in some contexts fixed effects estimators may be helpful (for example, Behrman, Ii and Murillo 1995; Behrman, Rosenzweig and Taubman 1996).

CONCLUSIONS

The development of skills and other human resources is seen increasingly as critical in international competitiveness and economic development. This increased emphasis originates in part from applied analysis of the roles of human resources in developing countries and in part from the 'new economic growth' literature in which human resources play a critical role in productivity growth because of externalities and increasing returns to scale to human resources and learning-by-doing associated with certain products.

This literature and casual observations have spawned a rich range of hypotheses about the determinants of human resources and the impact of skills and other human resources. There have been a myriad of empirical studies, both using micro and using aggregate data, that purport to investigate these hypotheses, and further such studies become available at an increasing rate. As a result, we can be confident about many *associations* between human resources and various background factors, policies, and market and non-market outcomes of interest.

Yet we know surprisingly little about *causality*, both regarding what are the magnitudes of factors that determine human resources and what are the magnitudes of the effects of skills and other human resources on different outcomes in various contexts, including international competitiveness. We know so little because so many of the studies are based on inadequate analytical frameworks and data with no or limited efforts to control for estimation problems – such as omitted variables, simultaneity, selectivity and measurement errors – that may cause substantial biases in empirical estimates. In a

number of cases in which there have been controls for such possible problems, comparison of the resulting estimates with standard estimates suggest
that such controls affect importantly our understanding of human resources
and development both from a positive perspective and in terms of possible
policy prescriptions. With regard to policy evaluations and recommendations,
moreover, the existing literature also lacks clarity, particularly regarding
efficiency reasons for policy interventions.

Often, for example, it reads as if it were sufficient to show an impact
(preferably a large impact) of human resources on desired outcomes to warrant policy support, with little or no attention paid to the need to identify
distortions between private and public incentives to justify considering such
interventions on efficiency grounds. It is true that there is frequent appeal to
externalities, but repeating the mantra 'externalities' is not a good substitute
for systematic analysis of what constitute externalities, what are their
magnitudes, and what policies are likely to be high in the policy hierarchy.

Looking forward, the limited present knowledge regarding causal relations
between human resources and development would seem to have two major
implications.

First, given present imperfect information and that information is always
likely to be imperfect, asymmetrical and not necessarily timely, in terms of
policies it seems desirable to develop and support human-resource-service-
related institutions that are more incentive compatible. This probably means
relying more on markets and improving markets when the social returns of
doing so are high rather than engaging in so much direct production and
regulation of human-resource-related services and the uses of human resources. But it also means focusing governmental activities where the government is likely to have a comparative advantage because of distributional
concerns or market failures – such as providing and analysing information,
preventing unregulated local monopolies, providing essential infrastructures,
supporting experiments regarding the development of human resources and
publicizing their results, subsidizing human resource activities where there is
good evidence of externalities and supporting human resource investments in
the poor through schemes such as vouchers, which increase the pressures for
efficiency. For many governments such foci would represent a considerable
shift of approaches to human resources, international competitiveness and
development.

Second, there is scope for considerable improvements of analysis of the
impact of skills and other human resources on international competitiveness
and development by building better on the foundations of improved analytical frameworks, better data, and better control for estimation problems, as
well as by being more systematic about inferring possible policy implications
of such analysis. Given the public good aspect of such knowledge and par-

ticularly of the information required for good analysis, there is a strong argument for public support for this process, both at the national and at the international level. More systematic studies with better data could be enlightening on a range of important questions regarding the impact and the determinants of human resources in developing countries and international competitiveness and other goals. How important are training, adult education and other human resource investments beyond schooling? How does the impact reflect the context in regard to physical investments, market development, macro strategy and international economic policy? What is the relation to sustainable growth? Are there important gender, ethnic or other demographic differences in the impact of human resources? Can human resource explanations of the impact be distinguished from other possibilities, such as screening and signalling? What is evidence regarding externalities or other market failures? What is the nature of interactions among human resources? Are there important productivity–equity tradeoffs in human resource investments? What are the political economy dimensions of human resource investments? How important is family background in the determination of human resources? How important is the state of credit and labour-markets? What are the origins of gender, race and other differences in human resource investments? To what extent are preference differences versus price differences important? How effectively are human-resource-related services provided? What determines the effectiveness of such service provision?

NOTES

* This chapter builds on Behrman (1990a, 1995, 1996a–c) and Behrman and Rosenzweig (1993, 1994). The author thanks Martin Godfrey for useful comments on an earlier version of this paper, but he alone is responsible for all 'interpretations' given in this chapter.

1. From the perspective of standard Ricardian comparative advantage the term 'international competitiveness' is an oxymoron – every country has comparative advantages in production of some goods and services. But this term has become a shorthand expression for being competitive (a net exporter) in international markets in certain goods and services that are thought to be of particular interest, perhaps because they are viewed as 'modern', more productive, or as leading to ongoing productivity growth (for example, through positive externalities). For the purpose of this chapter it is a maintained assumption that 'international competitiveness' is desirable.

2. Some commentators question how much is new in this literature (for example, Raut and Srinivasan 1993).

3. For more details, see the articles indicated in the text or the surveys in Bardhan (1995), Behrman (1990a), Lucas (1993), Raut and Srinivasan (1993), Pack (1994), and Romer (1989, 1993, 1994)

4. This assumption assures the existence of an optimum with a finite objective function in a dynamic optimizing model with increasing returns (see assumption 3).

5. If the increasing returns are external to the firm, a competitive equilibrium can exist.

6. Romer emphasizes that the idea of increasing returns being central to the growth process

goes back at least to Adam Smith. But this insight was not incorporated explicitly into prominent formal dynamic growth models until recently because of difficulties in such modelling.

7. She demonstrates that if such externalities are not too large, the equilibrium growth path is unique and the effect of various parameters on the equilibrium growth rate can be determined.

8. 'Endowments' is used to mean characteristics that are given independent of behavioural decisions (for example, genetically-determined ability). Behrman, Hrubec, Taubman and Wales (1980), Behrman, Rosenzweig and Taubman (1994, 1996), Miller, Mulvey and Martin (1995, 1996) and the references therein give evidence of the importance of endowments.

9. For the last three of these comparisons the otherwise identical individuals would have to live in different economies.

10. Therefore to obtain estimates of the impact of human resource investments on some outcome, one cannot just consider the association between the human resource investment and the outcome (that is, the association between years of schooling and wage rates), but one must control for the endowments underlying the human resource investments.

11. Behrman and Birdsall (1983) emphasize that publicly-subsidized school quality, if complementary with time in school, induces greater schooling attainment. If investors pay for greater quality, investment does not necessarily increase with higher-quality options; the equilibrium investment depends upon where the marginal cost curve for the higher-quality option is in addition to the location of the marginal benefit curve. Behrman and Birdsall (1983), Behrman, Birdsall and Kaplan (1994), and Behrman, Ross, Sabot and Tropp (1996) present estimates that suggest that the social rates of return to investments in school quality are at least as high as to those to increasing the quantity of schools with average current quality. These results raise questions about the efficiency of current allocations between schooling quality and quantity and about possible equity–productivity tradeoffs (that is, productivity gains may be larger from concentrating schooling resources among fewer individuals). The nature of equity–productivity tradeoffs, moreover, may have subtleties because some quality improvements may require more household inputs from poor households and others may free such resources for poor households (Barros and de Mendonca 1992). Stokey's (1991) emphasis on high-quality goods, production of which requires high-quality labour (see subsection on aggregate models) raises related questions about the role of quality (also see Wood 1994).

12. In this case, schooling or formal training is partly serving to signal for these attributes. Even if that is all that schooling or formal training is doing, there still are private returns to schooling or formal training through the returns from signalling one's attributes. If schooling or formal training is also associated with other characteristics (say, with family background independent of such attributes) that also affect directly the expected benefits, within a pure signalling model omitted variables also lead to biases in standard estimates of the private returns to schooling or formal training.

13. And for understanding under what conditions there may be efficiency reasons for governments or for private firms to subsidize human resource investments.

14. With bargaining, identification of who controls resources may be critical. Schultz (1990) and Thomas (1990) give estimates relating to human resource investments that are interpreted to imply disaggregation of sources across individuals. Behrman (1996c) provides further discussion and references.

15. Thomas, Strauss and Henriques (1991) give such an interpretation based on how schooling coefficient estimates decline as they include use of information sources in their conditional demand relations.

16. The public marginal financial cost may not be identical to the social marginal cost if there are distortions in prices paid by the public sector.

17. Schools are often characterized by the levels of test scores or other outcomes, but what is of interest in assessing school performance if schools serve roles beyond screening/signalling is the 'value added' (that is, *increases* (not the levels) in cognitive achievements or other measures of relevant skills). The distinction is important because schools with

selective admissions may have high cognitive achievement students but not much value added (and vice versa).

18. The economic definition of efficiency differs from the use of 'efficiency' in the educational literature, which often refers to promotion rates or dropout rates. Some grade repetition and some dropouts in fact probably are economically efficient. In almost any school system there are some students who are not yet mature enough to be promoted or who have a variety of learning disabilities so that they would benefit sufficiently from repetition, that it is efficient in an economic sense for them to repeat grades. Also it may be sensible from the point of view of households in an uncertain world to enrol a student in school with the intent of keeping the child in school through the year if health, weather, harvests and labour markets are normal, but to withdraw the child during the school year so that he or she can work if during the school year weather, harvest or labour markets turn out to be abnormal or if serious illness strikes – and then to re-enrol the child the next year. Likewise no repetition is not necessarily an indication of a good situation; no repetition can be obtained simply by automatically promoting all students whether or not they learn anything.

19. Other goals that are annunciated for developing countries often are closely related to these two economic goals. For example, the background papers for the United Nations Social Summit held in March 1995 in Copenhagen point to three foci: employment creation, poverty alleviation and social integration. All three of these foci (particularly since the third has important components of increasing participation in the economic system and of increasing command over resources for disadvantaged groups) are closely related to these two economic goals (Behrman 1995c).

20. I present a more extensive discussion in Behrman (1990a).

21. The systematic estimation of externalities does not seem to be an easy task with available data (also see Manski 1993), though one can think of conceptual experiments that would help (for example, randomly changing the schooling composition of communities). Some progress might be made by exploiting the observation that what is an externality at one level of aggregation is internal at another level of aggregation. For example, if carefully estimated micro private rates of return to schooling and carefully estimated rates of return to schooling based on aggregate data are compared, the differences would seem to reflect that the micro externalities are internal to the aggregate estimates. There would remain other estimation problems, such as controlling for simultaneity and unobserved factors, but perhaps careful analysis could isolate their effects. I note, however, that the standard micro estimates such as those that are summarized in Psacharopoulos (1994) tend to indicate much higher private rates of return to schooling than do aggregate estimates. If there were no estimation problems in either the micro or the aggregate estimates, this would imply that the externalities are negative, which is contrary to the priors of most people who work in this area.

22. For more details, see Ahmad (1994), Behrman and Rosenzweig (1993, 1994), Chamie (1994). Heston (1994) and Srinivasan (1994). To explore relations between human resources and development, indicators of development are also needed. The most common indicator, per-capita income, also has a number of problems of comparability that are discussed by Ahmad, Heston and Srinivasan. To explore relations between human resources and international competitiveness, empirical measures of such concepts as 'openness' are desirable, but the indicators used by various researchers are not all that highly correlated across countries (Harrison 1993).

23. Recent information collected in a special UNESCO/OREALC survey on repetition rates in Latin America and the Caribbean, for example, suggests that official-reported repetition rates for primary schooling are only about half the survey rates, though with a lot of variations across countries in the discrepancies between the official and the survey rates (Schiefelbein and Wolff 1992).

24. Deaton (1995) provides a more extensive discussion of these and other estimation issues with a focus on analysis of development issues.

25. Estimates in Behrman and Rosenzweig (1993) indicate that the association of schooling with per-capita income in cross-country estimates is only about half as large if there is

control for unobserved country fixed effects (perhaps representing cultural differences in materialism and work ethics) than without control.

26. Data on identical twins have the advantage over other data that they permit control for all unobserved genetic endowments by estimating the impact of the difference in human resources between twins on some outcome of interest. I am unaware of any studies that use identical twins data to estimate the impact of skills on indicators of international competitiveness. But there have been several studies that have used twins data to estimate the impact of schooling attainment (and, in one case, indicators of college quality) on wages (for example, Behrman, Hrubec, Taubman and Wales 1980; Ashenfelter and Krueger 1994; Behrman, Rosenzweig and Taubman 1994. 1996; Miller, Mulvey and Martin 1995, 1996) all but one of which (Ashenfelter and Krueger) find that the control for unobserved genetic endowments reduces substantially and significantly the estimated impact of schooling on wages.

27. Behrman and Lavy (1994, 1995) provide an example with their estimation of the dependence of child cognitive achievement on child health (and other factors including schooling) with Ghanaian data. If community prices and other characteristics are used as first-stage instruments, the health effects (as indicated by child height and other anthropometric indicators) appear much larger than in ordinary least-squares estimates. But if there also is control for unobserved family and community effects the estimated health impact (but not the schooling impact) falls considerably, suggesting that the first-stage instruments for the 'simultaneous' estimates are representing in important part other unobserved factors, and not just child health (that the estimated schooling effects do not fall as well suggests that these results do not only reflect exacerbation of biases towards zero due to measurement errors).

REFERENCES

Ahmad, Sultan (1994), 'Improving Inter-Spatial and Inter-Temporal Comparability of National Accounts', *Journal of Development Economics*, **44** (l), June, 53–76.

Ashenfelter, Orley and Alan Krueger (1994), 'Estimates of the Economic Return to Schooling from a New Sample of Twins', *American Economic Review* **84** (5) December, 1157–74.

Azariadis, Costas and Allan Drazen (1991), 'Threshold Externalities in Economic Development', *Quarterly Journal of Economics*, **105** (2), May, 501–26.

Bardhan, Pranab (1995), 'The Contribution of Endogenous Growth Theory to the Analysis of Development Problems: An Assessment', in Jere R. Behrman and T.N. Srinivasan (eds), *Handbook of Development Economics*, Volume 3B, Amsterdam: North-Holland, 2983–99.

Barro, Robert J. and Jong-Wha Lee (1993), 'International Comparison of Educational Attainment', *Journal of Monetary Economics*, 32:3, (December), 363–94.

Barros, R.P de and R.S.P. de Mendonca (1992), 'The Quality of Education in Brazil', Rio de Janeiro, Brazil: IPEA, mimeo.

Becker, Gary S. (1967), 'Human Capital and the Personal Distribution of Income: An Analytical Approach', Ann Arbor: University of Michigan, Woytinsky Lecture, republished in Gary S. Becker, *Human Capital*, New York: NBER, 2nd edn 1975, 94–117.

Behrman, Jere R. (1990a) *Human Resource Led Development?* New Delhi, India: ARTEP/ILO.

Behrman, Jere R. (1990b), *The Action of Human Resources and Poverty on One Another: What We Have Yet to Learn*, Washington, DC: Population and Human Resources Department, World Bank.

Behrman, Jere R. (1990c), 'Women's Schooling and Nonmarket Productivity: A Survey and A Reappraisal', Philadelphia: University of Pennsylvania, mimeo (prepared for the Women in Development Division of the Population and Human Resources Department of the World Bank).

Behrman, Jere R. (1995a), 'The Contribution of Improved Human Resources to Productivity', Philadelphia, PA: University of Pennsylvania, mimeo (prepared as Background Paper for UNDP Human Development Report 1996).

Behrman, Jere R. (1995b), 'The Impact of Distributive Policies, Governmental Expenditure Patterns and Decentralization on Human Resources', Philadelphia, PA: University of Pennsylvania, mimeo (prepared as Background Paper for UNDP Human Development Report 1996).

Behrman, Jere R. (1995c), 'Industry and Social Integration', Chapter 5 in UNIDO Position Paper for Social Summit, March 1995, Philadelphia, PA: University of Pennsylvania, mimeo.

Behrman, Jere R. (1996), 'Conceptual and Measurement Issues and Policies', in Jere R. Behrman and Nevzer Stacey (eds), *Social Benefits of Education*, Ann Arbor, MI: University of Michigan Press, 17–67.

Behrman, Jere R. (1996), 'Measuring the Cost-Effectiveness of Schooling Policies in Developing Countries: Revisiting Issues of Methodology', *Economics of Education Review*, 15:4, forthcoming.

Behrman, Jere R. (1996), 'Intrahousehold Distribution and the Family', in Mark R. Rosenzweig and Oded Stark (eds), *Handbook of Population and Family Economics*, Amsterdam: North-Holland Publishing Company, forthcoming.

Behrman, Jere R. and Nancy Birdsall (1983), 'The Quality of Schooling: Quantity Alone is Misleading', *American Economic Review*, **73**, 928–46.

Behrman, Jere R., Nancy Birdsall and Robert Kaplan (1994), 'The Quality of Schooling and Labor Market Outcomes in Brazil: Some Further Explorations', in Nancy Birdsall, Barbara Bruns and Richard Sabot (eds), 'Opportunity Foregone: Education, Growth and Inequality in Brazil', Washington, DC: Inter-American Development Bank, mimeo.

Behrman, Jere R., Z. Hrubec, Paul Taubman and T.J. Wales (1980), *Socioeconomic Success: A Study of the Effects of Genetic Endowments, Family Environment and Schooling*, Amsterdam: North-Holland Publishing Company.

Behrman, Jere R., Masako Ii and David Murillo (1995), 'How Family and Individual Characteristics Affect Schooling Demands in Urban Bolivia: Multiple Schooling Indicators, Unobserved Community Effects, Nonlinearities and Interactions', La Paz, Bolivia: UDAPE/Grupo Social, mimeo (original 1992)

Behrman, Jere R. and Victor Lavy (1994), *Child Health and Schooling Achievement: Association, Causality, and Household Allocations*, World Bank Living Standards Measurement Study Paper, No. 104, Washington, DC: World Bank.

Behrman, Jere R. and Victor Lavy (1995), 'Production Functions, Input Allocations and Unobservables: The Case of Child Health and Schooling Success', Philadelphia: University of Pennsylvania, mimeo.

Behrman, Jere R. and Mark R. Rosenzweig (1993), 'Aggregate Data on Schooling Investments and Stocks: Data Problems and Comparisons Cross Countries and Over Time', Philadelphia, PA: University of Pennsylvania, mimeo.

Behrman, Jere R. and Mark R. Rosenzweig (1994), '*Caveat Emptor:* Cross-Country Data on Education and the Labor Force', *Journal of Development Economics* , **44** (1), June, 147–72.

Behrman, Jere R., Mark R. Rosenzweig and Paul Taubman (1994), 'Endowments and the Allocation of Schooling in the Family and in the Marriage Market: The Twins Experiment,' *Journal of Political Economy*, **102** (6), December, 1131–74.

Behrman, Jere R., Mark R. Rosenzweig and Paul Taubman (1996), 'College Choice and Wages: Estimates Using Data on Female Twins', *Review of Economics and Statistics*, 73:4 (November), forthcoming.

Behrman, Jere R., David Ross, Richard Sabot and Matthew Tropp (1996), 'Improving the Quality Versus Increasing the Quantity of Schooling', Philadelphia, PA: University of Pennsylvania, mimeo.

Chamie, Joseph (1994), 'Population Databases in Development Analysis', *Journal of Development Economics*, **44** (1), June, 131–46.

Corden, Max (1974), *Trade Policy and Economic Welfare*, Oxford: Clarendon Press.

de Mello, Guiomar Mamo and Rose Neubauer da Silva (1992), 'Politica Educacional No Governo Collar: Antecedentes e Contradicoes', ('Education Policies of the Collar Government: Antecedents and Contradictions') Rio de Janerio, mimeo.

Deaton, Angus (1995), 'Data and Econometric Tools for Development Analysis', in Jere R. Behrman and T.N. Srinivasan (eds), *Handbook in Development Economics, Vol. 3A*, Amsterdam: North-Holland Publishing Co., 1785–882.

Diamond, Peter (1965), 'National Debt in a Neoclassical Growth Model', *American Economic Review*, **55**, 1026–50.

Hanushek, Eric (1986), 'The Economics of Schooling', *Journal of Economic Literature*, **24**, 1141–77.

Hanushek, Eric A. (1995), 'Interpreting Recent Research On Schooling in Developing Countries', *World Bank Research Observer*, **10** (2), August, 227–46.

Harbison, Ralph W. and Eric A. Hanushek (1992), *Educational Performance of the Poor: Lessons from Rural Northeast Brazil*, New York: Oxford University Press.

Harrison, Ann (1993), *Openness and Growth: A Time-Series, Cross-Country Analysis for Developing Countries*, Washington, DC. World Bank.

Heston, Alan (1994), 'A Brief Review of Some Problems in Using National Accounts Data in Level Comparisons and Growth Studies', *Journal of Development Economics*, **44**, (1), June, 29–52.

Lau, L.J., D.T. Jamison and F. Louat (1991), *Education and Productivity in Developing Countries: An Aggregate Production Function Approach*; PRE Working Paper, No. 612, Washington, DC: World Bank.

Lucas, Robert E. (1988), 'On the Mechanics of Economic Development', *Journal of Monetary Economics*, **21**, 3–42.

Lucas, Robert E. (1990), 'Why Doesn't Capital Flow from Rich to Poor Countries?', *American Economic Review*, **80** (2), 3–42.

Lucas, Robert E. (1993), 'Making a Miracle', *Econometrica*, **61** (2), March, 251–72.

Manski, Charles F. (1989), 'Anatomy of the Selection Problem', *Journal of Human Resources*, **24** (3), Summer, 341–60.

Manski, Charles F. (1993), 'Identification of Endogenous Social Effects: The Reflection Problem', *Review of Economic Studies*, **60**, 531–42.

Miller, Paul, Charles Mulvey and Nick Martin (1995), 'What Do Twins Studies Tell Us About The Economic Returns to Education? A Comparison of US and Australian Findings', *American Economic Review*, **85** (3) 586–99.

Miller, Paul, Charles Mulvey and Nick Martin (1996), 'Family Characteristics and the Returns to Schooling: Evidence on Gender Differences from a Sample of Australian Twins', *Economica*, forthcoming.

Mincer, J.B. (1974), *Schooling, Experience, and Earnings*, New York: NBER.

Nehru, Vikram, Eric Swanson and Ashutosh Dubey (1995), 'A New Data Base on

Human Capital Stock: Sources, Methodology and Results', *Journal of Development Economics*, **46** (2), April, 379–401.

Pack, Howard (1994), 'Endogenous Growth Theory: Intellectual Appeal and Empirical Shortcomings', *Journal of Economic Perspectives*, **8** (1), Winter, 55–72.

Psacharopoulos, George (1994), 'Returns to Investment in Education: A Global Update', *World Development*, **22** (9), September, 1325–44.

Raut, Lakshmi K. and T.N. Srinivasan (1993), 'Theories of Long-Run Growth: Old and New', in Kaushik Basu, Mukul Majumdar and Tapan Mitra (eds), *Capital, Investment and Development*, Cambridge: Basil Blackwell, pp. 3–32.

Romer, Paul M. (1986), 'Increasing Returns and Long-Run Growth', *Journal of Political Economy*, **94** (5), 1002–36.

Romer, Paul M. (1989), 'Human Capital and Growth: Theory and Evidence', Chicago, IL: University of Chicago, mimeo.

Romer, Paul M. (1993), 'Two Strategies for Economic Development: Using Ideas and Producing Ideas', *Proceedings of the World Bank Annual Conference on Development Economics*, 1992, Washington, DC: World Bank, 63–116.

Romer, Paul M. (1994), 'The Origins of Endogenous Growth', *Journal of Economic Perspectives*, **8** (1), Winter, 3–22.

Rosenzweig, Mark R. (1995), 'Why Are There Returns in Schooling?', *American Economic Review*, **85** (2), (May), 153–8.

Rosenzweig, Mark R. and T. Paul Schultz (1988), 'The Stability of Household Production Technology: A Replication', *Journal of Human Resources*, **23** (4), 535–5.

Schiefelbein, Ernesto and Laurence Wolff (1992), 'Repetition and Inadequate Achievement in Latin America's Primary Schools: A Review of Magnitudes, Causes, Relationships and Strategies', Washington, DC: World Bank, mimeo.

Schultz, T. Paul (1990), 'Testing the Neoclassical Model of Family Labor Supply and Fertility', *Journal of Human Resources*, **25** (4), Fall, 599–634.

Schultz, Theodore W. (1975), 'The Value of the Ability to Deal with Disequilibria', *Journal of Economic Literature*, **13** (3), 827–46.

Solow, Robert (1956), 'A Contribution to the Theory of Economic Growth', *Quarterly Journal of Economics*, **70**, 65–94.

Srinivasan, T.N. (1994), 'Data Base for Development Analysis: An Overview', *Journal of Development Economics*, **44** (1), June, 3–26.

Stokey, Nancy L. (1991), 'Human Capital, Product Quality, and Growth', *Quarterly Journal of Economics*, **106**, 587–616.

Thomas, Duncan (1990), 'Intra-household Resource Allocation: An Inferential Approach', *Journal of Human Resources*, **25** (4), Fall, 635–64.

Thomas, Duncan, John Strauss and Maria Helena Henriques (1991), 'How Does Mother's Education Affect Child Height?', *Journal of Human Resources*, **26** (2), Spring, 183–211.

UNESCO (1991), *Statistical Yearbook, 1991*, Paris: UNESCO.

Wood, Adrian (1994), *Skill, Land and Trade: A Simple Analytical Framework* Working Paper No. 1, Brighton, Sussex, UK: Institute of Development Studies, University of Sussex.

Young, Alwyn (1991), 'Learning by Doing and the Dynamic Effects of International Trade', *Quarterly Journal of Economics*, **106** (2), May, 369–406.

2. Does educating girls improve export opportunities?

Kersti Berge and Adrian Wood*

INTRODUCTION

Manufactured exports from developing countries grew from about $1 billion in the mid-1950s to about $380 billion in 1990. However, this success has been very unequally distributed among developing countries. Two major explanations have been offered for this uneven export performance. The first sees differences in trade policies as the cause (for example, Balassa 1982; World Bank 1987). The second sees trade as determined principally by resource endowments (for example, Keesing and Sherk 1971; Leamer 1984), and in particular regards human resources as the basis of success in exporting manufactures (Bruchmann 1989; Wood and Berge 1994).

Two characteristics of the human resources engaged in export-oriented manufacturing in developing countries stand out: the workers are mainly educated, and they are mainly female. Case studies from the 1970s and 1980s show that workers who produce manufactured goods usually have (and require) at least a basic education – defined as completing primary school or becoming literate (Lim 1980: 11; Lee 1984: 82 and 175; Pearson 1991: 150). The case studies also reveal the female intensity of the labour force in developing-country export-oriented manufacturing. The studies focus mainly on workers in export processing zones (EPZs) and multinational corporations. An overall estimate is that women comprise between 70 and 90 per cent of the labour force in EPZs (UNIDO 1988: 7).

Moreover, the East Asian newly-industrialized countries (NICs) which have led the field in export-oriented industrialization clearly started with relatively large supplies of educated labour, including educated *female* labour. In 1965 Hong Kong, Korea and Singapore had already achieved universal primary enrolment, well ahead of other developing countries (World Bank 1993: 43). Between 20 and 40 per cent of women had completed primary school, compared to less than 5 per cent in most other developing countries. By the mid-1980s, average years of schooling for women had reached 6.6 in

Korea, 6.5 in Hong Kong and 5.7 in Taiwan, not far short of the OECD average of 7.5 years (Barro and Lee 1993: Table A.5).

This chapter asks whether the apparent importance of female human resources for trade performance can be observed in more systematic cross-country comparisons. To our knowledge there has not been much statistical work on the links between gender and exports. Wood (1991) found that developing countries which exported a rising proportion of their manufacturing output to the North also tended to employ an increasing proportion of females in their manufacturing sectors. More importantly in relation to the present study, he found a positive but weaker relationship in the mid-1980s between the level of the export performance variable and the level of female intensity.

The structure of the chapter is as follows. The next section outlines the trade model, with and without the gender dimension. The third derives regression specifications and reports on the empirical results. The final section draws conclusions and outlines ideas for further research.

A SIMPLE MODEL OF TRADE

This chapter takes the view that factor endowments are the most important determinant of the extent to which countries export manufactured goods. Our model of trade is a standard Heckscher–Ohlin (H–O) framework, in which the factors of production are simply human resources and natural resources. Capital is excluded from the model on the grounds that it is mobile between countries. Within the general framework, there are two distinct submodels to explain: (a) the share of manufactured, as opposed to primary, exports in total exports; and (b) the composition of manufactured exports.

In the rest of this section, the two submodels are first outlined without any reference to gender (for a fuller statement and more empirical testing, see Wood 1994b and Wood and Berge 1994). The theoretical basis for introducing a gender dimension into the models is then developed.

Manufactured Versus Primary Exports

This submodel has two goods, manufactures and primary products; and two factors of production, human resources (or skill) and natural resources (or land). The essential distinction between the two goods is that production of manufactures requires a higher ratio of skill to land than does the production of primary products. What determines a country's comparative advantage as between manufactures and primary products is therefore its relative endowments of skill and land.

In both submodels, human resources are for simplicity divided into three skill categories. The first contains workers with no education (NO-EDs), who are not employable in manufacturing. The second category consists of workers with a basic general education (BAS-EDs). The final category includes all workers with substantial post-basic education and training (SKILDs). The average skill level of a country's labour force (and hence its ratio of skill to land) thus depends on the relative sizes of these three categories: it can be thought of as a weighted average of the skill levels within each category, with their labour force shares as weights.

Composition of Manufactured Exports

Manufactured exports are a far-from-homogeneous category: there is clearly a lot of difference between cheap shirts or shoes and expensive machines or pharmaceuticals. The essential respect in which manufactures are taken to vary in the present model concerns their skill intensity: the production of machines and chemicals needs a higher ratio of SKILD to BAS-ED labour than the production of shirts and shoes. (For simplicity, we may assume that there are only two manufactured goods: skill-intensive and labour-intensive.) Each country's comparative advantage within manufacturing is thus determined by its relative supplies of SKILD and BAS-ED labour.

Introducing a Gender Dimension

If it is true, as the case studies mentioned above suggest, that workers producing manufactured exports in developing countries are predominantly female, as well as literate, how should the theoretical framework sketched above be modified? The first step, following H–O logic, is to differentiate both goods and human resources not only by skill but also by gender; the second is to think about the underlying causes of comparative advantage.

The minimum accounting modification is to add one more good and one more factor. Thus, as regards goods, we may distinguish three rather than two types of manufactures: a skill-intensive good and two types of labour-intensive good – those which use female BAS-EDs intensively (textiles and electronics, say), and those which use male BAS-EDs intensively (other low-skilled manufacturing activities). The difference might be rationalized in terms of the common view that women's nimble fingers and docility make them more suited than men to meticulous, repetitive assembly-line work.[1] Correspondingly, we split BAS-ED labour into two distinct factors: literate females (BAS-ED$_F$), and literate males (BAS-ED$_M$).

Having made these modifications to the categories, it is then important to ask why, from a theoretical point of view, developing countries might have a comparative advantage in female-intensive manufactures. H–O logic tells us that this must be because female labour, relative to male labour, is cheaper in developing countries than in developed countries, so we need to look for reasons why this might be the case.

The usual H–O explanation of differences in relative factor prices (in the absence of trade) is differences in relative factor supplies or endowments. However, this explanation does not seem plausible here: in the population at large, the ratio of females to males is much the same in developing as in developed countries; moreover, if attention is restricted to the literate population eligible for employment in manufacturing, the ratio of females to males is actually lower in developing than in developed countries (as will be documented below).

None the less, if two of the usual H–O assumptions are modified, developing countries may still plausibly be argued to have a comparative advantage in female-intensive manufactures. The two assumptions are: identical demand patterns in all countries (given the relative prices of goods); and perfect factor mobility among sectors within each country.

First, the sectoral composition of demand differs between developed and developing countries. In particular, services account for a much larger share of employment in developed countries. Services are generally non-tradable and female-intensive, and so their larger share raises the demand for (and hence the relative wages of) female relative to male workers. In other words, a large share of the female workforce in developed countries is absorbed by services, thereby reducing the supply of female labour to the rest of the economy. By contrast, in developing countries, where the service sector is smaller, so is the economy-wide demand for female labour, and hence the supply of female labour to the tradable sectors is relatively cheaper.[2]

The intersectoral factor mobility assumption needs to be relaxed because women and men do not have equal access to all spheres of economic activity. Institutional constraints in all countries restrict women's access to many economic activities, and in particular tend to confine women to a limited set of occupations.[3] This restriction of opportunity tends to reduce the wages paid to females in these occupations.[4] It is plausible to suppose, moreover, that these restrictions are more severe in developing than in developed countries, both for cultural reasons and because of practical obstacles to female participation in modern-sector employment (such as poor transport facilities and little mechanization of domestic chores). This, too, could help to explain why the wages of females, relative to males, tend to be lower in developing countries, thus giving these countries a comparative advantage in female-intensive traded goods.[5]

Whether, and how widely, the wage gap between males and females is greater in developing countries ought to be tested empirically. However, there is a problem in doing so directly, since in principle the comparison of wages should be made *in the absence of trade* (since expansion of female-intensive manufactured exports tends to close the gap).[6] The approach to be taken in this chapter, instead, is to ask whether the pattern of trade is consistent with the hypothesis of a difference in (autarky) relative wages.

In this regard, we will examine the two aspects of trade distinguished in the submodels of the original framework, both of which are affected if a relatively low price of female labour confers a comparative advantage in labour-intensive manufactured exports. Among developing countries, those with larger endowments of female, relative to male, human resources would be more likely to have a comparative advantage in manufactured goods relative to primary products. Similarly, as regards the composition of manufactured exports, countries with larger endowments of literate females, relative to SKILD labour, would be expected to have more of a comparative advantage in labour-intensive, relative to skill-intensive, manufactures.

REGRESSION SPECIFICATION AND EMPIRICAL RESULTS

This section consists of four subsections. The first tests how far the ratio of manufactured to primary exports can be explained by relative endowments of human and natural resources. The second examines the relationship between the composition of manufactured exports and the skill composition of the educated labour force. The third is a hybrid, examining the effect of resource endowments on exports of labour-intensive manufactured goods relative to primary products. Within each subsection, the tests are first specified with respect to human resources in general, and then to human resources differentiated by gender. The fourth section incorporates demand-side factors into the three basic models tested in the previous sections.

Manufactured Versus Primary Exports

This submodel suggests that the ratio of a country's exports of manufactured goods (X_m) to its exports of primary products (X_p) is determined by its relative endowments of human resources (HR) and natural resources (NR). For many purposes, it is more convenient to express this endowment ratio in terms of skill *per worker* $(hr = HR/L)$ and land *per worker* $(nr = NR/L)$, making these variables independent of population size. A simple and flexible specification of the relationship is then

$$(X_m/X_p) = A(HR/NR)^\alpha = A(hr/nr)^\alpha \qquad (2.1)$$

where A and α are parameters. Equation (2.1) can be estimated in (natural) logs – denoted by $\wedge$ over the variable – as

$$(\hat{X_m/X_p}) = a + b(\hat{hr/nr}) + u \tag{2.2}$$

or equivalently,

$$(\hat{X_m/X_p}) = a + c.\hat{hr} - d.\hat{nr} + u \tag{2.3}$$

where a should be A (or $\hat{A}$) b, c and d should be estimates of α, and u is the error term.

Equation (2.3) is estimated for the largest possible number of countries (114) with a population more than one million, in the most recent available year. The trade data are from the UNCTAD *Handbook of International Trade and Development Statistics* (1991: Table 4.1), using the conventional division between primary exports (SITC 0–4 plus 68) and manufactured exports (SITC 5–8 minus 68). Human resources are measured by years of schooling, mainly from Barro and Lee (1993), while natural resources are measured by total land area. For a defence of these crude measures of skill and land, see Wood and Berge (1994: Section IIIc).

The estimated OLS regression of equation (2.3) is

$$(\hat{X_m/X_p}) = 0.88 + 0.81\hat{hr} - 0.69\hat{nr} \qquad R^2 = 0.57 \tag{2.3a}$$
$$(0.46)\ (0.14) \qquad (0.09)$$

with standard errors in parentheses. The coefficients on both independent variables are significantly different from zero at the one per cent level. This confirms that the ratio of a country's manufactured to primary exports is determined both by its natural resources and by the skill level of its labour force. The proportion of variance in trade composition which the model explains is quite high, as indicated by an R^2 of 0.57

Incorporating gender

To examine the influence of gender on export composition, we include a gender-gap variable, *FEMSHARE*, which measures the share of female school years in each country's total school years (average years of schooling multiplied by number of people). Thus, in two countries with the same ratio of human to natural resources, we expect the country with the higher proportion of *female* human resources to have a greater comparative advantage in manufacturing. There are other possible ways of measuring the gender gap in education (for example, the difference in average years of schooling of the two sexes), but this one seems the most appropriate in the present context.[7]

The estimated OLS regression including FEMSHARE is

$$(X_m/X_p) = 0.05 + 0.58\hat{h}r - 0.68\hat{n}r \qquad (2.3b)$$
$$(0.67)\ (0.20)\quad (0.09)$$

$$+\ 0.027 FEMSHARE \qquad R^2 = 0.59.$$
$$(0.016)$$

The coefficient on the gender-gap variable is positive and significant at the 10 per cent level, indicating that a one per cent change in the share of females increases the export ratio by 0.03 per cent. However, the fall in the coefficient on hr and the increase in its standard error indicate collinearity between hr and $FEMSHARE$ $(R = 0.7)$, which makes it difficult to distinguish between the effects of total human resources and female human resources.

Developing countries only

The case-study literature suggests that female human resources are particularly important in the production of *labour-intensive* manufactured goods.[8] While developing-country manufactured exports are predominantly labour-intensive, manufactured exports from developed countries are more skill-intensive. We would therefore expect gender to have a stronger effect on developing countries' export composition. To test this, regression (2.3b) was re-run for developing countries only.

The OLS regression for developing countries, without a gender variable, is

$$(X_m/X_p) = 1.15 + 0.54\hat{h}r - 0.74\hat{n}r \qquad R^2 = 0.53 \qquad (2.3c)$$
$$(0.52)\ (0.17)\quad (0.10)$$

and, with the gender-gap variable:

$$(X_m/X_p) = 0.68 + 0.42\hat{h}r - 0.73\hat{n}r \qquad (2.3d)$$
$$(0.72)\ (0.21)\quad (0.10)$$

$$+\ 0.15 FEMSHARE \qquad R^2 = 0.53.$$
$$(0.17)$$

Thus, contrary to expectations, for developing countries the gender-gap variable is insignificant. Moreover, the coefficient on *hr* drops even further, while the correlation coefficient (R) between *FEMSHARE* and *hr* remains at 0.7. It thus appears that the reduction of the sample size has accentuated the problem of collinearity to the point where it is impossible to distinguish a specific gender effect from the effect of human resources as a whole.

Composition of Manufactured Exports

The second submodel postulates that the skill composition of a country's manufactured exports depends on its ratio of SKILD to BAS-ED labour. For example, assuming the same general relationship as in the other submodel,

$$(X_{ms}/X_{mb}) = B(N_s/N_b)^\beta \qquad (2.4)$$

where X_{ms} and X_{mb} are, respectively, skill-intensive and (unskilled or BAS-ED) labour-intensive manufactured exports, and N_s and N_b are the numbers of SKILD and BAS-ED workers. X_{ms} are crudely measured as SITC 5 + 7 (chemicals and machinery and equipment) and X_{mb} as SITC 6 + 8 (everything else). A rough adjustment is made for exports of electrical equipment from the South to the North, which are classified as labour-intensive. SKILD workers are imperfectly measured as those with a complete secondary or tertiary education, and BAS-ED workers as those with more than zero but less than complete secondary schooling. (For further discussion of the data, see Wood 1994b: Section 7.)

This submodel is estimated in unlogged form, because β is approximately unity, and because the logged form generates an unreadable scatter. Using a reduced (because of data availability) sample of 73 developed and developing countries, the regression is:

$$(X_{ms}/X_{mb}) = 0.50 + 1.00(N_s/N_b) \qquad R^2 = 0.21. \qquad (2.4a)$$
$$(0.13) \ (0.23)$$

The fit of the composition of manufactures regression is much worse than that of the manufactured-versus-primary export regression, probably mainly because of data problems – the rough categorizations of the skill intensity of manufactured goods and the skill composition of the labour force.[9] (Studies for specific countries suggest a stronger association between their skill endowments and the skill intensity of their manufactured exports, see Wood 1994a: Chapter 3). Regression (2.4a) indicates that a unit increase in the ratio of SKILD to BAS-ED labour leads to a unit increase in the ratio of skill- to labour-intensive exports. Although the fit is poor, the coefficient on the skill-intensity ratio is robust (that is, not much affected by changes in the sample).

To test the effect of gender on the composition of manufactured exports, the gender-gap variable $FEMSHARE_{be}$ (the share of females in each country's BAS-ED labour force) is added to equation (2.4a). Note that, in this specification, if educated females confer a comparative advantage in labour-intensive manufacturing, we expect $FEMSHARE_{be}$ to have a *negative* effect on the dependent variable, which measures the ratio of skill-intensive to labour-intensive exports.

$$(X_{ms}/X_{mb}) = -1.02 + 0.82(N_s/N_b) \qquad (2.4b)$$
$$(0.47)\ (0.23)$$

$$+ 0.04 FEMSHARE_{be} \qquad R^2 = 0.32.$$
$$(0.01)$$

The fit of the regression is improved, but the coefficient on $FEMSHARE_{be}$ is positive (and significant), the opposite of what we expected.

The explanation seems to be that $FEMSHARE_{be}$ is highly correlated ($R = 0.7$) with average years of schooling, which may in practice be a better proxy for the skill level of the educated labour force than the measure that we are using, based on the numbers above and below the complete secondary school line. In other words, differences among countries in average years of schooling usually reflect differences *both* in the size of the NO-ED share of the labour force *and* in the average years of schooling of non-NO-ED workers. The latter may be a better measure of the relative supply of highly-skilled labour, and hence of comparative advantage in skill-intensive manufactures, than our simple ratio of SKILD to BAS-ED numbers.

An alternative test is to run two simple regressions, with different independent variables, the first excluding $BAS\text{-}ED_M$ and so defining the skill ratio as $SKILD/BAS\text{-}ED_F$, the second excluding $BAS\text{-}ED_F$ and defining the skill ratio as $SKILD/BAS\text{-}ED_M$. The fit of the first of these regressions (using BAS-ED females only) should be better if the number of literate females is truly a more important determinant of comparative advantage in labour-intensive manufacturing than the number of literate males.

The two OLS regressions are

$$(X_{ms}/X_{mb}) = 0.47 + 0.52(SKILD/BAS\text{-}ED_F) \qquad R^2 = 0.21 \qquad (2.5a)$$
$$(0.13)\ (0.12)$$

and

$$(X_{sk}/X_{be}) = 0.56 + 0.42(SKILD/BAS\text{-}ED_M) \qquad R^2 = 0.18. \qquad (2.5b)$$
$$\phantom{(X_{sk}/X_{be}) = }(0.12) \ (0.11)$$

The fit of the first regression is indeed better than that of the second, but only marginally so, mainly because $SKILD/BAS\text{-}ED_F$ and $SKILD/BAS\text{-}ED_M$ are highly correlated ($R = 0.9$). The coefficient on the independent variable in the first regression ($SKILD/BAS\text{-}ED_F$) is also larger: this probably reflects the fact that in countries with low levels of literacy there tends to be a greater literacy gap between males and females.

As before, the regressions were re-run for developing countries only. This experiment yielded no significant results, even using the initial gender-free skill ratio, N_s/N_b. This outcome is not surprising, since the equation for the full sample does not fit well, and since the bigger differences in the skill intensity of manufactured exports are *between* developed and developing countries. Thus within the developing-country subsample, the slighter true differences are swamped by the errors of measurement in both the dependent and the independent variables.

Hybrid Specification: Labour-intensive Versus Primary Exports

Another possible reason (in addition to collinearity) for the insignificance of *FEMSHARE* in the primary versus manufactured exports regression (2.3d) using the developing-country-only sample is that developing-country manu-factured exports are less labour-intensive (and thereby less female-intensive) than is usually assumed. To test this we can omit exports of skill-intensive manufactures entirely, in order to assess the impact of gender on exports of labour-intensive manufactures relative to primary products. Thus regression (2.3d) is re-run using (X_{mb}/X_p) as the dependent variable. The OLS regression for developing countries is:

$$(X_{mb}/X_p) = 0.70 + 0.44\hat{hr} - 0.75\hat{nr} \qquad (2.6)$$
$$\phantom{(X_{mb}/X_p) = }(0.90) \ (0.45) \quad (0.13)$$

$$+ \ 0.01\,FEMSHARE \qquad R^2 = 0.44.$$
$$(0.03)$$

The gender-gap variable is still not significant, and its inclusion renders the coefficient on human resources insignificant. Otherwise, there is little differ-ence between the regression coefficients of regressions (2.3d) and (2.6), and the fit of regression (2.6) is worse, perhaps because of misclassification of skill-intensive and labour-intensive exports.[10]

A recurring problem in interpreting the results reported above is the collinearity between total human resources and the gender gap. Countries with more educated people also tend to have smaller differences between male and female educational levels. Although the gender variable was significant in regression (2.3b), this multicollinearity renders the coefficients on *hr* and *FEMSHARE* unreliable. Figure 2.1 shows the relationship between the gender gap and the overall level of human resources. There is a clear positive relationship between average years of schooling and the share of females in total human resources. However, once the population has achieved an average of six years of schooling, the share of females in total human resources hovers around 50 per cent.

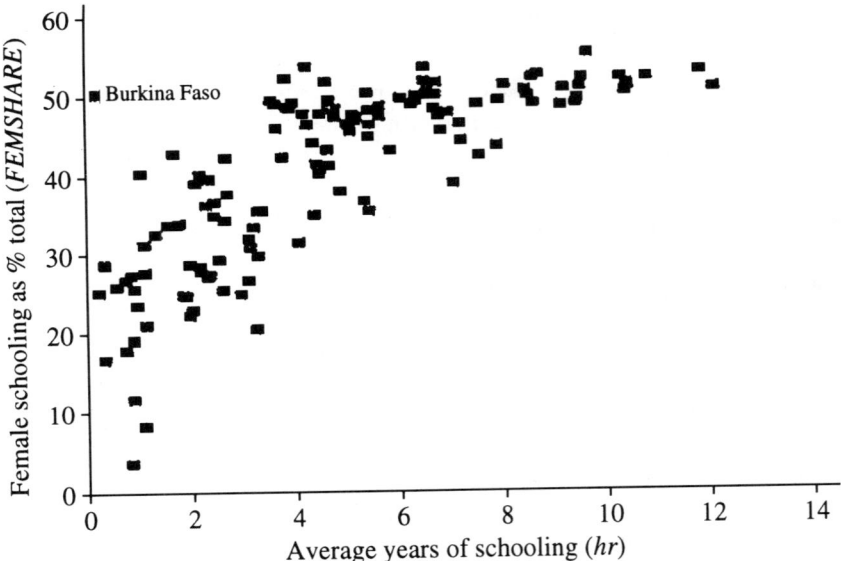

Figure 2.1   Female and average schooling

Including Demand-side Influences

It was argued above that although the relative *supply* of educated female labour is lower in developing countries, differences in *demand* for female labour may still result in relatively lower female wages. The above three models tested whether differences in the supply of educated females affect export composition. However, a better specification should also control for differences in demand.

The most conspicuous such difference concerns the demand for female labour generated by the service sector. Developed countries tend to have larger service sectors and thus a higher demand for female labour, putting upward pressure on relative female wages in the traded sectors. We therefore include the share of services in GDP as an additional independent variable.[11]

Cultural factors also influence the demand for female labour, and may particularly affect women workers' intersectoral mobility. In many countries, social conventions restrict women's access to waged employment in general and certain types of employment in particular. This tends to reduce women's wages across the board, as women workers are crowded into sectors deemed suitable for them. Furthermore, where social and cultural practices dictate women's activities, direct downward pressure on women's wages is less likely to be countered by opposition from female employees.

As one possible rough proxy for cultural influences on the demand for female labour, we include variables measuring the percentage of the population adhering to the major world religions: Christianity (Catholic and non-Catholic), Islam, Hinduism, Buddhism, and the residual category 'other religions'. We would expect countries with stricter religious restrictions on women's economic activity to have greater comparative advantage in labour-intensive manufacturing – provided of course that there are relatively few restrictions on factory employment.

In addition to restrictions on occupational mobility, women's geographical mobility is often limited. In many countries, it is considered inappropriate for women to travel long distances to their workplace. To allow for this, we also include urbanization (percentage of the population living in urban areas) in the regression. A higher level of urbanization should enable more women to enter the manufacturing labour market.

We tried these several demand-side variables in all three of the submodels explaining export composition – as between (a) manufactured and primary goods, (b) skill-intensive and labour-intensive manufactures, and (c) labour-intensive manufactures and primary goods.

The coefficients on service share and urbanization are not significantly different from zero, and the inclusion of these variables renders the coefficient on human resources insignificant. This reflects the high correlations between the service share, urbanization and human resources ($R_{hr,SERV} = 0.52$, $R_{hr,URB} = 0.62$ for the all-country sample), which cause collinearity in all three models. Including services and urbanization therefore does not improve the model specification.[12]

Since the sum of religious affiliations approximates 100 per cent for each country, we need to specify a reference category. 'Other religions' on its own is too small to be a meaningful reference category. We therefore chose to use the sum of Christianity, Buddhism and 'other religions' as the reference category, with dummy variables for the percentages of the population adhering to Islam (*ISLAM*) and Hinduism (*HINDU*).[13] We also included a dummy variable for oil exporting countries (= 1 for oil exporters, 0 otherwise), which is highly correlated with *ISLAM*.[14] The result for model (a) for 100 developed and developing countries is:

$$(X_m/X_p) = -1.02 + 0.78\hat{hr} - 0.57\hat{nr} + 0.034FEMSHARE \qquad (2.7a)$$
$$(0.90)\ (0.45)\quad (0.13)\quad (0.019)$$

$$+ 0.016HINDU + 0.011ISLAM - 1.72OIL \qquad R^2 = 0.69$$
$$(0.009)\qquad\quad (0.004)\qquad\quad (0.41)$$

and for 81 developing countries:

$$(X_m/X_p) = -0.93 + 0.73\hat{hr} - 0.56\hat{nr} + 0.028FEMSHARE \qquad (2.7b)$$
$$(0.87)\ (0.23)\quad (0.09)\quad (0.021)$$

$$+ 0.018HINDU + 0.011ISLAM - 1.57OIL \qquad R^2 = 0.66.$$
$$(0.009)\qquad\quad (0.004)\qquad\quad (0.44)$$

The coefficients on *ISLAM* and *HINDU* are all positive and significant (at the 10 per cent level), and their inclusion increases the size and significance of the coefficient on *FEMSHARE*. This tentatively suggests that the restrictions placed on women's activities in certain religions may indeed make female labour in manufacturing relatively cheaper in the countries concerned.

The inclusion of demand-side variables does not improve the composition-of-manufactured-exports submodel. In the earlier section, we found that *FEMSHARE* has a positive and significant coefficient (the opposite of what the model predicts) apparently because *FEMSHARE* is correlated with average years of schooling (which may be a better proxy for the skill level of the educated labour force than our SKILD/BAS-ED variable). The coefficients on *ISLAM* and *HINDU* were not significant in the composition-of-manufactured-exports model, and their inclusion raises the coefficient on *FEMSHARE* slightly.

In the labour-intensive-manufactured-versus-primary-exports model, the regression for 62 developing countries is:

$$(X_m/X_p) = -1.42 + 0.64\hat{hr} - 0.53\hat{nr} + 0.029FEMSHARE \qquad (2.7c)$$
$$(1.12)\ (0.44)\quad (0.12)\quad (0.030)$$

$$+ 0.024HINDU + 0.012ISLAM - 1.97OIL \qquad R^2 = 0.55.$$
$$(0.011)\qquad\quad (0.006)\qquad\quad (0.67)$$

The coefficients on *ISLAM* and *HINDU* are positive and significant (at the 5 per cent level), and the coefficients on human resources and *FEMSHARE* become more significant when demand-side factors are included (although they are still not significant at the 10 per cent level). As noted in the earlier section on labour-intensive-versus-primary-exports, the fit of this regression is worse than that of the total-manufactured-versus-primary-exports model (2.7a) because of possible misclassification of skill-intensive and labour-intensive exports.

Although the inclusion of demand-side influences did not improve the composition-of-manufactured-exports model, there was some improvement in the models explaining the composition of exports as between manufactures and primary goods. The increased significance of *FEMSHARE* in regressions (2.7a) to (2.7c) suggests that, when demand-side influences are controlled for, educating more females does give countries more of a comparative advantage in manufactured goods.[15]

CONCLUSIONS AND FURTHER RESEARCH

Overall, the cross-country regressions give only weak support to the view that manufactured exports depend more on the education of women than of men. Some of the results show a significant relationship in the expected direction (particularly when we control for demand-side influences), but many are insignificant or have the wrong sign. The weakness of the results is surprising, given the case-study evidence of the predominance of female workers in labour-intensive manufacturing for export.

There are two alternative interpretations of these findings. First, a country's supply of educated women is truly more important in determining its export performance than its supply of educated men, but collinearity in the data makes it impossible to isolate this effect. We cannot be sure whether the effect is due to the gender gap or to the overall level of human resources. Alternatively, the lack of significance of the gender-gap variable could indicate that the underlying hypothesis is false: that the gender composition of a country's human resources has little or no impact on its exports.

In principle, collinearity might be less of a problem if we had a larger sample. For each ratio of human to natural resources we might then have more variation in the proportion of females in total human resources. (See Figure 2.2 for the scatter of *FEMSHARE* against *hr/nr*.) In practice, however, we cannot increase the sample size. Moreover, even if we could do so, there are good reasons for believing that the problem would not be much reduced: the collinearity between overall education and the male–female gap is not

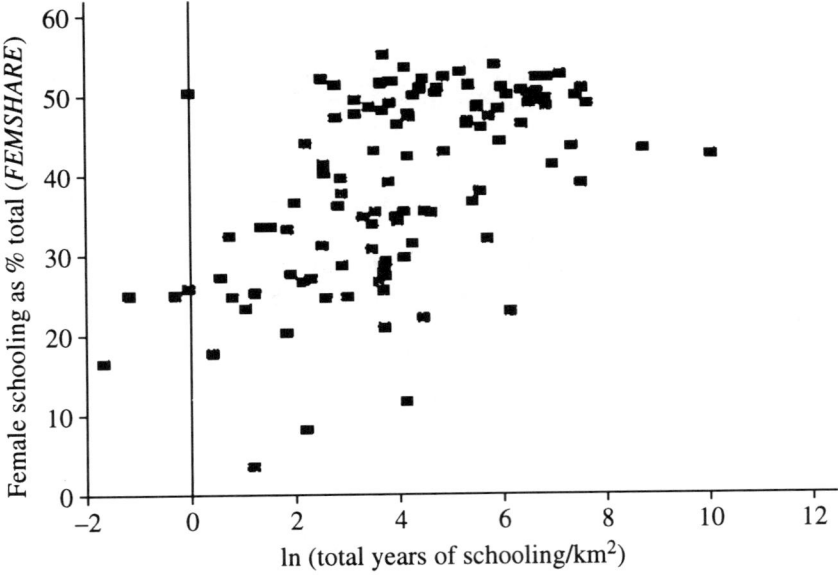

Figure 2.2   Female schooling and resources

coincidental, but largely the result of both variables being influenced by national attitudes, culture and politics.

Why might the gender composition of human resources not matter for exports, contrary to the findings of the case-study literature? One possible reason is that developing-country manufactured exports are less female-intensive than the case studies suggest. Most of these studies draw their findings from export-processing zones, and there are few if any data on the employment of women in developing-country export-oriented manufacturing as a whole.[16] A second possible reason for the insignificance of the gender-gap variable is that there are large differences in the female intensity of particular industries across countries. This may not have been picked up by the case studies, which have focused mainly on the East Asian and Latin American NICs.[17]

The current state of the evidence on the importance of female education for export-oriented manufacturing is thus unsatisfactory: case studies which say it is important, cross-country regressions which say maybe not. The most appropriate direction for further research is thus probably the analysis of data at a level intermediate between the case studies and the cross-country regressions. In particular, it would be well worth examining national data from household or labour-force surveys, which provide full coverage of all workers and sectors in a country (unlike the EPZ studies), linked up with trade data on each sector's exports. This should ideally be done for a representative selection of countries (developed as well as developing).

In addition to cross-country comparisons using the intermediate-level data, it might also be illuminating to see how the female intensity of sectors evolves over time within countries as their trade patterns change. For example, do sectors which were previously male-intensive become female-intensive as export opportunities increase?[18] It is possible, among other things, that rapid *change* in the female intensity of developing-country exports is taking place (as Wood 1991, found) which is not yet fully reflected in *levels*. In other words, countries with well-educated women may be in the process of increasing their manufactured exports, but for most countries this linkage is still not a major influence on exports.

NOTES

* The research on which this chapter is based was financed by the UK Overseas Development Administration through ESCOR Research Scheme R5037 and the IDS Research Programme. However, the views expressed are those of the authors, who are grateful for comments from Robert Cassen, Chris Colclough, Martin Godfrey and other participants at an IDS workshop on Skill Development for International Competitiveness.

1. Pearson (1992) summarizes the literature on the preference for women workers. Lee (1984) cites the case of US multinationals moving production out of Malaysia and Singapore because of shortages of female labour. Hein (1986) reports on employers in Mauritius going to great lengths to hire women. Pearson (1991) suggests that the potential pool of female labour was a major inducement for North American firms setting up production in the *maquiladoras* of Mexico.

2. Moreover, services are more female-intensive in developed countries than in developing countries, perhaps because of the institutional constraints discussed below. This implies that an even greater share of the female labour force is absorbed by the service sector in developed relative to developing countries. Einhorn (1994) estimates that between 75 and 80 per cent of women workers in industrialized market economies are in the service sector.

3. For example Islam in general and *purdah* (female seclusion) in particular constrains women's employment opportunities, by restricting women's mobility and visibility (Kabeer 1991) – though Kabeer stresses the interaction between cultural and economic forces. The notion that a family's honour resides in the virtue of its women demands constant surveillance of women so that they do not bring shame on the family. The preference is thus for women to work in the seclusion of their own homes (which may be accommodated by textile-industry outsourcing) or in situations where they are under constant supervision (factories).

4. Institutional norms also act directly on wage levels. Women's work is often valued less than men's work (for non-economic reasons) and women are therefore paid less. Moreover, since men are considered the family bread-winners, they are paid a family wage whereas a women's wage is considered supplementary 'pocket money'. This is true in both the North and the South, but the effect may be stronger in the South.

5. It is possible, however, that among developing countries, those with more institutional compartmentalization of employment opportunities for women also tend to be those with relatively low female literacy rates. If so, lower relative demand for literate female labour might be offset by lower relative supply, without much net effect on relative wages.

6. Some evidence of such a closing of the gap is provided by Addison and Demery (1989: 3, Table 3).

7. To illustrate the appropriateness of the share variable, consider two countries, A and B. In country A, women and men have an average of two and three years of schooling, respectively. In country B, women and men have an average of five and six years, respectively. Land per worker in country A is much lower, giving both countries the same human to natural resource ratio. Suppose also that only females can be employed in export-oriented manufacturing. The ratio of manufactured to primary exports is thus determined by the ratio of female years of schooling to land. The share of female years of schooling in total years of schooling (*FEMSHARE*) is higher in country B, and the ratio of female years of schooling to land is therefore also higher. The latter implies that country B has a greater comparative advantage in manufacturing (as indicated by a higher *FEMSHARE*). However, if the gender gap were measured by the difference in average years of schooling, the two countries would appear to have the same comparative advantage, which is not the case. If the gender gap were measured by the *ratio* of average female to average male years of schooling, the difference would be in the right direction, but the share measure more accurately captures its magnitude. (We experimented with the difference in average years of schooling and the ratio of average years of schooling as alternative gender-gap variables. Neither worked as well as the *FEMSHARE* variable.)

8. The gender composition of skilled labour, which is more relevant to developed than developing countries, lies beyond the scope of this chapter.

9. As reported in Wood (1994b: Section 7), the fit is even worse ($R^2 = 0.10$) if the US is excluded. The tests reported below were therefore also run excluding the US, but this made no material difference to the conclusions regarding gender.

10. Because it is BAS-EDs who are used intensively in the production of X_{mb}, we also experimented with the number of literate adults as the human resource variable (and the share of women in literate adults as the gender-gap variable). However, the coefficients on these variables were not significant.

11. The best measure would probably be the share of females employed in the service sector. Second best is the share of services in employment, which is closely related to our measure (services/GDP).

12. We also included services and urbanization separately, but this had the same effects as including them together.

13. If we use Islam, Hinduism and 'other religions' as the reference category, the coefficient on Christianity is negative. The coefficient on Buddhism is insignificant whatever the reference category.

14. Without the oil-exporter dummy, the coefficient on Islam would be negative (contrary to expectations). Oil exporters are countries in which oil and gas accounted for more than 50 per cent of exports in 1989, as defined in the *World Development Report 1991 (World Bank 1991)*. More information on our experiments with including oil and other specific natural resources in the regressions is available from the authors on request.

15. The low significance level and relatively unstable coefficients on *hr* and *FEMSHARE* underscore the tentativeness of these results. In the labour-intensive-manufactured-versus-primary-exports model the inclusion of *FEMSHARE* still leaves the coefficient on *hr* insignificant.

16. Although women make up about 80 per cent of the labour force in EPZs, these zones employed only about 1.9 million workers in the mid-1980s. By comparison, multinational corporations (MNCs) employed 7 million workers in developing countries, approximately 20 per cent of whom were women (Kreye et al. 1985: 15). (According to the same source, approximately 70 per cent of MNC production in developing countries was in manufacturing.)

17. Intraregional comparisons would be revealing in this respect. It may be inappropriate to include African and East Asian countries, with drastically different human to natural resource ratios, in the same regression.

18. Preliminary evidence for this is provided by Joekes (1982) for Morocco and Hossain et al. (1990) for Bangladesh.

REFERENCES

Addison, T. and L. Demery (1989) 'Labour Standards or Double Standards? Worker Rights and Trade Policy', Overseas Development Institute Briefing Paper, London, April.

Balassa, Bela (1982), *Development Strategies in Semi-industrial Economies*, Washington, DC: World Bank.

Barro, R. and J.W. Lee (1993), *International Comparisons of Educational Attainment*, NBER Working Paper No. 4349, Cambridge, MA: National Bureau of Economic Research.

Bruchmann, Kathrin (1989), 'Trade Policy and Manufactured Export Performance in Developing Countries: An Econometric Analysis', unpublished M.Phil. dissertation, Institute of Development Studies, University of Sussex, Brighton.

Economist (1989), *The Economist Atlas*, London: Hutchinson for Economist Books.

Economist (1990), *Vital World Statistics*, London: Hutchinson for Economist Books.

Einhorn, Barbara (1994), 'Productive Employment: Women Workers in a Changing Global Environment', in *1994 World Survey on the Role of Women in Development*, Geneva: ILO (forthcoming), pp. 51–68.

Hein, Catherine (1986), 'The Feminisation of Industrial Employment in Mauritius: A Case of Sex Segregation', in R. Anker and C. Hein (eds), *Sex Inequalities in Urban Employment*, Basingstoke: Macmillan, pp. 277–311.

Hossain, H., R. Jahan and S. Sobhan, (1990), *No Better Option? Industrial Women Workers in Bangladesh*, Dhaka: University Press.

Joekes, S . (1982), *Female-led Industrialization. Women's Jobs in Third World Export Manufacturing: The Case of the Moroccan Clothing Industry*, IDS Research Report No. 15, University of Sussex, Brighton: Institute of Development Studies.

Kabeer, Naila (1991), 'Cultural Dopes or Rational Fools? Women and Labour Supply in the Bangladesh Garment Industry', *European Journal of Development Research*, **3** (1), 133–60.

Keesing, D.B. and D.R. Sherk (1971), 'Population Density in Patterns of Trade and Development', *American Economic Review*, **61** (5), 956–61.

Kreye, O., J. Heinrichs and F. Fröbel (1985), *Multinational Enterprises and Employment*, Multinational Enterprises Working Programme Working Paper No. 55, Geneva: ILO.

Leamer, E.E. (1984), *Sources of International Comparative Advantage: Theory and Evidence*, Cambridge, MA: MIT Press.

Lee, Eddy (ed.) (1984), *Export Processing Zones and Industrial Employment in Asia*, International Labour Organization Asian Employment Programme (ARTEP), Bangkok: ILO.

Lim, Linda (1980), *Women in the Redeployment of Manufacturing Industries to Developing Countries*, UNIDO Working Papers on Structural Change, No. 18, Vienna: UNIDO.

Pearson, Ruth (1991), 'Male Bias and Women's Work in Mexico's Border Industries', in D. Elson (ed.), *Male Bias in the Development Process*, Manchester: Manchester University Press, pp. 133–63.

Pearson, Ruth (1992), 'Gender Issues in Industrialization', in Tom Hewitt, Hazel Johnson and David Wield, *Industrialization and Development*, Oxford: Oxford University Press, pp. 222–47.

UNCTAD (various years), *Handbook of International Trade and Development Statistics*, Geneva: UNCTAD.

UNDP (United Nations Development Programme) (1990), *Human Development Report*, Oxford: Oxford University Press.

UNIDO (1988), *Women and Human Resource Development for Industry*, Working Paper, Regional and Country Studies Branch, Studies and Research Division, and Unit for the Integration of Women in Industrial Development, Vienna: UNIDO.

Wood, Adrian (1991), 'North–South Trade and Female Labour in Manufacturing: An Asymmetry', *Journal of Development Studies*, **27** (2), 168–89.

Wood, Adrian (1994a), *North–South Trade, Employment and Inequality: Changing Fortunes in a Skill Driven World*, Oxford: Clarendon Press.

Wood, Adrian (1994b), *Skill, Land and Trade: A Simple Analytical Framework*, IDS Working Paper No. 1, University of Sussex, Brighton: Institute of Development Studies.

Wood, Adrian and Kersti Berge, (1994), *Exporting Manufactures: Trade Policy or Human Resources?*, IDS Working Paper No. 4, University of Sussex, Brighton: Institute of Development Studies.

World Bank (various years), *World Development Report*, New York: Oxford University Press for the World Bank.

World Bank (1991), *World Tables 1991*, World Bank Data on diskette, Washington, DC: World Bank.

World Bank (1993), *The East Asian Miracle. Economic Growth and Public Policy*, New York: Oxford University Press for the World Bank.

PART II

Labour-market Issues

3. From cheap labour to skill-based competitiveness: some labour-market aspects of the transition

Martin Godfrey*

INTRODUCTION

This chapter uses an old framework – the classical model of economic development with unlimited supplies of labour originated by Lewis forty years ago – to analyse a new phenomenon – the transition of a growing number of developing economies from a process of internationally–competitive growth based on cheap labour to one based on skill.

The Lewis model (Lewis 1954) shows how unlimited supplies of labour in an economy's subsistence sector contribute to growth of output and employment in the other, capitalist, sector. The availability of labour to the capitalist sector at a constant real producer wage (measured in units of output of the capitalist sector) yields a reinvestable surplus to profit earners, and growth and reinvestment become a continuous process.

However, this unlimited-labour-supply phase does not last for ever. Lewis identifies two 'turning points'. First, as the capitalist sector increases in size, relative to the subsistence sector, beyond a certain point, the terms of trade will turn against it. A shortage of the goods produced in the subsistence sector (wage goods for the capitalist sector) will push up their prices, which means that capitalists will have to pay higher real wages. In other words, the labour-supply curve will begin to slope upwards. The second turning point occurs when average product in the subsistence sector (on which the supply price of labour to the capitalist sector is based) begins to rise as a result of a fall in the number of workers in that sector. Again the capitalists will have to pay higher real wages along the now upward-sloping supply curve of labour.

The assumption of this chapter is that it is necessary for an economy to reach this second, labour-shortage, turning point before transition to skill-based competitiveness can occur. The case of Indonesia, an economy which has emerged fairly recently as an internationally-competitive exporter of manufactured goods, is explored in the light of this assumption. The reasons for Indonesia's success in international markets are analysed, and the question of how close it is to a transition from labour surplus to labour shortage (or from cheap labour to skill-based competitiveness) is addressed. In the course of this analysis it is hoped to identify a range of necessary conditions for this transition, with emphasis on conditions in the labour market.

INDONESIA'S EMERGENCE AS A COMPETITIVE MANUFACTURER

Indonesia has emerged as an internationally-competitive exporter of manufactured goods only in the past ten years. Its success in world markets can be attributed to several factors.

One is the programme of deregulation and institutional reform implemented by the government. Successive 'packages' over this period have reshaped the banking and financial system, customs arrangements, tax laws, protection against imports, import monopolies, licensing of investment and production, sea communications and state enterprises.

A second element has been the relative orthodoxy of fiscal policy. The word 'relative' is used because policy has not been as orthodox as it has looked. Although commitment to a balanced budget has been scrupulously honoured, 'balance' is defined to include external expenditures, such as debt servicing, and revenues raised externally, such as foreign aid and oil revenues. This has meant that net injections into the domestic circular flow of income have been considerable, in spite of the 'balanced' budget, but also that, as oil revenue has fallen, expenditure has been cut, so that the net domestic impact of the government budget has fallen. In general the main preoccupation of financial policy makers has been to avoid a return to the hyperinflation of the early years of independence, and in this they have been successful.

The third, and arguably most spectacular, influence on Indonesia's competitiveness in this period has been changes in factor prices. Broadly speaking, interest rates have been raised, the rupiah has been devalued and real wages have been restrained. Table 3.1 summarizes trends in some key factor prices since 1985.

Until 1984 a combination of low nominal interest rates and a high rate of price inflation meant that bank depositors had to endure negative real interest rates. Since then, a major reform of the financial sector and the reduction in inflationary pressures have allowed them to enjoy positive real rates for several years. One factor in this has been the authorities' determination to maintain an open capital account. Thus the supply price of capital to the Indonesian economy has been set by international interest rates (high over

Table 3.1   Indonesia: factor price trends, 1983–1991

	1985	1986	1987	1988	1989	1990	1991
Interest rate (nominal) %	18	15	17	18	19	17	23
Rate of increase in CPI %	5	6	9	8	6	7	9
Interest rate (real) %	13	9	8	10	13	10	14
Real effective exchange-rate index (1985 = 100)	100	76	58	56	57	54	54
Real producer wages agriculture (1985 = 100)	100	97	95	90	96	96	96
Real producer compensation costs industry (1985 = 100)	100	116	113	115	121	115	126

Notes: Interest rate (nominal) is the commercial bank deposit rate (IMF, IFS, line 601); CPI is for 17 cities (IMF, IFS, line 64); interest rate (real) is interest rate (nominal) deflated by the CPI; the real effective exchange rate is a trade-weighted exchange rate adjusted for relative inflation – see formula below (Asian Development Bank, *Asian Development Outlook*, Table A22); real producer wages agriculture is an unweighted index of agricultural wages for planting, weeding and hoeing in East, West and Central Java, deflated by the producer price index for the farmers who employ them (BPS); real producer compensation cost industry is an index of average annual labour costs in manufacturing (from BPS, *Survei Industri*), deflated by the wholesale price index for the manufacturing sector (BPS).

this period) plus premia for domestic inflation and (more important) for devaluation and other political risks. Since, on top of this, intermediation costs are relatively high (adding 7 to 8 percentage points to state banks' interest rates, for instance), both nominal and real rates to borrowers have been extremely high over this period. Also, since 1991, monetary policy has been tightened, in an attempt to reduce inflationary pressures, and interest rates have been given a further boost.

At the same time, the rupiah has undergone a steady devaluation since 1983. More important, since Indonesian prices have been rising at a relatively moderate rate, this has been a *real* devaluation. As can also be seen, agricultural real wages (deflated by producer prices) have stagnated and labour costs in manufacturing have risen only slightly since 1986. This combination of currency devaluation and wage restraint has made Indonesian labour among the cheapest in the world, in dollar terms, as Table 3.2 shows.

At less than 60 cents an hour, compensation costs (that is, wages and salaries in cash or kind and employers' expenditures on social security and payroll taxes) in Indonesian manufacturing are about 3 per cent of Western European and less than 4 per cent of American levels. Moreover, Indonesia's competitive position, compared not only with the highest-wage economies but with most of the rest of the world, improved significantly in the second half of the 1980s. Against the background of low and steady compensation

Table 3.2   *Hourly compensation costs for production workers in manufac-*
turing, selected countries, 1986–1992 (US dollars)

	1986	1987	1988	1989	1990	1991	1992
Indonesia	0.40	0.34	0.36	0.39	0.41	0.47	0.59
India	0.39	0.38	0.37	..	..	..	..
Korea	1.31	1.59	2.20	3.17	3.71	4.46	4.93
Singapore	2.23	2.31	2.67	3.15	3.78	4.35	4.95
Sri Lanka	0.29	0.30	0.31	0.31	0.35	0.40	0.40
Mexico	1.06	1.01	1.25	1.48	1.64	1.95	2.35
Austria	10.28	13.09	13.93	13.59	16.95	17.41	19.65
Netherlands	12.21	15.15	15.84	15.05	18.30	18.44	20.72
Czechoslovakia	1.33	1.49	1.81	1.87	1.62	1.17	1.32
Hungary	1.25	1.28	1.51	1.55	1.77	1.93	2.42
Poland	1.30	1.05	1.18	1.36	1.05	1.63	1.73
Romania	1.34	1.35	1.44	1.42	1.13	0.80	0.56
United States	13.26	13.52	13.91	14.32	14.91	15.60	16.17

Sources: For exchange rates, IMF *International Financial Statistics*. For hourly compensation
costs: for Indonesia, BPS. *Survei Industri*; for Hungary, national sources; for Czechoslovakia,
Poland, Romania, ILO *Yearbook* and *Bulletin of Labour Statistics*, and US Department of
Health and Human Services, *Social Security Programmes throughout the World*; for others, US
Department of Labor, Bureau of Labor Statistics, Office of Productivity and Technology.
Hourly Compensation Costs for Production Workers in Manufacturing, 1993, June 1994.

costs in Indonesia and Sri Lanka in this period, Table 3.2 shows Singapore's
and Korea's transition from labour surplus to labour shortage, and perhaps
the beginnings of a similar process in Mexico. It also shows the divergence in
Eastern Europe between Hungary, where dollar labour costs are matching
those of Mexico, and Romania, which is falling towards Asia.

Underlying the trends in Table 3.2 are changes not only in hourly compensation costs but also in nominal exchange rates. A more thorough analysis of
changes in international competitiveness involves the use of a measure, real
effective exchange rate, which takes into account inflation both in the country
concerned and in its trading-partner and competitor countries. There are
various definitions of real effective exchange rate, but the most widely accepted is that of the International Monetary Fund, as follows.

$$E_{reh} = \frac{E_{nh} P_h}{E_{no} \cdot P_o} \cdot 100$$

where

E_{reh} is index of real effective exchange rate;

E_{nh} is index of nominal exchange rate of home currency;

E_{no} is index of weighted geometric average of exchange rates of selected partner or competitor countries;

P_h is index of cost (for example, value-added deflator) in home country;

P_o is a weighted geometric average of the corresponding cost indices in selected partner or competitor countries.

Table 3.3 shows trends in real effective exchange rates for fourteen selected economies between 1986 and 1992.

Figure 3.1 shows the same information in the form of a graph for six of the economies in the table. Having fallen fast from 1985 to 1988, the real effective exchange rate of the Indonesian rupiah has remained relatively steady since then. As Table 3.3 and Figure 3.1 show, this has not put Indonesia at a disadvantage compared with the newly-industrialized countries and many European economies, but several direct competitors, such as India and (since 1989) China, have been following Indonesia's earlier example and reaping the gains of substantial real devaluations.

The data on exchange rates can be combined with those on compensation costs and value added per employee to yield indices of real manufacturing

Table 3.3   Index of real effective exchange rates, selected countries, 1986–1992 (1986 = 100)

	1986	1987	1988	1989	1990	1991	1992
Indonesia	100	76	73	75	72	70	68
China	100	94	108	121	92	99	96
India	100	93	88	83	76	63	58
Korea	100	100	112	131	129	130	125
Singapore	100	94	92	107	112	97	106
Sri Lanka	100	93	93	90	96	98	98
Mexico	100	103	125	122	124	134	..
Austria	100	81	78	76	77	74	75
Netherlands	100	103	104	101	105	103	107
Czechoslovakia	100	105	95	91	124	79	..
Hungary	100	90	92	93	97	110	116
Poland	100	73	66	74	63	97	97
Romania	100	106	106	97	71	57	47
United States	100	85	79	84	80	78	72

Source: IMF, *International Financial Statistics.*

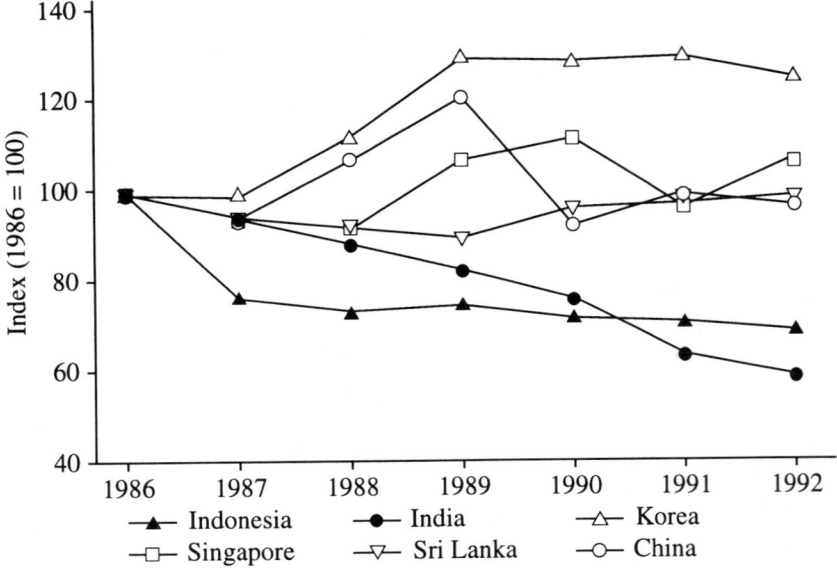

Figure 3.1   Real effective exchange-rate index, 1986–1992

labour cost per unit of output, expressed in foreign currencies. Real labour cost per unit of output in foreign currencies is equal to: real annual compensation cost per employee multiplied by the real effective exchange rate divided by real value added per employee. More formally

$$U = \frac{W_{nh}}{V_{nh}} \cdot E_{reh}$$

where

U is real labour cost per unit of output in foreign currencies;
W_{nh} is nominal annual compensation cost per employee in home economy;
V_{nh} is nominal value added per employee in home economy.
E_{reh} is index of real effective exchange rate.

The calculation of real labour cost per unit of output can, therefore, be reduced to four steps.

1. Calculate nominal annual compensation cost per employee in the home economy.
2. Calculate nominal value added per employee in the home economy.

3. Divide (1) by (2).
4. Multiply (3) by the real effective exchange rate.

As a first step, Table 3.4 assembles data on nominal annual compensation cost per employee in manufacturing in Indonesia and thirteen other economies. The increases in compensation cost in the table reflect both increases in real wages and in non-wage labour costs and inflation. Mexico, Poland and Romania, in particular, have had very high rates of increase in prices and wages.

Table 3.4   Index of nominal annual compensation cost per employee, manufacturing, selected economies, 1986–1992 (1986 = 100)

	1986	1987	1988	1989	1990	1991	1992
Indonesia	100	109	123	137	155	186	239
India	100	102	106	..	..	..	..
Korea	100	112	134	171	207	256	301
Singapore	100	102	108	127	141	155	167
Sri Lanka	100	118	125	146	180	213	233
Mexico	100	203	421	543	694	885	1,097
Austria	100	104	108	110	121	127	133
Netherlands	100	103	106	110	117	120	125
Czechoslovakia	100	102	130	133	137	160	174
Hungary	100	108	136	157	193	246	316
Poland	100	122	227	850	4,135	6,867	9,391
Romania	100	91	95	98	115	278	783
United States	100	103	109	112	114	115	117

Sources: ILO, US Department of Labor and national sources.

The next step is to divide nominal value added in the sector by the number of wage employees to get nominal value added per employee, as shown in Table 3.5. Once again, inflation rates have been a major influence on the numbers in this table which conceal wide differences in physical productivity trends.

The final stage is to divide the figures on compensation cost in Table 3.4 by the figures on value added per employee in Table 3.5, and then to multiply the resulting figures by the real effective exchange rate from Table 3.3. This yields the indices of real manufacturing labour cost per unit of output (in foreign currencies) shown in Table 3.6.

Figure 3.2 presents the same information in graphic form for five of the countries in the table. As can be seen, Indonesia's unit labour costs, which

Table 3.5   *Index of nominal value added per employee, manufacturing,*
               selected economies, 1986–1992 (1986 = 100)

	1986	1987	1988	1989	1990	1991	1992
Indonesia	100	114	122	153	171	181	226
India	100	119	141	163	..	..	..
Korea	100	113	116	121	128	150	159
Singapore	100	107	120	128	139	133	145
Sri Lanka	100	115	151	249	152	161	179
Mexico	100	253	540	621	786	1,009	..
Austria	100	101	107	115	125	129	114
Netherlands	100	98	103	106	105	110	112
Czechoslovakia	100	102	104	104	109	166	177
Hungary	100	110	119	134	156	205	242
Poland	100	132	225	722	4,211	5,289	7,655
Romania	100	101	107	101	93	212	631
United States	100	108	116	125	133	136	145

Sources: UN, ILO, Asian Development Bank, and national sources.

Table 3.6   *Index of real manufacturing labour cost per unit of output (in*
               foreign currencies), selected countries, 1986–1992 (1986= 100)

	1986	1987	1988	1989	1990	1991	1992
Indonesia	100	73	74	67	65	72	72
India	100	80	66	..	..	..	..
Korea	100	99	130	185	208	222	236
Singapore	100	89	83	106	114	113	122
Sri Lanka	100	96	77	53	114	131	128
Mexico	100	83	97	107	109	118	..
Austria	100	83	78	72	74	72	87
Netherlands	100	109	107	104	117	112	120
Czechoslovakia	100	105	119	116	157	76	..
Hungary	100	88	105	109	119	132	151
Poland	100	67	66	88	62	126	119
Romania	100	95	94	93	87	75	58
United States	100	80	74	76	69	66	58

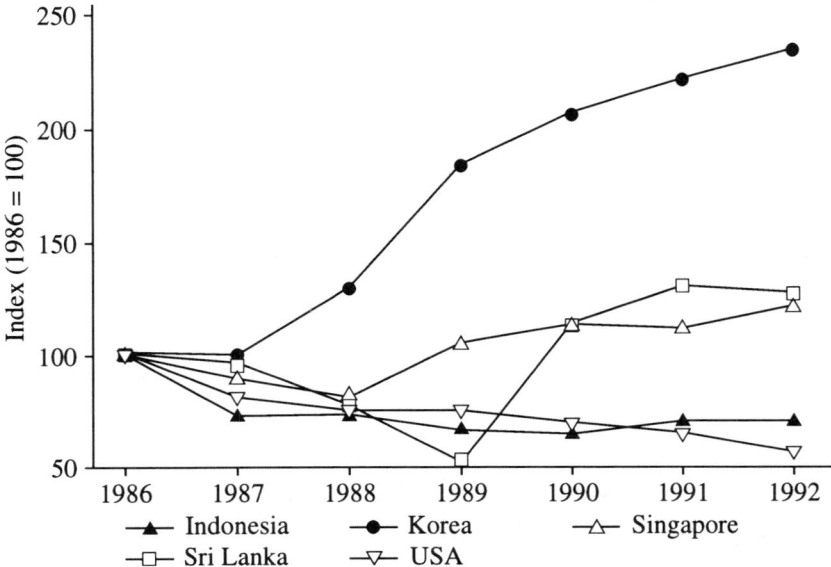

Figure 3.2   Real unit labour-cost (foreign currencies) index, 1986–1992

Table 3.7   Composition of exports, selected years, 1982–1983 to 1992–
1993 (per cent of total value)

		1982–83	1988–89	1992–93
Oil and gas exports		78.9	38.5	29.7
Non-oil exports		21.1	61.5	70.3
of which:	Agricultural	14.6	35.0	24.0
	Mineral	3.6	7.9	5.1
	Textiles and garments	0.8	7.9	16.9
	Handicrafts	0.1	0.9	1.8
	Electrical appliances	0.6	0.5	3.0
	Cement	0.0	0.4	0.3
	Fertilizer	0.1	0.7	0.6
	Other	1.1	8.2	18.6
Total exports		100.0	100.0	100.0
$ '000 million		18.6	19.8	35.3

Sources: World Bank (1994 and 1990).

fell in the late 1980s as a result of real devaluation, wage restraint and productivity increases have turned upwards again in the early 1990s. Data on close competitors are not available in this period, but the reform process in economies such as India, Bangladesh, China and Vietnam is having a favourable effect on their unit labour costs; competition is particularly fierce at the lower end of the garment market (Pangestu and Azis 1994: 20). The most striking aspect of Figure 3.2 (and a reminder that not only structurally-adjusting, developing economies can take this route) is the spectacular fall in US unit labour costs, due partly to productivity increases, but mainly to real effective devaluation of the dollar.

As might be expected, the fall in real unit labour cost in Indonesia has had a dramatic impact on labour-intensive exports. Between 1982–83 and 1992–93 total exports almost doubled, to more than $35,000 million. Non-oil exports grew particularly fast and by 1992–93 accounted for more than 70 per cent of the total. As Table 3.7 shows, export success was not confined to manufacturing: export earnings from agriculture tripled in ten years. But the most spectacular success was that of labour-intensive manufactured exports, particularly textiles and garments (which increased fortyfold in the period) and footwear.

Table 3.8   Population 10 years and over, by kind of activity during previous week, 1982–1993

(per cent of total)	1982	1986	1988	1990	1991	1992	1993
Labour force	54.0	57.3	57.6	57.3	57.1	57.3	56.6
of whom:							
working	52.3	55.8	56.0	55.9	55.7	55.8	55.1
of whom:							
employer/self-employed	10.6	12.2	11.8	11.4	10.7	11.7	12.0
self-employed + helper	12.3	12.9	12.9	13.2	12.8	13.0	12.5
employee	17.3	14.4	14.5	15.5	16.3	16.4	17.0
family worker	12.1	16.3	16.8	15.7	14.9	14.8	13.6
job seeking	1.6	1.5	1.6	1.4	1.5	1.6	1.6
Not in labour force	46.0	42.7	42.4	42.7	42.9	42.7	43.4
of whom:							
at school	20.5	21.5	22.1	21.1	20.5	20.3	20.5
housekeeping	18.5	14.4	13.4	14.8	15.4	15.2	15.4
other	7.0	6.8	6.8	6.8	7.0	7.2	7.4
Total	100.0	100.0	100.0	100.0	100.0	100.0	100.0
Total (million)	110.4	122.6	129.4	135.7	137.3	140.8	143.8
Unemployment rate (%)	3.0	2.6	2.8	2.5	2.6	2.7	2.8

Source: BPS, *Labour Force Survey.*

As far as impact on employment is concerned, the usual labour force survey measures shown in Table 3.8, are not very illuminating. As can be seen, with the unemployment rate never rising above 3 per cent in the 1982–90 period, the number working has been largely supply-determined and has grown at the same rate as the population in the economically active age group.

The most striking evidence of the beneficial impact of growth and structural change on the demand for labour is the fast rate of growth of wage employment. Overall, as the census data in Table 3.9 show, total employment grew at around the same rate as the labour force during the 1980s, but wage employment grew much faster, at an annual rate of 6 per cent, with manufacturing, construction and trade the most dynamic of the larger sectors. Female wage employment grew significantly faster than male – at an annual average rate of 7.5 per cent – particularly in manufacturing. Since 1990, to judge from the labour force survey data in Table 3.8, wage employment has continued to grow at an annual rate of more than 5 per cent.

Table 3.9   Employment by sector and employment status, 1980 and 1990

	Total employment			Wage employment		
	1980 ('000)	1990 ('000)	change p.a. (%)	1980 ('000)	1990 ('000)	change p.a. (%)
Agriculture	28,040	35,931	2.5	4,359	5,578	2.5
Mining	369	766	7.6	130	658	17.6
Manufacturing	4,361	8,340	6.7	2,191	5,820	10.3
Electricity	85	158	6.4	63	139	8.2
Construction	1,573	2,886	6.3	955	2,027	7.8
Trade	6,611	10,754	5.0	560	1,416	9.7
Transport	1,468	2,703	6.3	747	1,382	6.3
Banks/Finance	232	545	8.9	200	516	9.9
Services nec	7,787	9,901	2.4	4,752	7,737	5.0
Not stated	666	—		132	—	
Total	51,192	71,984	3.5	14,089	25,273	6.0

Sources: BPS, Population Censuses.

LABOUR COST, PRODUCTIVITY AND WAGE EMPLOYMENT

The factors underlying Indonesia's emergence as an internationally competitive labour-intensive manufacturer are, then, fairly clear: increasing productivity combined with real devaluation and wage restraint. What is less clear is whether the ground is being laid for the transition from labour surplus to labour shortage, or from cheap labour to skill-based competitiveness.

An important issue in this transition is the relationship between labour cost and productivity as the number of employees in manufacturing increases. In his pioneering paper Lewis (1954) described an economy in which employers in the capitalist sector are faced with a perfectly elastic supply curve of labour as having unlimited supplies of labour. However, as attempts to make the Lewis model more rigorous (for example, Ranis and Fei 1961) showed, the arithmetic of labour transfer is such that special assumptions are necessary to preserve the possibility of a perfectly horizontal labour-supply curve, even where there is surplus labour in the subsistence sector, potentially available for employment at the going wage.[1] This means that we should be fairly relaxed in allowing an economy with fluctuations in the supply price of labour still to be defined as a labour-

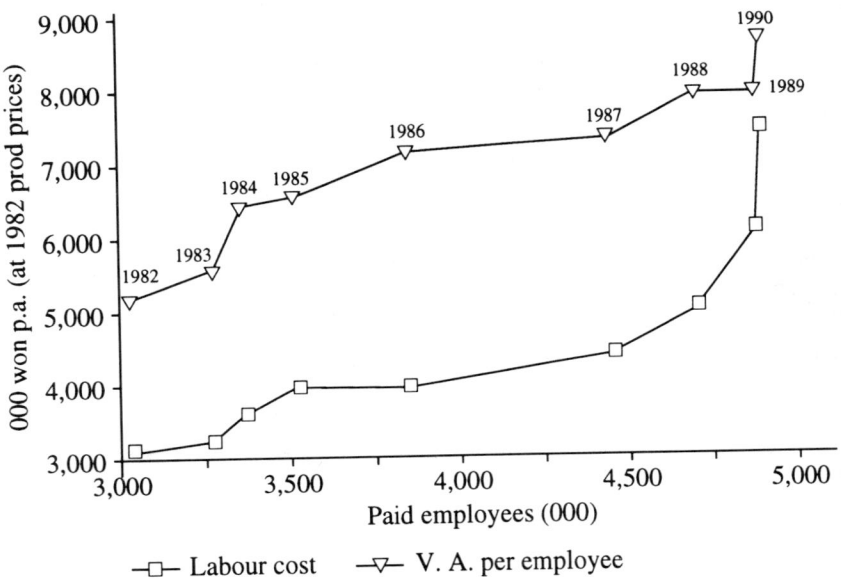

Figure 3.3   Korea: real labour cost, value added per employee and paid employment in manufacturing, 1982–1990

surplus economy, as long as those fluctuations are not occurring around a steeply rising trend.

Even if real labour cost rises steeply as employment increases this may just reflect segmentation, due to trade union power or government regulation. Only if these can be ruled out as important influences, and if wage increases are associated with productivity increases, can it be regarded as an unequivocal sign of an emerging shortage of labour. It is useful, in this respect, to look at the recent experience of two economies which have successfully made the transition – Korea and Singapore.

Figure 3.3 shows what happened in Korea to annual compensation cost per employee (labour cost) and value added per employee, both deflated by the producer price, in manufacturing, as paid employment in the sector changed, between 1982 and 1990. After years of fast productivity growth but relatively stagnant wages, labour cost in Korea began to rise from 1982 onwards. Until 1988, productivity and the demand for labour continued to increase and the transition to a higher-wage, skill-based economy appeared to be going smoothly. In 1989 and 1990, however, a wage explosion dramatically increased labour's share in value added, and expansion in the number of employees came to a halt.

Figure 3.4 shows the relationship between trends in the same variables in Singapore over the same period. As can be seen, employment in Singapore's

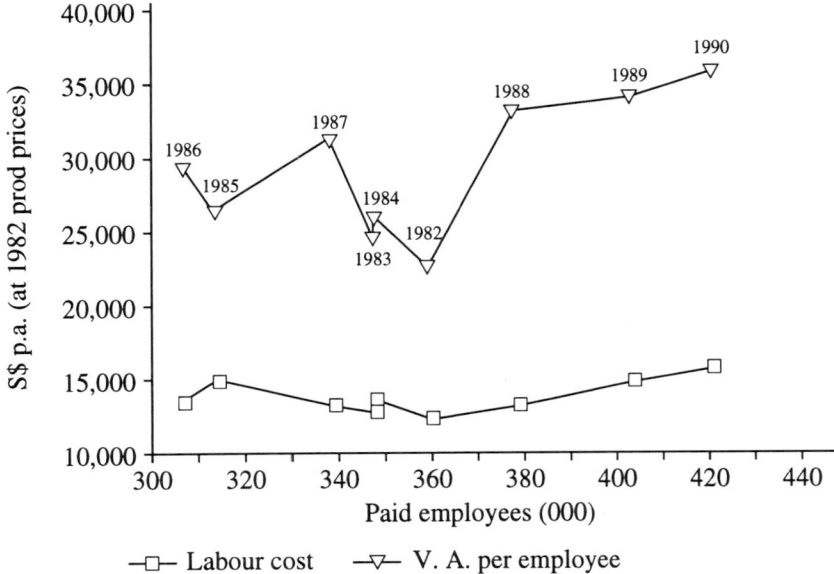

Figure 3.4   Singapore: real labour cost, value added per employee and paid employment in manufacturing, 1982–1990

Table 3.10 Indonesia: large and medium manufacturing, compensation cost and value added per employee, 1986–1992

	1986	1987	1988	1989	1990	1991	1992
Nominal compensation cost per employee (Rp'000)	1,116	1,219	1,374	1,524	1,730	2,075	2,669
Producer price index (1985 = 100)	101	113	125	132	151	166	174
Real compensation cost per employee (Rp'000)	1,105	1,080	1,098	1,152	1,146	1,248	1,535
Value added at current prices (Rp'000 m.)	9,348	11,279	13,882	19,046	25,171	29,926	41,438
Real value added (Rp'000 m.)	9,216	9,994	11,098	14,396	16,679	18,005	23,834
Number of employees ('000)	1,691	1,788	2,065	2,259	2,663	2,994	3,313
Real value added per employee (Rp'000)	5,450	5,589	5,374	6,373	6,263	6,014	7,194

Source: BPS, *Survei Industri.*

manufacturing sector actually fell between 1982 and 1986, while labour cost rose. This reflects an ill-advised attempt by the government, between 1979 and 1984, to push up wages in order to encourage employers to adopt more skill-intensive and technology-intensive methods. From 1986 onwards, however, after the abandonment of the centralized high-wage policy, the demand for labour recovered and, as manufacturing productivity steadily increased, so too, from 1988 onwards, did wages and compensation cost.

The experience of Korea, from 1982 to 1988, and Singapore, from 1986 to 1990, suggests that the transition to skill-based competitiveness in manufacturing involves, alongside expansion in the number of employees, sustained growth in value added per employee, followed, with a lag, by increases in wages and compensation cost. How promising is Indonesia's recent experience in this respect? Table 3.10 assembles data relevant to this question from the survey of large and medium manufacturing establishments. As can be seen, while the number of wage employees in large- and medium-scale manufacturing has increased steadily, at an annual average rate of 12 per cent between 1986 and 1992, both real compensation cost per employee and real value added per employee have also increased.

The relationship between these three variables is presented graphically in Figure 3.5. There is little doubt about the stage through which the Indonesian

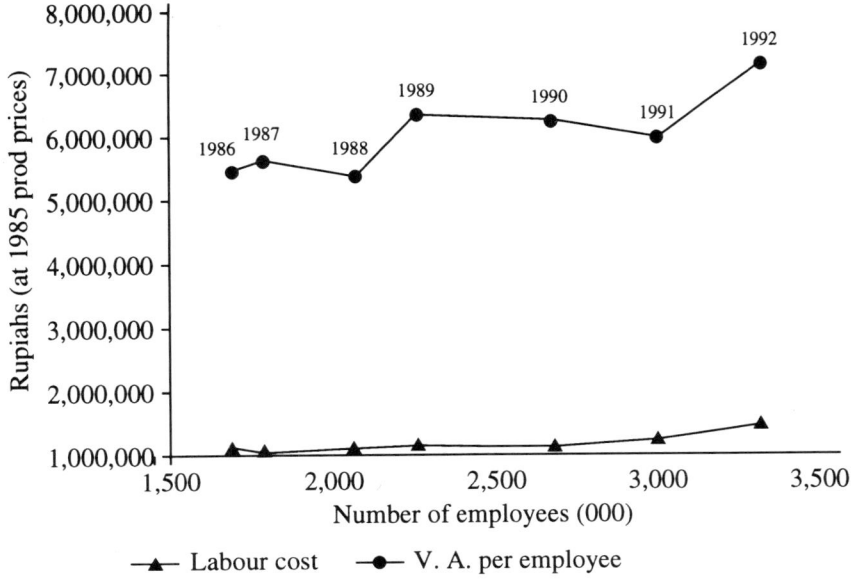

Figure 3.5   *Indonesia: real labour cost, value added per employee and employment in large and medium manufacturing, 1986–1992*

labour market was passing prior to 1990. As Figure 3.5 shows, fast expansion of wage employment in large/medium manufacturing (by 57 per cent between 1986 and 1990) was accompanied by a real labour-cost increase of less than 4 per cent. In agriculture, also, increases in wage employment in Java over the same period did not involve significant increases in the real producer wage (see Godfrey 1993). All this is consistent with a relaxed version of an unlimited-labour-supply model: in this phase Indonesia was still a labour-surplus economy, in the sense that increases in employment did not set off substantial increases in the supply price of labour.

In 1990–92, on the other hand, as Figure 3.5 shows, a 24 per cent increase in the number of employees in large/medium manufacturing went along with a large (34 per cent) increase in real compensation cost. In other sectors, also, there are signs of warming labour markets in the early 1990s. Figure 3.6, for instance, shows what has happened to real producer wages, agricultural real wages seen from the point of view of the producer, in Central, East and West Java over the past ten years. As can be seen, employers were favourably placed between 1985 and 1991, with no signs of steep upward pressure on

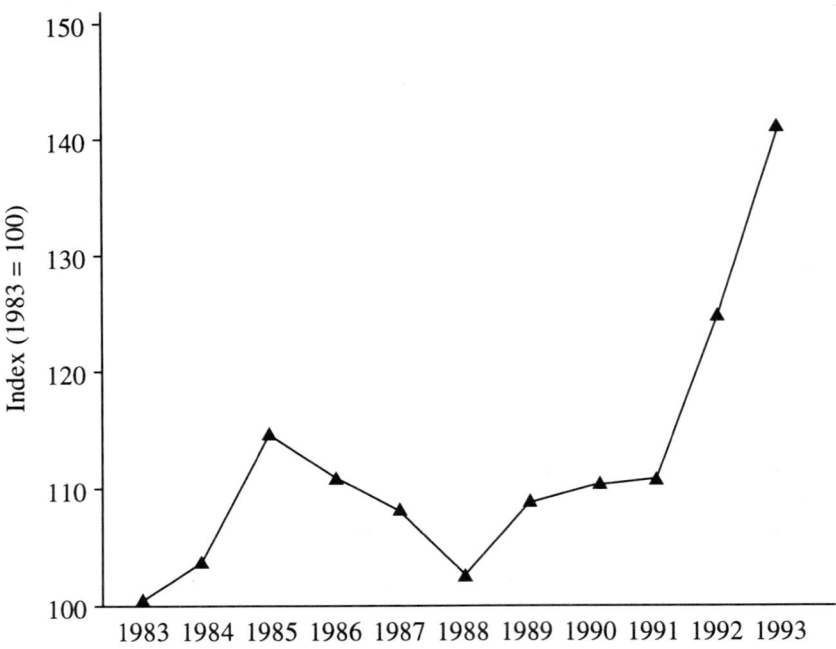

Figure 3.6   Agricultural real wage trends, Java 1983–1993 (deflated by producer prices)

real wages so defined. However, employers faced a sharp rise in real wages in 1992 and 1993.

Regional producer price indices are not available for other sectors but, with wage data available for the construction sector, deflation by regional consumer price indices reveals some interesting trends. Figure 3.7 shows a similar upturn in real wages in 1991–92 in the construction industry, to judge from the BPS data on bricklayers' wages in five Javanese cities. In all cases except Bandung construction wages were lower in real terms in 1990 than they had been five years earlier. In all cases they have risen since then, steeply except in the case of Surabaya.

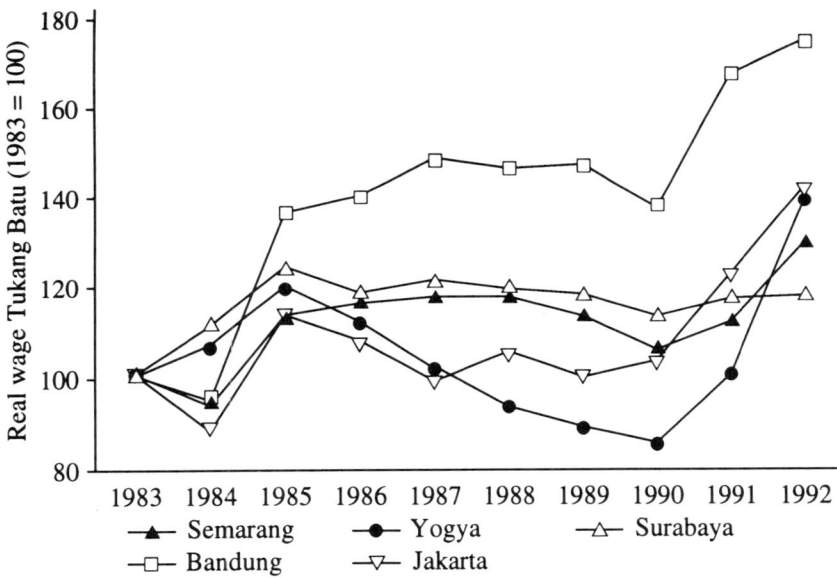

Figure 3.7   Construction real wage trends, five cities 1983–1992 (deflated by CPI)

Does all this signify a tightening of Indonesian labour markets, presaging the onset of the rising-real-wage turning point? The data, particularly the fact that the labour-cost increase in manufacturing has gone along with an increase in productivity, such that the absolute gap between the two has widened (see Figure 3.5), are consistent with such a hypothesis. But it must be admitted that they are consistent with other hypotheses also. Since 1989 the government has allowed a gradual demilitarization of industrial relations and the Department of Manpower has conducted a campaign against breaches of minimum wage regulations. Partly as a result, workers have begun to express their grievances over low pay and poor working conditions directly, by going on strike. The rise in real wages and labour costs in recent years may reflect a once-for-all adjustment to a new political situation rather than a fundamental change in labour market conditions. Wages are still desperately low and labour is weak.

Recent productivity increases, also, should be put into perspective. Table 3.11 compares productivity in manufacturing in 1987 in Indonesia, Korea, Australia, Japan and the United States. As can be seen, in 1987 Indonesian manufacturing productivity was 38 per cent of that in Korea (when, as Table 3.2 showed, its labour cost was 16 per cent of Korea's), 21 per cent of that in Australia, and only about 10 per cent of that in the US (but its labour cost was only 2.5 per cent. In comparison with Korea, the highest relative productivity is achieved in chemical products, metals and textiles.

Table 3.11   International comparisons of real GDP per person engaged in 1987 in six branches of manufacturing (US = 100)

Branch	Indonesia*	Korea	Australia	Japan	United States
Food, beverages and tobacco	5.4	12.8	47.2	29.1	100
Textiles, wearing apparel and leather	16.5	31.8	61.7	76.6	100
Chemicals, petroleum, coal, rubber and plastics	10.6	15.4	52.3	81.6	100
Basic and fabricated metals	25.2	45.0	54.1	104.3	100
Machinery, electrical machinery and transport equipment	15.3	42.4	43.0	114.1	100
Other manufacturing#	9.0	25.1	43.4	66.9	100
Total	10.0	26.4	48.4	81.8	100

Notes:
\#   Wood products, furniture and fixtures; paper, printing and publishing; non-metallic mineral products; precision instruments; and other manufacturing.
*   The Indonesia/US comparison is for establishments with more than 19 persons employed; other comparisons are for total manufacturing.

Source: Szirmai (1994).

The Indonesian branches in which the greatest improvements in relative productivity took place between 1975 and 1990 are tobacco products, textiles, wearing apparel, wood products and furniture, and paper products. By 1990, as Table 3.12 shows, overall manufacturing productivity was still only 11 per cent of the US's (labour cost, in Table 3.2, 2.7 per cent), and 36 per cent of Korea's (labour cost 11 per cent). Indonesia was still well ahead of

Table 3.12   Real GDP per person engaged in manufacturing (US = 100)

	India	Korea	Japan	Indonesia	United States
1970	7.0	13.8	58.9		100
1971	6.3	15.8	57.8		100
1972	6.1	14.5	59.9		100
1973	6.0	15.4	61.6		100
1974	6.0	14.3	63.4		100
1975	5.8	17.6	64.1	7.7	100
1976	5.7	17.3	66.8	8.0	100
1977	5.8	17.8	67.7	8.0	100
1978	6.2	20.6	71.6	9.4	100
1979	5.7	18.4	77.7	9.0	100
1980	5.6	20.4	82.3	10.6	100
1981	6.1	22.7	84.3	11.5	100
1982	6.9	23.9	88.3	10.5	100
1983	7.1	24.4	83.6	9.3	100
1984	7.1	25.3	83.7	9.9	100
1985	7.7	24.5	85.0	10.5	100
1986	7.9	25.4	79.7	11.5	100
1987		26.4	81.8	10.0	100
1988		26.7	83.1	11.0	100
1989		28.9	87.1	10.5	100
1990			89.4	10.9	100

Note: The India/US and Indonesia/US comparisons are for large and medium establishments, the Korea/US and Japan/US comparisons are for total manufacturing.

Source: Szirmai (1994).

India, but, relative to the US, was not yet at the stage reached by Korea in the early 1970s.

All this is consistent with the verdict of a recent review of industrial policy (World Bank 1993: 80) that: science and technology research efforts, limited in any case to the public sector, are below those of high-performance East Asian economies; government funding for such research and development has provided only limited commercial value added to industrial production; while it has produced cutting-edge capabilities in a few selected products, these capabilities have not yet been transformed into the capacity to produce these products competitively; while progress has been made in some process industries to world best-practice levels, engineering and electronics industries are extremely weak technologically; and Indonesia's private sector lags significantly behind competitor countries in its commitment to and capability of making effective use of foreign technology. Nevertheless, recent developments in Indonesia's enterprises and labour markets are interesting, and will repay the careful attention of labour economists.

THE SUPPLY OF EDUCATED LABOUR

Beside the emergence of a shortage of unskilled labour, another condition necessary for a transition to skill-based competitiveness, obviously, is an increase in the supply of more educated labour. This can be measured directly, by a variety of educational indicators, or indirectly, by the structure of wages and labour costs.

Table 3.13 assembles some educational indicators for the usual range of countries plus the Philippines and Thailand. The table mainly draws attention to the problems of trying to use aggregated educational statistics for this purpose. For instance, the indicator, mean years of schooling (used by UNDP in its index of educational attainment[2]) puts Singapore and Indonesia in the same category. This may reflect the reliance of Singapore on large numbers of unskilled immigrant workers; more generally, it suggests that an indicator of the level of education of the entire stock of a country's adult population is not suitable for detecting emerging trends. Mean years of schooling of recent entrants to the labour market in the 25–30 age group may be more relevant for this purpose. In the absence of such disaggregated data, it would be useful to have figures on output from the various levels of the educational system, in relation to relevant age groups. In the absence of output figures, we have to fall back on enrolment ratios, as in Table 3.13.

Here again problems arise, mainly from the differing definitions of educational levels used in different countries. Consider, for instance, the comparison of the tertiary enrolment ratios of Thailand and Singapore, or of the US and the Netherlands. Combining the ratios for secondary and tertiary education[3], as in the fifth column of the table, may reduce (though it does not eliminate) these comparability problems. It suggests, at least, some interesting categories: a group of countries in which the combined secondary and tertiary enrolment ratio is still low (about 25 per cent) – Indonesia, India and Thailand; an intermediate group with ratios of 34 to 40 per cent – Mexico, Singapore and Sri Lanka; and the remainder, with ratios of 45 per cent and higher. Significantly, this high-ratio group includes all the Central and Eastern European countries in the table, but only the Philippines and Korea of the Asian countries.

Table 3.13   Indicators of educational development

	% of age group enrolled				(2nd+ 3rd)÷2	Mean years of schooling	Science graduates as % of total
	Secondary		Tertiary				
	1970	1991	1970	1991	1991	1992	1990
Indonesia	16	45	4	10	28	4.1	11
India	26	44	6	..	25	2.4	20
Korea	42	88	16	40	64	9.3	29
Philippines	46	74	28	28	51	7.6	30
Singapore	46	70	..	8	39	4.0	53
Sri Lanka	47	74	3	5	40	7.2	12
Thailand	17	33	13	16	25	3.9	18
Mexico	22	55	14	15	35	4.9	32
Austria	72	104	23	35	70	11.4	34
Netherlands	75	97	30	38	68	11.1	32
Czechoslovakia	31	84*	17	18*	51*	9.2	48
Hungary	63	81	13	15	48	9.8	17
Poland	62	83	18	22	53	8.2	32
Romania	44	80	11	9	45	7.1	68
United States	..	90	56	76	83	12.4	24

Notes: Mean years of schooling is the average number of years of schooling received per person aged 25 and over. *1990.

Sources: World Bank, *World Development Report* , 1993; UNDP, *Human Development Report*, 1993.

The final column of Table 3.13 shows science graduates as a percentage of total tertiary graduates. Again, it suggests the dangers of oversimplified approaches. The importance of science (and, more generally, of numeracy) in skill-based industrialization is often emphasized, and the low percentages of Indonesia and Sri Lanka may be signs of a problem in this respect. Equally, however, the very high percentages found in some Eastern European countries are also problematic; re-education of the huge stock of engineers is a major task in Romania, for instance.

THE STRUCTURE OF EARNINGS

An important indirect indicator of what is happening in the market for more educated labour is the structure of earnings and labour costs. As the supply of qualified people increases in any economy, differentials in earnings between more- and less-qualified workers tend to fall. This is necessary for a shift in comparative advantage to take place from production based on cheap, unskilled labour to production based on skilled labour. For instance, Table 3.14 shows how differentials between occupational classes were compressed in Britain between 1913 and 1978. Before the First World War male professionals in Britain earned more than five times as much as unskilled manual workers; by 1978 the ratio had fallen to 2.4. In 1980, men with university degrees in the UK earned on average 53 per cent more than men with no advanced educational qualifications; by 1988, the premium (which fluctuates with changes on the demand as well as the supply side) had increased slightly but was still only 65 per cent (OECD, *Employment Outlook 1993*: Table 5.6).

Table 3.15 shows what has happened to wage differentials by schooling and gender in Indonesia as output from the educational system has increased since 1977. Differentials have narrowed at all levels, particularly for males, and are rapidly approaching the ratios found in industrialized economies. A male who has completed his upper-secondary schooling (taking at least twelve years) now earns, on average, little more than double the wage of an unschooled worker.

Table 3.14   Average earnings, males, seven occupational classes, Great Britain, 1913–1914 to 1978

	1913–14		1935–36		1960		1978	
	£	ratio	£	ratio	£	ratio	£	ratio
Professional								
Higher	328	5.2	634	4.9	2,034	3.8	8,286	2.4
Lower	155	2.5	308	2.4	847	1.6	5,435	1.6
Managers etc.	200	3.2	440	3.4	1,850	3.5	8,050	2.4
Clerks	99	1.6	192	1.5	682	1.3	3,701	1.1
Foremen	123	2.0	273	2.1	1,015	1.9	4,685	1.4
Manual								
Skilled	106	1.7	195	1.5	796	1.5	4,354	1.3
Semi-skilled	69	1.1	134	1.0	581	1.1	3,827	1.1
Unskilled	63	1.0	129	1.0	535	1.0	3,390	1.0

Source: Routh (1980: 120).

Table 3.15   Wage differentials by level of schooling and gender, Indonesia, 1977–1990 (indices, < primary = 100)

	Male				Female			
	1977	1982	1987	1990	1977	1982	1987	1990
< Primary	100	100	100	100	100	100	100	100
Primary	151	142	128	122	149	151	128	126
Lower secondary	275	203	170	158	396	290	225	203
Upper secondary								
General	245	249	212	214	380	368	304	287
Vocational	328	262	214	209	483	375	348	319
Tertiary	1,033	410	372	366	1,428	582	551	508

Sources: Manning (1994: Table 1), from Central Bureau of Statistics, *National Labour Force Surveys* (SAKERNAS), 1977, 1987, 1990, and *National Social Economic Survey* (SUSENAS), 1982.

Perhaps more relevant to the issue of transition are the ratios among the age groups that are entering the labour market. Table 3.16 shows how these have changed for urban males in recent years. The series show signs of statistical noise and of fluctuations from year to year reflecting fluctuations in demand, but in general they show falling premia for education among new entrants to the labour market in the face of fast expansion of enrolment and output. Urban labour markets no longer differentiate between those new entrants who have and those who have not completed primary schooling, and extend only a small premium to lower-secondary school leavers. At upper-secondary level vocational graduates do worse than general graduates. The only category with a relatively resilient premium is university graduates who continue to enjoy a wage about four times that of an unschooled worker at labour-force-entry age.

EDUCATIONAL QUALITY

The missing element in most discussions of the market for educated labour is quality. Through its effect on productivity, quality of education has an obvious impact on the timing of transition, but is very difficult to measure.

A worrying aspect of the recent fast expansion in educational enrolment and output in Indonesia is the fall in quality that has apparently resulted. At primary level (where the foundations for subsequent performance are laid), even though the number of qualified teachers has increased, a recent study

Table 3.16 Trends in annual average wage earnings, male urban employees, selected age groups, 1986, 1988, 1990 and 1992

Schooling	Age group	1986		1988		1990		1992	
		Rp '000	index	Rp '000	index	Rp '000	index	Rp '000	index
None	15–20	380	100	428	100	604	100	740	100
Primary	15–20	508	134	546	128	711	118	714	97
Lower Secondary General	15–20	649	171	1,058	247	732	121	916	124
Upper Secondary General	21–30	1,084	285	1,106	258	1,311	217	1,557	211
Upper Secondary Vocational	21–30	1,183	311	1,048	245	1,272	211	1,430	193
Academy	21–30	1,495	393	1,662	388	1,683	279	2,363	320
University	21–30	1,472	387	2,042	477	2,161	358	2,812	380

Sources: 1986, 1988: McMahon and Boediono (1992: Table III.1); 1990: private communication; 1992: McMahon (1994).

(Suryadi 1990) found 'profound problems' in teacher quality which was observed to be 'extremely low' (particularly in mathematics and science), insufficient educational resources (rooms, libraries, laboratories, cafeterias, toilets, classroom equipment, books), and a major problem of management quality.

All this is consistent with the findings of a rare in-depth study of what goes on inside Indonesian primary school classrooms by Djalil (undated), reported on by Kemmerer et al. (1990: 57):

> Djalil found that in Indonesian primary schools memorisation was the technique used more times than all others combined. The school day, designed to be four hours, was generally much shorter due to the late arrival of the teachers at school. Textbooks, learning materials and facilities such as libraries and laboratories were rare. Teachers were distracted by the need to make money on other jobs so they did not plan instruction or analyse homework carefully or diagnose and evaluate each pupil's progress. On average, they were not skilled in defining lesson objectives, explaining lessons, using relevant examples, or examining for comprehension of concepts. Feedback was not used to provide either positive or corrective reinforcement. Responses from pupils were often of the choral type, with some students wrong and some right. Students did not ask questions. Teachers did not teach to individuals but only to the large intact group of the entire class, which prevented them from assessing individual performance. They did not seem to know how to set objective criteria in order to measure the behaviour of pupils.

At secondary level, the education sector review, carried out in September–October 1985, found the average quality of graduates at both junior and senior secondary levels to be 'less than adequate' (IEES: Chapter 6, 75). The 'quality of the typical SMA [senior secondary school] graduate continues to decline to a level that is probably equivalent to that of the SMP [junior secondary school] before the beginning of rapid expansion of secondary education' (IEES: chapter 6, 77). English continued to be a particularly problematic subject (IEES: Chapter 6, 77) and standards in science and mathematics may have deteriorated further, to judge from recent performance in university entrance tests and average grades of first-year undergraduates. More recently, Somerset (1988: 54–74) reports on the poor quality of recruits to education programmes compared with those to non-education programmes in universities, as measured by their grades in the senior-secondary-school-leaving examination, and the poor quality of teaching in teacher education programmes.

In higher education there are spectacular internal inefficiencies, illustrated by the fact that the average age of graduates in non-educational subjects in 1986 was 29 (Study Team of Tracer Study of University Graduates 1986: 126) and the average time taken to finish a supposedly four-year course ranged from 7 to 10 years (IEES: chapter 9, 51). To a large extent the universities inherit the results of poor-quality schooling, at both primary and secondary levels. A 1986 study found that the 'quality of the raw input' was the main determinant of wide variations in internal efficiency and quality of graduates between universities (Research Team 1986).

Of course, the combination of deterioration in educational quality and expansion in quantity is not unique to Indonesia. It does, however, draw attention to the difficulties of quantitative analysis in this area. None of the usual proxies for educational quality (teacher/pupil ratios, class size, teacher qualifications, repetition and dropout, textbook availability, and so on) is wholly satisfactory as a determinant of educational outcome, let alone of labour-market outcome.

It is tempting to fall back on the perceptions of businessmen. For instance, Table 3.17 summarizes the views of a sample of international employers on the quality, availability and cost of production and managerial labour in eleven Asian countries. In most countries quality of production labour is not seen as a big problem (although it should be noted that Indonesia, together with China, is the worst placed in this respect). Availability and cost are, however, worrying employers in the obvious range of countries where labour shortage has emerged – Hong Kong, Japan, Singapore, Korea and Taiwan.

Table 3.17 Labour ratings in selected Asian countries

	Production labour			Managerial labour		
	Q	A	C	Q	A	C
China	5	1	1	10	10	1
Hong Kong	1	10	8	1	10	10
Indonesia	5	1	1	10	10	2
Japan	1	10	10	1	1	10
Malaysia	3	3	3	5	5	5
Philippines	3	1	2	3	1	1
Singapore	1	10	8	1	10	8
Korea	1	8	7	5	10	9
Taiwan	1	9	8	1	8	9
Thailand	4	2	1	10	10	4
Vietnam	3	1	1	10	5	1

Notes: Q = Quality; A = Availability; C = Cost; 1 = the best grade possible; 10 = the worst grade.

Source: Political and Economic Risk Consultancy Ltd., reported in *International Herald Tribune*, 29 July 1991.

Slight availability problems are beginning to arise in Malaysia and Thailand. As far as managerial labour is concerned, top quality ratings go only to Hong Kong, Japan, Singapore and Taiwan. Indonesia, along with China, Thailand and Vietnam, receives the poorest rating. The most interesting case in the table, with a better managerial quality rating than Korea, is the Philippines.

CONCLUSIONS

A number of necessary conditions for the transition from cheap labour to skill-based competitiveness in manufacturing have been identified in this chapter. These will now be summarized, and the extent to which they are present in Indonesia will be assessed.

First, the basis must be laid for the transition by a period of sustained growth in wage employment in manufacturing, accompanied by growth in real value added per employee, stability in the real producer wage, and a trend in the real effective exchange rate that ensures international competitiveness. There is no doubt that Indonesia has been going through this stage.

Secondly, demand for unskilled labour must increase at such a rate that a shortage of such labour begins to emerge, with the result that the real product wage begins to rise, alongside a continued increase in real value added per employee. Indonesia is showing some symptoms consistent with a move into this phase, but most observers doubt whether a shortage of unskilled labour is imminent.

A third condition necessary for the transition is an increase in the supply of better-educated labour, particularly at the senior secondary and tertiary levels. This will generally be reflected in a narrowing in earnings differentials between more- and less-qualified workers. Indonesia has experienced both these trends and earnings differentials are now quite narrow, but educational expansion, though fast, has not yet lifted it out of the category of countries with relatively low enrolment ratios at these levels.

Fourthly, not only must the quantity of educated people be sufficient to sustain the transition to skill-based competitiveness, so, too, must their quality. Here, it must be admitted that Indonesia has problems, reflected not only in assessments of the quality of its schooling but also in the views of employers on the quality of its labour and management.

In short, there is no doubt that Indonesia has laid the basis for transition and is on the way towards developing the shortage of unskilled labour that precedes it, but neither the quality nor the quantity of its better-educated labour, and of its management, yet look sufficient to sustain an early transition. The view of many observers that it must wait until the early years of the twenty-first century may be justified on these grounds alone.

Finally, what about those countries which have developed the necessary skills but nevertheless do not seem to have entered a phase of skill-based competitiveness? An obvious example is the Philippines[4], which is in the highest category of senior secondary and tertiary enrolment ratios and receives the highest rating from international businessmen for availability and quality of managerial labour.

Figure 3.8, which shows the relationship between the real producer wage, real value added and employment in manufacturing in the Philippines between 1986 and 1991, points to one aspect of the economy's problems. As can be seen, real compensation cost per employee increased in the Philippines over this period, just as it did in Indonesia. The difference is that real value added per employee has been on a downward rather than an upward trend. This combination is a sign not of emerging labour shortage but of labour-market segmentation. While workers in the larger establishments covered by the survey[5] enjoyed wage increases well ahead of the rate of inflation, wage employment grew only slowly and hundreds of thousands of Filipinos sought work overseas. The contrast with the comparable trends for Indonesia (in Figure 3.5) is telling.

In international markets, the unfavourable impact of wage and productivity trends has been compounded by trends in real effective exchange rates. This

Figure 3.8   Philippines: real labour cost and value added per employee
and employment in manufacturing, 1986–1991

has had contrasting implications for real unit labour costs in the Philippines and Indonesia, as Table 3.18 shows. While real wage growth in the Philippines in this period was slower than in Indonesia, the comparison of trends in productivity was very much in Indonesia's favour. And, while the Philippines shared in the Asian region's tendency towards falling real effective exchange rates, this was not enough to prevent its real unit labour cost from rising – again in contrast to its neighbour, devaluing at an even faster rate.

Table 3.18   *Manufacturing wages, value added per employee, exchange rates and unit labour cost: a comparison of the Philippines and Indonesia, 1986–1991 (Indices, 1986= 100)*

	1986	1987	1988	1989	1990	1991
Nominal compensation cost per employee						
Philippines	100	117	136	155	183	223
Indonesia	100	109	123	137	155	186
Nominal value added per employee						
Philippines	100	94	104	113	129	148
Indonesia	100	114	122	153	171	181
Real effective exchange rate						
Philippines	100	94	91	95	93	92
Indonesia	100	76	73	75	72	70
Real unit labour cost (foreign currencies)						
Philippines	100	117	118	131	132	139
Indonesia	100	73	74	67	65	72

Sources: As for Tables 3.3, 3.4, 3.5 and 3.6; Bot (1994).

The Philippines, thus, is an example of an economy with all the educational preconditions for transition to skill-based competitiveness, but without the necessary combination of wage, productivity and exchange-rate conditions. The sad conclusion is that skill-based competitiveness requires competitiveness as well as skill.

NOTES

*   Thanks are due, with the usual disclaimer, for helpful comments to participants in the IDS Workshop, particularly Adrian Wood.
1.   See Godfrey (1986: 125–34) for further discussion.
2.   Index of educational attainment = 2/3 × adult literacy rate + 1/3 × mean years of schooling.
3.   By merely adding up the ratios for 1991 (or the most recent year) and dividing by 2.
4.   Sri Lanka is another, but sufficient data for analysis are not available. Several Eastern European economies may also be in this category.

5. Those employing on average ten or more workers, or with average monthly receipts of 1 million pesos ($48,000 at 1989 exchange rates) or more.

REFERENCES

Bhattacharya, Amar, and Mari Pangestu (1993), *The Lessons of East Asia: Indonesia – Development Transformation and Public Policy*, Washington DC: World Bank.

Bot, Kees (1994), 'Notes on Wages and Earnings in the Philippines', Manila: ILO Employment Promotion Project, mimeo.

Godfrey, Martin (1986), *Global Unemployment: The New Challenge to Economic Theory*, Brighton: Wheatsheaf.

Godfrey, Martin (1993), *Employment Planning within the Context of Economic Reforms: A Case Study of Indonesia, World Employment Programme Research*, Working Paper No. 39, WEP 2–46/WP.39, Geneva: ILO.

IEES (1986), *Indonesia: Education and Human Resources Sector Review*, Jakarta: Ministry of Education and Culture/USAID.

Kemmerer, Frances, Dean Nielsen and Patrick Lynch (1990), *A Review of Teacher Education Issues in Indonesia*, Educational Policy and Planning Project, Jakarta: Ministry of Education and Culture.

Lewis, W. Arthur (1954), 'Economic Development with Unlimited Supplies of Labour', *The Manchester School of Economic and Social Studies*, **22** (2), May, 139–91.

Manning, Chris (1994), *Labour Market Developments in Indonesia during the New Order*, Economics Division Working Papers, Canberra: Research School of Pacific and Asian Studies, ANU.

McMahon, Walter (1994), 'The Contribution of Secondary Education to Economic Development in East Asia', Urbana: University of Illinois, mimeo.

McMahon, Walter and Boediono (eds) (1992), *Education and the Economy: The External Efficiency of Education*, Educational Policy and Planning Project, Jakarta: Ministry of Education and Culture.

Pangestu, Mari and Iwan Jaya Azis (1994), 'Survey of Recent Developments', *Bulletin of Indonesian Economic Studies*, **30** (2) August, 1–37.

Ranis, Gustav, and John C.H. Fei (1961), 'A Theory of Economic Development', *American Economic Review*, **51** (4) September, 533–65.

Research Team (1986), *Baseline Study on Internal Efficiency and Student Characteristics of Higher Education in Indonesia*, Jakarta: Department of Education and Culture, Director General of Higher Education.

Routh, Guy (1980), *Occupation and Pay in Great Britain, 1906–79*, London: Macmillan.

Somerset, H.C.A. (1988), 'Quality Issues in General Secondary Education', Jakarta: World Bank, mimeo.

Study Team of Tracer Study of University Graduates (1986), *Tracer Study of University Graduates, Final Report*, Director General of Higher Education, in cooperation with Demographic Institute, Faculty of Economics, University of Indonesia, Jakarta.

Suryadi, Ace (1990), *Improving the Educational Quality of Primary Schools*, Educational Policy and Planning Project, Jakarta: Ministry of Education and Culture.

Szirmai, Adam (1994), 'Real Output and Labour Productivity in Indonesian Manufacturing, 1975–90', *Bulletin of Indonesian Economic Studies*, **30** (2) August, 71–101.

World Bank (1990), *Indonesia: Foundations for Sustained Growth*, Report No. 8455–IND, Washington, DC: World Bank.

World Bank (1993), *Indonesia: Industrial Policy – Shifting into High Gear*, Report No. 12153–IND, Washington, DC: World Bank.

World Bank (1994), *Indonesia: Stability, Growth and Equity in Repelita VI*, Report No. 12857–IND, Washington, DC: World Bank.

4. Can governments engineer the transition from cheap labour to skill-based competitiveness? The case of Singapore

Cheah Hock Beng

The future now belongs to societies that organise themselves for learning. What we know and can do holds the key to economic progress, just as command of natural resources once did. ... More than ever before, nations that want high incomes and full employment must develop policies that emphasise the acquisition of knowledge and skills by everyone, not just a select few. The prize will go to those countries that are organised to learn and to act on what they learn. (Marshall and Tucker 1992: xiii)

INTRODUCTION

Following the success of its earlier development efforts, since 1979 Singapore has sought to transform her economy and society into that of a developed nation. The state has taken an active role in promoting economic development since the 1960s, and continues to be involved in diverse ways in its attempts to mould the country into a highly-competitive force in the international economy.

This chapter examines the process through which Singapore has attempted to manage the transition from a developing to a developed economy. In this process, competitive advantage is not simply a natural endowment, as has been generally assumed in orthodox economics textbooks under the concept of 'comparative advantage'. Competitive advantage can be created. In Singapore, the government actively sought to create competitiveness in various dimensions through a diverse range of measures.[1] This chapter focuses on the efforts to create competitiveness through skills development, and associated labour and wage policies.

This process of creating competitive advantage was not a smooth one. While there have been significant achievements for the economy and for labour in Singapore, difficulties were also encountered. The difficulties stemmed partly from the attempts of the government to determine the nature of behaviour and decisions at the enterprise level. Difficulties were encountered when these efforts were unable to match the complex needs and the diverse situations faced by enterprises. Nevertheless, the process of development and adjustment has until now been largely successful.

In the face of new domestic and external constraints, can the achievements be sustained and broadened in the longer term? Much depends on developments in the international economy upon which Singapore is very dependent but on which it is also unable to exert significant leverage. The outcome also depends partly upon the domestic capacity to resolve the contradictions that have been encountered, and upon the creativity of the city-state in responding to the new challenges. It also depends significantly upon the state–enterprise relationship, in particular, the creation of opportunities for decisions to be made more independently at the enterprise level in areas such as wage determination, employee motivation, work practices and industrial relations.

DEVELOPMENT STRATEGY IN SINGAPORE 1968–1984

Since 1968, the government has pursued a development strategy which emphasized export-oriented industrialization, based upon an open economy, substantial direct foreign investment by multinational corporations, and the transfer of technology and skills from abroad (Cheah 1980). As an integral part of this process, the demands of workers and trade unions were firmly restrained. Foreign labour (professionals as well as skilled and unskilled manual workers) was also imported to help fill the new jobs created by the export-oriented industrialization strategy.[2] The government contended that:

> An open door policy is one which at least ensures rapid growth right from the start. When foreign corporations bring their expertise, what we experience, as a developing nation, is a brain drain in reverse. Naturally we pay for this, we pay in the form of profits and know-how fees remitted abroad and high salaries to foreign management and technical personnel. ... [However] [i]t would be wrong for us to resent the inflow of management personnel, engineers and technicians from abroad. On the contrary, we could regard them as blazing the trail for the new industries which we do not have the knowledge and technology to set up ourselves. (Goh 1970; 30)

Indeed, the Prime Minister, stressing the contribution which the expertise of foreign professionals could make to a developing economy, pointed out that

> [W]e have never suffered from any inhibitions in borrowing capital, know-how, managers, engineers, and marketing capabilities. Far from limiting the entry of

Table 4.1 Development indicators and labour-force statistics, 1975–1993.

Year	Gross domestic product ($m.)	Per capita indigenous GNP ($)	Gross fixed capital formation ($m.)	Labour force ('000 persons)	Number employed ('000 persons)	Number unemployed ('000 persons)	Unemployment rate (%)	Labour-force participation rate (%)	Median monthly income($)	Median age (years)
1975	19,087.0	5,089	6,875.0	867.4	828.7	38.7	4.5	57.3	286	29.0
1976	20,515.0	5,496	7,445.0	904.2	864.4	39.7	4.4	57.6	307	28.8
1977	22,134.0	6,011	7,584.0	936.9	900.4	36.5	3.9	58.5	318	29.3
1978	24,046.0	6,303	8,652.0	991.0	955.6	35.3	3.6	60.0	329	28.9
1979	26,305.0	6,892	9,766.0	1,053.1	1,018.3	34.8	3.3	61.4	347	29.2
1980	29,025.0	8,343	11,126.6	1,102.5	1,068.9	33.5	3.0	62.7	377	29.1
1981	31,603.1	9,854	12,810.3	1,187.9	1,153.6	34.4	2.9	63.0	433	29.3
1982	33,772.3	11,085	15,405.7	1,253.2	1,221.2	32.1	2.6	63.4	511	29.8
1983	36,537.2	12,533	17,067.7	1,292.8	1,251.2	41.5	3.2	63.8	560	30.1
1984	39,572.5	13,599	18,677.4	1,304.3	1,269.1	35.1	2.7	63.4	613	31.0
1985	38,923.5	13,044	16,424.8	1,287.8	1,234.6	53.3	4.1	62.2	654	31.4
1986	39,641.4	12,824	14,540.2	1,298.5	1,214.4	84.0	6.5	62.3	667	31.8
1987	43,371.8	13,733	15,028.0	1,329.3	1,266.9	62.4	4.7	62.7	687	32.3
1988	48,203.4	15,424	16,259.6	1,377.7	1,331.6	46.1	3.3	62.9	721	32.6
1989	52,657.4	17,535	18,503.4	1,424.7	1,394.1	30.7	2.2	63.1	764	32.8
1990	57,271.9	20,090	21,004.5	1,494.4	1,469.2	25.2	1.7	63.1	818	33.9
1991	61,081.0	21,620	24,095.8	1,554.3	1,524.3	30.0	1.9	64.8	919	33.6
1992	64,771.0	22,839	26,532.5	1,619.6	1,576.2	43.4	2.7	65.3	1,002	33.9
1993	71,211.9	24,871	30,553.1	1,635.7	1,592.0	43.7	2.7	64.5	1,099	34.7

Annual growth rate (%)

1975–1978	8.0	7.6	7.3	4.4	4.8	−3.5	0.9	4.7	0.1
1978–1984	8.6	14.5	14.3	5.0	5.1	1.0	0.6	11.8	1.1
1984–1986	0.1	−2.9	−11.8	−0.2	−2.2	54.7	−0.6	4.3	1.3
1986–1988	10.3	9.7	5.7	3.0	4.7	−25.9	0.3	4.0	1.3
1988–1993	7.8	9.7	13.3	3.7	3.8	2.7	0.3	9.1	1.2

Notes: Gross domestic product and gross fixed capital formation are valued at 1985 market prices. Per-capita indigenous GNP is valued at current market prices. Population, labour-force, employment and participation rate refers to persons aged 15 years and over. Annual growth rate is computed on a least-squares basis, with the exception of those relating to employment rate and labour-force participation rate.

Sources: Singapore Department of Statistics, *Yearbook of Statistics* and Singapore Ministry of Labour, *Report on the Labour Force Survey of Singapore 1993*, p. 29.

foreign managers, engineers, and bankers we encourage them to come. ... Had we tried to go into industry on our own, working from first principles, we would never have made it ... to acquire the know-how, to develop the management and markets, would have cost us dearly. We would have had to learn the hard way, paying for every mistake. As it was, Singaporeans were being paid while learning, and their instructors were making a fair return on investments, while instructing them on the job. (Lee 1980)

This general approach brought significant benefits in terms of rapid economic growth and higher employment (Table 4.1). As a result, in the early 1970s, the government had already intended to promote a shift away from the predominance of labour-intensive manufacturing activities. However, it was deflected from these plans by the recession of 1975 and the instability of the international economy during 1973–75. It was subsequently acknowledged that excessive fear of rising unemployment in the domestic economy had caused the government to hold on to low-wage and labour-intensive manufacturing for too long. This helped to depress the rate of economic growth relative to those achieved by the other Asian newly-industrializing economies (NICs), and intensified the domestic labour constraints in the subsequent economic recovery.

Consequently, the government sought to resume its earlier efforts to restructure the economy, while recognizing that it would not be easy to make up for the lost time, because international economic conditions were generally less favourable and there was also greater competition from other countries attempting to undertake the same process of structural change at the same time. Indeed, the less favourable conditions convinced the planners that more direct and stronger measures were needed to promote the desired economic transformation.

The general objective of the Economic Restructuring Strategy (ERS) adopted in 1979 was to promote a 'second industrial revolution'. Its intention was to achieve an economy-wide shift towards higher-value-added activities. It was intended to encompass the service sector as well as manufacturing industry, and the public sector as well as the private sector. In 1986, a prominent government advisory body described the strategy as follows:

Restructuring meant two things: Firstly, upgrading *existing* economic activities by increasing the value-added of each worker; this entailed higher labour productivity and greater automation and mechanisation. Secondly, promoting *new* economic activities with higher value-added content; this meant more new investments in higher skilled and higher-technology manufacturing and service activities. (The Economic Committee, 1986: 25)[3] (original emphasis).

The ERS continued to rely on the multinational corporations (MNCs) for the transfer of skills and technology. However, the skills of the domestic workforce would also be enhanced by an increased output of trained manpower from various educational and training institutions, so as to achieve better-paid and higher-skilled full employment, and a rise in the general standard of living.

The planners perceived that, first, the rise in the general wage level, together with the reduction in the number of foreign workers, would encourage firms to rationalize and upgrade their operations in the officially recommended ways (that is, through greater mechanization, automation, computerization and increased use of robots); and second, higher productivity (based on better management, better industrial relations, better skills, and more capital-intensive methods of production) would promote efficiency and international competitiveness, and support continuing economic growth and a rising standard of living.

Wage Policy

Since the formation of the National Wages Council (NWC) in 1972, the government has sought to influence the general wage level on a tripartite basis (together with the representatives of trade unions and employers' organizations). During most years prior to 1979, the general effort was aimed at restraining the rate at which wages rose (Table 4.2).

By the late 1970s, however, the city-state was experiencing severe labour shortages. During that period, the government also perceived that excessive wage restraint in the previous years had promoted the retention of labour-intensive economic activities. This hindered the natural process of economic upgrading and restructuring, and made the economy more vulnerable to international competition from other developing countries, and to growing protectionism in developed-country markets.

To spur the process of economic restructuring in general, and productivity growth in particular, the government encouraged significant wage increases to 'correct' the perceived deficiencies of the previous wage-restraint policy, and to restore wages to their 'natural' market levels. This was achieved through the annual recommendations of the NWC during 1979–81. The NWC comprises representatives from employers, trade unions and the government. Its recommendations for higher wage increases during this period served to raise labour costs for all employers. However, the impact weighed most heavily upon firms engaged in labour-intensive activities. This measure was accompanied by the imposition of increased contributions to the Central Provident Fund (CPF),[4] and the introduction of the Skills Development Fund levy, all of which contributed to a significant rise in labour costs.

It was perceived that these measures would encourage employers to economize on labour through organizational rationalization, and the general restructuring of production. These measures were accompanied by government

Table 4.2   National wages council wage rise recommendations, 1972–1993

Year	Private sector	Public sector
1972	6% without offsetting of annual increments.	9% without offsetting.
1973	9% with varying rates of offsetting depending on salary.	
1974	$40 + 6% without offsetting of annual increments.	$40 + 6% without offsetting for employees earning less than $1,000 per month.
	$40 + 10% for employees who have not received an annual increment.	10% without offsetting for employees earning at least $1,000 per month.
1975	6% with full offsetting of annual increments, provided that those employees who are on incremental scales received a minimum increase after offsetting of 3%; for those at the maximum of their pay scales, the wage increase was 3%.	6% with full offsetting of annual increment provided that those on incremental scales received a minimum increase after offsetting of 3%; for those at the maximum of their pay scales, the wage increase was a full 6%.
1976	7% with full offsetting of annual increments on a group basis.	6% with full offsetting of all forms of increases in remuneration on a group basis.
1978	$12 + 6% with full offsetting of all forms of increases in remuneration on a group basis.	$12 + 6% with full offsetting of all forms of increases in remuneration on a group basis.
1979	$32 + 7% with full offsetting of all forms of increases in remuneration on a group basis.	$32 + 2.5% subject to minimum of 7%.
1980	$33 + 7.5% with full offsetting of all forms of increases on a group basis, and an additional 3% of the group monthly wage bill of June 1980, to be distributed only among above average employees.	$33 + 7.5% with full offsetting of all forms of increases on a group basis, and an additional 4% for above average employees.
1981	$32 + 6% to 10% with full offsetting of all forms of increases on a group basis, and an additional 2% of the group monthly wage bill of June 1981 to be distributed only among meritorious performers.	$32 + 5% subject to a minimum of 11%, an additional 5% of the group monthly wage bill of June 1981 to be distributed only among meritorious performers.

1982	$18.50 + 2.5% to 6.5% with full offsetting of all forms of increases on a group basis.	$18.50 for employees earning $568 per month or less, 3.25% for those earning more than $568 per month.
1983	$10 + 2% to 6% with full offsetting of all forms of increases on a group basis.	$10 + 1.3% for employees earning $604 per month or less, 3% for those earning more than $604 per month.
1984	$27 + 4% to $27 + 8% with full offsetting of all forms of increases on a group basis.	$27 + 4.2% for employees earning $680 per month or less, 8.2% for those earning more than $680 per month.
1985	3% to 7% with full offsetting of all forms of increases on a group basis	0% after offsetting.
1986+1987	Wage restraint.	
1988+1989	Total wage increase should be given in two parts – a moderate basic wage increase and a variable payment/bonus linked to company/individual performance or productivity. Total wage increase should lag behind productivity growth.	
1990	Built-in wage increase (annual increments plus wage adjustments) should lag behind productivity growth. Companies performing well should, however, reward employees with higher variable bonus.	
1991	Total wage increase should be lower than that of 1990, in line with the expected slower economic growth. Built-in wage increase should lag behind productivity growth. Companies performing well should, however, reward employees with higher variable bonus.	
1992	Total wage increase should be moderated in line with the expected slower economic growth. Built-in wage increase should lag behind productivity growth. Companies should pay as much of the wage increase as possible in the form of variable component.	
1993	Built-in basic wage increase should lag behind productivity growth. Total wage increase can, however, reflect the expected improved economic and business performance. Companies should pay as much of the total wage increase in the form of variable component. Those companies which had done exceptionally well should pay a special bonus.	

Sources: Singapore, Ministry of Labour, *Singapore Yearbook of Labour Statistics*, various issues.

efforts to reduce the number of foreign workers employed in the economy. However, since 1982, the NWC has moderated significantly the level of wage increases in its recommendations, and justified this in relation to the more difficult domestic and international economic situation.

Skill Formation

There has been a considerable expansion of the facilities for raising the skills of the labour force. The educational system had been substantially reorganized to provide more years of schooling for a greater proportion of youths (Soon 1988), to increase their levels of skill prior to as well as after their absorption into the workforce. In addition to the schools, there are 17 institutions managed by the Institute of Technical Education, and four polytechnics. At the tertiary level, there is the National University of Singapore, and Nanyang Technological University which incorporates the National Institute of Education. The Open University also began offering degree courses in January 1994 through the Singapore Institute of Management.

These have expanded the opportunities for continuing education and training. Measures have also been undertaken to improve the quality of public and corporate management through the expansion of postgraduate courses in management and business administration. This has also involved the import of foreign expertise (including professors from the leading American schools of management and business studies) to conduct courses in Singapore, in addition to sending students abroad on scholarships for such training.

In 1979, the Skills Development Fund (SDF) was established to finance measures intended to raise the skills of the workforce, to encourage the retraining of workers who might otherwise be retrenched in the course of the national economic restructuring drive, and to promote labour-saving and productivity-raising investments. It was constituted from mandatory contributions by employers, despite some misgivings about the scheme, particularly from small business enterprises. The contributions amounted to a percentage of the wage bill of those employees earning less than $750 per month.[5] Encouragement to employers to upgrade the skills of their workforce, and to expand both in-house and external training opportunities, was provided through the SDF's Training Grant Scheme, which awarded varying rates of subsidy according to the assessed merits of each funding application.

The National Productivity Board (NPB) also undertook numerous measures to expand training opportunities, and to instil greater awareness about the importance of measures to achieve higher productivity. It spearheaded the drive to establish quality control circles (QCCs) within companies, and to familiarize employees with QCC techniques, drawing on expertise in this field from Japan and the United States. The cost of attendance at numerous

NPB-sponsored training courses, on this and other subjects, was subsidized by the SDF. These efforts were a part of the overall national effort of human resource development.

As part of this general effort a host of skills development programmes were introduced. The Basic Education for Skills Training (BEST) programme was introduced in 1982 to raise the level of literacy and numeracy of persons in the workforce who had not been educated up to the Primary 6 educational level, as a consequence of the previously high rate of attrition in the educational system and the narrower structure of educational opportunities. In July 1984, a Modular Skills Training (MOST) programme was offered on a full-time basis and, from October 1986, also on a part-time basis, for graduates of the BEST programme and for persons who had completed the Primary School Leaving Examination (PSLE). Each module in the programme was a short, self-contained course leading to an employable skill. A further extension in skills development was introduced in the form of the Worker Improvement through Secondary Education (WISE) programme in September 1987. This aimed to prepare persons who had completed the PSLE, or the BEST programme, for the GCE 'N' Level examination in English and/or Mathematics. Finally, a programme for the improvement of basic work skills (in communications, personal effectiveness, problem solving, work economics and computer literacy), named Core Skills for Effectiveness and Change (COSEC), had been introduced in February 1986. This was targeted mainly at clerical and service workers. All these programmes were supported by the SDF.

Technological Upgrading

With the objective of improving operational efficiency and of raising the general level of productivity, various measures were introduced to promote mechanization, computerization, automation and the increased use of robots, where applicable. Fiscal measures encouraging investments in labour-saving and modern production machinery and equipment are contained in the investment allowance scheme offered by the Economic Development Board (EDB) as well as in the various provisions for accelerated depreciation. In addition, as the SDF expanded the scope of its operations, its Training Grant scheme was complemented by the Interest Grant for Mechanization Scheme, which provides financial support for capital investments in new labour-saving machinery and equipment, and the Development Consultancy Scheme, which assists local companies to seek expert advice to improve the efficiency of their operations.

With the labour shortages experienced in Singapore, these efforts did not arouse significant concern among the labour force. Labour-saving technology was promoted as a means of enhancing the capabilities and productivity of the workforce, and as an important factor in maintaining international com-petitiveness despite higher wage increases.

Initially, small local business enterprises benefited little from these new provisions. The assistance was more readily utilized by larger as well as foreign-owned enterprises, some of which would have been prepared to im-prove their production processes in the absence of any assistance. They thus received a bonus from the introduction of the new schemes. Subsequently, however, the EDB responded to requests for greater emphasis to be placed on promoting smaller enterprises, and it sought more actively to assist small local businesses to utilize the various schemes for improving the sophistica-tion of their production processes. This was also intended to assist the smaller local enterprises to become more efficient subcontractors to larger firms and, in this respect, the assistance of the larger foreign firms was also sought by the EDB.

Employment of Foreign Workers

The ERS also involved a major policy decision about the employment of foreign workers. In December 1981, it was announced by the Prime Minister that recruitment of foreign workers from non-traditional (that is, other than Malaysian) sources would soon cease. According to the then Prime Minister,

> Work permit holders from non-traditional countries have been allowed in as a temporary measure. This recruitment will stop in 1982. From January 1983, as their work permits expire, they will begin to leave. Thus, all non-traditional country workers will leave by December 31, 1984, except for [those engaged in] construction and shipyards, and domestics. In other words, 1982 is the last year manufacturers have to continue operations with their full complement of non-traditional work permit holders. Therefore, they must further mechanise, auto-mate, computerise, and improve management to cut down on workers; or they will have to relocate their factories [abroad]. (Lee 1982)

The then Prime Minister added that:

> [Foreign] Workers we want to retain beyond 1990 should be those who will raise our level of productivity. We shall give such workers permanent residence with a view to citizenship. Then we shall have a more homogeneous workforce, working together as a team, because they all feel committed to Singapore. Then the princi-ple, from each his best, to each his worth, which has been the basis of our progress, will work under optimal conditions.[6]

To ease the increasingly severe labour shortage, employers were encouraged to establish more creches and child-care facilities, to facilitate the absorption and retention of more local women in the workforce, as one alternative to the dependence on foreign labour.

Subsequently, however, the government's resolve weakened as the labour shortage persisted and as employers continued to appeal for the policy to be reconsidered. Various concessions were granted to employers. In November 1983, some foreign workers due to leave in 1984 were given a two-year extension. In February 1984, the government gave permission for the recruitment of workers from Hong Kong, Taiwan, Macau and South Korea. In November 1984, the Minister of Labour announced that the government would review the policy of phasing out foreign workers by 1991. In March 1985 the Minister of Finance reported that the policy would be administered with greater flexibility, and the government subsequently froze the foreign workers' levy at $200 a month instead of raising it to $350 by April 1986 as planned. This was a manifestation of the increased influence of employers in the tripartite relationship with the government and the trade unions.

Industrial Relations Policy

Industrial legislation, direct influence in the trade union movement, regulations by statutory and other state-dominated agencies, and frequent exhortations by the political leadership, have all played an important part in determining the industrial relations climate in Singapore since political independence was achieved. As Pang (1978: 435) noted,

> [t]he main actor in the Singapore industrial relations system is the Government and its agencies. Management is given a relatively free hand to maximise profits in the context of a market economy, while the labour movement is assigned the role of helping to preserve industrial peace, and to explain national programs and policies.

Leggett (1985: 8–9) also observed that 'during the 1970s ... the vigilance of the NTUC's Industrial Affairs Council in monitoring affiliates' disputes and the proscriptions contained in the Trade Disputes Act, the Criminal Law (temporary Provisions) Act, and the Trade Unions Act ... combined [to] make a legal strike virtually impossible in Singapore'.

In undertaking the ERS the government continued to monitor the industrial relations scene closely and introduced further innovations to the situation, in accordance with its perception of changing needs. The 1982 Trade Union (Amendment) Act modified the definition of a trade union, and altered the practice of industrial negotiations, so as to promote greater identification by the workers with their employers and the corporate interests. The Employment Act was also amended in 1984 so as to permit employers greater flexibility in defining the length of the working day and the working week, and the terms of employment, among other things. This was also intended to facilitate changes in work practices arising from the introduction of new technology.

These changes have been accompanied by a shift in philosophy from a Taylorist approach in the management of the workforce to a Human Relations approach for creating a more contented labour force, and greater emulation of the 'Japanese model' of labour management (see Leggett 1988, and Lim, C.Y. 1982: 101ff.).

In response to the persuasion of the political leadership, the National Trades Union Congress (NTUC) dissolved its two large omnibus (multi-industry) unions (the Singapore Industrial Labour Organization and the Pioneer Industries Employees Union) into industry unions. Since 1981, efforts were also directed towards the promotion of house (enterprise) unions. These moves were intended to strengthen the nexus of interests between employers and employees, and to foster a consensus approach to the management of industrial relations.

In this respect, the government also sought to promote the COWEC (company welfarism through employers' CPF contributions) scheme. This was intended to channel a part of the employer's CPF contribution into a scheme to be administered by the employer, with the interest derived from the investment of the principal sum, to be used for the provision of better welfare benefits to the employees of the company. It was perceived that this scheme would strengthen employee identification with and loyalty to the employer, and reduce popular expectations and reliance on the government for the provision of social welfare benefits. In relation to this and other measures, the Japanese pattern of development has been a significant influence on the political leadership (see Awanohara 1987, and Soesastro 1985). However, the COWEC scheme achieved only limited headway because of the uncertainties which employees and employers felt about the operation of the scheme, and about the value of the benefits from it. By January 1986, only eight companies had introduced the scheme. By 1991, only four of the twenty companies participating in the pilot scheme were still implementing it (Economic Planning Committee 1991: 105).

In summary, prior to 1979, Singapore's development strategy and labour policy was primarily directed at *job creation*. The principal premise then, it may be suggested, was that 'any job is better than no job'. And in that respect, the maintenance of relatively low wage levels was a major consideration in ensuring international competitiveness. Although some efforts were made to modify the general strategy in the early 1970s, it was only after 1978 that a concerted and determined effort was undertaken to formulate and implement a general strategy to upgrade the quality and the level of sophistication of economic activity in manufacturing industry in particular, and in the economy generally. In the government's view, improved skills among workers, better management, and the introduction of new technology would provide a firm basis for maintaining Singapore's international economic competitiveness, as well as providing better-paid jobs and a higher standard of living for the population. This strategy resulted in a number of significant achievements.

THE ACHIEVEMENTS AND CONTRADICTIONS OF THE ECONOMIC RESTRUCTURING STRATEGY

The industrial relations system created by the government resulted in industrial peace and an attractive investment climate. The substantial and continuing inflow of foreign investments has transformed Singapore into a renowned manufacturing centre, and contributed significantly to the high rate of economic growth. Foreign skills, management and technology have helped the city-state to progress towards the achievement of the objectives of the Economic Restructuring Strategy.

The ERS contributed to a significant increase in total output and employment (Table 4.3). Growth rates in these respects were greater during the period 1978–81, than in the previous three years 1975–78. Output increased by an average of 8.0 per cent between 1975 and 1978, and 9.5 per cent between 1978 and 1981, while employment increased by an average annual rate of 4.8 per cent and 6.4 per cent, respectively.

The rapid growth of employment in the years after 1975 had intensified demand pressures in the labour market. In response to this, one principal objective of the ERS was to reduce the demand for labour by encouraging firms to adopt more capital-intensive methods of production. During 1981–84, the changes that occurred were in accord with the objectives of the ERS. Total employment increased at a slower rate of 3.2 per cent per annum, while labour productivity rose to 4.4 per cent per annum. It is probable that employment growth would have moderated somewhat even without a change of policy, because of the constraints posed by the slower-growing labour pool and by a situation of full employment. Nevertheless, the ERS measures contributed partly to the reversal of the previous employment trend.

The unemployment rate declined from 4.5 per cent in 1975 to 3.6 per cent in 1978, to 2.6 per cent in 1982, despite the fact that an increasing proportion of persons of working age joined the labour force. In a situation where labour scarcity was the norm, the pressures on firms promoted mechanization, automation and computerization to supplement and to enhance the efforts of the limited workforce, rather than to diminish the size of that workforce.

In addition to the slower growth of employment, there have been significant improvements in the composition of the workforce since the introduction of the ERS. Between 1980 and 1986, the number of persons engaged in the two highest-paid occupational categories (administrative, managerial and

Table 4.3 *Output, employment and productivity by industry*

Industry	Gross domestic product (%)						
	1975	1978	1981	1984	1986	1988	1993p
Agriculture, fishing, quarrying	1.8	1.5	1.3	1.1	0.9	0.6	0.3
Manufacturing	25.9	27.4	29.4	25.0	25.1	28.6	27.6
Utilities	1.8	2.1	2.0	1.9	2.1	2.1	2.0
Construction	8.6	6.9	7.7	12.5	8.2	5.8	6.7
Commerce	20.7	19.6	18.2	17.0	16.8	17.8	17.9
Transport and communication	9.1	10.9	12.3	12.9	14.3	14.1	14.6
Financial and business services	15.9	17.9	21.7	23.9	26.4	25.3	26.9
Other services	13.5	12.5	11.1	11.0	12.1	10.9	9.8
Total	100.0	100.0	100.0	100.0	100.0	100.0	100.0
	($19,087m)	($24,046m)	($31,603m)	($39,573m)	($39,641m)	($48,203m)	($71,212m)

Industry	Annual growth rate (%)					
	1975–78	1978–81	1981–84	1984–86	1986–88	1988–93
Agriculture, fishing, quarrying	1.6	4.4	2.8	–10.8	–9.1	–6.2
Manufacturing	10.0	13.9	2.2	0.2	17.6	7.4
Utilities	13.7	7.8	6.4	5.0	9.7	7.5
Construction	0.4	13.6	26.5	–19.0	–6.9	11.2
Commerce	6.1	6.9	5.4	–0.7	13.5	8.3
Transport and communication	14.7	14.0	9.7	5.0	9.5	9.0
Financial and business services	12.4	16.8	11.2	5.3	6.0	9.4
Other services	5.3	5.3	7.6	4.8	4.4	5.9
Total	8.0	9.5	7.8	0.1	10.3	8.1

Persons employed (%)

Industry	1975	1978	1981	1984	1986	1988	1993
Agriculture, fishing, quarrying	2.5	2.0	1.2	0.9	0.9	0.5	0.3
Manufacturing	26.2	28.2	30.4	27.4	25.4	28.5	27.0
Utilities	1.1	1.0	0.7	0.8	0.7	0.6	0.5
Construction	4.7	5.4	6.0	8.5	8.9	6.7	6.4
Commerce	23.0	23.5	21.8	22.5	23.5	22.9	22.8
Transport and communication	11.7	11.4	11.4	10.4	10.1	9.7	10.5
Financial and business services	6.1	6.7	7.6	8.6	8.7	9.6	10.9
Other services	24.5	21.7	20.7	20.6	21.5	21.4	21.6
Total	100.0	100.0	100.0	100.0	100.0	100.0	100.0
	(833,525)	(958,948)	(1,153,600)	(1,269,100)	(1,214,400)	(1,331,600)	(1,592,000)

Annual growth rate (%)

Industry	1975–78	1978–81	1981–84	1984–86	1986–88	1988–93
Agriculture, fishing, quarrying	-2.7	-9.1	-7.0	-0.4	-23.7	-8.9
Manufacturing	7.4	9.0	-0.2	-6.2	11.2	2.5
Utilities	1.5	-7.1	8.7	-9.0	1.2	-2.2
Construction	9.7	9.9	16.1	-1.2	-7.7	2.6
Commerce	5.5	3.7	4.4	-0.9	4.2	3.6
Transport and communication	3.9	6.4	0.1	-4.5	3.5	5.2
Financial and business services	8.1	11.1	7.4	-1.6	9.9	6.3
Other services	0.6	4.6	3.2	2.3	1.9	3.9
Total	4.8	6.4	3.2	-2.2	4.7	3.6

Table 4.3 continued

Industry	GDP per person employed ($)						
	1975	1978	1981	1984	1986	1988	1993
Agriculture, fishing, quarrying	16,514	18,781	28,528	38,509	30,876	43,806	50,736
Manufacturing	22,649	24,350	26,516	28,462	32,472	36,331	45,749
Utilities	38,663	51,814	82,091	76,980	102,427	120,488	193,413
Construction	49,696	32,134	35,369	45,707	30,743	31,298	46,637
Commerce	20,643	20,960	22,916	23,579	23,662	28,077	35,073
Transport and communication	17,670	24,136	29,493	38,818	46,913	52,536	62,513
Financial and business services	60,132	66,862	77,842	86,615	99,084	95,672	110,410
Other services	12,586	14,459	14,714	16,707	17,527	18,400	20,261
Total	22,896	25,073	27,395	31,182	32,643	36,200	44,731

Industry	Annual growth rate (%)					
	1975–78	1978–81	1981–84	1984–86	1986–88	1988–93
Agriculture, fishing, quarrying	4.4	15.0	10.5	-10.5	19.1	3.0
Manufacturing	2.4	2.9	2.4	6.8	5.8	4.7
Utilities	10.3	16.6	-2.1	15.4	8.5	9.9
Construction	-13.5	3.2	8.9	-18.0	0.9	8.3
Commerce	0.5	3.0	1.0	0.2	8.9	4.6
Transport and communication	11.0	6.9	9.6	9.9	5.8	3.5
Financial and business services	4.0	5.2	3.6	7.0	-1.7	2.9
Other services	4.7	0.6	4.3	2.4	2.5	1.9
Total	3.1	3.0	4.4	2.3	5.3	4.3

Notes: The absolute figures for GDP are at constant 1985 market prices. GDP totals exclude imputed bank service charges and include import duties. Employment refers to persons aged 15 years and over. Employment totals include persons employed in activities not adequately defined. Employment figures for 1975 and 1978 are based on SSIC 1973, those for 1981 are based on SSIC 1978, and those for 1984 and later years are based on SSIC 1990. Annual growth rate is computed on a compound basis.

Sources: Derived from Singapore Department of Statistics, *Yearbook of Statistics*, and Ministry of Labour, *Yearbook of Labour Statistics*.

executive workers, and professional, technical and related workers) increased by an average of 4.5 per cent and 4.9 per cent a year, respectively; while the two lowest-paid occupational categories (production, transport and manual workers, and the miscellaneous category 'others', which includes agricultural, animal husbandry workers and fishermen) declined in absolute numbers (Table 4.4). These trends continued over the subsequent periods, 1986–88 and 1988–93 (Table 4.7).

The changes in the occupational structure resulted partly from the rise in the educational level of the population. Between 1983 and 1993, the number of persons in the workforce with tertiary-level qualifications increased by an average annual rate of 9.8 per cent, while the number of persons in the workforce possessing only lower-primary or no qualifications declined in absolute terms (Table 4.8).

The rise in the technical and professional skills of the local workforce and their substantial acquired experience in manufacturing industry has enabled them to take on positions of greater responsibility. In almost every case, junior and middle-level supervisory positions are filled by local personnel. At the same time, an increasing proportion of local personnel has been promoted to senior executive and managerial positions even among wholly-foreign-owned subsidiaries of large multinational corporations (MNCs). These appointments extend beyond the Personnel Department, into areas of corporate production, marketing, finance, design and development, and even to the position of managing director of local and (in some cases) regional operations. It is, by now, not unusual to encounter a wholly-locally-managed subsidiary of a large American MNC in Singapore.

Finally, the ERS contributed to significant improvements in the standard of living of the general population and, in particular, to the reduction of poverty. Over the period 1973–82, the proportion of the population living below the poverty line, as measured by the minimum monthly household requirement (MMHR),[7] declined significantly – from about 30 per cent to about 8 per cent. The proportion of the population receiving incomes ranging from the MMHR to twice the MMHR, has also declined, from about 40 per cent to less than 30 per cent. There was a corresponding rise, from about 30 per cent to more than 60 per cent, in the proportion of the population whose incomes were more than twice the MMHR.

Thus, the ERS was associated with a continued rise in the general standard of living. Not only did poverty diminish, but the proportion of the population receiving incomes which are more realistically in line with their normal needs had increased. This resulted from the rising wage levels in the economy, the rise in the employment rate, as well as the increase in the labour force participation rate. More families had multiple income earners, labour scarcity intensified the upward pressures on wages, rising productivity made employ-

Table 4.4 Distribution of all employed persons by occupation, 1980, 1983 and 1986

Occupation	1980 %	1983 %	1986 %	Absolute change ('000)			Annual growth rate (%)			Average wage in 1985 ($)
				1980–83	1983–86	1980–86	1980–83	1983–86	1980–86	
Administrative, managerial and executive workers	4.8	5.3	5.9	10.1	5.8	15.9	6.1	3.0	4.5	2,950
Professional, technical and related workers	8.8	9.5	11.0	16.3	15.0	31.3	5.4	4.3	4.9	1,883
Clerical and related workers	15.6	16.8	15.7	28.6	−15.5	13.1	5.4	−2.7	1.3	852
Sales workers	12.3	13.9	13.5	29.9	−6.3	23.6	7.0	−1.3	2.8	778
Service workers	10.4	10.8	11.9	13.9	10.4	24.3	4.0	2.7	3.3	676
Production, transport and other manual workers	40.4	37.8	35.8	6.0	−30.0	−24.0	0.5	−2.3	−0.9	659
Others*	7.7	5.9	6.2	−14.3	1.9	−12.9	−6.1	0.9	−2.7	666
Total ('000)	100.0 (1,077.1)	100.0 (1,167.6)	100.0 (1,149.0)	90.5	−18.6	71.9	2.7	−0.5	1.1	1,106

Notes:
The data is classified according to Singapore Standard Occupational Classification (SSOC) 1978.
The data refers to persons aged 15 years and over. Annual growth rate is computed as a simple average between the respective years. Average growth rate is computed on a compound basis. Average wage refers to average monthly basic wage in the manufacturing sector.
* This includes agricultural, animal husbandry workers and fishermen, and workers not classified in any other category.

Source: Singapore Ministry of Labour, *Yearbook of Labour Statistics*.

Table 4.5 Educational qualifications of the Singapore workforce, 1981–1985

Highest qualification attained	1981 (%)	1982 (%)	1983 (%)	1984 (%)	1985 (%)	1981–1985 Absolute change	1981–1985 Annual growth rate (%)
No qualification*	24.5	24.9	23.3	20.7	22.8	–8,479	–2.1
Primary	31.8	30.0	30.2	31.9	30.9	2,342	–1.0
Post primary	0.9	0.8	0.8	0.4	0.6**	–3,032	–13.5
Secondary	30.1	30.4	30.4	30.1	29.2	2,413	0.7
Post secondary	9.1	9.7	10.5	10.6	11.0	25,138	5.7
Tertiary	3.6	4.1	4.6	4.9	5.2	20,209	11.0
Others	0.1	0.2	0.3	0.4	0.4	2,852	33.2
Total	100.0	100.0	100.0	100.0	100.0	41,442	1.0
('000)	(1,112.8)	(1,140.5)	(1,167.7)	(1,174.8)	(1,154.3)		

Notes:
The data covers employed persons aged 15 years and over.
'Others' refers to persons with qualifications not classified elsewhere.
Annual growth rate is computed on a least-squares basis.
*   Includes persons who never attended school.
** Includes persons with N-level qualifications.

Source: Singapore Ministry of Labour, unpublished data.

Table 4.6   Earnings and performance of all employed persons, 1981–1993

| | Earnings indicators | | | | | | Performance indicators | |
| | Real average monthly earnings | | Real total wage increase | | Overall unit labour cost | | GDP per employed person | |
Year	($)	Annual change (%)		Annual change (%)		Annual change (%)	($)	Annual change (%)
1981	805	n.a.		n.a.		n.a.	27,395	0.9
1982	898	11.6		n.a.		12.2	27,655	0.9
1983	978	8.9		n.a.		7.1	29,202	5.6
1984	1,055	7.9		n.a.		4.3	31,179	6.8
1985	1,133	7.4		n.a.		1.1	31,527	1.1
1986	1,159	2.3		3.0		−12.7	32,643	3.5
1987	1,189	2.6		3.6		−4.1	34,235	4.9
1988	1,268	6.6		6.7		3.3	36,200	5.7
1989	1,360	7.3		7.4		8.9	37,774	4.3
1990	1,437	5.7		6.4		9.2	37,262	−1.4
1991	1,517	5.6		4.7		8.3	40,072	7.5
1992	1,604	5.7		5.8		3.2	41,093	2.5
1993	1,665	3.8		5.2		−0.6	44,731	8.9

Average annual change (%)

1981–85	9.0	n.a.	6.2	3.1
1986–87	2.5	3.3	–8.4	4.2
1988–93	5.8	6.0	5.4	4.6

Notes:
Real average monthly earnings are deflated by the corresponding year's Consumer Price Index (September 1987–August 1988 = 100). They include bonuses, if any, but exclude employers' CPF contributions.
Real total wage increase refers to the increase in basic wage and the variable wage component of employees in the private sector who are eligible to join trade unions.
Overall unit labour cost refers to the unit labour cost of the overall economy.
GDP per employed person is based on constant 1985 market prices.
Average annual change is computed as the simple average of the number of years in the period for which data is available. n.a. indicates that the data is not available.

Sources: Derived from Singapore Department of Statistics, *Yearbook of Statistics* various issues; Ministry of Labour, *1993 Yearbook of Labour Statistics*, p. 25; and Ministry of Labour, *Report on Wages in Singapore 1993*, p. 12.

ers willing to provide higher wage increases, and the National Wages Council's recommendations helped to increase wages more rapidly for the lower-paid groups in comparison to the higher-paid occupations. All these resulted in substantial benefits for the low-income group while also promoting the upgrading and restructuring of the economy.

The relative success of Singapore's development efforts in most years since 1965, can be attributed partly to favourable external conditions. These included a moderately stable and relatively liberal international economic environment, the relatively high growth rates in developed-country economies and in countries in the neighbouring region, which produced positive effects for international trade; as well as the rapid growth of direct foreign investment and the global spread of manufacturing activities by American, European and Japanese MNCs, which facilitated the transfer of skills and technology and helped to provide access to foreign markets (see Dicken 1986). On the domestic scene, the government perceived that the economic achievements vindicated the numerous measures which it had undertaken to promote harmonious industrial relations, to improve productivity, and to restructure the economy. However, the process was not entirely free of problems.

Contradictions in Labour Policy

Various observers have focused on the significant costs which they perceive to exist in the development strategy that has been adopted. Heyzer (1983) argued that the dominance of the state, and the pursuit of policies favouring foreign direct investments by MNCs have resulted in 'structural dualism' in the economy, and 'class polarisation' in the society, with the majority of the industrial workforce being employed as 'cheap labour'. Lin (1986) focused attention on the health hazards for workers in the large electronics industry. In the construction industry, Wilkinson et al. (1986) observed that technical change tends to promote de-skilling rather than to enhance the skills of the workforce. Islam and Kirkpatrick (1986) have also suggested that the previous trend towards more equal income distribution has been reversed since 1979.

It has also been argued that developments in Singapore have resulted in a situation which restricts the room for manoeuvre of trade unions not closely affiliated to the ruling party, and in a compliant labour movement. According to Leggett (1988) the symbiotic relationship between the ruling party and the NTUC has led the trade unions to socialize the workforce into adopting attitudes and behaviour congruent with the economic and social imperatives identified by the government. 'Compliance is justified by the need for economic survival and progress and the inevitability of technological change'.

Deyo (1984) also noted that the composition of the industrial workforce (which includes a large number of female workers employed in relatively unskilled labour-intensive assembly operations) has contributed to the compliant state of the labour movement. This situation has resulted in worker demoralization and lack of commitment to the institutional norms emanating from above (Deyo 1981), and a membership crisis for the trade unions (Leggett 1988).

Labour Turnover and the Controversy over 'Job-hopping'

The economic policy changes since 1978 also caused several other difficulties. One of the problems encountered in the structural adjustment process which arose from attempted adjustments in the labour market was the controversy over 'job-hopping'. The controversy arose from allegations by some government officials and some employers of job-hopping by employees. The phenomenon could be addressed in more neutral terms as one of frequent job changes ('job mobility') by some employees. But to the authorities concerned and to the employers affected, it was a worry that the continuing situation of labour scarcity had generally increased the leverage of employees (particularly of skilled and professional persons, but also for young female operatives with limited skills), thus tipping the balance of bargaining power in their favour; and that the availability to employees of a range of (competing) job offers had enabled them to make higher demands in relation to wage levels, working conditions and employment fringe benefits. Employers were concerned that these demands and the rising expectations that fuelled them would directly reduce the profitability of their operations. The government was also concerned that economic success was making the workforce 'soft', promoting bad work attitudes and practices, and unduly high demands and expectations among the workforce, which would lead directly to the loss of international competitiveness of economic activities in the city-state.

Consequently, job mobility of employees was perceived and labelled as job-hopping by 'choosy' workers, merely 'for a few dollars more'. A strong public campaign was undertaken to chastise the job-hoppers. The state also campaigned strongly for the adoption of Japanese work practices, in particular, that workers should be loyal to their employers, diligent in their jobs, engage in 'teamwork' with their colleagues and superiors, and be patient and reasonable in their expectations over reward. Moreover, the government rushed into a flurry of measures to combat the perceived problem. This included, just within the month of January 1981 alone, a scheme which made available to employers the computerized Central Provident Fund records on the employment history of prospective job applicants, to assist them 'to check if the prospective employee is guilty of excessive job-hopping', a survey to obtain a 'demographic and socio-economic profile' of 6,600 persons who were each noted, from CPF records, to have changed jobs three times within the past year, and a proposal for a 'special fund' to be set up in conjunction with the CPF, to reward employees who remain with the same employer for a minimum period, varying from five to ten years (see Soh 1981a, 1981b, and Tan 1981). Some employers took these and other related developments as cues to continue the torrent of public criticisms about the 'bad' Singapore worker. Unfavourable comparisons with the Japanese (or sometimes, the European) worker were made.

The controversy over job-hopping, the 'choosy' Singapore worker, his/her reluctance to undertake shift-work, his/her excessive expectations and other bad work habits, had in fact been growing since the early 1970s, when the domestic economy began to experience labour shortages. But in 1981, the recriminations reached fever-pitch proportions. Employers also used the opportunity to pressure the government to ease its efforts to phase out the continued employment of ('more reliable') foreign workers. In this respect, they achieved some success (see Awanohara 1981, and Ambalam 1984).

The situation was one in which the measures undertaken by the government to achieve its objectives under the ERS, were increasingly working at cross-purposes. On the one hand, the 'corrective wage policy' raised wage levels and enhanced the leverage of workers *vis-à-vis* employers in the situation of labour scarcity. Indeed, the ERS was founded on the premise that workers (and other productive resources) would be transferred from lower-paid jobs to higher-skilled and better-paid jobs, that is, the general level of job mobility *should* rise. Employers who resisted or were unable to pay the higher wage levels, and to undertake other measures of job enhancement, *should* be driven out, and replaced by others who possessed the capacity and willingness for this. Moreover, as the Chairman of the NWC himself had explained, the rationale for the application of a *general* rather than a *selective* policy was that 'a national general wage policy ... is least discriminatory. It is non-directional. It allows the operation of market forces for all industries and all establishments in the same industry' (Lim 1979a).

On the other hand, as it turned out, the government did not trust 'market forces' to be sufficiently discriminating, to be able to distinguish an 'excessive job-hopper' from an ERS-conforming job-changer. In addition to profuse exhortations, it sought to introduce direct administrative measures to distinguish the 'sheep' from the 'goats', and to apply different treatments to the two groups. In fact, however, the government was itself unable to define and to distinguish clearly *who* was a job-hopper, and *what* were the defining characteristics of 'excessive job-hopping'. Somehow, it was decided that individuals who had undertaken three job changes in the course of a particular year would be likely candidates, and efforts were initiated to conduct a survey to establish their 'demographic and socio-economic profile'.

In certain respects, the survey findings were irrelevant. For government officials subsequently realized that these developments were beginning to affect adversely the image of the local workforce in the eyes of potential foreign investors, and to have a bearing on their investment decisions. Gross generalizations by some national leaders, officials and employers were in danger of creating an unfavourable stereotype of the whole workforce. What had begun as a strictly domestic campaign to shame the local worker into further improving his/her skills, his/her work habits and his/her attitudes, so as to facilitate the success of the ERS, had snowballed (as local retorts in response to perceptions of unfair accusations mounted) into a heated controversy, which may have deterred some of the higher-technology investments the government and the ERS had desired to attract. Furthermore, the relaxation of the policy relating to the employment of foreign labour weakened the implementation of the ERS. More fundamentally, as one observer noted, 'there is a danger that the apparent lack of consistent long-range objectives and policies might confuse participants in the Singapore economy, including foreign investors, and affect growth' (Awanohara 1981).

Subsequently, various efforts were undertaken to extricate the ERS from the confusions that had resulted. Reports began to appear in the press proclaiming that the labour shortage and the problem of job-hopping had eased. Favourable comments, and reports on the investment and labour situation, and on the positive qualities of the workforce, were publicized. Negative comments and criticisms from employers and public figures diminished. Some employers found, to their surprise, that their disparaging remarks had actually soured their relationship with their employees, and tried to explain what they had *really* meant to say (see Lim 1982). The Prime Minister, in a major speech, reiterated the government's commitment to 'a wholly Singaporean workforce without any work permit holder at all by 1991' and reaffirmed the previous policy relating to the (temporary) employment of foreign workers (*Straits Times*, 1 January 1982). And in January 1984, the Ministry of Labour rejected a call from an employer for the government to impose curbs on the mobility of workers, arguing that 'the answer to job-hopping or high labour turnover is for management to look critically at the problems within their own companies and see what is causing their employees to resign and to find a remedy for them ... [it is] a problem for management to resolve and not for the government to prescribe measures against' (*Straits Times*, 4 January 1984).

These difficulties indicated some of the problems faced by the state in its attempts to prescribe the parameters of behaviour at the enterprise level. Subsequently, the government itself appeared to realize some of the limitations in its capacity to direct changes in the labour market. For in this situation the advantage had swung significantly in favour of labour. Market forces combined with the imperatives of the ERS to provide workers with substantial leverage in their relations with employers. However, this situation was altered dramatically by a severe downturn in the economy.

THE 1985 ECONOMIC DOWNTURN AND ITS AFTERMATH

The various difficulties encountered earlier were submerged by a larger problem which occurred with the severe downturn of the Singapore economy in 1985. The annual GDP growth rate declined from 10.2 per cent in 1980 to −1.8 per cent in 1985. During the same period, the growth rate of exports fell from 34 per cent to −2.3 per cent, while the growth rate of net investment commitments in manufacturing plunged from 50.2 per cent to −37.9 per cent. In 1985, domestic demand declined by 3 per cent and trade also contracted by 4 per cent. A total of 101,700 jobs were lost (42 per cent in construction, 38 per cent in manufacturing, and 21 per cent in commerce) and the unemployment rate had risen to 6 per cent at the end of 1985.

Although the NWC had moderated its wage increase recommendations since 1982, the general level of wage increase between 1982 and 1984 was higher than that of previous years. The reasons for this may be attributed to the relatively high rates of economic growth in the early 1980s which increased demand for workers, together with government efforts to reduce the number of foreign workers, and heightened expectations among the workforce stemming from the previous NWC wage recommendations. In combination, these factors contributed to continued strong upward pressures on wages. In addition, other government measures contributed significantly to the higher costs of housing, transportation and public utilities. These, and other financial impositions, raised the costs of undertaking economic activity and the general cost of living in the city-state.

This was partly intended. For the policy makers had earlier believed that if firms encountered higher operating costs and lower profitability, they would turn more to mechanization, computerization and automation. Consequently, it was expected that the economic restructuring process would be speeded up, with substantial benefits perceived to accrue in the long run.

However, the problems had not been fully anticipated. One problem was a significant rise in unit labour costs. The Economic Committee, a high-level advisory committee established to review the economic restructuring strategy, reported that unit labour costs in Singapore, taking productivity changes into account, had risen 39 per cent between 1980 and 1984. This increase was significantly higher than that in Taiwan, Hong Kong and South Korea. It even exceeded similar growth rates in Japan, the United States and the United Kingdom. However, the Economic Committee recognized that the substantial rise in wage costs was only one part of an escalation of cost increases over a broad front (see Cheah 1986).

Remedial Measures

In the course of 1985 and 1986, the government introduced several measures in an attempt to steer the economy back on to its original course. Among the most important were a range of cost-cutting measures intended to restore international competitiveness. In March 1985, the 2 per cent payroll tax was suspended, and the Skills Development Fund levy was reduced from 4 per cent to 2 per cent for three years. The policy on foreign workers was also amended to permit more flexible implementation of the policy to repatriate foreign workers, with special attention to the needs of manufacturers, hotels, shipyards, construction companies and working mothers.

In February 1986, the Economic Committee submitted a host of recommendations for additional cost-cutting measures, as well as numerous other suggestions for economic reform, some of which overturned a number of fundamental tenets of earlier government policy. In this respect, the Committee's recommendations also brought into question some key assumptions underlying the ERS, for example, the need to raise the general wage level to promote economic upgrading and restructuring, the need to maintain a high level of domestic savings, the need for a substantial government direction of the economy and direct government involvement in economic activity, and the need to phase out foreign workers completely.

The government accepted and implemented many of the Economic Committee's recommendations.[8] A significant development was the government's endorsement of the Economic Committee's call for wage restraint for at least two years, and for a reform of the existing wage system. In the public sector the half-month incentive payment for 1986 was cancelled. In addition, the number of employees in government and statutory boards was to be reduced by 10 per cent over a 5-year period, through attrition and more selective recruitment.

Thus, following the downturn in the economy in 1985, there were substantial changes in several aspects of labour policy and of the ERS itself. Among other things, these involved the imposition of restraints on wage increases, a significant reduction in the level of employers' CPF contributions, and a relaxation of the restraints on employment of foreign workers. In addition, the government deemed that a temporary fall in the general standard of living was necessary and unavoidable. Finally, in keeping with the recent fashion in economic policy, the government also placed greater emphasis on market deregulation, and expressed its intention to reduce its involvement in the economy. Nevertheless, the numerous means for ensuring peaceful industrial relations remained in place, and employees and trade unions were still expected to arrive amiably at a consensus with employers on ways to improve production efficiency and international competitiveness.

These measures introduced by the government accompanied a recovery from the recession over the period 1986–88. With the recovery the government regained its confidence and began to focus its efforts on achieving bigger and better things.

THE GRAND VISION FOR THE NEXT LAP – BECOMING A DEVELOPED NATION IN THE FIRST LEAGUE

Planning and strategy formulation during the period of economic recovery culminated in the appearance of three significant reports in 1991. These were *Singapore: the Next Lap* (Government of Singapore 1991), *The Strategic Economic Plan: towards a Developed Nation* (Economic Planning Committee 1991), and *Science and Technology – Window of Opportunities: National Technology Plan 1991* (National Science and Technology Board 1991). Together, these reports present the principal ideas, and directions for the city-state to focus its efforts in the years ahead, as well as the strategies and means to achieve the higher goals that have been identified.

The principal goal is 'to attain the status and characteristics of a first league developed country within the next 30 to 40 years' (Economic Planning Committee 1991; 2). To achieve this goal, 'the basis of international competitiveness will have to change substantially. It will have to shift from maintaining a substantial cost differential between Singapore and the developed countries, to matching the capabilities of the other developed countries, at least in certain key areas of economic importance' (Economic Planning Committee 1991: 42). The Committee identified three principal deficiencies hindering the process of closing the gap with the developed countries. These were the relative weakness of local enterprises, the low level of the indigenous technology base and the comparatively lower educational level.

Increased Investment in Education and Skills Development

All three reports placed strong emphasis on the need for increased investment in education and skills development. First, the government (1991: 15) pledged that 'Education will receive the highest emphasis as it is resourcefulness, not resources, that will increasingly determine winners and losers in the future'. Consequently, it was stated,

> We will invest heavily in our people, to enable them to move up to higher value added and hence better paid jobs. The key is higher productivity. Labour productivity must improve by at least 3 to 4 per cent per year for the next decade. We have moved from labour-intensive industries to skill- and knowledge-intensive industries and services. In the next lap, skills and knowledge will become even more crucial in determining winners and losers. We need to work smarter, be better organised and discover new work methods. We can achieve this through innovation, technology and teamwork. (Government of Singapore 1991: 59)

The Economic Planning Committee (1991: 28) noted that 61 per cent of the non-student population in Singapore had achieved an education level of only Primary 6 or less, compared with 'the better developed countries', where 90 per cent or more of the population have completed 10 years of education. It emphasized the need to give all Singaporeans at least ten years of quality basic education. Furthermore, it reported that the Ministry of Education aims to increase the proportion of each Primary One cohort entering tertiary institutions to 60 per cent by the Year 2000 (Economic Planning Committee 1991: 56).

In justifying the need for strategic planning in this and other areas, the Committee argued that 'the reason for such a long-term perspective is that some of the major attributes needed to be successful depend on educational, social or organisational programmes. These require a long lead time. To raise the educational level, for example, from 40 per cent with secondary education to 90 per cent would take about 30 years. Unless the right policies are introduced now, such a situation would be almost impossible to achieve' (Economic Planning Committee 1991: 40). Even more ambitiously, it advocated that 'Singapore's educational and training programmes should adopt a life cycle perspective for the individual, from cradle to retirement' (Economic Planning Committee 1991: 57).[9]

The National Technology Plan elaborated on the need to rely more on innovation as the basis for international competitiveness, and the means for Singapore to achieve that. It noted that Singapore needed to catch up not only with the developed countries, but also with the higher achievements of Taiwan and South Korea in technology promotion (National Science and Technology Board 1991: 7).

The Technology Plan set targets to raise the number of research scientists and engineers from 28 per 10,000 persons in the labour force in 1990 to 40 per 10,000 in 1995;[10] and to double national expenditure on research and development from 1 per cent of GDP in 1990 to 2 per cent of GDP by 1995 (divided in equal proportions between the public and private sectors). It recommended the introduction of various training programmes and scholar-ship schemes to attract graduates into the R&D field, the enhancement of career prospects in this field, and the promotion of an attractive working and living environment for this group.

Attraction of Foreign Talents

While higher investment in education and skills development for the local workforce was strongly emphasized, it was believed that this would not be sufficient to satisfy the skilled manpower requirements of the growing and maturing economy.[11] Consequently, all three reports expressed an urgent need to attract larger numbers of foreigners with technical skills and profes-sional qualifications.

The Government (Government of Singapore 1991: 15) argued that 'Singa-pore is what it is today because we have been able to attract talent from all over the world to work and live here. We must attract more world talent, especially Asian talent. Our city can accommodate them, and we will be the richer for it'.[12] More specifically, the Economic Planning Committee (1991: 8) noted that

> With its size constraint, Singapore can only hope to become a developed country if it taps from the world the best of its talent and technology. ... In order to do this, Singapore needs to ... [a]dopt an immigration policy involving an intake, tenta-tively estimated at around 0.4 per cent per annum of the population, of high quality professional and skilled persons to augment existing low growth rates in the labour force, as well as to refresh and renew the higher echelons of the talent pool in Singapore. This strategy must continue even beyond the year 2030.

The Committee (1991: 57) also supported the establishment of an Interna-tional Manpower Division in the Economic Development Board to attract talented and professional persons to work and live in Singapore. Similarly, the National Technology Plan advocated a liberal foreign recruitment pro-gramme to supplement the recruitment of locals for R&D work. It argued that

> To succeed in reaching our target (of 40 research scientists and engineers per 10,000 persons in the labour force), we need to depend significantly on foreign recruitment of talent. Just as we opened our doors to foreign investors in the manufacturing and service sectors, and benefited from the new technology, mar-kets and business practices they brought with them, we must do the same for R&D. ... Well-qualified and experienced foreign researchers bring with them knowledge and skills which we would take years to develop if we go it alone. They can help to build up a critical mass of talent and a research reputation, both of which will further enhance Singapore's standing as a R&D centre. Local researchers and aspiring researchers will have role models to emulate. *This is a propitious time for Singapore to look out for foreign talent as economic slowdown*

in the developed countries have cut research budgets, leading many researchers to look for alternatives. (National Science and Technology Board 1991: 38, emphasis added)

Both the Strategic Economic Plan and the National Technology Plan also identified specific areas in industry and technology for promotion and assistance.[13]

These are some of the most significant measures that have been advocated and implemented to achieve the principal goal set for Singapore.[14] They represent an effort to continue the process of upgrading Singapore's economic capabilities by tapping domestic as well as external labour, investments, technology and skills. The results are striking.

PERFORMANCE SINCE 1988

Between 1988 and 1993, Singapore's GDP grew by an average of 7.8 per cent annually, while per-capita indigenous GNP rose by 9.7 per cent annually to reach $24,871. Investment rose more significantly, as indicated by an annual growth rate of 13.3 per cent in gross fixed capital formation. Over the same period, median monthly income rose by 9.1 per cent annually (Table 4.1), or 6.0 per cent annually in real terms. While the National Wages Council continued to try to moderate wages increases (see Table 4.2), the rise in income was higher than the average annual increase of 4.3 per cent in productivity, represented by GDP per person employed (Table 4.3. See also Table 4.6). This is a reflection of the pressures on wages resulting from a low level of unemployment (less than 3 per cent) and only a moderate increase (3.8 per cent annually) in the size of the labour force (Table 4.1).

In terms of changes in the occupational structure, the better-remunerated occupational categories expanded more rapidly. Thus 'legislators, senior officials and managers' increased in numbers by 9.7 per cent annually between 1988 and 1993, while 'production workers, cleaners and labourers' experienced an average annual growth rate of only 1.3 per cent (Table 4.7). This indicates a general shift towards higher-paid, and generally better-skilled occupations. This shift corresponds directly with a shift in the educational qualifications of the workforce, in which higher qualification categories expanded in numbers more rapidly than lower qualification categories. For instance, over the period 1983–93, persons with tertiary qualifications increased at an average annual rate of 9.8 per cent, compared to a rise of only 1.7 per cent annually for persons who possess primary or lower secondary qualifications, and a corresponding fall of 1.8 per cent in the category of persons who possessed only lower primary qualifications or never attended

Table 4.7 Occupations and wages of employed persons

Occupations	Distribution (%)				Absolute change ('000)			Annual growth rate (%)			Monthly Gross Wage ($)
	1984	1986	1988	1993	1984–86	1986–88	1988–93	1984–86	1986–88	1988–93	1993
Legislators, senior officials and managers	7.7	7.4	7.9	10.5	–8.5	15.3	62.1	–4.4	8.2	9.7	5,317*
Professionals	4.5	4.5	4.6	6.1	–2.5	7.1	35.3	–2.2	6.3	9.5	3,264
Technicians and associate professionals	9.6	10.2	11.5	14.1	2.2	29.3	71.4	0.9	11.2	8.0	2,494
Clerical workers	14.8	14.3	14.0	14.7	–14.0	12.3	46.9	–3.8	3.5	4.6	1,314
Service, shop and market sales workers	15.4	15.4	15.1	13.5	–7.4	13.5	14.6	–1.9	3.5	1.4	1,377
Agricultural and fishery workers	1.1	1.1	0.7	0.1	–0.3	–3.9	–7.3	–1.1	–15.7	–24.9	n.a.
Production workers, cleaners and labourers#	42.9	42.0	41.6	37.1	–35.0	44.0	35.8	–3.3	4.2	1.3	1,255**
Others	4.0	5.0	4.6	3.9	10.7	–0.3	1.5	10.1	–0.2	0.5	n.a.
Total	100.0	100.0	100.0	100.0	–54.8	117.2	260.4	–2.2	4.7	3.6	1,918***
	(1,269,200)	(1,214,400)	(1,331,600)	(1,592,000)							

Notes:

Occupations are classified according to Singapore Standard Occupational Classification 1990.

Gross wage includes basic wage, overtime payments, commissions, allowances, and any other monetary payments with the exception of bonuses.

Annual growth rate is computed on a compound basis.

\# Refers to production craftsmen, plant and machine operators, cleaners and labourers.

* Refers to managers only.

** Gross wages vary from $1,501 for production craftsmen, to $1,234 for plant and machine operators, to $1,029 for cleaners, labourers and related workers.

*** Refers to the average monthly earnings of all employed persons. This includes all remuneration received before deduction of CPF contribution and personal income tax. It includes annual wage supplement, and variable payments/bonuses.

Source: Derived from Singapore Department of Statistics, *Yearbook of Statistics 1993*, pp. 56, 61, 62.

school (Table 4.8). This rise in the general level of qualifications in the workforce resulted from the significant increase in the number of graduates from universities, polytechnic and other vocational education institutions (Table 4.9).

Table 4.8   Educational qualifications of the Singapore labour force

			1983–1993	
Highest qualification attained	June 1983 (%)	June 1993 (%)	Absolute change	Annual growth (%)
Never attended school/				
Lower primary	23.2	15.4	–48,800	–1.8
Primary/Lower secondary	31.3	29.2	73,000	1.7
Secondary	30.4	29.9	97,300	2.2
Post-secondary/Diploma	10.6	16.4	130,400	6.9
Tertiary	4.5	9.1	91,000	9.8
Total	100.0	100.0	342,900	2.4
(Number)	(1,292,800)	(1,635,700)		

Note: The data covers persons aged 15 years and over. Annual growth rate is computed on a compound basis.

Source: Derived from Ministry of Labour, *Report on the Labour Force Survey of Singapore 1993*, p. 17.

The significance of these changes can be observed in the change in the structure of exports. Agricultural-intensive exports, the least sophisticated product category of exports, declined from 45.9 per cent of total exports in 1970 to 19.7 per cent in 1980 to 6.8 per cent in 1993. In contrast, technology-intensive exports, which is the most sophisticated export product category, increased its share of total exports from 6.2 per cent in 1970 to 16.4 per cent in 1980 to 43.2 per cent in 1993 (Table 4.10).

In these respects we can observe a significant transformation of Singapore's capabilities, associated with the improvements in educational and skill levels, as well as with changes in the occupational structure. The pressures on wage levels are also supporting the shift towards more human-capital-intensive and technology-intensive economic activities.

Nevertheless, it may be argued that the pace of these changes could have occurred more rapidly if various policy measures had not had the unintended effects of slowing the speed of the transformation. One of these measures relates to the previous restraints on wage levels. Another relates to the

Table 4.9 Graduates from post-school educational and training institutions

Institution/Course	1983	1984	1985	1986	1987	1988	1989	1990	1991	1992	1993	Annual growth rate* (%)
Universities	3,497	4,276	4,546	5,245	5,447	5,703	6,062	6,327	7,013	7,854	8,417	8.1
Polytechnics	3,454	4,056	4,409	5,173	6,436	6,879	6,753	7,384	7,539	8,445	9,900	10.1
ITE courses	n.a.	n.a.	n.a.	21,180	23,963	26,026	26,911	27,425	27,644	67,519	58,904	16.1
NPB courses	n.a.	n.a.	n.a.	n.a.	12,804	13,175	20,608	21,823	18,991	26,013	30,062	14.7
SIM courses	578	794	903	950	1,053	1,278	1,905	2,092	2,366	2,725	3,221	18.4
SIHRM courses	n.a.	n.a.	n.a.	47	147	116	27	298	160	215	299	24.2
ISS courses	379	570	780	967	1,734	1,214	1,763	1,487	1,932	1,840	1,616	15.2
Ministry of Labour OS&H courses	n.a.	n.a.	n.a.	n.a.	n.a.	16,702	20,899	25,680	31,076	38,309	86,902	34

Notes:
Figures for universities include graduates from the National Institute of Education.
* Average annual growth rate is computed on a least-squares basis for the period 1983–1993, or for the years when data is available.

Acronyms
ITE: Institute of Technical Education. In April 1992, the ITE took over the functions of the former Vocational and Industrial Training Board (VITB). The figures for graduates from the ITE's courses in 1992 and 1993 are not strictly comparable to those of earlier years, which are derived from the VITB.
NPB: National Productivity Board.
SIM: Singapore Institute of Management.
SIHRM: Singapore Institute of Human Resource Management
ISS: Institute of Systems Science.
OS&H: Occupational safety and health.

Sources: Derived from Singapore Department of Statistics, *Yearbook of Statistics*, various issues, and Ministry of Labour, *1993 Singapore Yearbook of Labour Statistics*, pp. 131–44.

Table 4.10 Changes in the composition of Singapore's exports, 1970–1993

Type of exports	Composition of Singapore's exports (%)				Absolute change (US$million)			Annual growth rate (%)		
	1970	1980	1990	1993	1970–80	1980–90	1990–93	1970–80	1980–90	1990–93
Agricultural-intensive	45.9	19.7	8.4	6.8	3,112	571	637	18.3	1.4	4.6
Mineral-intensive	25.2	28.2	15.9	13.9	5,067	2,885	1,919	30.1	4.3	7.1
Unskilled-labour-intensive	10.7	15.5	16.1	17.8	2,828	5,470	4,702	33.5	11.0	15.9
Human-capital-intensive	8.1	11.9	19.8	15.9	2,181	8,098	1,327	33.7	16.3	4.1
Technology-intensive	6.2	16.4	38.1	43.2	3,083	16,865	11,873	41.8	20.2	16.8
Others	3.5	8.3	1.8	2.3	1,556	−638	738	40.4	−4.9	21.2
Total	100.0	100.0	100.0	100.0	17,822	33,251	21,251	28.7	10.5	12.0
(US$million)	(1,554)	(19,376)	(52,627)	(73,876)						

Notes:
For descriptions of export categories refer to Tyers and Phillips (1984: 43–5).
Annual growth rate is computed on a compound basis.

Source: United Nations trade statistics.

previous import of unskilled foreign labour, and a third factor is related to previous education structure and policies. The effects of these factors can be explained only by referring to events that occurred earlier.

The Effects of the Wage Restraint Policy

First, apart from a brief period (specifically during 1979–81) when wage levels were boosted significantly by design, wage levels in Singapore have for decades been restrained (with varying degrees of success), through the recommendations of the National Wages Council, which continues to pronounce on these matters even now. It has been argued that these restraints dampened the pace of adjustment to a situation of increasing labour scarcity (Cheah 1988). Earlier recognition of this fact led the NWC itself to introduce its 'wage correction policy' recommendations to boost wage levels during 1979–81. However, the publicity (domestically and especially abroad) associated with this policy change was counterproductive, and created an adverse (but incorrect) perception of Singapore as an exceptionally high-cost location for economic activity. Consequently, when Singapore experienced an unexpected severe economic recession in 1985, local and foreign observers (especially employers) were quick to blame the earlier recommendations which boosted wages,[15] and to call strongly for wages to be restrained.

By February 1986, the Economic Committee was recommending 'severe' wage restraint, arguing that 'there should be no net increase in average wage costs after the CPF cut. This severe restraint should continue for two years. Even after economic recovery, wage increases should as a rule not exceed productivity increases' (Economic Committee 1986: 8). Shortly after, the government accepted and emphasized the need for a two-year period of wage restraint. This was subsequently endorsed by the NWC in April 1986. Thus, a 'temporary' general wage restraint became an expedient answer to the problem of the country's declining international competitiveness. It was argued that Singapore should practise wage restraint for two or three years (or 'as long as necessary'), allowing wage increases among its competitors to close the gap and enable it to regain international competitiveness.

However, the imposition of a general wage restraint (together with a reduction in the employer's CPF contribution rate) was problematic in several respects. First, a severe wage restraint policy constituted intervention by the state in the workings of the labour market, in a manner inconsistent with the expressed policy preference in Singapore for the freer operation of market forces. Furthermore, wage restraint was counterproductive for the future, just as the wage restraint policy of the late 1960s to mid-1970s was previously held responsible for the slow productivity growth during that period. In short, a general wage restraint was a backward step in relation to Singapore's own earlier experiences of wage policy.

The Economic Committee had itself argued, but subsequently neglected, the point that

> The basic problem with the NWC guidelines is that it is almost impossible to find one figure which is suitable for all companies and all jobs. Each set of circumstances is unique, and must be individually taken into account. When managements and unions are still inexperienced in wage bargaining, a strong guideline like the NWC enables them to reach a reasonable, if not optimal, solution. As managements and unions grow more mature and confident of each other, there comes a point when it is better to leave them to sort out their wage increases by themselves. The Committee is therefore of the view that the NWC should cease issuing a quantitative annual wage recommendation. (Economic Committee 1986: 103)

However, the Economic Committee's recommendation of severe general wage restraint, which resulted in strong pressures for virtually all organizations to freeze or cut wages, was no less arbitrary than those of the NWC in the past.[16] The Economic Committee failed to realize that the criticisms which it had levelled against the NWC guidelines, could be applied with equal force against its own recommendations for wage restraint. In short, on this issue, the Committee ignored its own recommendations and policy prescriptions.

The efforts which aimed to enforce wage restraint, based on the prevailing wage level until the wage levels in competing countries 'catch up', seemed to overlook the fact that Singapore's wage level could be expected to be higher than those of Hong Kong, Taiwan and South Korea, in part because of the inherently greater labour scarcity in Singapore. Given the declining trend in Singapore's birth rate, and the difficulties that would be associated with any attempt to resort to a large-scale import of foreign workers, the situation of relative labour scarcity was unlikely to change significantly. Consequently, it would be unwise to wait for wages in those countries to catch up, just as it would be folly to wait for wages in Indonesia, Bangladesh and China to catch up. Based on the inherently greater relative scarcity of labour and, thus, inherently higher wage level, Singapore should learn to do different things, or perform them better relative to its competitors. Indeed, with the greater relative scarcity of labour in Singapore compared to its principal Asian competitors, these efforts to artificially restrain wages in Singapore served also to distort market signals.

Evidence that such a distortion occurred may be found in the fact that, following the new wage restraints, the post-1985 economic recovery resulted in a recurrence of the labour shortage in service activities as well as in manufacturing. There were also difficulties in recruiting more teachers and nurses, and increased difficulties in recruiting foreign professional expertise.[17] These difficulties led to a renewed clamour by employers for a further relaxation of restrictions on the import of foreign workers.

The Effects of the Import of Foreign Labour

The second factor which slowed down the adjustment process in Singapore was a substantial reliance on foreign labour, especially large numbers of unskilled or low-skilled foreign workers for factory work, construction, and even domestic services. As upward pressures on wage levels intensified, employers made repeated demands for restrictions on the use of lower-cost foreign workers to be eased, and for the charges imposed to be reduced.

In 1984, after numerous representations by employers, the earlier objective of phasing out such workers completely by 1991 became doubtful (see *Sunday Times*, 26 February 1984: 6, and Ambalam 1984). In March 1986, the Finance Minister conceded that the government would exercise greater flexibility in the repatriation of foreign workers, giving greater consideration to the needs of manufacturers, hoteliers, shipyards, construction companies and working mothers. Thus, the policy of wage restraint combined with the continued reliance on large numbers of non-professional foreign workers in Singapore to delay further the shift away from jobs which required these workers. This situation retarded the incentives for firms to press forward more vigorously with efforts to upgrade their activities and to restructure their operations.

The Effects of the Earlier Educational Structure

Finally, earlier deficiencies in Singapore's education structure also contributed to the slower shift towards higher-value-added economic activities. In the 1960s and early 1970s, this was associated with the excessively academic-orientated and elitist nature of education, which resulted in substantial numbers of students being 'pushed out' of the education system, with few options for continuing or resuming their education later (Cheah 1977). This system was responsible for the fact noted by the Economic Planning Committee (1991: 28) that 61 per cent of the non-student population in Singapore had achieved an education level of only Primary 6 or less.

When the education system was reformed in the 1970s and 1980s, substantially increased emphasis was given (correctly) to the promotion of vocational education. However, the new bias against tertiary education was sustained for too long. Only in the 1990s was a second university formally established, and more recently, in 1994, the Open University began operating. During the earlier absence of these new institutions, the only alternative for those unable to gain access to the limited places in the local university was to seek tertiary education abroad, at considerably greater expense. These constraints help to account for the fact reported by the National Science and Technology Board (1991: 7, 17) that Singapore lags significantly in the proportion of research scientists and engineers, compared not just with developed countries such as Japan, the United States, Germany, Sweden and Switzerland, but also in comparison with Taiwan and South Korea.

From this perspective, the recent substantial investments in the tertiary education sector represent an effort to 'catch up' with those countries, and to correct for the relative neglect of tertiary education in earlier decades. That neglect has also contributed to the slower transition towards more skill-intensive and technology-intensive activities in recent times. The attempt in recent years to attract significant numbers of qualified professionals to Singapore is another part of the effort to make up for lost time and lack of foresight (see Pearson 1985).

CONCLUSION: 'WHATEVER THE FUTURE BRINGS, WE WILL BE READY'[18]

The answer to the question posed in the title of this chapter is a qualified 'yes'. Singapore's experience demonstrates that competitiveness can be created, and not just be endowed. More specifically, this experience shows that a government can successfully promote competitiveness through skills development.[19] The government has been successful, despite the difficulties and controversies.[20] Skills development has played an important part in facilitating a technological catching-up process in Singapore. The successes experienced in this process have contributed to Singaporeans' growing confidence and pride in their capabilities and their achievements. This growing confidence lies behind increasingly assertive expressions of views and positions by government officials and others. However, the following caveats are necessary.

First, the achievements of the government's policies can be attributed partly to the soundness of many aspects of the Economic Restructuring Strategy, and partly to favourable domestic and external economic circumstances (see Cheah 1993).

Second, in Singapore skills development occurred concomitantly with, and has been only one part of, a wider range of associated measures and conditions which, in combination, produced the present results.

Third, the process of establishing competitiveness, even now, remains a taxing and, in various ways, problematic one. The various policy zigzags represent a process of trial-and-error correction.[21] It has been a learning process to establish both the possibilities and the limits of particular courses of action, which are not always unambiguously apparent or adequately appreciated *ex ante*.[22]

Fourth, the process of skills upgrading is far from complete and, inevitably, will never be completed. It is a part of the 'race without a finish line'. In this process, competitiveness may be acquired and lost, and is always relative and temporary.[23]

Fifth, these developments are drawing Singapore closer to big league competition,[24] where the rewards and the risks are substantially greater.

Finally, in its efforts to guide the economy successfully through the transition from a developing to a developed economy, the government has intervened extensively in the labour market and in other areas of the economy and society, both directly and indirectly. It is clear that where the market rules it is with the approval of the government. Approval can be withdrawn or altered if and when the authorities deem it necessary. For, despite its fallibility, the government perceives itself as the principal arbiter of the development process. Its efforts have resulted in significant achievements in some respects, and generated difficulties and controversy in other instances. These twin aspects reveal the tremendous possibilities as well as the serious problems that may be associated with a state-dominated development effort.

These caveats should be heeded by others who seek to follow in these footsteps, and who may try to replicate the successes.

NOTES

1. These include development of physical infrastructure, development of production capabilities, skills development, technology acquisition, and through the formation and shaping of economic, social and political institutions (see, among others, Goh 1970, 1977; Chan 1976; Economic Committee 1986; National Science and Technology Board 1991; Economic Planning Committee 1991; Government of Singapore 1991; Soon and Tan 1993; and various contributions to Rodan 1993).

2. For earlier writings on employment, labour conditions, the trade union movement and the state of industrial relations, see Pang (1978 and 1981), Pang and Tan (1976 and 1983), Pugh (1984), Tan (1984) and Cheah (1988).

3. One specific objective of the ERS was to achieve annual growth of 8 per cent to 10 per cent in the 1980s, so as to raise per-capita income to between $15,000 and $18,000 (at 1979 prices) in 1990. As per-capita GNP was $8,220 in 1979, this required an average annual increase of $616 to $889 in real terms. This was to be associated with a productivity increase of 6 per cent to 8 per cent per year. At the same time, the number of foreign workers would be reduced to a level not exceeding 15 per cent of the Singaporean labour force.

4. The Central Provident Fund is a mandatory savings scheme based on contributions from employees and their employers. The principal aim of the scheme is to try to ensure that workers possess adequate savings for their retirement needs. Extensions of the scheme have enabled it to be used for purchasing public housing, payment of major medical expenses, investment in government-approved corporate shares, insurance and educational purposes.

5. The levy was set initially at 4 per cent of the employers' payroll costs. It was subsequently lowered to 2 per cent and then 1 per cent.
6. Quoted in *Straits Times*, 1 January 1982.
7. An earlier study by Cheah (1977) had established a subsistence level measure of the minimum monthly household requirements (MMHR) for households of different sizes and composition in Singapore, and was able to derive estimates of the number of households and persons living below the established subsistence level. By adjusting the level of MMHR established for that year, to take inflation into account, it was possible to establish similar indicators for subsequent years. By this means, it was possible to derive estimates of the extent of poverty for subsequent years.
8. The cost-reduction measures that were adopted included a reduction in employers' CPF contributions from 25 per cent to 10 per cent for two years, a 25 per cent rebate on personal income tax in assessment year 1986, reduction of the top income tax rate from 40 per cent to 33 per cent and the lowest tax rate from 4 per cent to 3.5 per cent in assessment year 1987, and reduction of the corporate tax rate from 40 per cent to 33 per cent in assessment year 1987. The government also reduced further the SDF levy from 2 per cent to 1 per cent. These and related measures were estimated to amount to more than $3 billion in terms of annual public revenue forgone.
9. In July 1994, three new schemes were introduced, drawing on the Skills Development Fund, to provide training opportunities for retrenched workers (the Retraining Voucher Scheme), employees in small and medium-sized enterprises, and employees in high-value-added manufacturing activities (the SDF Training Award Scheme in Core Skills). These schemes were expected to cost S$20 million and to generate 30,000–40,000 additional training places over the next three to four years, above the existing 400,000 training places (*Straits Times*, 9 July 1994, weekly edition: 24).
10. It was highlighted in the Plan that Singapore needed to catch up not only with developed countries such as Japan, the United States, West Germany, Sweden and Switzerland in this respect, but also with Taiwan and South Korea whose research scientists and engineers in 1988 already amounted to 43 per 10,000 and 33 per 10,000, respectively.
11. The Government of Singapore (1991: 25) had contended, 'we need to increase our natural population growth rate. Broadly speaking, we need 50,000 babies a year'.
12. 'Studies have concluded that, with careful use of land, we can comfortably house 4 million people, 50 per cent more than now, and still improve our quality of life' (Government of Singapore 1991: 24)..
13. The Economic Planning Committee (1991: 64) advocated that government 'selecting niches, or targetting or picking winners' should be avoided. Instead it recommended 'evolving highly developed niches in which Singapore can match the countries of the first league of developed nations … based on a high level of participation with the private sector'.
14. In support of such measures Marshall and Tucker (1992: 56) contended that 'key differences in the organisation of the society as a whole, as well as within the firm, appear to account for substantial differences in the capacity of the economy to perform well, given the challenge presented by the newly integrated world economy. … *'These patterns of organisation do not automatically emerge as a result of the actions of market forces, but rather as a result of conscious choices made by governments, managers, and labor, choices that could spell the difference between national success and failure'* (emphasis added). See also Pfeffer (1994). For contrary views, see *The Economist*, 12 March 1994: 19–26, and 26 March 1994: 81–2.
15. By then the NWC had returned to more modest wage-increase recommendations for several years. Nevertheless, the adverse perception persisted, perpetrated by particular interest groups.
16. The perceived importance of such measures was strengthened by the Economic Committee's perception that, after experiencing wage increases higher than productivity growth for several years, 'We cannot … solve our problems simply by restraining wages and waiting for our productivity to catch up. In a recession, the prospects of high productivity growth restoring our competitive position are remote' (1986: 41). The government, the

NWC and employers' associations, in a concerted fashion, strongly urged employers to implement the wage freeze (cut). Employers who did not conform, as well as those who did but who sought to lay the blame for their actions elsewhere, were subjected to public criticism.

17. Special arrangements had to be made for expatriates employed in tertiary institutions of learning, the Mass Rapid Transport project and the public service so that they would not be adversely affected by the reductions in the CPF contribution rate, through conversion to a gratuity payment scheme (*Straits Times*, 30 July 1986: 26). Recruits to elite groups in the civil service were earlier exempted from the reductions in their starting pay (*Straits Times*, 24 October 1985: 1).

18. Comment by Prime Minister Goh Chok Tong in his foreword to Government of Singapore (1991: 13).

19. For recent efforts to convince the American administration to place greater emphasis on the upgrading of workforce skills and capabilities, see Marshall and Tucker (1992) and Reich (1991).

20. Success serves to mute or to deflect criticism of the policies that have been adopted and the means employed in the development process. It serves also as the principal justification, *ex post*, for having done things 'our way'.

21. This point tends to be overlooked or underemphasized by those (most recently, Huff 1994: 369) who attribute success to 'sensible politics and good public administration'.

22. It may be argued that in many (perhaps most) cases this is a necessary process though, obviously, not sufficient to ensure success. Emphasis of this point is needed against the simplistic propositions of (a) those who proclaim that the market mechanism is always superior to government intervention, as well as (b) those who proclaim the opposite. In this respect, Huff (1994: 368–69) provides a useful comment.

23. In this respect, the concept differs significantly from the static orthodox concept of comparative advantage.

24. See *Straits Times*, 16 August 1995, weekly edition: 4.

REFERENCES

Ambalam, G. (1984), 'Phase-out of Foreign Workers by 1991 is to be Reviewed', *Sunday Monitor*, 18 November, 1.

Awanohara, S. (1981), 'Singapore Opens Doors', *Far Eastern Economic Review*, 10 July, 40–41.

Awanohara, S. (1987), '"Look East" – the Japan Model', *Asian–Pacific Economic Literature*, **1** (1), 75–89.

Beer, M., B. Spector, P. Lawrence, D.Q. Mills and R. Walton (1984), *Managing Human Assets*, New York: Free Press.

Chan, H.C. (1976), *The Dynamics of One Party Dominance: The PAP at the Grass-roots*, Singapore: Singapore University Press.

Cheah, H.B. (1977), 'A Study of Poverty in Singapore', M.Soc.Sc. dissertation, University of Singapore, Department of Sociology.

Cheah, H.B. (1980), 'Export-oriented Industrialisation and Dependent Development: the Experience of Singapore', *IDS Bulletin*, **12** (1), 35–41.

Cheah, H.B. (1986), 'The Downturn in the Singapore Economy: Problems, Prospects and Possibilities for Recovery', *Southeast Asian Affairs 1986*, Singapore, Institute of Southeast Asian Studies.

Cheah, H.B. (1988), 'Labour in Transition: the Case of Singapore', *Labour and Industry*, **1** (2), 258–86.

Cheah, H.B. (1993), 'Responding to Global Challenges: the Changing Nature of

Singapore's Incorporation into the International Economy', in Garry Rodan (ed.), *Singapore Changes Guard: Social, Political and Economic Directions in the 1990s*, Melbourne: Longman Cheshire, 101–15.

Deyo, F. (1981), *Dependent Development and Industrial Order: An Asian Case Study*, New York: Praeger.

Deyo, F. (1984), 'Export Manufacturing and Labour: the Asian Case', in Charles Bergquist (ed.), *Labour in the Capitalist World-Economy*, Beverly Hills: Sage, pp. 267–88.

Dicken, P. (1986), *Global Shift: Industrial Change in a Turbulent World*, London: Harper & Row.

Economic Committee (1986), *The Singapore Economy: New Directions*, Singapore: Ministry of Trade and Industry.

Economic Planning Committee (1991), *The Strategic Economic Plan: Towards a Developed Nation*, Singapore: Ministry of Trade and Industry.

Economist, The (1994a), 'O Brave New World', 12 March, 19–26.

Economist, The (1994b), 'Investing in People', 26 March, 81–2.

Goh, K.S. (1970), *Decade of Achievement*, Singapore: Ministry of Culture.

Goh, K.S. (1977), *The Practice of Economic Growth*, Singapore: Federal Publications.

Government of Singapore (1991), *Singapore: the Next Lap*, Singapore: Times.

Heyzer, N. (1983), 'International Production and Social Change: an Analysis of the State, Employment, and Trade Unions in Singapore', in Peter S.J. Chen (ed.), *Singapore: Development Policies and Trends*, Oxford: Oxford University Press, pp. 105–28.

Huff, W.G. (1994), *The Economic Growth of Singapore: Trade and Development in the Twentieth Century*, Cambridge: Cambridge University Press.

Islam, I. and C. Kirkpatrick (1986), 'Export-led Development, Labour-market Conditions and the Distribution of Income: the Case of Singapore', *Cambridge Journal of Economics*, **10** (2), 113–127.

Kantrow, A. (1985), 'America's Industrial Renaissance', in Federal Reserve Bank of Atlanta, *How to Compete Beyond the 1980s*, Westport, Conn., Quorum Books, pp. 97–110.

Lee, K.Y. (1980), in A. Senkuttuvan (ed.), *MNCs and ASEAN Development in the 1980s*, Singapore: Institute of Southeast Asian Studies, pp. 191–204.

Lee, K.Y. (1982), '1982: a Good Year for Us, Barring Global Upsets', broadcast New Year message.

Leggett, C. (1985), 'Singapore's Dual Functioning Trade Unions', paper presented at Institute of Southeast Asian Studies (Singapore) Occasional Seminar on 18 May.

Leggett, C. (1988), 'Industrial Relations and Enterprise Unionism in Singapore', *Labour and Industry*, **1** (2), 242–57.

Lim, C.Y. (1979a), 'Economic Restructuring and the Trade Union Movement in Singapore', Paper presented at the NTUC Seminar and Triennial Delegates Conference, 8–11 November.

Lim, C.Y. (1979b), 'Economic Restructuring in Singapore', in Central Executive Committee of the People's Action Party, *Petir*, 25th anniversary issue.

Lim, C.Y. (1979c), 'Restructuring the Singapore Economy', English version of the National Day special supplement, published in *Sin Chew Jit Poh*, 9 August.

Lim, C.Y. (1982), *Learning from the Japanese Experience*, Singapore, Maruzen Asia.

Lim, I. (1982), 'Silent Protest at Plant over Remarks by MD', *Straits Times*, 13 May, 38.

Lin, V. (1986), *Health, Women's Work, and Industrialization: Women Workers in the Semiconductor Industry in Singapore and Malaysia*, Working Paper no. 130, Michigan State University, Office of Women in International Development.

Marshall, R. and M. Tucker (1992), *Thinking for a Living: Education and the Wealth of Nations*, New York: Basic Books.

National Science and Technology Board (1991), *Science and Technology – Window of Opportunities: National Technology Plan 1991*, Singapore: National Science and Technology Board.

Pang, E.F. (1978), 'Changing Patterns of Industrial Relations in Singapore', in Peter S.J. Chen and H.D. Evers (eds), *Studies in ASEAN Sociology*, Singapore: Chopman Enterprises, pp. 422–36.

Pang, E.F. (1981), 'Economic Development and the Labour Market in a Newly Industrializing Country: the Experience of Singapore', *The Developing Economies*, **19** (1), 3–16.

Pang, E.F. and L. Lim (1982), 'Foreign Labour and Economic Development in Singapore', *International Migration Review*, **16** (3), 548–76.

Pang, E.F. and C.H. Tan (1976), 'Foreign Investment, Unions and the Government in Singapore', in *Foreign Investment and Labour in Asian Countries*, Tokyo: Japan Institute of Labour.

Pang, E.F. and C.H. Tan (1983), 'Trade Unions and Industrial Relations', in P. Chen (ed.), *Singapore: Development Policies and Trends*, Oxford: Oxford University Press, pp. 227–39.

Pearson, R. (1985), 'Avoiding Skill Shortages in the New Technologies', *Long Range Planning*, **18** (4), 33–8.

Pfeffer, J. (1994), *Competitive Advantage through People: Unleashing the Power of the Work force*, Boston, Mass.: Harvard Business School Press.

Pugh, C. (1984), 'Trade Unions, Welfare, and Co-operative Organizations in Singapore', *Southeast Asian Journal of Social Science*, **12** (2), 68–87.

Reich, R. (1991), *The Work of Nations: Preparing Ourselves for 21st Century Capitalism*, New York: A. Knopf.

Rodan, G. (ed.) (1993), *Singapore Changes Guard: Social, Political and Economic Directions in the 1990s*, Melbourne: Longman Cheshire.

Saw, S.H. (1984), *Labour force projections for Singapore*, Institute of Southeast Asian Studies, Research Notes and Discussion Paper no. 47.

Singapore Department of Statistics (1981), *Census of Population 1980*, Release No. 4, Singapore: Singapore National Printers.

Soesastro, H. (1985), 'Japan "Teacher" – ASEAN "Pupils": Can it Work?', in R.A. Scalapino, S. Sato and J. Wanadi (eds), *Asian Economic Development – Present and Future*, Berkeley: Institute of East Asian Studies.

Soh, T.K. (1981a), 'CPF Check on Job Hop: Govt. Scheme Starts Today', *Straits Times*, 7 January, p. 1.

Soh, T.K. (1981b), '6,600 Face Job Hop Quiz: Govt. Move to Check Bad Work Habit', *Straits Times*, 13 January, p. 1.

Soon, T.W. (1988), *Singapore's New Education System: Educational Reform for National Development*, Singapore, Institute of Southeast Asian Studies.

Soon, T.W. and C.S. Tan (1993), *Singapore: Public Policy and Economic Development*, Washington, DC: World Bank.

Stahl, C.W. (1984), 'Singapore's Foreign Workforce: Some Reflections on its Benefits and costs', *International Migration Review*, **18** (1), 37–49.

Tan, B.H. (1981), 'Hoppers: Carrot and Stick Plan', *Sunday Times*, 25 January, 1–6.

Tan, C.H. (1984), 'Towards better Labour-management Relations', in P.S. You and C.Y. Lim (eds), *Singapore: Twenty-five Years of Development*, Singapore: Nan Yang Xing Zhou Lianhe Zaobao, pp. 189–205.

Tyers, R. and P. Philips (1984), 'Australia, ASEAN and Pacific Basin Merchandise Trade, Factor Composition and Performance in the 1970s', *ASEAN-Australia Economic Papers* No. 13, Canberra: ASEAN-Australia Joint Research Project.

Wilkinson, B., C. Leggett and S. Patarapanich (1986), 'National Ideology, Technology and Employment: the Construction Industry in Singapore', *New Technology, Work and Employment*, **1** (1), 67–76.

PART III

The Role of Education and Training

5. Education and training for manufacturing development

Robert Cassen and George Mavrotas*

INTRODUCTION

Two developments have lit up the stage of research on human resources and manufacturing. One has been the new growth literature, with its emphasis on the production of knowledge and the ways it can be endogenized.[1] New cross-section estimates such as those of Barro incorporate education variables which explain a considerable share of growth.[2]

The other has been the world of manufacturing itself, where first, competition has been widely seen to have been affected by 'lean production', 'flexible production' and other changes, and secondly, countries facing new lower-cost producers as their own wages rise have had to 'upgrade' their products and product-mix to succeed in world markets. It is well known that this has much to do with human skills; even in the industrial countries, or some of them, falling behind in the skilling of the labour force has been a frequent topic in the media as well as in academic research.[3]

Our concentration is on *training*, which is somewhat the poor relation of this literature. It does not appear at all in any of the growth regressions, because quantitative data about it are hard to come by; this means that the contribution of human resources to growth may well be being underestimated. In a highly significant study, firms in selected industries in Japan, Malaysia and Thailand were minutely examined; they made the same product, and the technology was *more* modern in the latter two countries; yet 'labor productivity in these industries in Thailand and Malaysia ranges from one fourth to one third that of the Japanese plants'. The authors attribute the difference mainly to Japanese methods of on-the-job training.[4]

One of the few countries for which there is an estimate of the cost of firm-level training (albeit an insecure one) is the US, where figures published in 1990 suggest a total in the range of $180–200 billion.[5] Most of the literature, too, concentrates on the training of the workforce; that of *managers* is another less well-documented topic, as is that of productive service personnel (professional – accounting, finance, law – and other), but we do not do much to fill the gap.

ROLE OF EDUCATION AND TRAINING

There is much evidence of rises in educational enrolment *pari passu* with increasing output and exports of manufactures. In all the East Asian 'Miracle' countries, educational levels have risen well above what would be predicted by per-capita income. There have been considerable advances even in Japan recently: between 1970 and 1988, the percentage of the male labour force with only junior high school education halved (from 47 per cent to 23 per cent); the proportion with college or university education almost trebled, from 6 per cent to 16 per cent.[6] The model employed by the World Bank's *East Asian Miracle* study explains a large share of growth in those countries by the extent of education; different parts of education are associated with growth in each country (primary education is highly significant in all these economies; secondary education is most powerful in Japan, least in Indonesia, and Thailand, where indeed secondary education has been lagging and skill shortages are apparent. Malaysia also has skill shortages, but mainly because of a lack of tertiary education in technical subjects, and weaknesses in training [7]). For the economies studied, excepting Hong Kong, 60 per cent or more of economic growth is 'explained by the accumulation of physical and human capital, initial income levels and population growth'; primary education is 'by far the largest single contributor to [their] predicted growth rates'.[8] And as we show below, education is strongly linked to training.

But what exactly have education and training to do with manufacturing? Considerable survey evidence at the firm level attributes to education and training both the ability to adopt new technology by firms, and the ability to make other productivity advances.

Take the technology issue first. Japan's ability to introduce robotics and microelectronics in industry has been related to the educational improvements of the 1970s and 1980s. Studies for Taiwan and a number of other countries show similar findings.[9] One of the few econometric studies has suggested the importance of education to the adoption of new technology; it measured the relations between labour-force education and age of equipment. The authors estimated a model of the demand for highly-educated workers on a panel of 61 US manufacturing industries observed in 1960, 1970 and 1980. Their results are consistent with the central hypothesis of their study on the link between education and technical change.[10] A large number of studies have explored the acquisition of technological capacity by developing countries, and testify to the importance of human resources for the purpose.[11]

An important consideration here is the very large body of evidence about the changing character of manufacturing production and trade. Fewer and fewer products are made first and then sold to whoever will buy them; they are made to client specifications. (One estimate is that 60 per cent of all production and sales in OECD countries are to client-specific orders.[12]) One should not exaggerate; there is still a range of products and processes which do not have these characteristics. Manufacturing of many products splits into production stages, the less skilled of which go to low-wage countries. And some products are little affected by new technology: a can of peaches is still a can of peaches. If this were not so, there would be little opportunity for the less-advanced countries.

But the effect of the changes is to put a premium on information and other skills for marketing, design and quality control. Statistical process control is an increasingly demanded skill. A range of cost-reducing innovations in production such as JIT inventory are increasing the demand for skills. Automated and machine-controlled production techniques are affecting an ever-widening number of products; even those such as garments which were traditional points of entry into manufacturing for developing countries are for all these reasons becoming increasingly skill-intensive. Another requirement of the 'new competition' is speed of response; this as well as having implications for skills affects the location of skilled and low-skill activities,[13] and places demands on transport capacity, communications and infrastructure generally. It is, in sum, becoming increasingly difficult for countries without a range of skills and productive services to compete internationally in manufactures.

This evidence, however, tells us only a part of *how* the skills provided by education and training are used. There remain the other productivity effects. They come from such things as shop-floor efficiency, the adaptive innovations which demand both higher- and lower-level skills, and which are responsible for a major share of productivity growth in manufacturing; as has been noted, 'The economic benefits from the acquisition of a new technology are generally less than the cumulative benefits from gradual improvements made after its introduction'.[14]

A number of different views about productivity benefits are found in the literature. Obviously a degree of knowledge is required to organize production and install a new process; but once it is operating, it might be thought that continuing use would become routine. But this is not so. Close observation of Japanese manufacturing has indicated that a critical need for skills is not just in running a process normally as in coping with changes, or putting it right when it goes wrong. Power, mechanical, or parts failures, the absence of particular workers with particular skills, variations in the product – the more adaptable the worker, the better he/she is able to remedy a problem. Downtime is expensive, and the more complex and expensive the production process, the more important it is not to interrupt it. This is why the Japanese training method puts such emphasis on equipping the worker to perform a range of related functions in the production process. The advent of flexible, small-batch production where the product and associated tools and equipment are subject to frequent change adds to the value of this training.

Another point is costs. There have been a number of studies of sub-branches of UK business, especially by Sig Prais. They show the disadvantage of the British worker, who commonly has less education and training than his/her counterpart in competitor countries. His/her wage may be lower, but he/she is more expensive to employ because he/she needs more expenditure on management, supervision and quality control.[15] The costs may be even higher since the evidence shows that available skills to some extent determine technology, and firms with low-skill labour cannot adopt new techniques.

Under what he calls the 'white-collarisation of the blue-collar worker' in Japan, Koike has shown that the Japanese worker will have a good education to start with, will get training within the enterprise, principally on the job, and will spend time in a variety of workshops within a given manufacturing process until he/she has a thorough understanding of the products and the machinery and organization which produce them. His/her skills are little lower than those of a technician with higher qualifications and greater theoretical knowledge. According to this and some other studies, the Japanese system of seniority wages and lifetime employment are not cultural features of Japanese manufacturing, but sensible rewards for experience and usefulness to the firm.[16] Japanese workers acquire greater breadth and depth of experience, that is, they can operate in a range of workplaces, and can do more tasks in each workplace; their pay is in fact not based purely on seniority, but often related to the difficulty of the tasks they can accomplish, which have great value to the firm.[17]

TRAINING

So far we have been talking generically about the uses of education and training. Now we will discuss training itself more specifically: evidence, theory, determinants, markets and market failure, and policy implications. We concentrate on training provided by firms; vocational training outside the firm will be addressed in the final sections of the chapter.

Evidence

The relationship between training, innovation and productivity has long been a subject of study. Enos (1962) and Hollander (1965) concluded that training effort is essential to make the most of new technologies, resulting in increased productivity and trade competitiveness. The relationship between training and technological change has recently been supported by a number of empirical studies.[18] The main conclusion is that workers in industries experiencing high rates of total factor productivity growth get more training, have more rapid wage growth, more experience and less job turnover.

A good deal of the evidence comes from industrial countries; but the findings are similar to those already noted. A study comparing UK and German manufacturing firms has argued that the higher productivity of the latter can be attributed to the superior level of the training of shopfloor workers, particularly that of foremen, who in Germany would typically have an advanced craft qualification, unlike their British counterparts.[19] According to Dougherty (1989) there are two types of effects: first, German workers were able to use any given type of equipment more productively in the sense of exploiting the technical capabilities of machines; abuses were less frequent and faults more likely to be diagnosed correctly and cured; and second, management in Germany was willing to install more advanced equipment. The average age of UK machinery appeared similar to that in the German firms, but it was less sophisticated. This X-inefficiency effect is also present in developing countries.[20]

Dertouzos et al. (1989) concluded that the shortcomings of the system of human resources training in the United States had a considerable impact on the economy's relative loss of competitiveness in recent years. Davies and Caves (1987) found that the UK underinvests in human capital in terms of both technical and managerial skills. In another study, Schott (1981) comparing the determinants of innovations in the UK, Canada and the United States, concluded that, despite cultural differences, at least part of the relatively poor performance of the UK in terms of innovative capacity lies in the quality of its managers. (The proportion of managers with university degrees is 90 per cent in Japan, 40 per cent in the US, and 35 per cent in the UK.[21]) Greenhalgh and Mavrotas (1993) derive similar conclusions concerning the UK's performance in training provision during the Thatcher years. Other comparisons between the United States and Japan and between Germany and France arrived at similar conclusions, that is, that better training permits the optimal use of new technologies.

A number of studies show that in-firm training pays off well in developing countries in some circumstances. For example, enterprise and pre-employment training have produced social rates of return of 20 per cent in Malaysia;[22] in-plant training for welders in Korean shipbuilding had a social rate of return of 28 per cent, higher than in non-firm training institutions;[23] on-the-job training was 'an extremely systematic and powerful ingredient in the rapid growth of Japanese companies'.[24] But much depends on the conditions. 'A large body of evidence, based largely on worker-level data of training and earnings, shows that enterprise training yields higher private returns than training from other sources, and that these returns are higher when they occur in industries with a relatively well educated labour force, experiencing rapid technological change'.[25]

Obviously demand and supply conditions for skilled labour will affect the rewards of training to the individual, in more ways than one. Koike and Inoki (1990) observe that with a premium on scarce educational qualifications in Malaysia, firms will often hire on the basis of credentials; this frustrates promotion and training within the firm, and is bad for worker morale. Since other firms do the same, there is more worker mobility, which again may militate against training. Private returns to the acquisition of skills may be higher than social returns when there is a queue of workers for good jobs and selection is by hierarchy of educational or training credentials; or if growth is constrained by skill shortages, but individuals are uncertain about which skills to invest in, there may be high social returns but low (perceived) private returns. Care may thus be needed in interpreting estimates of private returns, as far as public policy is concerned, especially in developing countries interested in promoting manufacturing development.

Determinants

Macroeconomics, exports and the competitive environment

It is clearly necessary from all points of view that policies should encourage growth and exports, and a competitive environment. Progress in manufacturing requires increasing demand, stimuli to efficiency and adoption of new technology. Reliance on the domestic economy alone will not afford the available potential economies of scale, or, if it is a heavily protected one, the necessary competitiveness. The developing countries which have been successful in manufacturing in the last twenty-five years have stressed export orientation and been open to foreign investment, at least on a selective basis, even if they have not been all that liberal in financial and trade policies. Rapid employment growth that comes in particular from exporting successfully provides the incentive to families to educate their children and acquire qualifications.

A recent study provides some evidence for these linkages. Focusing on six developing countries in the 1980s with different trade policies, the study concluded that countries with outward-oriented policies (South Korea, Thailand and Malaysia) did better than countries with inward-focused strategies (Nigeria, Egypt, Tunisia) as far as human capital development was concerned, in the sense that an outward orientation encouraged higher levels of private-sector vocational education and training, and internal and external efficiency in public-sector vocational education and training that more closely matched that of the private sector.[26]

Although the study argues for a causal link between trade regime and human resource development, the direction of causality is subject to debate. It is true that exporting will be difficult with the kinds of labour-market distortions that discourage training. But the study does nothing more than show that the inward-looking economies had these distortions. It is possible to ask whether outward-oriented strategies were responsible for both the outstanding export performance of the East Asian NICs and their efficiency in human capital development, or whether their success should in fact be attributed to an initial combination of high literacy rates and few natural resources, with subsequent massive investment in secondary and higher education.[27] Exporting may well do more for training by the incentives it provides to introduce new technology and hence to train, and the contact with overseas buyers, suppliers, firms and agencies which help them to know what has to be done.

Training incidence and education

An empirical study of training provision in Peru (Arriagada 1989) concluded that 'workers with less than secondary schooling, which constitutes over 50 per cent of the urban male labour force in Peru, do not receive job-skills from the institutional training system. Moreover, ... the probability of receiving [institutional] training is largely determined by educational attainment, where secondary schooling is the lowest entry level into training courses, revealing that in the case of Peru, training and formal education are indeed complementary' (p. 44). The study also reports empirical evidence associated with the impact of different types of institutional training on wage rates. 'Job-related' training (that is, institutional training associated with specific employment) increased wage rates more than 10 per cent, 'post-secondary' training (that is, training in technical institutes) 20 per cent; but training in 'academes' (vocational schools) had no impact at all on wages. Table 5.1 reports the effect of different levels of school attainment on the probability of training by type of institution.

Another empirical study for the US confirms theoretical predictions of a strong complementary relationship between education and training (Tan 1990). The probability of training incidence was higher for more educated workers (male and female) and increased with schooling attainment. A World Bank study of Indonesia (World Bank 1991), following a survey of 142 firms and

Table 5.1   Effects of educational attainment on the probability of training incidence by type of institution in Peru

Educational attainment	Job based (JBP)	Post-secondary training (PST)	Academes (ACT)
Some secondary[1]	0.095	0.265	0.065
(6–9 years)	(1.52)	(1.57)	(0.91)
Secondary complete	0.302*	0.529*	0.133*
(10 years)	(5.10)	(3.59)	(1.89)
Some post-secondary	0.160*	0.754*	1.145*
(11–13 years)	(2.00)	(4.88)	(2.87)
Post-secondary complete	0.114	0.583*	–0.003
(14+ years)	(1.39)	(4.35)	(0.97)

Notes:
1. Excluded category is primary schooling.
* Statistically significant at the 5 per cent level or better.
t-values in parentheses

Source: Arriagada (1989)

1,900 workers, confirmed the complementarity between education and off-the-job training – see Table 5.2 for a summary of the results. The table also summarizes the relationship between different types of training (on the job, off the job and so on) and educational attainment. The above strong positive relationship is also present in a study of Mexico.[28] Table 5.3 summarizes the main findings. The probability of training incidence is very low for non-

Table 5.2   Training incidence by level of education of surveyed workers in selected Indonesian industries, 1989 (per cent)

Educational attainment of surveyed workers	Proportion getting training	Type of worker training			
		Watching only	OJT	OFT and OFFJT	OFFJT
Primary education	46	18	76	6	1
Lower secondary	42	13	76	8	3
Upper general secondary	55	23	68	5	3
Upper vocational secondary	51	13	71	10	6
Post-secondary	48	31	41	19	9

Source: World Bank (1991)

Table 5.3   *Training by level of education of employed males in Mexico,*
1991 (per cent)

Educational attainment	Percentage with training	Source of training	
		On the job	Off the job
Average	15.25	12.48	2.77
No schooling	1.13	0.83	0.30
Primary incomplete	4.27	3.41	0.86
Primary	9.42	8.14	1.28
Secondary incomplete	12.49	9.94	2.55
Secondary	13.83	11.45	2.38
High school	21.86	17.73	4.13
College	27.40	21.79	5.61
Postgraduate	32.66	26.75	5.91

Source: Mexico Secretariat of Labour and Social Welfare, 'Encuesta Nacional de Empleo Urbano', Modulo de Capacitacion (1991), cited in Sabot (1993).

educated workers (1–4 per cent), rises to 14 per cent for workers with secondary education and to more than 27 per cent for college graduates, to reach 33 per cent for postgraduate education workers. A series of recent studies in the UK have also reached similar conclusions, that is, that more educated workers receive more training.[29]

While this is the general finding, it is not universal. A study in Zambia found a *negative* relation between training duration and education in many high-level occupations; the author suggested that this indicated both an absence of fixed qualifications for entry to particular occupations, and a tradeoff between education and training.[30] While the study in question refers to an earlier period, and thus may not be relevant to current manufacturing, there clearly is truth in the observations. In fact relatively little is known about the actual skill content of a wide range of occupations, or the need for specific capacities provided by education or training as they relate to specific jobs or tasks. While the bulk of available studies points to a relationship between secondary education and training, the macro findings on the importance of primary education, cited above, must have some bearing on the issue – undoubtedly there are many jobs for which primary rather than higher levels of education makes a critical difference to worker productivity. Raw, uneducated labour, however low cost, has little value in manufacturing today, for any degree of sophisticated production. Until new studies focus precisely on this topic, however, we will remain in the dark about it.

Firm size and training

At the firm level, an important determinant of training incidence is firm size. Small firms often find that the average cost of training workers is much higher than that incurred by larger firms. The fixed costs of training distributed across a smaller number of employees and the production loss associated with a worker being away from the workplace can be higher in small firms than in large firms. Furthermore, large firms may be in a better position to cope with potential 'poaching' problems because they can provide attractive packages of job promotion.[31]

Technology and training

Another important training determinant is technological change, as has already appeared above. Rapid technological change leads to more training effort in order to improve trade competitiveness. A study in Taiwan concluded that enterprise-based training is related to high levels of productivity and innovation in the industries involved.[32] The study surveyed 48,000 manufacturing firms, and explored *inter alia* the hypothesized positive relationship between industries that do 'TECH' (expenditure on R&D and purchased know-how) and training incidence. Table 5.4 summarizes the main findings. As is obvious from the table, there exists a positive relationship across industries in the proportion of firms that train and those that do TECH, something that confirms the predictions of the theory. This finding was also made in Ghana.[33]

Table 5.4   Training and technology expenditures in Taiwan, selected manufacturing industries, 1986

Two-digit manufacturing industry	Sample size (firms)	% Firms training	% Firms doing TECH	Spending ($m.)	
				Training	TECH
22 Textiles	7,772	3.79	4.14	507	2,394
23 Apparel	3,308	4.72	4.56	564	1,463
26 Paper and Publishing	9,176	1.42	1.35	316	1,771
27 Chemicals	986	8.01	12.17	1,241	11,386
31 Plastics	10,505	2.59	3.64	258	2,365
36 Electrical/Electronics	7,566	8.06	10.98	532	7,880
37 Transport Equipment	4,108	4.48	5.01	457	9,021

Notes:
1. TECH are expenditures on in-house R&D and purchased know-how.
2. Training and TECH spending are conditional on positive values.

Source: Aw and Tan (1993).

Other empirical studies have also confirmed the impact of technological change on training incidence. Tan (1990) using US data found a higher training probability in high-tech manufacturing sectors. Greenhalgh and Mavrotas (1996) using UK data from labour-force surveys in 1984 and 1989, reached similar conclusions. All the technology variables used in the study proved to be significant as determinants of training incidence in the UK. Other studies in developed countries have produced similar results.

Unionization and training
Union membership might be expected to have a negative impact on training given the low wages paid to trainees during the training period. However, two factors are likely to work in the opposite direction: first, both the training and the introduction of new technology related to it may raise wages in the longer run, and second, the lower labour turnover of union members which increases the return from training. These aspects may explain the findings of an empirical study on the issue, which reported estimates confirming a positive relationship between training incidence and union membership for the United States, Australia and the United Kingdom.[34] Empirical studies in developed and developing countries have also concluded that related variables are important as determinants of training incidence. Self-employed workers for instance have a low training incidence. The same conclusion holds for female workers relative to males, as well as for older workers.[35]

Market Failure and Government Failure

We describe in an Appendix the main aspects of the theory of training. Theory suggests that training will be inadequate because of free-rider problems and information problems. These are borne out in practice: where labour turnover is high there is obviously less incentive to firms to provide training, unless it pays off very quickly – as seems to be the case with simple and low-cost forms of training. Risk factors (whether the worker will stay with the firm, or complete his/her training) are part of the problem. The theoretical properties of information asymmetry also indicate potential market failure. In practice there are other information problems: firms may simply be unaware of the need for and the effects of training, and how to go about providing it or having it provided. And without some form of standardization and certification of institutional training, firms and individuals will not know the value of training provided, especially when provided privately.

One can add to these reasons, which pertain to incentives to *firms*, further factors which affect incentives to *individuals*. The latter affect principally education and training outside the firm, since within the firm training normally has only benefits and no costs to the individual. Depending on circumstances, individuals may lack information about the returns to acquiring qualifications; even if they have the right information, it is notorious that capital markets are deficient in providing credit to individuals for increasing future earnings. (Firms of course can pay for training outside the firm, but then the risk factor enters in.) Lastly there may be economies of scale in training itself, which can imply that atomized training provision is inefficient: this is particularly likely to be the case at early stages of manufacturing development when enterprises are typically small.

While all these reasons suggest a considerable role for government in training provision, there is ample evidence of the lack of success of government-provided training in many contexts, as examples below will demonstrate. A lack of testing of effectiveness of the public role in training is a key factor – without it, publicly-provided training may fail to respond to changing needs.

In addition, the success of training provision is highly context-dependent: a range of conditions affect it, from the social regard for the jobs to which training leads, to the institutions which surround the operation of firms. It has been argued on the basis of German experience that traditions of cooperation between companies, the presence of well-endowed employer organizations, and long-term links between companies and banks all affect the willingness of the private sector to engage effectively in training.[36]

Financing of training

For all these reasons it can be seen that except in the case of completely firm-specific skills, there may be an insufficiency of training, possibly leading to a 'low skills equilibrium'.[37] Such considerations constitute a case for government intervention in training, provided government can prove successful. One could add another point: if governments can identify training needs which are not apparent to individual firms, particularly regarding the development of skills for future expansion, they may be able to 'lead' the market. This is closely related to current arguments about industrial policy and the role of government; certainly some governments have been able to 'pick winners' when it comes to promoting skill development. Perhaps the outstanding example has been that of Singapore in information technology;[38] though such programmes are by no means easy to get right, as the Korean case has shown.[39]

Schemes adopted by developing countries to help finance training have taken several forms. The most common is the levy system where 1–2 per cent of the wage bill is levied to finance training. Such a scheme may be ineffective if public or semi-public training centres and institutes simply receive a fixed budget from the levy fund, irrespective of whether they are or are not adjusting their training programmes to changing needs. A levy system has to be regarded by firms as investment, not as an additional tax.[40]

Other schemes for financing training programmes involve tax rebates, special financing focused on particular target groups, contract training by either the government or the firm, or taxes imposed on firms which fail to train. (The latter can misfire, as happened in Korea in the 1970s, where firms preferred to pay the tax.[41]) Tax rebates can be a strong incentive, provided the process of getting the proposed training activity approved for a tax rebate is not so slow and bureaucratic that it discourages firms from using it.

As noted earlier, labour turnover may be the enemy of training. This may be hard to prevent when skills are highly transferable, as is often the case at relatively low levels of technology and where much training is for basic assembly skills and the like. Lall's (1994) study of Malaysia suggests rates of turnover in excess of 100 per cent in some firms – even so, it still pays them to train: either they are public spirited, or the costs of training are small and the rewards high. (High turnover is only one source of a generally poor record in training in Malaysia. Lall's data suggest a relative lack of attention to training by government.)

If training costs are substantial, firms may try to restrict turnover. Contract training constitutes an important means for firms to protect themselves from losing the workers they train. Contract schemes may take several forms, such as a seniority wage system, company pension plans and so on. Available empirical studies suggest that such methods can work.[42] Finally, payroll tax levies have the advantage of providing a stable source of funding support for the development of national systems of training.

POLICIES

Training policies need a broad and long-term perspective. They must also be evaluated in the light of the evidence on training determinants reviewed above. They will differ considerably depending on the stage of development. And there is a close relationship with educational policies: some of the most difficult issues are resolving possible conflicts among priorities in education.

Improving Responsiveness to Demand

The first requirement is an accurate assessment of training needs. Many countries – not only developing ones – have long relied on manpower planning, but these have frequently resulted in large errors. The standard method has been to employ output forecasts and some form of input–output coefficients of skill requirements and match these with state provision of training or inducements to individuals and training institutions to provide training. They have gone wrong in part because the manpower forecasts thus obtained have been highly inaccurate, in part because there is often little relation between education and training received and the jobs those trained actually go on to do.

The leading candidate to replace manpower planning is 'labour-market monitoring'. Tanzania's experience affords an example. In the early stages of independence it relied on manpower requirements forecasting to guide its investment in post-primary education and training. Its policy makers were not just motivated by egalitarian zeal; they were advised by the World Bank, in the light of forecast 'requirements', to favour primary over secondary education. The result was a shortage of educated and skilled personnel in a large number of fields over the 1980s.[43] In general, policies that facilitate short-term adjustment through labour-market information, linkages between training institutions and employers as well as incentives to guide the size and the occupational content of training are likely to be much more effective, as has been discussed for Thailand, which has also encountered shortages in secondary education.[44] The movement of wages and employment offer a better guide to trends in the demand for skills.

One of the most striking examples has been provided by studies of Indonesia. Labour-market signals produced quite different conclusions from manpower forecasting requirements, as indicated in a 5-year planning exercise known as Repelita V (1989–93). The manpower forecast projected a large

Table 5.5   Labour-market signalling in Indonesia

| Level of education | Market signals for 1988 | | | Manpower requirements |
	Real rate of return (%)	Unemp. age 26–35 (%)	Median job search time (months)	Repelita V for 1989–93 (000's)
Primary and under	13	0.7	1.0	–5,217
Junior Secondary	13	2.6	1.2	–289
Senior Secondary General	13	3.7	2	+779
Senior Secondary Vocational	10	2	2	+491
Academy	12	6.5	2	+50
University	6	7.8	2	+457

Source: Adams, Middleton and Ziderman (1992).

shortage of primary education graduates, a small shortage of junior secondary graduates and a surplus of graduates above this level, particularly among
senior general secondary graduates. However, labour-market monitoring (which
relied on social rates of return, unemployment for 26–35-year-olds, and median job search time) yielded a different picture: what was needed was a more
balanced allocation of spending on primary, junior secondary and senior
general secondary education. The manpower forecast failed to anticipate the
strong demand for general secondary graduates (see Table 5.5).[45]

A key role in ensuring a relationship between training and demand, as far
as concerns government-provided training, must be played by the private
sector. Such reforms of government training as have been conducted with a
degree of success in recent years have usually included roles for private-
sector representatives on boards of training institutions and policy-making
bodies.

Links Between Education and Training

There is a division of labour between the educational system, free-standing
(government or private) training institutions, and training provided by firms.
For a number of reasons, vocational training in schools is not often cost-
effective. Low rates of return have been found in most developing countries.
It tends to be expensive when based on equipment, out of date, and the skills
it teaches are often not what firms want.[46] On the whole firms that train prefer
well-educated school leavers who are adaptable and learn quickly.

This is not to say that there is no role for free-standing training institutions,
which may enjoy economies of scale. These may teach relatively low-level
skills such as auto and appliance repair, metal and wood working, office
functions and the like. Aid agencies have even experimented with mobile
training workshops teaching welding or simple mechanical skills. At the
higher-tech end of the spectrum, there are clear roles for institutional training. A case in point is the Clothing Industry Training Institute in Sri Lanka;
established with the help of German aid in 1984, it has brought modern
management, supervisory, technical and productive skills to the garment
industry, which has become a successful exporter.[47] Singapore's Centre for
Computer Studies is another example.[48]

(Industrial countries have been able to make use of 'group' training schemes
to encourage training in small firms. Group training for small firms can take
the form of a group training association. The aim is to make available the
same range and quality of training advice that a large firm would expect to
get from its own training department. Involved firms can benefit in a number
of ways: (i) advice and assistance in the identification of occupational training needs, (ii) design of appropriate training programmes, (iii) participation

in specialized programmes arranged for the group in local technical institutions and (iv) continuous evaluation of training performance within individual firms.[49] This form of training provision has been standard practice in developed countries for a number of years (the UK for example) but not as far as is known in developing ones, for reasons apparently related to implementation difficulties in practice, high transport costs, communication problems and so on.)

Most of the available studies suggest that increasingly it is *secondary* education that is associated with training in manufacturing firms. In the studies already referred to for Indonesia, Mexico and Peru, which show a correlation of training with education, secondary education is commonly the most powerful correlate, if not the minimal level. In addition a study for Zimbabwe showed craft apprenticeships to be more cost-effective than school-based or pre-employment artisan training: but the apprentices were highly selected secondary school-leavers, and worked with the biggest firms (which pay more).[50] Production operators in most automated assembly plants need a minimum of secondary education to service and repair machinery, and provide feedback to engineers to make modifications and improvements.[51] In a further study of Indonesia, the *only* post-employment training found to have significant positive benefits (measured by wage-differentials) was that offered to senior secondary-school graduates.[52] There is also, obviously, a need for highly-qualified technicians and engineers, varying with the technological level and extent of manufacturing – even the poorest countries need at least a modest layer of well-qualified people in 'high-tech' occupations.

As noted above, however, the links with education are far from well understood. This is not only true of primary education, which was discussed above, but also with different levels of secondary education. The role of educational *quality* has also made little appearance in the 'skills' literature, though elsewhere it is being found to be of great significance. Quality is so variable that much empirical study which simply correlates years of education with a variable of interest, or uses years of education as the basis of rate of return estimates, may be seriously flawed. There is also still considerable uncertainty about what within education are the important factors for productivity – the specific subjects and cognitive skills taught, or attitudes engendered towards work, cooperation. Altogether, with the exception of a few very detailed studies, we are a long way from knowledge with a desirable fineness of discrimination.

Information

An important part of policy must be to ensure a better flow of information to all parties about training. The Ghana study referred to earlier found firms quite lacking in knowledge about the training requirements of new technology, and other aspects of training.[53] Firms in Malaysia attempted to introduce technology which their labour was not skilled enough to use efficiently.[54] Even in the Netherlands, one of the countries with a successful training record by European standards, firms were found to know little about the costs and benefits of their own training schemes.[55]

But the information problem is not restricted to firms: potential trainees, parents, schools, and training institutions all need information about changing labour-market conditions. Certification of training courses is part of the information problem. A training system which produces qualifications needs accepted standards and controls – otherwise the informational value of any certificates provided will be minimal. (This has been a problem in India recently, where a host of private institutions have grown up to train IT professionals – the government has been forced to step in and introduce standards, examinations and so on.)

All the evidence points to an important role for government as a provider of information – but not government alone. Representatives of the private sector are needed at various points in public training activities to ensure that the education and training system is responsive to current and future demands.

Picking Winners

As has already been noted, it may be possible for countries to lead in skills development by identifying potential growth sectors or products and facilitating their development by fostering appropriate education and training. The case of the Sri Lankan garment industry was mentioned, as was informatics in Singapore. There is probably no more important single area than information technology for succeeding in modern manufacturing – every country needs it, but needs and capacities differ.

Singapore's programme was based on higher education and training institutions and sending students overseas; continuing education for IT professionals subsidized by government; raising IT literacy throughout the workforce by incorporating IT in education at several levels and encouraging programmes for office workers; introducing IT in most government offices; and continuous monitoring of labour-market trends and requirements. The Port of Singapore Authority alone employed nearly 300 IT professionals by 1989. The country aims to have 30,000 such professionals by the year 2000 – it had only 800 in 1980.[56]

While Singapore had perhaps the most outstandingly successful programme of its kind anywhere, the same elements are pertinent in all countries: private-sector development, human resource creation, and public-sector management. Examples of strategies for other countries are available.[57] Some very salutary experience has been gained, however, in attempts to introduce IT programmes in difficult settings, where institutional, human resource and other constraints abound. The poorer the country, the less it can afford to make mistakes, and the more careful it must be to plan and to learn from the past. There are, however, good as well as bad experiences, and there is plenty of scope for promoting IT economically within the limits of a particular setting.[58]

STRATEGIES

We assume the better-off countries with advanced manufacturing sectors can solve their own problems. Problems are not unknown: as already noted, some of the successful exporters of manufactures are experiencing human resource shortages – Malaysia and Thailand are two very different examples of countries which failed to anticipate the growth of demand.

The poorest countries have the greatest difficulties in ensuring appropriate levels of training. Firm size, which – as noted – correlates with training, is typically small. Technology is not advanced. Secondary education levels are low, and technicians and engineers are in short supply. For these countries the highest priority is to increase the coverage and quality of education up to the secondary level. In many of them this can be accomplished by reallocation from tertiary education to primary and secondary, and reallocation within tertiary education to more practical subjects – especially those countries with tertiary education patterns left over from colonial days, weighted towards arts and law graduates hoping (without much prospect today) for government jobs.

In these countries the types of encouragement to enterprise training described above are essential, and the role of free-standing training institutions has to be considered with care. Because firm-level training is likely to be restricted, there will be more opportunity for them, especially for teaching lower-level skills; the less-expensive forms of vocational education can also be promoted. But much depends on the ability to foresee labour-market trends reasonably well.

It must be recognized that if demand for skills is not adequate, taught skills decay and training institutions fail. A Bangladesh study illustrates several of the problems. Vocational and technical training institutions were found to have low rates of return. Partly the problems were remediable – class sizes were too small, course durations were too long (averaging three years, most should have been halved), entry-level qualifications were too high. But some relate to the labour market: the opportunity costs of these institutions for their trainees were too high given the expected rewards. More than half of each cohort of trainees dropped out before qualifying; of 500 interviewed, 50 per cent said they would not take employment in the skill for which they were being trained. These institutions, it should be noted, were providing training for some 25,000 enrollees annually, for a labour force numbering 30,000,000; informal training from government, private and non-governmental organization (NGO) sources was available to a further 20,000.[59]

These problems are not confined to the poorest countries. Government training institutions in Indonesia were found to have the same problems as those in Bangladesh: low capacity utilization, inadequate training methods and uncertain usefulness.[60] As a result of such observations, government training institutions were moving towards providing 'third-party training', that is, training facilities to complement those of other (private or official) bodies, paid for by the latter, though still subsidized by government.

A study of Ghana has shown the importance of education and training of entrepreneurs and production managers – to university degree level in the technically more advanced firms. Firms without such leadership showed little capacity to introduce new technology and methods. Firms did little formal (off-the-job) training. Apprenticeships worked well for transmitting traditional craft skills, but were not suitable for teaching the skills necessary for more advanced technologies – these required classroom training. One thing which the study showed was the importance of 'technological catalysts', often foreign or foreign-trained personnel at different levels; firms with such people present were better both at organizing training and at enabling firms to introduce new techniques.[61]

Different problems are found in the three South Asian low-income countries which have more established manufacturing sectors and considerable layers of trained and qualified personnel at all levels: India, Sri Lanka and Pakistan. While there is educated unemployment and underemployment in these countries, this is to some extent misleading. Many of the paper qualifications do not reflect high standards, and if India and Pakistan at least were to experience the beginnings of rapid growth of manufacturing, they would soon run into skill shortages; their secondary enrolment rates for 1990 were 44 per cent and 22 per cent, respectively, and the quality of much secondary education is low. In Sri Lanka the problem is perhaps the other way round: high levels of educational enrolment have existed for some time, but policies have prevented the country from being a significant player in the world of manufacturing domestically or internationally. In all three countries the training record is very uneven.

In Latin America, training is relatively well established in many countries, with a diversity of types of funding and institutions and a considerable volume of in-firm training, but, as one might expect, some preponderance of public training institutions.[62] Several countries are still quite deficient in education, however. The most egregious for its income level is Brazil, where only 39 per cent of the age group was enrolled in secondary education in 1990.

In many of these countries there is more scope for stimulating manufacturing and exporting, but education and training needs still require careful monitoring. The countries deficient in secondary and higher technical and engineering skills must pay attention to them, as well as to policies to enhance enterprise-based training.

The Sri Lankan example reminds one that human resources are a necessary but not a sufficient condition. To some extent there is a chicken and egg problem. Foreign direct investment has been responsible for much Third World manufacturing success, but it, too, is in part attracted by the presence of skilled labour.[63] Everything to do with manufacturing and technology adoption has a human resource background, and growth itself provides the resources to promote better education and training. But most countries have scope for reallocation of resources between and within educational sectors, and if skill and training requirements were forecast within a reasonably realistic range, they could meet a large part of their needs.

Is there a conflict of priorities? After all, education has so many roles to play. There are demands for universal primary education, for greater equality of male and female education at all levels. Education, especially of females, plays a major part in improving health and contributing to fertility decline. Are there more objectives and constraints than the solution can satisfy? Probably. But some of the constraints in the educational system itself have to be removed by favouring secondary education, to provide the teachers for the future. And countries have to satisfy the imperatives of growth to provide the resources for public services. As has been seen, what look like egalitarian strategies in education sometimes turn out to have inegalitarian results. Maximizing welfare over time is the goal, not satisfying some subsidiary goal immediately.

It is far beyond the scope of this chapter to elucidate such problems generically. Our purpose has been more modest: to illuminate the role of education and training in manufacturing, and give some pointers as to how it should be fitted into the policy process. The lessons of experience could assist many countries to do better than they have so far.

NOTES

*   The authors are indebted to Christine Greenhalgh in Oxford and to participants at the IDS Workshop for valuable comments, and offer special thanks to Adrian Wood for his particularly thorough attention. The usual disclaimer applies.
1. Romer (1986, 1990) and Lucas (1988) Easterly, King, Levine and Rebelo (1993) have

extended their models by introducing the 'technology adoption' hypothesis into their model. The main assumption is that the economy does not create new goods, it simply adopts goods and technology produced elsewhere. However, this adoption process is costly since it requires skilled labour to use new technologies.

2. Barro (1991).
3. The World Bank's *East Asian Miracle* study emphasizes the role of human resources in these economies' success (World Bank 1993a); Dertouzos et al. (1989) analyse US failings in this regard.
4. Koike and Inoki (eds) (1990).
5. US Congress (1990). The figure splits into $30–45 billion annually for formal classroom training within firms, and $150 billion or more for informal training.
6. Konishi (1989).
7. World Bank (1993a). For Malaysia, see additionally Lall (1994) and Lim and Toh (1992).
8. World Bank (1993a: 51–2). The study expresses some puzzlement at the strong showing of female education in the growth regressions despite low female participation rates in the labour force. The explanation may lie not just in the non-market benefits of female education (the study's suggestion), but also in the importance of female workers in exports of manufactures – though as Chapter 2 by Berge and Wood in the present volume makes clear, further research is needed on this topic.
9. On Japan, see Koike (1987), Konishi (1989), Taira and Levine (1992); on Taiwan see Aw and Tan (1993); more generally see various studies cited in Middleton et al. (1993).
10. Bartel and Lichtenberg (1987). They concluded that 'government subsidies and other policies which tend to encourage the acquisition of education ... will ... accelerate the rate of adoption of new technologies by lowering the costs of adjustment and implementation' (p. 10). There is, it must be said, an alternative explanation of their correlation, namely that skill- and education-intensive industries were growing faster and had progressively younger capital stocks.
11. See, for example, Lall (1989, 1990), and numerous detailed studies, some of which will be referred to below.
12. World Bank (1992: Chapter 3).
13. A large amount of the (relatively unskilled) sewing stage of shoe manufacture transferred virtually overnight from Bangladesh to the Dominican Republic to be close to American markets (World Bank 1992). Final assembly and processing of shoes for OECD country markets often now take place in those countries, for related reasons. For other aspects of the 'new competition', see Michael Best's well-known work of that title (Best 1990).
14. Dahlman and Westphal (1982). This was also found in earlier studies, for example, of the introduction of steamships on the Ohio and Mississippi rivers (Mak and Walton 1972), or of petroleum refining (Enos 1962).
15. Prais (1990).
16. Koike (1987). There is a debate in the literature on Japan: are long-term contracts designed to reduce the costs of labour turnover? Japanese workers are paid less than their marginal product at the early stage of their career, and more than the marginal product later. This certainly reduces the incentive to quit. But there is an alternative view: investment in human capital by the firm is greater if the worker's tenure is longer. The evidence does suggest that earnings profiles are less steep when the mandatory retirement age is higher – this is consistent with the long-term contract theory. (But it need not be inconsistent with human capital theory – it depends *which* theory. We return to this issue below.) On this discussion see Clark and Ogawa (1992) and Lazear (1979).
17. Koike and Inoki (eds) (1990).
18. For example, Lillard and Tan (1986), Tan et al. (1991) and Mincer (1990). Enos (1993) has a number of further interesting observations, although its forecasting method is in the 'manpower-planning' mode.
19. Daly, Hitchens and Wagner (1985).
20. However, it has been argued by Kelly (1986) that the problem is rather a qualitative lack of motivation and performance than a quantitative shortage of specific skills, in the sense that the job gets done, eventually, but not well.

21. UNDP (1992).
22. Cohen (1985), cited in Middleton et al. (1993).
23. Lee (1985), cited in ibid.
24. Konishi (1989).
25. Aw and Tan, (1993).
26. Adams, Goldfarb and Kelly (1992).
27. See Chapter 2 by Kersti Berge and Adrian Wood in this book.
28. Green (1991), Booth (1991) and Greenhalgh and Stewart (1987).
29. Colclough (1971).
30. Lynch (1993). Lim and Toh (1992) find the same result in Malaysia.
31. Aw and Tan (1993).
32. Lall et al. (1994).
33. Tan et al. (1991).
34. The relationship between training incidence and mobility of the workforce is also impor-
    tant. A study of the impact of human capital variables on earnings and mobility in
    segmented labour markets in India has concluded that 'vocational or technical training
    helps allocate men more in the self-employed and unprotected wage-sector than the wage-
    sector. Training also helps women to be self-employed ... Thus, although employers
    determine which workers are to be allocated to which sector, improving education and
    training of an individual may increase her/his probability of being employed in a better
    salaried and more secure job' (Khandker 1992: 24).
35. David Soskice, 'UK's wrong turning on training', *Financial Times,* January 1990.
36. Finegold and Soskice (1988).
37. Wong (1992).
38. Kim et al. (1992).
39. See Kanawaty and de Moura Castro (1990).
40. Kim (1987).
41. Schiller and Weiss (1979) and Tan et al. (1991).
42. UNESCO (1981), cited in Adams, Middleton and Ziderman (1992). Knight and Sabot
    (1990) have also shown that the policies produced an *in*egalitarian result.
43. Middleton et al. (1991).
44. Adams, Middleton and Ziderman (1992).
45. Middleton et al. (1993). Vocational education in developed countries is a different story,
    though its success varies from country to country.
46. Lall and Wignaraja (1992).
47. Wong (1992).
48. Greig (1989).
49. Bennell (1993).
50. Godfrey (1993).
51. Lall et al. (1994).
52. Lim and Toh (1992).
53. De Koning (1993).
54. W.B. Tan et al. (1991).
55. See, for example, World Bank (1993c) on Turkey.
56. World Bank (1990).
57. Godfrey (1993).
58. Lall et al. (1994).
59. World Bank (1991).
60. See Wheeler and Mody (1991).

REFERENCES

Adams, A., R. Goldfarb and T. Kelly, (1992), *How the Macroeconomic Environment Affects Human Resource Development*, WPS No. 828, Washington, DC: World Bank.

Adams, A., J. Middleton and A. Ziderman (1992), *Manpower Planning in a Market Economy with Labour Market Signals*, WPS No. 837, Washington, DC: World Bank.

Arriagada, A. (1989), *Occupational Training among Peruvian Men*, WPS No. 207, Washington, DC: World Bank.

Aw, B.-Y. and H. Tan (1993), 'Training, Technological Capability, and Productivity: A Firm-Level Analysis of Taiwanese Manufacturing', Paper presented to the World Symposium on the Economics of Education, Manchester, May (processed).

Barro, R.J. (1991, 'Economic Growth in a Cross Section of Countries', *Quarterly Journal of Economics*, **106**, May.

Bartel, A. and F. Lichtenberg (1987), 'The Comparative Advantage of Educated Workers in Implementing New Technology', *Review of Economics and Statistics*, February,

Becker, G. (1964), *Human Capital*, Chicago: Chicago University Press.

Bennell, P. (1993), 'The Cost-Effectiveness of Alternative Training Modes in Zimbabwe', *Comparative Education Review*, **37** (4) November.

Best, M. (1990), *The New Competition*, London: Polity Press.

Booth, A. (1991), 'Job-related Formal Training: Who Receives it and What is it Worth?', *Oxford Bulletin of Economics and Statistics*, **53**.

Chapman, P. (1991), 'Institutional Aspects of Youth Employment and Training Policy in Britain: A Comment', *British Journal of Industrial Relations*, **29**.

Clark, R. and N. Ogawa (1992), 'The Effect of Mandatory Retirement on Earnings Profiles in Japan', *Industrial and Labour Relations Review*, **45** (2) January.

Colclough, C. (1971), 'Manpower Planning in Developing Countries: Some Problems – an Empirical Analysis of Occupation, Education and Training with Special Reference to Zambia', Doctoral thesis, University of Cambridge.

Dahlman, C. and L. Westphal (1982), 'Technological Effort in Industrial Development: an Interpretative Survey of Recent Research', in Stewart and James (eds) (1982).

Daly, A., D. M. W. N. Hitchens and K. Wagner (1985), 'Productivity, Machinery and Skills in a Sample of British and German Manufacturing Plants: Results of a Pilot Study', *National Institute Economic Review*, **111**, February.

Davies, S. and R. Caves (1987), *Britain's Productivity Gap*, Cambridge: Cambridge University Press.

De Koning, J. (1993), 'Evaluating Training at the Company Level', *International Journal of Manpower*, **14** (2/3).

Dertouzos, M.L., R.K. Lester, R.M. Solow and the MIT Commission on Industrial Productivity (1989), *Made in America: Regaining the Productive Edge*, Cambridge, MA: MIT Press.

Doeringer, P. and M. Piore (1971), *Internal Labour Markets and Manpower Analysis*, Lexington: D.C. Heath.

Dougherty, C. (1989), *The Cost-Effectiveness of National Training Systems in Developing Countries*, WPS No. 171, Washington, DC: World Bank.

Easterly, W., R. King, R. Levine and S. Rebelo (1993), 'Policy, Technology Adoption and Growth', in R. Solow and L. Pasinetti (eds), *Economic Growth and the Struc-*

ture of Long Term Development, International Economic Association Conference volume.

Enos, J.L. (1962), 'Invention and Innovation in the Petroleum Refining Industry', in K. Arrow (ed.), *The Rate and Direction of Inventive Capacity*, Princeton, NJ: Princeton University Press.

Enos, J.L. (1993), *The Creation of Technological Capability in Developing Countries*, London: Pinter.

Feuer, M., H. Glick and A. Desai (1991), 'Firm Financed Education and Specific Human Capital', in D. Stern and J. Ritzen (eds), *Market Failure in Training*, Berlin: Springer-Verlag.

Finegold, D. and D. Soskice (1988), 'The Failure of Training in Britain: Analysis and Prescription', *Oxford Review of Economic Policy*, **4**.

Godfrey, M. (1993), *Labour Market Monitoring and Employment Policy in a Developing Economy: A Study of Indonesia*, New Delhi: ILO/ARTEP.

Green, A. and H. Steedman (1993), *Educational Provision, Educational Attainment and the Needs of Industry*, Report Series No. 5, National Institute of Economic and Social Research.

Green, F. (1991) *The Determinants of Training of Male and Female Employees in Britain*, Discussion Paper No. 153, University of Leicester.

Greenhalgh, C. and G. Mavrotas (1993), 'Workforce Training in the Thatcher Era: Market Forces and Market Failures', *International Journal of Manpower*, **14** (2/3).

Greenhalgh, C. and G. Mavrotas (1996), 'Job Training, New Technology and Labour Turnover', *British Journal of Industrial Relations*, **34** (1), March, 131–50.

Greenhalgh, C. and M. Stewart (1987), 'The Effects and Determinants of Training', *Oxford Bulletin of Economics and Statistics*, **49**.

Greig, F. (1989), *Enterprise Training in Developed and Developing Countries*, PHREE Paper, September, Washington DC: World Bank.

Hashimoto, M. (1981), 'Firm-specific Human Capital as a Shared Investment', *American Economic Review*, June.

Hollander, S. (1965), *The Sources of Increased Efficiency*, Cambridge: MIT University Press.

Kanawaty, G. and C. de Moura Castro (1990), 'New Directions for Training: An Agenda for Action', *International Labour Review*, **129** (6).

Katz, E. and A. Ziderman (1990), 'Investment in General Training: The Role of Information and Labour Mobility', *Economic Journal*, **100**.

Kelly, T. (1986), 'Labour Market Efficiency', Paper presented to the ARPLA symposium on Labour Market Information Functions of Labour Administration, Indonesia.

Khandker, S. (1992), *Earnings, Occupational Choice, and Mobility in Segmented Labour Markets of India*, Discussion Paper No. 154, Washington DC: World Bank.

Kim, C.-O., Y.K. Kim and C.-B. Yoon (1992), 'Korean Telecommunications Development: Achievements and Cautionary Lessons', *World Development*, **20** (12) December.

Kim., S. (1987), *In-service Training as an Instrument for the Development of Human Resources in Korea*, Paris: OECD Development Centre.

Knight, J.B. and R.H. Sabot (1990), *Education, Productivity and Inequality: The East African Natural Experiment*, Oxford: Oxford University Press.

Koike, K. (1987), 'Human Resource Development and Labour-Management Relations', in K. Yamamura and Y. Yasuba (eds) *The Political Economy of Japan*, Stanford University Press.

Koike, K. and T. Inoki (eds) (1990), *Skill Formation in Japan and Southeast Asia*, Tokyo: University of Tokyo Press.

Konishi, Y. (1989), *A Quantitative Analysis of Educational Policies in Postwar Japan*, Kobe, Japan: Research for Economics and Business Administration, Kobe University.

Lall, S. (1989), 'Building Industrial Competitiveness in Developing Countries', Development Centre Studies, Paris: OECD.

Lall, S. (1990), 'Explaining Industrial Success in the Developing World', in V.N. Balasubramanyam and S. Lall (eds), *Current Issues in Development Economics*, London: Macmillan.

Lall, S. (1994), *Malaysia's Export Performance and its Sustainability*, Report to the Asian Development Bank, Manila.

Lall, S., G.B. Navaretti, S. Teitel and G. Wignaraja (1994), *Technology and Enterprise Development: Ghana under Structural Adjustment*, London: Macmillan.

Lall, S. and G. Wignaraja (1992), *Foreign Involvement by European Firms and Garment Exports by Developing Countries*, Development Studies Working Papers No. 54, Queen Elizabeth House (Oxford)/Centro Studi Luca d'Agliano (Turin), November.

Lazear, E. (1979), 'Why is There Mandatory Retirement?', *Journal of Political Economy*, **87** (6) December.

Lillard, L. and H. Tan (1986), *Private Sector Training: Who Gets it and Why?*, The Rand Corporation.

Lim, T.G. and K.W. Toh (1992), *Industrial Restructuring and Skills Enhancement in Malaysia*, ILO/ARTEP, Working Paper, New Delhi, December.

Lucas, R. (1988), 'On the Mechanics of Economic Development', *Journal of Monetary Economics*, **22**.

Lynch, L. (1993), 'The Economics of Youth Training in the United States', *Economic Journal*, **103**, September.

Maizels, A. (1992), *Commodities in Crisis*, Oxford, Clarendon Press.

Mak, J. and G.M. Walton (1972), 'Steamboats and the Great Productivity Surge in River Transportation', *Journal of Economic History*, **32** (3) September.

Middleton, J. and T. Demsky (1988), *World Bank Investment in Vocational Education and Training*, WPS No. 24, Washington, DC: World Bank.

Middleton, J., N. Poapongsakorn, O. Regel and C. Sujatanond (1991), *Vocational Training in a Changing Economy: The Case of Thailand*, PHREE Paper, January, Washington, DC: World Bank.

Middleton, J., A. Ziderman and A. Adams (1993), *Skills for Productivity: Vocational Education in Developing Countries*, Baltimore, MD: Johns Hopkins University Press.

Mincer, J.B. (1990), 'Labour Market Effects of Human Capital and of its Adjustment to Technological Change', Department of Economics, Columbia University, New York.

Prais, S. (1990), *Productivity, Education and Training*, London: National Institute of Economic and Social Research.

Romer, P. (1986), 'Increasing Returns and Long-Run Growth', *Journal of Political Economy*, **94**.

Romer, P. (1990), 'Endogenous Technological Change', *Journal of Political Economy*.

Sabot, R.H. (1993), 'Skills Development in East Asia: Some Evidence and Comparative Perspectives', Washington DC: World Bank.

Schiller, B. and R. Weiss (1979), 'The Impact of Private Pensions on Firm Attachment', *Quarterly Journal of Economics.*

Schott, K. (1981), *Industrial Innovation in the U.K., Canada and the U.S.A.*, London: British North American Committee.

Soskice, D. (1993), The German Apprenticeship Model: A Simple Model, Paper presented to the International Conference on The Skills Gap and Economic Activity, Birkbeck College, University of London, April.

Steedman, H. (1993), 'The Economics of Youth Training in Germany', *Economic Journal*, **103**, September.

Stern, D. and J. Ritzen (1991), 'Introduction and Overview', in D. Stern and J. Ritzen (eds), *Market Failure in Training*, Berlin: Springer-Verlag.

Stevens, M. (1993), 'Transferable Training and Market Failure', paper presented in the International Conference on The Skills Gap and Economic Activity, Birkbeck College, University of London, April.

Stewart, F. and H. James (eds) (1982), *The Economics of New Technology in Developing Countries*, Boulder, Colo: Westview Press.

Taira, K. and Levine, S. (1992), 'Education and Labour Skills in Postwar Japan', in R. Leestma and H.J. Walberg (eds), *Japanese Educational Productivity*, Michigan Papers in Japanese Studies No. 22, Center for Japanese Studies, Ann Arbor.

Tan, H. (1980), 'Human Capital and Technological Change', Ph.D. Thesis, Yale University.

Tan, H. (1990), *Private Sector Training in the U.S.: Who Gets It and Why?*, The Rand Corporation.

Tan, H., B. Chapman, C. Peterson, and A. Booth (1991), 'Youth Training in the U.S., Great Britain and Australia', *Research in Labour Economics*, **13.**

UNDP (1992), *Human Development Report*, New York: UNDP.

US Congress (1990), Office of Technology Assessment, *Worker Training: Competing in the New International Economy*, OTA–ITE–457, Washington, DC.

Wheeler, D. and A. Mody (1991), 'International Investment Location Decisions', Industry and Energy Dept., World Bank, Washington, DC (processed).

Wong, S.H. (1992), 'Exploiting Information Technology: A Case Study of Singapore', *World Development*, **20** (12) December.

World Bank (1990), *Bangladesh: Vocational and Technical Education Review*, World Bank Country Study, Washington, DC.

World Bank (1991), 'Indonesia: Employment and Training Foundations for Industrialisation in the 1990s', Population and Human Resources Division, The World Bank, Washington DC.

World Bank (1991), *Vocational Training on the Threshold of the 1990s*, Vols I and II, February.

World Bank (1992), *Global Economic Prospects and the Developing Countries*, Washington, DC: World Bank.

World Bank (1993a), *The East Asian Miracle: Economic Growth and Public Policy*, A World Bank Policy Research Report, Oxford University Press.

World Bank (1993b), *World Development Report*, Washington, DC: World Bank.

World Bank (1993c), *Turkey: Informatics and Economic Modernization*, World Bank Country Study, Washington, DC.

Ziderman, A. (1988), *Social Rates of Return to Manpower Training Programmes: The Policy Context*, PHREE Paper, Washington, DC: World Bank.

APPENDIX

Theory of Training Provision by the Firm

The economic theory of training descends in the modern literature from Becker (1964) and his 'human capital' model. The distinction between 'general' and 'specific' training is of paramount importance in this tradition. General training is defined as portable skills which command an equal return in other firms. Becker concludes that since generally-trained workers are paid their marginal product, the return to general training accrues to the individual worker. This has important implications for the financing of this type of training: because individual workers reap the benefits of the investment, employers will not be inclined to finance it.

At the other end of the spectrum, specific training, that is, training that is of value only to the firm providing it, is financed by the firm, which can later pay the trainee less than the value of his/her output to recoup the cost, as firm-specific skills do not give the trainee any opportunity to sell his/her skills elsewhere at a higher price. The underlying assumptions for the operation of the above two training markets are: no uncertainty as to the value of future returns, no borrowing limitations restricting the private financing of human capital and no turnover of workers who have received firm-financed specific training.

This dichotomy of training markets has been criticized in the relevant literature.[1] First, it has been argued that Becker's model is unable to explain many types of training which could reasonably be described as generating occupationally-specific but not firm-specific skills (Greenhalgh and Mavrotas 1996). Most skills can only be characterized as 'locally general' (more than one employer will value the skills at the same price) even if they are 'globally specific' (not all employers in the whole economy will value them equally).

Second, uncertainty about productivity after training provides another argument against the Becker model. Uncertainty and transaction costs may lead to sharing of specific training investment, where the sharing ratio is chosen to minimize losses due to labour turnover (Hashimoto 1981). Third, information asymmetry can also reverse the conclusions of the model (Katz and Ziderman 1990). It has been argued that even general training can be financed partly by employers if there is an information asymmetry between the trainee's current employer and alternative employers as to the value of training. Katz and Ziderman support the idea that potential recruiters do not possess much information on the extent and type of workers' on-the-job training. This results in substantial information-based costs for firms that recruit rather than train (for example, opportunity costs, actual expenses and increased exposure to risk). The final result is that the recruiting firm places a lower value on a recruited worker with general training than the firm that trained him/her. The above informational asymmetry implies that a firm may find it feasible to finance part or even all of a worker's general training.

Stevens (1993) has considered the case where any training provided by the firm has both general and specific features, but the balance can be altered in one or other direction. The concept of 'transferable training' is of relevance here. It is defined as 'training for skills which are of some potential value to other firms in addition to the training firm, but for which there is no assumption about the nature of labour market competition'.[2] Within this framework of analysis, both parties bear some of the costs, with the cost-sharing ratio as well as the balance between general and specific elements in the training programme being endogenously determined. The exogenous factors are the *ex ante* uncertainty to the individual of the value of the skills inside and outside the firm, and the conditional probabilities of quits or layoffs for workers of given skill types. In this context, it is shown that labour turnover is higher for workers who are less specifically trained under plausible assumptions.

It has also been argued that many skills may not be specific to firms but may, instead, be specific to the technologies used by firms (Tan 1980). In a technology-specific skills model, skills derived from new technologies are firm-specific to the innovating firm as long as it is able to monopolize that technology; as that technology diffuses to other firms able to use the new skills, the skills become increasingly transferable.

Finally, Koike and Inoki (1990) observe that there are many determinants of workers' loyalty to their firm, including the longevity of the firm and its likelihood of survival in the marketplace, as well as pay and other standard features. Further, it is not necessary that *all* the skills workers acquire by training have to be firm-specific in order for workers to have incentives to stay with a firm; in their study, it suffices if 10–20 per cent of skills are firm-specific.

NOTES

1. Complementarity between general and specific training is also possible and has been emphasized by Stern and Ritzen (1991) and Feuer, Glick and Desai (1991). The result is underinvestment in general skills. Chapman (1991) has also criticized the neoclassical model of Becker as too simplistic and developed instead an eclectic approach which incorporates efficiency wage theory and emphasizes the problems associated with imperfect information.
2. Stevens (1993: 5).

6. State failure or market failure? The ten steps to a levy-grant system of vocational training

Chris Edwards*

INTRODUCTION

This chapter is about the theory and practice of vocational training (VT). I start by looking at the economics of VT and at ten steps which lead logically to a levy-grant system. A levy-grant system is defined as one where companies (whether public or private) have to pay a training tax or levy into a fund and then get the whole or part rebated in the form of grants for expenditure on approved training schemes.

Economists differ considerably about the desirability of levy-grant systems for VT. Right-wing economists emphasize state failure and advocate leaving VT to the market. Shackleton (1993) is one of these and argues that the strong pressures behind a state push for training can be explained by public choice analysis – namely that 'many interest groups stand to gain from government regulation or funding for training' (Shackleton 1993: 37). Many of the writings on VT from the World Bank also take a pro-free-market, anti-interventionist line emphasizing the likelihood of state rather than market failure (see Dougherty 1989; Dougherty and Tan 1991; and World Bank 1991; for a critical review of World Bank 1991, see Lauglo 1992). By contrast, Keynesian economists put the emphasis on market failure and the desirability of state intervention to correct for market failure (see Hutton 1995 and Stewart 1993; 97). On the Marxist left, there has been something of a neglect of VT. In the 1960s and 1970s, this was due to an emphasis on Fordism and the associated focus on deskilling by Braverman (Braverman 1974). By the 1980s, the left pendulum had swung well away from Fordism and deskilling and has been in danger of *over*emphasizing general skills (as opposed to industry-specific skills) in the context of flexible specialization (see Murray 1985 and, for a non-leftist source, Piore and Sabel 1984).

In this chapter I attempt to look at some of the arguments for particular VT arrangements in the light of economic theory and then at the practices or experiences of a range of countries. But first it is necessary to answer the question, *what is vocational training?*

A *vocational skill* is generally defined as a skill *specific to a particular occupation*. Thus the term can embrace skills *specific* to a particular employer[1] or skills which are *transferable or marketable* across an 'industry' – that is, where a number of employers produce similar goods and/or are involved in similar production processes. If the skills are totally transferable and can be used in any industry, they are not vocational skills but are general educational skills. Thus vocational training can be defined as training which imparts employer-specific skills or skills which are transferable between employers within an industry. For the design of a VT system, this distinction is important as are *two further* distinctions, namely:

1. that between the skills required by *existing* employers and industries and skills likely to be demanded in the *future*; and
2. that between skills imparted to *new* entrants to the labour force and skills required by the *existing* labour force.

The second distinction is important because it is estimated that in the UK more than 80 per cent of the workforce likely to be working in the year 2000 was already in work by the end of 1993 (TIC 1993/94: 85).

Although in theory these three distinctions are quite clear, in practice they are quite difficult to make. Thus employer-specific and marketable skills may be complementary; skill accumulation may lead to, as well as follow from, new production processes; and skills acquired by one employee may be transferred to new entrants without any 'formal training'. For these reasons, and others such as the problems of measuring training costs (for example, the opportunity cost of trainers' time) and benefits or returns (not least the in-training returns), it is perhaps not surprising that estimates of net VT expenditure vary widely.

Many but by no means all estimates put British VT expenditure as well below that of its industrial competitors. Thus in Finegold and Soskice we are told that British firms have been estimated to devote 0.15 per cent of sales turnover to training compared with 1–2 per cent in Japan, France and West Germany (1988: 23) while the TIC quotes figures that put UK expenditure well below that of France and slightly below that of Germany (TIC 1993/94: 85). An estimate by Dolton puts the expenditure by the average British company as only a third of that in Germany and only a fifth of that in Japan (Dolton 1993: 1266). By contrast, Dore and Sako estimate that Japanese employers spend well below 1 per cent of GNP on VT whereas British public and private employers spend 1.85 per cent (1989: 144) and Lynch (1994: 12) quotes figures for the mid- to late-1980s of training expenditure as a percentage of the total wage bill as follows: UK 1.3; West Germany 1.8; France 1.6; US 1.8; and Japan 0.4.

Clearly the estimates of total training expenditure vary considerably, but measuring the training input is not the only problem. What also matters is the cost-effectiveness of the expenditure. In this respect, because of the lack of tracer or longitudinal studies, the information is even more crude.

Given the problems of specifying in practice what are, and what are not vocational skills and what is and what is not VT, it is almost impossible to identify such a thing as a 'VT system' (see Twining 1993: 2). Nevertheless, in this chapter, I attempt to look first at the economic principles behind VT and then to look at the greatly differing VT practices in a number of countries to see how their 'systems' relate to the theory. Does this considerable variation in VT structures mean that some countries have followed wrong policies? Or does it mean that different training structures are appropriate to different political and economic conditions or both? And, if so, what factors are important? Does it mean that countries have structures which are inappropriate even to their particular political and economic conditions? These are the questions that I try to address in the final section of the chapter. The first stage in an attempt to answer them is to take a closer look at the ten steps leading to a levy-grant system, which I do in the next section.

STATE FAILURE OR MARKET FAILURE? THE TEN STEPS TO A LEVY-GRANT SYSTEM

Step 1 in Box 1 sets out the assumption that *an employer's competitiveness is an (inverse) function of the cost per unit of production which in turn is an (inverse) function of productivity.* This simply states that those producers are the most competitive who can produce at the lowest unit cost. Cost here includes a rate of profit that will keep the producer in the market. Thus a reasonable long-term assumption is that those employers who produce at the lowest cost of production will be most competitive. To produce at lower and lower cost over time means that employers have to increase total factor productivity or, with a given capital stock, increase labour productivity.

Step 2 assumes that, for any given physical capital stock, *labour productivity is a function of skill in the labour force.* Thus higher labour productivity is assumed to be generated by higher skills and if the higher labour productivity outweighs the higher wage rates which may be paid for higher skills, then there will be a lower labour cost per unit of output and a lower cost of production per unit (allowing for product quality and capital intensity).

Step 3 simply assumes that *skill in the labour force is a function of training and qualifications* and step 4 assumes (from steps 2 and 3) that *productivity*

Box 1   The ten logical steps to a levy-grant system

Start with 4 assumptions:

1   competitiveness = f(costs) = f(total factor productivity)
2   for a given capital intensity, productivity (and wages) = f(skill in labour force)
3   skill in labour force = f(training, qualifications)

and from 2 and 3:

4   productivity (and wages) = f(training, qualifications).

Therefore, from 4, there is an incentive for both employers and employees to promote training and the acquisition of qualifications. But these incentives are conditional on how the particular labour market works and on *who finances the acquisition of skills/ qualifications*. Is it:

5   **The employee?**
   ● by taking a 'low' wage apprenticeship, or:
   ● by paying for the training outside the workplace (assuming the qualification is widely accepted); or is it:

6   **The employer?**
   ● this is the more likely, the lower the training costs, the more the skills are specific to the employer and/or the lower the labour turnover from the employer.

From 5 and 6 it follows that if there is:
   ● no low-wage apprenticeship system, and
   ● no certainty of the value of the qualification; and if:
   ● the skills are not firm-specific and there is a high rate of labour turnover, then:

7   Training is likely to be *socially suboptimal* and there will be an incentive for free-riding, '*poaching*' or 'cherry-picking'.

Solutions?

8   **The government provides and pays for the training**
   ● advantages; such central (supply-led) provision
      – can take advantage of any economies of scale in training;
      – may be able to 'pick winners' (anticipate new skills);
   ● disadvantage;
      – the training may be 'supply-led' and not match the needs of the employers (whether in the public or private sectors).

9   **Employers provide but government pays for the training**
   ● advantage:
      – more incentive than under 8 to provide 'suitable' (demand-led) training; but
   ● disadvantage:
      – problems of 'moral hazard' (the employer may oversupply at the cost of public finance) or, if the skills are employer specific, the government may be supplying skills which the employer would have provided anyway.

So

10   **Is a levy-grant system the final solution?**
   ● a levy-grant system is where either employers or the state (or both in close conjunction) provide the training but where employers pay for the training through a payroll levy or tax and are then reimbursed through grants to cover part or whole of the cost of 'approved' and certifiable training
   ● advantages:
      – training is 'demand-led';
      – there is an incentive for firms to adopt a 'training culture' since they have to pay for training anyway;
      – problems of bureaucratic expense in ensuring that the training is 'approved', that is, that the training has been provided at the right level.

(and wages) are a function of skill and therefore of training and qualifications.

There are, of course, a huge number of questions raised by steps 2 and 3. Step 2 raises questions about the role of skills and 'human capital' in economic growth. The answer to this is not at all clear. In neoclassical growth theory, it has been assumed that as physical and human capital accumulate, their incremental contribution to output diminishes. An alternative ('endogenous growth') model is one in which there are dynamic economies of scale so that increments to physical and human capital make increasing contributions to output as economies get richer. Thus high education and skill *levels* give rise to the adoption and adaptation of better technology which generates growth (see OECD 1994, 115). Perhaps, not surprisingly, given these different formulations, there is no firm conclusion about the precise role of human capital in economic growth.

In Solow's neoclassical model (Solow 1957), there was a significant residual component which was unexplained by growth in physical capital and labour. Since this was correlated with measures of educational achievement (such as primary and secondary school enrolment), it was inferred that human capital generally plays an important role in economic growth. More recently, the World Bank's study of growth in eight high-performing Asian economies (HPAEs) concluded that primary school enrolment played a statistically significant role in cross-economy regression tests of growth, but only a small part of the *differences* in growth between the 8 HPAEs and more than 100 other economies could be explained by conventional economic variables (World Bank 1993, 51 and 54). Thus there is something of a black hole in the explanation of growth, but the belief is widespread that skill is an important component of growth, particularly in the 'endogenous' models (see OECD 1994: 115 and Pack in Helleiner (ed.) 1992).

From steps 2 and 3, an important additional question that arises is, how do we measure skill in the labour force? Clearly, in terms of step 2, the argument is circular if we measure skills by wage rates. Then do we measure skills by qualifications? What if the qualifications, however, are not adding to productivity but are simply a function of screening or credentialism? (see Perlman 1988: 84). And if screening or credentialism are thought to be prevalent, then using years of schooling as a measure may be equally suspect[2]. In this context, the cross-sectional studies carried out by the London-based National Institute of Economic and Social Research (NIESR) over the past decade seem to be on firmer ground. These studies have looked at plants producing similar goods in different countries and after making due allowances for differences in the age and composition of physical capital stock, the productivities of the plants are compared together with the skills or qualifications of the workers.[3] The conclusions are generally that the productivity differences are due to differences in qualifications, although Shackleton (1993: 30) is sceptical, raising the possibility that the productivity differences may be due to differences in physical capital (in spite of the attempts to control for these) or to 'managerial cultures'.

If from steps 2, 3 and 4, we can say that labour productivity (and wages) are a function of skills, that skill is a function of training and qualifications, and that therefore productivity (and wages) are a function of training and qualifications, then there may be a clear *incentive for either employers or employees (or both) to promote the acquisition of those qualifications*. This leads us to the questions: how do the incentives occur and how can and do employees and employers respond to the incentives?

The neoclassical argument derived from Becker (1964) has been that only under certain special conditions will employers have an incentive to invest in 'marketable skills' but that employees are likely to see training as an investment in human capital and be willing to make the sacrifice of having lower earnings during the training period in return for a higher wage in the future. A large literature and numerous empirical studies on rates (both private and social) of return to education and training have followed Becker with some writers (for example, Eckaus in 1993 in response to a 1992 Becker paper) emphasizing the importance of incorporating uncertainty, instability and market friction into the Becker-type analysis.

Thus in a Becker-type analysis, *employees may be prepared to take a low net income now in return for a higher wage promised by a higher qualification in the future*. This is step 5. If the qualification is likely to give rise to a higher wage and/or status in the future, there is an incentive for individual employees to accept a lower net income now by either

i.   accepting a lower wage now in return for an 'apprenticed' training provided by the employer and a reasonable assurance of a higher wage in the future; or
ii. paying the costs of training themselves (including the cost of a reduction in leisure and the fees for training courses) outside or alongside the direct employment.

In a Becker-type model, the employee is more likely to be willing to make the sacrifice to achieve the qualification

● the less specific the qualification is to a particular employer;
● the more likely the qualification is to be recognized outside the employer;
● the higher the future wage (and or job status, security and/or satisfaction); and

- the lower the cost of the training (the 'imputed' cost will be lower the greater the enjoyment of the training process itself).

Thus step 5 sets out the incentive for the employee to undergo training. But there are also *possible responses by employers*. This is step 6. An employer is more likely to be willing to pay for the employee's training the higher the discounted surplus from training over the costs. The discounted surplus will be greater

- the lower is the wage rate after the training period relative to the higher productivity attributable to the employee;
- the more likely it is that the employee will remain with the employer; and
- the lower the costs of training, where these include any difference between the employee's net output and wage costs during training as well as the more obvious resource costs of training. Thus a low-wage apprenticeship is likely to mean lower net costs associated with training.

Logically steps 5 and 6 take us on to step 7 which is the possibility that *the level of training will be socially suboptimal*, that is, that the incentive for training on the part of both employees and employers may be too weak to achieve the level of training which gives the best return to society. Thus for skills which are not firm specific, each firm will hope that other firms undertake training so as to provide a pool of skilled labour which it can tap. At the same time it may want to avoid incurring the costs of training itself; that is, it will want to be a 'free-rider' and to be able to 'poach' or 'cherry-pick' qualified labour away from other firms.

This is a notable example of the 'Prisoner's Dilemma' type of game which as Hargreaves and Varoufakis put it: 'fascinates social scientists because it is an interaction where the individual pursuit of what seems rational produces a collectively self-defeating result' (Hargreaves and Varoufakis 1995: 146).

In the particular context of training (see Chapman 1993: 97 and 98), the best collective solution may be for all employers to train and yet individual 'rationality' leads to a situation in which employers are reluctant to train since, if they do, they subsidize the 'poachers'. Training is therefore socially suboptimal – that is, although there are high social returns to training, the training does not take place although, as we shall see, different institutional structures are more or less successful in overcoming potential market failures in the provision of general training (see also Lynch 1994 (ed.): 22). The problem of suboptimal training may occur even in the case of skills which are firm-specific if labour turnover is high or expected to be so (see OECD 1994,

146) but sub-optimality is most likely where the skills are not firm-specific. In this case (of transferable skills), there is an incentive to poach.

Dougherty and Tan (1991: 50) cast doubt on whether poaching takes place since, they argue, the trainee gets the benefit of the training, not the employer who is allegedly doing the poaching. But this argument makes the extremely strong (pre-capital-theory) assumption that the trained worker is paid not only a wage higher than a trainee, but a wage equal to the value of his/her marginal productivity.[4] At the level of the aggregate economy, this assumption is theoretically fragile, to say the least. However, even if the marginal productivity theory is thought to hold, the employer who is alleged to be poaching will gain a competitive edge if there are net costs in training. The arguments of Dougherty and Tan are *theoretically* weak and *practically* fly in the face of numerous allegations of poaching by employers.

The likelihood of poaching and of a socially suboptimal outcome is the more likely:

- the less employer-specific (or the more industry-specific) the skills;
- the higher the job mobility between firms;[5]
- the greater the uncertainty about the future demand for qualifications (skills); and
- the harder it is to get information about training, qualifications and so on (see OECD 1994: 149).

Under these assumptions, there is a strong case for an interventionist policy designed to create a better training market as well as to correct for market imperfections. Two possible training models may be thought to provide a solution to the problem.

First (and I call this step 8), there is the *state training model*. Under this model, the government not only pays for but also runs the training centres for each industry. The case for this will be stronger the less employer-specific are the skills and the greater the economies of scale in training. Also the case for state provision or coordination is stronger if the skills are not now in demand but likely to be required by industries emerging in the future. But the more the skills *are* in demand now, and the more they are employer-specific, the greater is the danger either that the state-provided skills will be inappropriate to employers (whether in the public or private sector) or that the training will constitute a specific subsidy to a particular employer. Thus government skill centres make more sense the more the skills are general and transferable – that is, where there is a strong felt need for 'flexible specialization'. Thus government training centres may have an advantage in being able to anticipate future skills, but they have a disadvantage in not being sufficiently accountable to the firms demanding the skills. As a result, the model may suffer from being excessively 'supply-led' and from producing skills which are not wanted by employers.

A second possible solution to the 'poaching' problem goes to the other extreme of state provision. This is where the training is provided by employers but where finance comes from government grants. This I call the *voluntarist model* (step 9). In this model, training is demand-led (unlike the supply-led state model) and 'free-riding' and 'poaching' are avoided, inasmuch as (in the absence of fraud), employers do not gain if they do not train. Nevertheless the problem of 'unfair competition' may arise where the training is employer specific and there is the problem of 'moral hazard' where employers are tempted to oversupply the training which they are being paid to provide (and a possible public finance problem).

An attempt to avoid the supply-led disadvantage of step 8 and the oversupply disadvantage of step 9 leads us on to step 10 – the *levy-grant system*. Under this scheme, the supply-led problem of the state model is avoided by employers providing the training themselves or being heavily involved in the training provision, while the moral hazard problem of the voluntarist model is avoided by employers paying for training through a levy. And in paying a levy, they are discouraged from being free-riders or from poaching.

Thus the problem of vocational training revolves around the provision of marketable skills (in this context skills that are common to an industry) both for the present and the future. As we have seen, Becker's model may provide a solution to this problem, namely that, under certain very specific conditions, the market generates an investment in industry-specific skills. But if these specific conditions do not hold, there may be a case for state intervention to correct for the inadequacies of the market and it may be that a levy-grant system provides the correct intervention. In the light of this theoretical framework, the sections which follow look at VT in a number of countries. I start with Germany, widely reckoned to have a highly successful VT system but one which is not a levy-grant system. What are the secrets of its success? This is the issue looked at in the next section.

VOCATIONAL TRAINING IN GERMANY[6] – THE 'CORPORATIST' MODEL

The German system of VT is often referred to as a 'dual' system. It is dual in the sense that training takes place at two places: the vocational school and the place of work. Learning on the job is organized mostly on the basis of a contract between the employer and the trainee. The off-the-job learning takes place mostly within part-time vocational schools (*Berufsschule*), although some training (about 8 per cent in 1991–92) takes place in full-time vocational schools (*Berufsfachschule*). The legal basis for the training of young persons is the Vocational Training Act of 1969.

Unlike the UK where apprenticeships are limited to few sectors of the economy, VT covers almost all sectors of the economy in Germany including banking and insurance, health and personal social service, and retailing as well as industry and agriculture (Casey 1986: 64). The Chambers of Commerce (*Kammer*) in Germany (to which employers have to belong – see Tonge 1993: 12) are heavily involved in registering the apprentices and setting standards for the qualifications. It is fair to say that the system is 'employer-run'. The coverage of the 'dual system' is considerable, not only in terms of sectors but also in terms of the proportion of youths that enter the system. About half of the persons reaching school-leaving age go into apprenticeships in Germany compared with less than one-sixth in France and the UK (see Casey 1986: 64 and Steedman 1993: 1284).

Most young people start their 'dual training' at the end of full-time compulsory education although the average age of apprentices has risen from 16.6 years in 1970 to 18.5 years in 1987 (Casey 1991: 208) and the training takes about three years. The examination standards apply throughout the country and ensure minimum qualifications for each occupation.

Most of the financing (in the early 1980s about two-thirds of the total) for VT comes from the employers. The part-time vocational schools are funded by the state governments (*Länder*) and some training centres are supported by Federal and regional grants.

With the unification of East and West Germany, there was no great upheaval because, although there were some differences, the system of VT in the German Democratic Republic had the same roots (Casey 1991: 221).

The German system of VT is recognized as a successful one with a long record of continuity and stability dating back at least a century. It is reflected in (relative to the UK) low youth unemployment (Casey 1986: 63) and, together with the compulsory educational system, it seems to produce superior results in terms of productivity (see Prais 1981; Prais and Wagner 1983, and 1988; Steedman and Wagner 1987, 1989). It emerged intact after something of a crisis in the early 1980s (Casey 1991: 218) and has been so successful that the 1993/94 Report of the Trade and Industry Committee of the UK's House of Commons called for it to be copied in the UK.

In a later section I discuss whether the German system can be copied in the UK. Here in the rest of this section, I address two linked questions. First what makes the German system so successful? And secondly what is the training incentive structure for employees and employers?

For *employees*, there is the knowledge that the qualifications will be worth a lot and will pay off at the end of the training period. The contents of the qualifications are set out in the Regulations of the Vocational Training Act (as revised) and the standards are set nationally and examined by the local chambers of industry and commerce. The system has had a great deal of continuity so that the trainee has a strong expectation that the qualification that he or she expects to get at the end of three years will be accepted. The 'information imperfections' are small (see Steedman 1993: 1283). In addition precisely because the system is so widespread, there are very few unskilled, well-paid jobs. All of this means that, as Crouch puts it: 'The majority of young people accept the trade-off between low wages in the short term and the acquisition of a useful skill in the long term' (Crouch 1992: 34 and 35).

The wages of the apprentices are low. They are paid training allowances which are only about a third of adult rates – whereas in the UK the proportion is well over half (see Casey 1986, 66; Chapman 1993: 122; OECD 1994: 143; and Steedman 1993: 1283). These low training allowances provide *employers* with an incentive to train or at least reduce their reluctance not to train. Casey has estimated that even the net costs of training to employers are quite low and that, allowing for a likely overstatement of costs and under-statement of returns from apprentices, training might well be costless or even profitable for many enterprises (Casey 1986, 67 and 70).

Nevertheless for large companies, with net costs of training, employers have some disincentive to train. Why, then, do the large employers pay for what appears to be transferable training? One part-answer is that German companies are locked into high-skill, high-value-added production and can only hope to retain competitiveness both nationally and internationally by obtaining the most able of the young people seeking apprenticeship. Because of the strong collectively-organized employers and employees, the coopera-tive industrial relations and the tightly regulated wages structure, the chances of later recruiting the best of those trained by others is low (Franz and Soskice 1994: 20 and 21 and Winkelman 1994: 7). 'Poaching' is small. A second part of the answer is that the transferable skills and employer-specific skills are complementary (Franz and Soskice 1994: 15 and 19).

Thus the incentive structure interlocks with institutional factors to encour-age employers in Germany to train (Finegold 1991). *First* there is a strong collective pressure (though no formal sanctions) from the Associations or Chambers to train (see Crouch 1992: 35) and the VT system is buttressed by a set of detailed regulations. *Secondly* there seems to be a general willingness on the part of companies in Germany to take 'risky', long-term decisions to invest in research and development and to train, protected as they are from hostile takeover bids and other short-termist influences. This contrasts sharply with the British economy (see Eltis et al. 1992) and is a factor emphasized by Finegold in his D.Phil. study of education and training (see Finegold 1992: Chapter 2). *Thirdly* the job turnover rates of the companies investing most heavily in training are small (see Casey 1986: 67 and 68).

It is the strong collective pressure that induces Colin Crouch to refer to the German model as a corporatist model but he emphasizes that it is not a model which has been widely copied. He points out that it is found in Austria and Switzerland but they have emerged 'within similar histories'. As Crouch puts it: 'Real institutional imitation is very difficult' (Crouch 1992: 35).

Furthermore it is worth asking whether it is even worth attempting to copy, since there are a number of weaknesses that have been identified by various researchers, namely:

1. the system is said to be inflexible due to the high degree of regulation to which it is subject (Casey 1991: 214);
2. the training is said to be too specific and not transferable and is said to be based less on standards than on time-serving; and,
3. there is no guarantee of employment following the apprenticeship and the unemployment rate is higher for 20–24 year olds than for those under 19 (Casey 1986: 72 and 74).

The first may be said to be a price worth paying to achieve the confidence in which the system is held by apprentices and employers. The evidence for the second is said to be that many companies train beyond the standards set by the qualifications but this may be a necessary adjustment to changing circumstances. The alternative of changing the Regulations frequently might shake the confidence of the 'market' in the acceptability of the qualifications, although the Regulations have been periodically modified in the light of the changing skill composition of occupations (Casey 1991, 215). Thirdly, by the end of the 1980s, the problem was less severe as the average duration of unemployment after an apprenticeship had shortened (Casey 1991: 206).

In brief, in spite of these weaknesses, the German system is generally acknowledged to have operated successfully and to have adapted to changing needs with the use of outside training establishments (subsidized by the state) and group-firm training where firms are too small or too specialized to provide all the relevant training required by the state regulations. As Steedman puts it: 'it is difficult for an outside observer to perceive any fundamental weakness in its massive institutional underpinning and firm public support' (Steedman 1993: 1288).

Therefore, the German system meets the conditions of steps 5 and 6 in Box 1. The incentive structure is sufficiently strong and stable so that when combined with the institutional factors of long-term corporate finance, strong collective employer and employee organizations and a cooperative industrial relations structure, it encourages a successful apprenticeship system. As a result it has not been thought necessary to introduce a levy-grant system although, in the mid-1970s a law was put on the Statute Book authorizing the

Federal government to impose a levy on firms not offering apprenticeships if the supply of apprenticeships was below a certain level. In fact the levy was not enforced and the law was abolished in 1980 (Franz and Soskice 1994: 7). By the end of the 1980s, the calls for a statutory obligation to provide apprenticeship places and for a levy-grant scheme to finance training activity were no longer heard (Casey 1991: 218). In the mid-1980s, a crisis shortage of apprenticeships which had been exacerbated by a demographic rise in the 16–19 age group (Casey 1991: 206) was averted by a collective effort from the employers, backed by the Christian Democratic Party. Later, in the 1990s, a different sort of demographic pressure – a drop in the 16-19 age group – has been averted by immigration from East Germany (Casey 1991: 218) and the 'dual system' remains intact.

VT IN JAPAN – THE 'COMPANY' MODEL

It is somewhat ironic that in the 1870s a delegation of Japanese statesmen visited the US and the UK for almost a year to see what made Britain and America so prosperous while Japan remained so poor (Dore and Sako 1989: ix). A little over a century later, the tables were turned and economists were spending much time trying to understand the source of the Japanese miracle and what the US and the UK could learn from Japan. By the 1990s, Japan's average income (GNP) per capita was more than a quarter higher than the US's and almost three-quarters up on the UK's (see World Bank 1995: Table 1). Japan had succeeded in more than just catching up following the 'unequal treaties' of the 1850s.

Various studies have emphasized the high standards of full-time education in Japan and in particular the high standards in mathematics and engineering (see, for example, Dore and Sako 1989: 1 and Prais 1987). Employers in Japan can therefore build on this to get the multiskilled and adaptable workforce needed, as Prais points out, for a world of rapidly-changing technology. Dore and Sako argue that the tremendous effort and expenditure on education and the well-defined educational structure in Japan stem from the national effort to catch up and the Confucian respect for education, although they stress that some Confucian Analects (such as the distaste for manual labour) have been rejected (Dore and Sako 1989: 4 and 13).

A well-developed system of VT builds on the foundation laid by the basic education. The state plays a prominent role and selection for VT takes place at both the high-school and university levels (Dore and Sako 1989: 21). However, there is strong competition in the provision of VT both between ministries and between the state and the private sector (Dore and Sako 1989, 57 and 60), although the latter is not heavily subsidized. By contrast with the system in the US, the Japanese system is particularly good at educating and training the bottom half in the ability range (Dore and Sako 1989, xii).

The training structure is highly functional to the needs of industry because of the detailed structure of tests administered generally not by the training institutions but by users or customers (Dore and Sako 1989: xiv, 101 and 118). Certification by the state (as opposed to professional associations) dates back to the Meiji Restoration of the 1870s (Dore and Sako 1989, 119). However, the most significant aspect of Japanese training is the on-the-job training in the context of the tradition of lifetime employment. It is this combination of lifetime employment and a culture of national education that makes companies into teaching/learning organizations (Dore and Sako 1989: xvi). Lifetime employment is especially important for the large firms (each employing more than a thousand workers) which employ something like a fifth of all workers in Japan (Dore and Sako 1989: 76). For Japanese companies as a whole, labour-force turnover averages only about 10 per cent a year and is considerably less in the large companies. However, it is important to emphasize that, in terms of labour turnover, there is *not* a sharp dichotomy between large and small firms in Japan. Instead there is a spectrum and even the smaller firms have low labour turnover rates compared with other industrial countries (Dore and Sako 1989, 110). In addition, subcontracting by large companies to small and the close links between them are important in helping to keep up skill levels in small firms (Dore and Sako 1989: 110).

Thus most employers are happy to provide training and retraining in both marketable (industry-specific) skills as well as firm-specific skills and in Japan there is a strong commitment to VT similar to that to basic education. The strong VT system builds on a strong foundation of basic education. As a result, Dore and Sako claim, Japanese companies probably spend no more and probably less on training than their British counterparts (1989: 144 – but, as pointed out earlier, the statistics are shaky). Certainly, it seems that the training is much more cost-effective.

Nevertheless the system is not beyond criticism. The basic education and the formal VT are said to be lacking in creativity, and in recent years there has been a greater emphasis on retraining and on what has been called 'vocational ability development' and 'self-enlightenment' (Dore and Sako 1989: 150). In spite of this, an extensive 1984 Review of Education recommended few changes (Dore and Sako 1989: 11) and the VT system continues to be widely acknowledged as successful. Its basis is the intensity of the basic education, the continuity of its standards and testing structure but above all the teaching/learning culture of the Japanese companies in the context of the lifetime employment system. This is why it seems sensible to refer to it as a 'company' as opposed to the German 'corporatist' model.

THE STATE-DIRECTED MODEL OF VT – LESSONS FROM SRI LANKA AND MALAYSIA

In both Sri Lanka and Malaysia, VT has been state dominated in that a large number of VT institutes have been financed and run by government agencies. In both countries these state-run systems have been strongly criticized.

In *Sri Lanka*, there has been considerable criticism of the government-dominated VT structure. Kelly has estimated that there are more than 3,000 publicly-supported training programmes in the country being operated by 20 different ministries (Kelly 1992: 24) and, not surprisingly, it is widely argued that there is considerable duplication between the programmes. In addition, most training centres are criticized for being too small to achieve economies of scale and for having inadequate links with industry. The latter criticism, namely, that the VT training system has been supply-led and that it has not provided the skills needed by employers, has been particularly prominent and those few VT institutes (notably the Clothing Industry Training Institute and the National Textile Training Centre) which do seem to have had some success in placing their trainees in jobs, are striking exceptions in that they do have close links with industry.

In 1990, in an attempt to rationalize the situation, the government established the Tertiary and Vocational Education Commission (TVEC) through the Tertiary and Vocational Education Act. At the same time, in attempts to reduce the high (more than 30 per cent) dropout rate of apprentices, to increase the proportion of apprentices who are retained by enterprises at the end of their training and to move towards a national certification scheme, the National Apprenticeship and Industrial Training Authority (NAITA) was established to replace the former National Apprentice Board. NAITA's role is to plan, organize and provide VT, to set standards, to conduct trade tests and to advise the TVEC on VT, but some observers have been critical of the overlap between NAITA and the TVEC.

Apprentices in Sri Lanka are paid by the government (in 1994, SL Rs 450 or about $9 per month) and since there is no contributory requirement from enterprises and no obligation on the part of enterprises to employ the apprentices at the end of the programme, the accusation is that apprentices simply constitute a source of cheap labour.

The cost to the government of the vocational training is estimated to be something like SL Rs 420 million (World Bank 1992, 3). This is about 1 per cent to 1.5 per cent of value added in the manufacturing sector and the system is widely accused of being wasteful since more than half of the trainees fail to get jobs within one or two years of completing training,[7] which is partly a reflection of the lack of linkages between the training suppliers and users (Kelly 1992: 14 and 15).

As a result of these inadequacies, the establishment of a Skill Development Fund has been under discussion for some time in Sri Lanka. In February 1992, the government announced its intention to establish such a fund with an initial budget of SL Rs 1 million (see *Daily News*, 1 February 1992: 1 and 14) and in September–October 1992, a World Bank paper argued that such a fund might be set up initially from government funds with, later, the cost being wholly or partially transferred to industry (World Bank 1992: 5). However, at the time of writing, this fund has still not been established, partly it seems because of the lack of a competency-based testing and certification scheme.

In *Malaysia*, there have been similar criticisms of the VT system. The main conclusions of a study of industrial training carried out in 1984 were:

- most industrial training in Malaysia was on the job; less than 5 per cent of skilled workers obtained their skills before joining industry (see Scott 1984: para. 103);
- most on-the-job training was unstructured and led to low productivity (para. 104);
- the use of off-the-job training (in government-run Industrial Training Institutes – ITIs) by firms was limited because the manufacturing sector perceived the courses as being not immediately applicable to their needs (para. 106);
- in general, firms had not been involved in planning and funding VT and ensuring a major role for industry was seen as a prerequisite for facilitating effective vocational training in the future (para. 107);
- the ratio of skilled to unskilled workers in Malaysia was only about a quarter of that in Japan or the US (para. 109);
- vocational training in Malaysia would have to improve in terms of both quantity[8] and quality if the Malaysian manufacturing sector was to be upgraded.

To promote this improvement the Scott report recommended that:

- a National Vocational Training Board (NVTB) be created and, under it, Industrial Training Councils be established for subsectors of manufacturing industry (para. 112);
- norms for training spending by firms be set by the ITCs.

The Scott report hinted at the desirability of a levy-grant system but did not go so far as to recommend one.

The recommendations of the Scott report were not implemented. In 1985 and 1986, there was a sharp recession in the Malaysian economy but with the resumption of a rapid rate of growth in the second half of the 1980s, considerable skill shortages in the Malaysian economy were evident. In 1989, a study by Guy Standing for a Human Resources Development project observed that the majority of manufacturing enterprises in Malaysia conducted no formal training of their employees and only about 15 per cent did any training at all (see MHR 1991: 17). Standing's study was followed by a study of VT by the Malaysian government (the Economic Planning Unit) and the Asian Development Bank in 1991 and in May of the same year a Cabinet Committee on Training under the chairmanship of the Minister of Education issued a report. The Committee, which had been established in March 1990, collected (through Working Groups) information on the skills required in six areas (electrical and electronic, textile, construction, information technology, wood-based and a group of five other manufacturing subsectors) and made recommendations on how to overcome any skill shortages. A common weakness identified in these sectors was the lack of public–private sector collaboration in training and the prevalence of poaching (MHR 1991: 8, 28 and 30). The Committee argued that:

> The majority of the public educational and training institutions lack the mechanism of feedback response which could enable them to detect and respond to changes in the labour markets. ... Courses offered by many of these training institutions are too basic and not job-specific. ... Contacts with the private sectors or industries are not institutionalised in advisory committees for the majority of training institutions. (MHR 1991: 32)

In short, the Committee argued, 'Existing government training institutions are not market driven' and there was a need for 'much greater inputs from the private sector which, after all, is the major user of skills' (MHR 1991: 43 and 53).

The Committee concluded that 'there is thus a need for governmental interventions to stimulate a greater level of investment in skill training. Intervention could be in the form of *providing better financial incentives for employers and employees for manpower training and development*' (MHR 1991: 36; added emphasis).

Thus this time there was a stronger hint at the need for some sort of levy-grant or pay-and-play system and finally a Human Resources Development Levy was introduced with effect from January 1993, levied at the rate of 1 per cent of the payroll on all manufacturing enterprises employing more than 50 employees. The levy was to be administered by a Council, with a majority of the members coming from the private sector. A paper produced by the Ministry of Human Resources and outlining how the scheme would work emphasized the importance of generating a training culture through a 'critical mass' of companies involved in training and retraining. The paper, quoting a 1988 study by Daniel Bas in support (see Bas 1988), argued that such a culture would be encouraged by a training levy and proposed that companies would be encouraged to train through grants to be administered by a Human Resources Development Council. These grants would reimburse between 60 per cent and 80 per cent of the training costs depending on the type of training (MHR 1991).

Thus in Malaysia dissatisfaction with a supply-led model of VT and a high level of poaching has led to the introduction of a levy-grant system, a system which had long been in existence in Singapore, as discussed in the next section.

A LEVY-GRANT SYSTEM IN OPERATION – A CASE STUDY OF SINGAPORE

In 1990, levy-grant systems were reported to be in operation in more than 30 countries, most of which were in the lower- to middle-income bracket (see Middleton et al. 1993: 123). As we have seen, a levy-grant scheme was introduced in Malaysia in 1993.[9]

Bas claims that 'levies to finance training have generally had positive results. They have made it possible to redistribute costs among the principal beneficiaries and have made all the parties involved more aware of the problems of training' although he concedes that small and medium-sized employers have often been neglected by such schemes (Bas 1988: 367).

The reaction of a World Bank paper to levy-grant systems is more circumspect than Bas when it states that:

> there has been mixed success in establishing training funds. ... Where governments have set up such funds, without clear plans for training or adequate training capacity in industry and without full participation of industry, the results have usually been failures and have not led to any significant improvement or expansion in enterprise training. (World Bank 1992: 5)

One country in which a levy-grant funding scheme seems not to have been a failure is *Singapore*. There, a Skills Development Fund was established. This was financed from a levy at the rate of 4 per cent of payroll in 1979 which was then, at the time of the recession in the mid-1980s, reduced first to 2 per cent (in 1985) and then to 1 per cent (in 1986). It was introduced in 1979 as part of the government's attempts to restructure the economy away from labour-intensive industries to high skill-intensive, high-value-added industries, that is to promote a shift towards a high-skill, high-wage economy. This was part of a move away from a growing dependence on low-wage imported labour. The levy in 1979 was accompanied by a sharp rise in wages recommended by the National Wages Council and by an increase in the employers' contribution to the national superannuation scheme (the Central Provident Fund-CPF) (see Chapter 4 by Cheah in this book and Rodan 1989: 144).

The levy was, and is, payable only on low-wage workers – those paid *less than* S$750 a month – in 1991 this lower limit was raised to S$1,000 a month (SDF 1990/91: 3). The objective of the Skills Development Fund was to encourage employers to train employees and to retrain retrenched workers and the levy is a tax without a *quid pro quo*, meaning that for any given employers the benefits are not related to contributions. In recent years SDF grants have exceeded the income from levies – for example in 1990–91 grants totalled S$60 million compared with a grant income of S$20 million with most of the balance being covered by interest on the large reserves built up through the early 1980s when the levy was at a higher rate.

The levy proceeds are used to finance grants from the Skills Development Fund to which employers are encouraged to apply. The *main* grant scheme has been the Training Grants Scheme, Under this, grants are given for all types of skill training programmes with an emphasis on the upgrading of workers earning S$1,000 a month or less. The grants cover between 50 per cent and 80 per cent of the public courses, and grants are payable up to certain maxima for in-house training programmes. In 1988, a *second* scheme was introduced called the Emerging/Critical Skills Programme, replaced in 1993 by a "High-End Skills' Programme. Under these schemes, grants have provided enhanced incentive funding for training in skills which have a strategic impact on the economic development of Singapore – that is, for skills which were likely to be in demand in the future. A *third* scheme (the Training Leave Scheme) was designed to encourage the training of older workers. *Finally* grants have been provided for the development of training infrastructure – one example being an Increasing Training Opportunities (INTRO) scheme which was launched in 1987 and was designed to encourage employers to share their in-house expertise, facilities and training programmes with other companies (see Cheah, Chapter 4 in this book, for details of further SDF programmes introduced in the first half of the 1980s).

The grants in Singapore are provided only for employer-based training to ensure (as the SDF puts it) 'the accountability of the workplace' (SDF 1992: 1), but in the late 1980s, the emphasis of the SDF changed from one of generating a high level of specific-skill training activity among employers to encouraging them to boost the transferable skills of existing workers through planned training (and retraining) programmes so that the workforce is more flexible and responsive to new work processes. Finally, in addition to the schemes for improving the training infrastructure, some of which are designed to help small and medium businesses, in 1990 the SDF introduced a Training Voucher System (TVS) with an emphasis on employers with less than 50 workers. It allows such employers to pay only 50 per cent or 80 per cent of training costs while the SDF pays the balance.

The Skills Development Fund in Singapore was introduced at a time when the Singaporean economy was facing a critical labour shortage and when it was relying increasingly on imported labour. The SDF has been comprehensive inasmuch as it has encouraged the development of skills:

- in existing processes for existing workers;
- in existing processes for new entrants;
- in emerging processes and technologies for both the new and existing labour force;
- for small and medium-sized employers through the INTRO scheme; and finally,
- for the older workers.

In this way Singapore has retained a competitive advantage for many existing products but has also created a competitive advantage in new higher-skilled, higher-valued products. In so doing it has moved towards a sort of 'high-skill equilibrium' similar to that in Germany, but quite dissimilar to that of the UK which is said to be in a 'low-skill equilibrium'. It is the British 'system' that is discussed in the next section.

VOCATIONAL TRAINING IN BRITAIN – FROM VOLUNTARISM TO A LEVY-GRANT SYSTEM AND BACK TO VOLUNTARISM

In the UK, there has been a widespread argument for some time that skilled labour is, and has been, in short supply and that this shortage goes a long way to explaining the weak performance of the British economy. Eric Hobsbawm has argued that 'The British ... entered the twentieth century and the age of modern science and technology as a spectacularly ill-educated people' (1968: 169) and turn-of-the-century complaints about how Britain's poor training record limited economic competitiveness can be found in the report of the 1884 Royal Commission on Technical Instruction (see King 1993: 216).

Almost a century later, in 1993–94, the lack of skills was still being cited as a major problem. Thus a House of Commons Trade and Industry Committee stated that: 'Many of our witnesses regarded the level of skills in the workforce as the central problem affecting UK manufacturing. Given that it is becoming ever easier to transfer capital and technology around the world, the skills of the workforce will increasingly be the determining factor in the competitiveness of different countries' (TIC 1993/94, 81).

The low level of skills in Britain is derived from weaknesses in both general education and in VT. At the level of general education, there are indications that:

- at the primary and secondary levels, British children perform relatively poorly in internationally comparable tests. With regard to science, English 10 year olds and 14 year olds on average lag behind children of the same age in most of 17 other countries (see Finegold and Soskice 1988: 223 and TIC 1993/94: 83);
- compared to competitor nations, higher education participation rates are low in the UK (see TIC 1993/94: 84; although see Williams 1992).

Not only does Britain lag behind competing industrial countries in general education, but also, as we have seen, expenditure in Britain on VT lags behind its competitors.

Given the weakness of both general and vocational education, it is perhaps not surprising that the British workforce is poorly qualified (see TIC 1993/ 94: 84), comparing unfavourably with Canada, Germany, the Netherlands, France and Japan (see Green in Glyn and Miliband (eds) 1994: 69). These studies claimed to show a relationship between the low education-and-qualifications level and low labour productivity. The TIC report on the *Competitiveness of UK Manufacturing Industry* in 1993–94 pointed out that the principal conclusion of the studies carried out by the NIESR – comparing performance in a range of matched industries in the UK, Germany, France, the Netherlands, Switzerland and the US – was that it was not equipment that accounted for the UK's poor competitiveness but lack of training, qualifications and skills at all levels in the workforce (TIC 1993/94: 82).

Thus it seems that there are deficiencies *both* in full-time British education *and* in VT (in terms of both quantity and quality). As a result, far from VT in Britain compensating for the deficiencies of general education, if anything, it has made the situation worse.

What, then, is the 'British model' of VT? The first point to make is that there has been no one model of British VT. Indeed a major problem of British VT has been the enormous number of changes in the training structure that have taken place over the past four decades.

The history of British VT since 1945 has been one of 'from voluntarism to voluntarism'. Before 1964 there was a reliance on an apprenticeship system which was inadequate because, at the factory level, the apprentice/skilled-labour wage ratio was too high and the qualification system too fragmented. At the aggregate level, the stop–go economic policy and short-termist outlook of employers combined to discourage significant investment in human capital. The situation was critical as neither step 5 nor step 6 in Box 1 were operative.

In 1964, policy shifted to step 10, with the introduction of a levy-grant system. The advocates of the system have argued that:

- the quality if not the quantity of training was improving, and
- a training culture was being created;

while the detractors have emphasized that:

- a cumbersome bureaucracy emerged as a result of the excessive number of Training Boards, and
- the training provided was too narrow and specialized.

In 1973, with the establishment of the Manpower Services Commission, there was a move to coordinate national training needs, but at the same time the levy-grant system was diluted. In terms of Box 1, there was a move from step 10 to a mixture of steps 8 and 9, with the government financing the training but with both the government and the employers providing the training, and the move away from the levy-grant system was completed in 1981 when the Boards were largely wiped out. Finally, the move back to voluntarism went further in the late 1980s when semi-autonomous Training and Enterprise Councils (TECs) were set up.

In the eyes of many of the economists and industrial sociologists who have looked at VT in Britain, the structure does little to alleviate the critical skill shortage. It is widely argued that the starting point is weak inasmuch as the system of general education is largely irrelevant to the needs of industry.[10] But far from VT compensating for these inadequacies, if anything, VT has made the situation worse. Relative to the wages of skilled labour, trainees' wages have been driven down over the past 20 years (Green in Glyn and Miliband (eds) 1994: 77), but this wage reduction has not been sufficient to entice a large increase in training by employers. The financial structure within which industrial Britain operates is so short term, labour turnover so fast, and the manufacturing sector so subject to a low and volatile demand for skills that the economy is described as being in a 'low-skill equilibrium' (see Finegold and Soskice 1988 and Keep and Mayhew 1993).

This 'low-skill equilibrium' is both a consequence and a cause of the poor economic performance. It is a *consequence* because Britain was the first industrialized economy and as such produced mass-production goods using 'Fordist' techniques which required only a small number of skilled workers. It is a *cause* because the absence of a well-educated and trained workforce has given the British economy little capability to respond to new economic conditions. Thus the low-skill economy in the UK is in a sort of equilibrium with the policy emphasis being on deregulation and 'labour-market flexibility', of lowering real wage rates and encouraging labour-intensive, low-value-added sectors rather than knowledge-intensive, high-value-added manufactures. As Mason et al. point out: 'given the present structure of workforce skills in Britain – heavily polarised between a small minority of highly-qualified personnel and a large majority of low-skilled workers – it is understandable that many branches of British manufacturing have tended to specialise in highly automated mass production of relatively low value added goods' (1994: 76). One concern about this pattern of specialization must be the limitations it places on the future growth in real incomes in Britain especially as competition is increasingly with the newly-industrialized countries (NICs) which have cheaper social infrastructures (Crouch 1992: 44).

There is considerable agreement that the UK's skills level has to be raised. It was with this aim in mind that National Education and Training Targets were drawn up by the CBI in 1989 and endorsed by the government in 1991. These set out various targets for new entrants and for the existing labour force in terms of NVQs up to the year 2000 (see CBI: 1989 and TIC 1993/94: 97).[11] Although the CBI's report referred to 'world class targets' it has been admitted that the targets are well below the plans and targets of competing countries (see TIC 1993/94: 99).

The CBI set out a number of conditions for the targets to be reached: educational reform; establishment of a national framework of qualifications and standards; effective local delivery of VT; employers taking their full responsibility for training; and employers, individuals and the government meeting their share of the cost (CBI 1989: 7, and 11–12).

But what is meant by effective local delivery of VT and how should the cost be shared? These are two of the crucial questions. In other words what changes to the VT system in Britain are necessary?

The TIC report's recommendation was that 'the Government consider ways of developing Youth Training into a system similar to Germany's dual system covering all 16 to 18 year-olds whether employed or not' (TIC 1993/94: 103) but David Soskice rejects this as a serious possibility. He argues that 'the UK should hold no serious hope of emergence from its low skill equilibrium via the route of company-based initial training' (Soskice 1993: 111). Soskice's argument is that this is the route that has been tried for some years in the UK and failed. He also argues that this failure has been inevitable given the lack of underlying institutions (long-term financial provision, cooperative industrial relations systems and powerful collectively-organized employers) appropriate to a successful company-based training structure (Soskice 1993: 111). The long-term finance is necessary to encourage the employers to risk long-term investments in human capital; the collectively-organized employers are necessary to enable training expertise to be shared and to deter 'poaching'; and cooperative industrial relations are necessary to enable employees and employers to have trust that the reward structure for training will be stable (see Soskice 1993: 103).

Thus Soskice's argument (see also Steedman 1993: 1289) is that for training to operate in the UK along German lines requires the creation of *institutional structures* similar to those in Germany. He argues that such radical institutional restructuring is unlikely and that since the institutional structure in the UK is somewhat similar to that in the US (short-term finance and weak collective organizations of capital and labour), then his tentative conclusion is that there is a strong case for a reorientation of labour-market policy and of policy-related research away from initial VT and towards mass post-16 and higher education (Soskice 1993: 102). In brief, his argument is that the UK has institutions similar to those of the US and therefore it should have a system of vocational education and training similar to that of the US (for a summary of the latter, see Box 2). He argues that not only is this – sharply increasing post-16 staying-on and university participation rates – consistent with the latest shift in UK policy but also that such a move will provide the social, organizational and computing skills required in an increasingly service and client-dominated economy (Soskice 1993: 101 and 111).

However, Soskice admits that this policy suggestion may seem odd and that it invites criticisms which highlight the weaknesses of the US approach. These weaknesses are the neglect of the bottom third or so of the labour force – of lower-level employees and of youth in some inner city and rural areas; the waste of the educational system in the US; an inadequate creation of the capacity for incremental product and process innovation within manufacturing; and the low academic attainment in many subjects (Soskice 1993: 104). He counters that in the UK there is already an underclass (which has been failed by the VT systems of the past two decades or so), but he also recognizes that in ruling out a company-based training route he is rejecting 'what some have seen as the most hopeful way of reducing this underclass' (Soskice 1993: 112). To help the underclass, he argues that alongside the mass higher education for the top two-thirds, there would need to be a restructuring of education and training for the bottom third 'if we are not to end up in an American situation' (Soskice 1993: 112 and 113).

Thus in arguing that 'effective initial training systems in which private companies play a central role require fundamental socio-economic institutions which the UK does not have' (Soskice 1993: 102), Soskice provides a stark choice, namely, either reform the institutional structure or go down an education and training route which is appropriate to the broader institutional structure.

One way of attempting to alter the institutional structure would be to reintroduce a levy-grant system. There are many such calls in the UK for such a reintroduction. The major political opposition parties – that is, Labour

**Box 2	Vocational training in the US – a model for the UK?**

Apprenticeships in the US are few and far between and of low quality. There is a low completion rate (see Lynch 1993: 1293) and high (geographic) mobility, and relatively high wages for apprentices (at 60 per cent of the adult rate) have meant that employers are discouraged from taking on apprentices (Lynch 1993: 1293 and 1294). Less than 3 per cent of labour-force entrants go into apprenticeships (Lynch 1993: 1294).

The most common way for those of the 140 million labour force in the US who get training and education is through further education following high school (Lynch 1993: 1295 and 1994: 6). In 1985, 58 per cent of the high school graduates went on to further education (Perlman 1988: 82) – a rapidly increasing percentage of women (see Lynch 1993: 1295). This training is provided by the public and private sector, but about 80 per cent is in a highly decentralized public sector (Perlman 1988: 91). However, progress through higher education is slow because of the necessity for students to work their way through and there is a high dropout rate (Perlman 1988: 92). Because of the high dropout rates, almost 60 per cent of young men and women by the age of 25 have received no formal training after completing school (see Lynch 1993: 1296).

Private rates of return to training are higher than another year of schooling (Lynch 1993: 1297) but Perlman (1988: 84) raises the question as to whether the social rate of return is much lower, the difference being due to the training acting as a manifestation of credentialism. Because of this and the high dropout rates, there are widespread allegations of waste (Perlman 1988: 85 and 92). The trend in colleges towards occupational (vocational) training may (Perlman claims) add to productivity (1988, 85), but at the same time the number of years of schooling for most jobs has increased and overeducation is widely adduced (Perlman 1988: 86).

In brief the 'school-to-work' transition in the US is 'chaotic' (Heckman 1993: 7) and part of the reason given for the weakness of the VT institutional structure in the US is the historical dependence on immigrant skilled labour (Lynch 1994: 6). In addition to the waste (due to the dropout rate and the credentialism), there is a significant undereducated underclass (OECD 1994: 123 and Perlman 1988: 93).

Most private-sector training does not provide nationally-recognized qualifications and most company training is highly firm-specific (Lynch 1993: 1297 and 1299).

It is in the context of these weaknesses of the US system that there has been some discussion of the introduction of an employer-training tax in the US (see Lynch 1993: 1299).

and the Liberal Democrats – have argued for the imposition of such a system, with the Liberal Democrats arguing that a remissible Training Levy is backed by the OECD's 1994 *Jobs Study* (see Liberal Democrats 1994: 11 and Senker 1995: 3). The Trades Union Congress and many of the affiliated Unions are also in favour of a levy-grant system (see TUC 1994: 13 and MSF 1992: 12) as are some employers (see TIC 1993/94: 104).

By contrast, the CBI (the major employer's organization in the UK) is not convinced that a levy-grant system is needed (see TIC 1993/94: 104) and, as we have seen, nor is the Conservative Party which favours a 'voluntarist' approach. However, given the broader institutional structure in the UK, I agree with Soskice that a company-based VT is unlikely to be any more successful in the future than it is at present or has been in the past.

CONCLUDING COMMENTS

I started this chapter by setting out a Becker-type model through which human capital may be generated through vocational training 'using market forces'. However, in looking at the case studies of a number of countries, it is clear that the original Becker model was too neo-liberal in its formulation. It was too neo-liberal not only in assuming a marginal productivity theory of wage determination (with or without increasing returns to scale) but also because of its assumptions about the way in which markets work. Becker's model needs to be modified to recognize that the incentives for the creation of human capital (as set out in steps 5 and 6 of Box 1) will only be operative if the market signals are sufficiently strong to be heard and acted on. Thus employers and employees need to know that the incentives are in existence and that they will remain in existence. This trust will be a function of both the stability and continuity of the incentives and the institutional context of which the market is a part.

Thus in the case of Germany, which was discussed in the third section, the 'dual' system operates highly successfully. The system has operated for some decades with the incentive system working well because of the trust built up over time as a result of the institutional context within which it operates, namely long-term corporate finance, strong collective employer and employee organizations and a cooperative industrial relations structure – in short, a 'social market' (see Hutton 1995).

In Japan (discussed in the fourth section) the VT system, though quite different from that of Germany, works equally well if not better. The VT system in Japan has a good foundation in terms of basic education but the 'VT market' works well precisely because of a major market imperfection, namely the lack of job mobility. As a result the VT is employer-led with few transactions and monitoring costs.

It is clear, then, that the incentives set out in steps 5 and 6 of Box 1 work well in Germany and Japan. This is not the case in Sri Lanka and Malaysia, the country case studies discussed in the fifth section. In both countries, the VT system has been state-led, largely through VT institutes. The potential defects of state-led systems are twofold: that employers are not encouraged to be active in training provision and, precisely because they are not, the VT is criticized for not being geared to the needs of employers. Both defects have been all too apparent in Sri Lanka and Malaysia, where levy-grant systems have been under discussion for some time. To date, no such system has been set up in Sri Lanka but a levy-grant system has been in operation in Malaysia since 1993.

Similarly (as described in the sixth section) a Skills Development Fund has been in operation in Singapore since 1979, with the grants from the fund being aimed at generating skills for existing workers and new entrants in relation not only to existing processes and products but also to emerging processes and products. Thus the SDF in Singapore is recognized to have played a major role in the restructuring of the economy towards high-skill, high-value-added manufacturing and service sectors.

By contrast, the UK is trapped in a 'low-skill equilibrium'. The seventh section discussed the immense number of changes that have taken place in the VT structure in the UK over the past four decades. The structure has gone from a voluntarist in-company VT system, through a levy-grant scheme and then back to voluntarism. The most recent moves in the 1990s have been the setting up of Training and Enterprise Councils with a more recent policy shift towards increasing post-16 staying-on and university participation rates.

It is not surprising that a recent report states that 'Britain's education and training is an inefficient and confusing mess' (Bennett et al. 1992). Most researchers who have studied the TECs are highly critical of them, and in a recent provocative paper David Soskice argues for the adoption of a VT structure similar to that of the US. His reasoning is that not only would such a structure (VT through mass post-16 and higher education) provide the social, organizational and computing skills likely to be in demand in the UK economy but that such a VT structure would be consistent with British institutions.

Where I agree with Soskice is that the voluntarist system in Britain has not succeeded and cannot succeed in overcoming the acute skill shortage. I also agree that the institutional structure is such that a dual system along German lines is not workable. However, the American and German systems are not the only alternatives. I view the recommendation of an American system as a 'counsel of despair' in that it would not be cost-effective and would perpetu-ate, as Soskice admits, the inequalities in the UK – what Hutton calls the '30–30–40 society' (Hutton 1995). A superior third option is the reintroduction of a levy-grant system for, as in Sri Lanka, Malaysia and Singapore, the necessary market conditions (as in steps 5 and 6 of Box 1) do not exist for the creation of skills in the right quantity and quality.

In the UK, as in many other countries, the market structure has to be modified in order to work effectively. As Hilary Metcalfe has put it: 'It is ... clear that reliance on market forces alone will not work when the market is imperfect' (Metcalfe 1993: 56). Thus the VT market in the UK needs modifying. However, the paradoxical situation is that the modification will have to remain in existence for some time for it to work effectively and for it to pull the UK economy out of its low-skill equilibrium. In the same way that for steps 5 and 6 in Box 1 to work, the incentives have to be stable, so too is the same stability required for step 10 – a levy-grant system. The paradox in the economics of VT, as in so many other areas of economics, is that imperfect markets need to be moulded and modified to work effectively but at the same time the modifications need to be infrequent if the markets are to work effectively.

NOTES

* The assistance of Maureen Fell in writing this chapter is gratefully acknowledged, as are the comments of Martin Godfrey, Rosalind Malt and numerous others, although I take full responsibility for the views expressed.

1. Here I use the term 'employer' to denote a 'firm' or 'company' employing wage labour in the pursuit of profit. It is important to note that in this chapter I am discussing the incentives and arrangements for VT in the production of *traded, manufactured goods*.

2. However, various studies have found rates of return to schooling to be as high among self-employed workers, implying that schooling does contribute to productivity and is *not* merely a screening device (OECD 1994: 119).

3. For a good discussion of these studies, see Ashton et al. in Green (ed.) 1989: 134 and 135.

4. It is important to note here that Becker also makes this assumption, which I reject. This is why I refer in this chapter to a 'Becker-type' analysis.

5. Thus the *greater* the contractual and legal barriers to job mobility and worker layoffs, the more likely it is that the training market will work *efficiently* (OECD 1994: 148).

6. In this chapter I look at the VT 'systems' in two member countries of the European Union, namely, Germany and the UK. In this context, it is important to note that the principle of 'subsidiarity' applies – that is, under the Treaty of Rome (establishing the EEC) and the Treaty on European Union (signed at Maastricht in December 1991) the organization and content of VT is the primary responsibility of the member countries.

7. One major problem of assessing the efficiency of VT in Sri Lanka is the lack of longitudinal or tracer studies so that little is known about where skilled labour comes from and how it is trained, although Kelly (1993: 31) reported that a number of tracer studies had been initiated by the World Bank through the TVEC.

8. It is worth noting that although in the early 1980s government-run schemes dominated VT, the amount spent on such training in Malaysia was small, being less than 5 per cent of the amount spent on 'mainstream secondary education' (see Bas 1988: 357).

9. In 1990 a Training Guarantee Scheme was introduced in Australia. Under this, employers were required to spend 1 per cent of their payroll on training with any shortfall having to be paid to the government. In 1994 the Scheme was suspended after numerous criticisms from employers (see Senker 1995: 29–32).

10. Given the Conservative Party's strong ideological commitment to voluntarism in vocational training, it is perhaps not surprising that most policy interventions in recent years have been in the area of general education policy, which has been notable for its rapidity and frequency of change (Crouch 1992: 46).
11. New targets were set out in a 1995 White Paper entitled *Competitiveness: Forging Ahead* (see DTI 1995).

REFERENCES

Bas, D. (1988), 'Cost-effectiveness of Training in Developing Countries', *International Labour Review*, **127** (3), 355–369.

Becker, G. (1964), *Human Capital: A Theoretical and Empirical Analysis with Special Reference to Education*, New York: NBER.

Bennett, R., H. Glennerster and D. Nevinson (1992), *Learning Should Pay*, Dorset: BP Educational Service.

Braverman, H. (1974), *Labour and Monopoly Capital: The Degradation of Work in the Twentieth Century*, New York: Monthly Review Press.

Casey, B. (1986), 'The Dual Apprenticeship System and the Recruitment and Retention of Young Persons in West Germany', *British Journal of Industrial Relations*, **24** (1), March, 63–81.

Casey, B. (1991), 'Recent Developments in the German Apprenticeship System', *British Journal of Industrial Relations*, Vol 2, June, 205–22.

CBI (1989), *Towards a Skills Revolution*, London: Confederation of British Industry.

Chapman, Paul G. (1993), *The Economics of Training*, New York/London: Harvester Wheatsheaf.

Crouch, C. (1992), 'The Dilemmas of Vocational Training Policy: Some Comparative Lessons', *Policy Studies*, **13** (4), Winter, 33–48.

Department of Education and Science (1991), *Education and Training for the 21st Century*, London: HMSO.

Dolton, P.J. (1993), 'The Economics of Youth Training in Britain', *Economic Journal*, **103**, September, 1261–78.

Dore, R. and M. Sako (1989), *How the Japanese Learn to Work*, London: Routledge.

Dougherty, C. (1989), *The Cost-Effectiveness of National Training Systems in Developing Countries*, World Bank Working Paper No. 171, Washington, March.

Dougherty, C. and Tan (1991), *Financing Training, Issues and Options*, World Bank Working Paper No. 716, Washington, July.

DTI (Department of Trade and Industry) (1995), *Competitiveness: Forging Ahead*, London: HMSO.

Eckaus, R.S. (1963), 'Investment in Human Beings: A Comment', *Journal of Political Economy*, **LXXI** (5), 501–4.

Finegold, D. (1991), 'Institutional Incentives and Skill Creation: Preconditions for a High-Skill Equilibrium', in P. Ryan (ed.), *International Comparisons of Vocational Education and Training for Intermediate Skills*, London: Falmer Press, pp. 93–116.

Finegold, D. (1992), *The Low-Skill Equilibrium: An Institutional Analysis of Britain's Education and Training Failure'*, University of Oxford, D.Phil. thesis.

Finegold, D. and D. Soskice (1988), 'The Failure of Training in Britain: Analysis and Prescription', *Oxford Review of Economic Policy*, **4** (3), 21–53.

Franz, W. and D. Soskice (1994), *The German Apprenticeship System*, Discussion Paper FS 1 94 302, Wissenschaftszentrum Berlin für Sozialforschung, Berlin.

Glyn, A. and D. Miliband (eds) (1994), *Paying for Inequality: The Economic Cost of Social Injustice*, London: IPPR/Rivers Oram Press.

Green, F. (ed.) (1989), *The Restructuring of the UK Economy*, Hemel Hempstead: Harvester Wheatsheaf.

Hargreaves, H.P. Shaun and Y. Varoufakis (1995), *Game Theory: A Critical Introduction*, London: Routledge.

Heckman, J. (1993), *Assessing Clinton's Program on Job Training, Workfare and Education in the Workplace*, Working Paper No. 4428, National Bureau of Economic Research, Massachusetts.

Helleiner, G. (ed.) (1992), *Trade Policy, Industrialisation and Development*, Oxford: Clarendon Press.

Hobsbawm, E. (1968), *Industry and Empire*, Harmondsworth: Penguin.

Hutton, W. (1995), *The State We're In*, London: Jonathan Cape.

International Association for the Evaluation of Educational Achievement (1988), *Science Achievement in Seventeen Countries*, Oxford, Pergamon Press.

Keep, E. (1986), *Designing the Stable Door: A Study of How the Youth Training Scheme was Planned*, Warwick Papers in Industrial Relations, No. 8, May.

Keep, E. and K. Mayhew (1993), 'UK Training Policy: Assumptions and Reality', paper presented to the Centre for Economic Policy Conference, The Skills Gap and Economic Activity, London, April.

Kelly, T. (1992), ' A Strategy for Skills Development and Employment Policy in Sri Lanka', Institute of Policy Studies, Colombo, Sri Lanka.

Kelly, T. (1993), 'Labour and the Numbers Racket', Institute of Policy Studies, Colombo, Sri Lanka.

King, D. S. (1993), 'The Conservatives and Training Policy 1979–1992: From a Tripartite to a Neo-Liberal Regime', *Political Studies*, **XLI**, 214–35.

Lauglo, J. (1992), 'Vocational Training and the Bankers' Faith in the Private Sector', *Comparative Education Review*, **36** (2), 227–36.

Lees, D. and B. Chiplin (1970), 'The Economics of Industrial Training', *Lloyds Bank Review*, April, 29–41.

Liberal Democrats (1994), *Working for Change: Promoting Jobs and Employability*, Policy Paper No. 9, Brighton Conference, September.

Lynch, L. (1993), 'The Economics of Youth Training in the United States', *Economic Journal*, **103**, September, 1292–302.

Lynch, L. (ed.) (1994), *Training and the Private Sector*, Cambridge, Mass: NBER.

Mason, G., B. Van Ark and K. Wagner, (1994), 'Productivity, Product Quality and Workforce Skills: Food Processing in Four European Countries', *National Institute Economic Review*, February, 62–83.

Metcalfe, H. (1993), 'Training and Education in Britain: A New Study', *Policy Studies*, **14**, 56–9.

MHR (Ministry of Human Resources) (1991), *Private Training Initiatives in Relation to the Proposed Human Resources Development Fund*, Kuala Lumpur, Malaysia: Ministry of Human Resources.

Middleton, J., A. Ziderman and A. Van Adams, (1993), *Skills for Productivity*, Oxford: Oxford University Press.

MSF (1992), *Manufacturing Matters*, London: Manufacturing, Science, Finance (MSF).

Murray, R. (1985), 'Benetton Britain', *Marxism Today*, November, 28–32.

Nolan, P. (1994), 'Labour Market Institutions, Industrial Restructuring and Unemployment in Europe', in J. Michie and J. G. Smith (eds), *Unemployment in Europe*, Academic Press, London: Harcourt, Brace and Co, pp. 61–71.

OECD (1994), *The OECD Jobs Study: Evidence and Explanations*, Paris: OECD.

Perlman, R. (1988), 'Education and Training: an American Perspective', *Oxford Review of Economic Policy*, **4** (3), 82–93.

Piore, M. and C. Sabel (1984), *The Second Industrial Divide*, New York: Basic Books.

Prais, S. (1981), 'Vocational Qualifications of the Labour Force in Britain and Germany', *National Institute Economic Review*, **98**, 47–59.

Prais, S. (1987), 'Educating for Productivity: Comparisons of Japanese and English Schooling and Vocational Preparation', *National Institute Economic Review*, **119**, February, 40–56.

Prais, S. and K. Wagner (1983), *Schooling Standards in Britain and Germany: Some Summary Comparisons Bearing on Economic Efficiency*, NIESR Discussion Paper, No 60.

Prais, S. and K. Wagner (1988), 'Productivity and Management: the Training of Foremen in Britain and Germany', *National Institute Economic Review*, **123**, 34–47.

Rodan, G. (1989), *The Political Economy of Singapore's Industrialization*, Kuala Lumpur, Malaysia: Forum.

Scott, W. D. (1984), *Industrial Training Schemes in the Manufacturing Sector*, Kuala Lumpur, Malaysia: Ministry of Human Resources.

SDF (1990/91), *Annual Report 1990/91*, Singapore: Skills Development Fund.

SDF (1992), *An Applicant's Guide to the Training Grant Scheme*, Singapore: Skills Development Fund.

Senker, P. (1992), *Industrial Training in a Cold Climate*, Aldershot: Avebury.

Senker, P. (1995), *Training Levies in Four Countries: Implications for British Industrial Training Policy*, Engineering Training Authority/Science Policy Research Unit, University of Sussex.

Shackleton, J. R. (1993), 'Investing in Training: Questioning the Conventional Wisdom', *Policy Studies*, **14** (3), Autumn, 29–40.

Solow, R. (1957), 'Technical Change and the Aggregate Production Function', *Review of Economics and Statistics*, **XXXIX**, August, 312–30.

Soskice, D. (1993), 'Social Skills From Mass Higher Education: Rethinking the Company-Based Initial Training Paradigm', *Oxford Review of Economic Policy*, **9** (3), 101–13.

Steedman, H. (1993), 'The Economics of Youth Training in Germany', *Economic Journal*, **103**, September, 1279–91.

Steedman, H. and K. Wagner (1987), 'A Second Look at Productivity, Machinery and Skills in Britain and Germany', *National Institute Economic Review* (122) 84–96.

Steedman, H. and Wagner, K. (1989), 'Productivity, Machinery and Skills: Clothing Manufacture in Britain and Germany', *National Institute Economic Review* (128) 40–57.

Stewart, M. (1993), *Keynes in the 1990s*, Harmondsworth: Penguin.

Streeck, W. et al. (1987), *The Role of Social Partners in Vocational Training in the Federal Republic of Germany*, Berlin: CEDEFOP.

TIC (Trade and Industry Committee) (1993/94), *Competitiveness of UK Manufacturing Industry*, Second Report, Session 1993/94, London: HMSO.

Tonge, J. (1993), 'Training and Enterprise Councils: the Privatisation of Britain's Unemployment Problem', *Capital and Class*, Autumn, 9–16.

TUC (1994), *A New Partnership for Company Training*, London: Trades Union Congress, August.

Twining, J. (1993), *Vocational Training and Education in the UK*, Berlin: CEDEFOP.

Williams, G. (1992), 'British Higher Education in the World League', *Oxford Review of Economic Policy*, **8** (2), 146–58.

Winkelman, R. (1994), *Training, Earnings and Mobility in Germany*, Discussion Paper, Centre for Economic Policy Research, London.

World Bank (1991), *Vocational and Technical Education and Training*, World Bank Policy Paper, Population and Human Resources Department.

World Bank (1992), *Sri Lanka; Proposed Skills Development Project*, Aide-mémoire, September/October.

World Bank (1993), *The East Asian Miracle*, New York: Oxford University Press for the World Bank.

World Bank (1995), *World Development Report*, Washington, DC: Oxford University Press.

PART IV

Structural Adjustment

7. Skill development and structural adjustment

Robert E.B. Lucas*

INTRODUCTION

This chapter explores the interconnections between structural adjustment, skills and skill generation, and considers issues in the design, promotion and implementation of skill acquisition during adjustment. The chapter begins with a general consideration as to why some form of policy intervention may be recommended, in the interests of static and dynamic efficiency as well as on grounds of equality, in the simultaneous interface between structural adjustment and skill accumulation. This theme is developed not only with respect to training and the labour market, but also with respect to such issues as investment incentives and aggregate demand management since these broader issues are central to the process of structural adjustment. Later sections of the chapter turn to the difficulties of information gathering for training policy decisions and hence to the more pragmatic issues of designing and implementing a training-education strategy in an economy undergoing adjustment.

SKILLS, COMPARATIVE ADVANTAGE AND STRUCTURAL ADJUSTMENT

In a world of increasingly sophisticated technologies, it has become more difficult to discern a country's competitive advantage in foreign trade simply in terms of labour abundance and labour intensity of alternative production activities. The profile of skills embodied in the labour force has assumed an increasing importance in shaping cost competitiveness, and not merely the size of the labour force in relation to other available inputs.

The skills of the labour force interact with the amount and composition of the capital stock, with natural resource endowments, and the state of technology available, to define the range of production in which a country is able to compete on the world market.

While some skills are highly specific to particular spheres of production, others can be transferred across a more or less extensive range of industries. Both ranges of skills help in defining competitive advantage. A labour force well endowed with basic skills and education normally means that a country will be competitive in the skill-intensive range of industries (though this may not be true if the existing capital equipment fails to take advantage of their skills, for instance). Moreover, the prior possession of highly-specific skills does help to render production in the relevant activity cheaper.

Yet the mere possession of certain skills is obviously no guarantee that the production which draws upon those skills will remain cost-effective as prices alter. The structural adjustment following a trade liberalization episode, or indeed in response to evolving shifts in the world terms of trade, will normally diminish the demand for certain skills or even render them redundant while enhancing the demands for other skills.

If the many markets drawn upon during structural adjustment each worked perfectly, then an efficient rate of retraining would be enjoyed without need for policy action. The more general forms of training, which raise productivity in jobs performed for more than one potential employer, would be financed by workers themselves, either out of savings or in the form of diminished pay while training. The costs of more specific training would typically be shared between employer and employee, with the resultant productivity gains being shared in the form of enhanced pay for the employee and rents received by the employer.

Even such an efficient process of retraining and shift towards newly-competitive industries would not result in gains for all. In the short run, we should expect real losses for workers with skills specific to declining industries (and indeed to capital owners more generally in these activities). Conversely there may be substantial windfall gains to those with skills (and capital) specific to the newly-competitive spheres, at least during the transition period. Whether this results in a widening in income inequality depends very much upon in whom the specific skills are embodied (and who possess the specific capital). For instance, if skilled workers in the previously protected, declining industries were a relatively privileged group and those enjoying windfall returns on their newly-demanded skills are less privileged, this will tend to generate a more even distribution of income even while pursuing greater efficiency, though the converse is also entirely possible.

Although perfect markets may offer an efficient pattern of retraining, this will be drawn out over a more or less extended period for two reasons. First, training itself requires time: some speeding up may be feasible but in the end there is a tradeoff between skill absorption and compression of training. Second, structural adjustment in labour and other associated markets (such as switching to new investments and penetrating product markets) is normally spread out over time. The most common explanation for decisions to defer adjustments is rising costs of adjusting rapidly. There are certainly adjustment costs inherent in both hiring and laying off workers: besides training costs there are costs of searching for and screening among new employees, and implicit or explicit contractual terms commonly impose a severance payment on employers. Thus the pressure to pursue retraining quickly may be diminished if costs of screening and search for promising trainees is high or if severance arrangements leave employers more dependent upon natural turnover. The latter may well, for instance, depend upon the age structure of the labour force in declining industries: an employer faced with costly early retirement arrangements versus retaining older workers until normal retirement age despite a declining market, may well opt for the latter, thus diminishing the difficult task of retraining older dismissed workers.

In very broad terms there are essentially three interrelated sets of reasons, emerging from the foregoing discussion, why some form of policy action may be recommended with respect to training during structural adjustment: (a) for efficiency reasons because markets are not perfect; (b) for dynamic efficiency reasons because retraining may not occur on a sufficient scale within a given time scope; (c) for reasons of income distribution.

In the following sections, these three elements must be borne in mind while examining some implications of various alternative imperfections in markets. It should be emphasized at the outset that it is normally critical to consider carefully the nature of specific market failures before proceeding to design and implement corrective measures. The most effective policies are typically those which, within the range of potential effective administration, target the identified problem most directly. Our discussion of these issues is here divided into two sections. The following section deals with a number of aspects both in the provision of training itself and in labour markets. The subsequent section then more briefly addresses some important links with other related areas of policy concern, such as the link with trade policy, with the promotion of capital investments, and with aggregate demand management.

TRAINING AND THE LABOUR MARKET

Training

General training and, to a lesser extent, specific training call for workers to finance investments in their own training in the context of competitive labour markets. The returns are in the form of subsequently enhanced wages. Yet capital markets in most economies are not well suited for lending to trainees. Future earnings do not represent credible collateral against which to secure a loan. As a result, members of more affluent families are typically better placed to finance their own training. This disparity in capacity to undertake training may not only render job opportunities and hence income distribution more unequal but may also be inefficient – denying training to bright but poor individuals.

To the extent that too little training ensues, especially of disadvantaged groups, a potential exists for policy intervention to improve both the efficiency of structural adjustment and the income distribution generated by that adjustment. Since the ultimate difficulty stems from inadequacies in the capital market, the appropriate policy response is one of making loans available to trainees. By adopting a strategy of requiring loan repayment upon future employment, such a programme could in principle be made largely self-financing, thus enabling financing training of the next generation. It should, however, be recognized that training loans are likely to suffer from high default rates precisely for the reason that private markets prove reluctant to lend for training. Default may be particularly problematic in situations where international migration is common, for emigrants are normally beyond the effective reach of creditors. In other contexts self-defined group accountability for debts has proved very successful in limiting default rates, and some potential presumably therefore exists for exploiting this – for example, in integrated rural development schemes when existing rural production patterns are disrupted during a structural adjustment.

Frequently, in developing countries, trade liberalization lowers effective protection offered to more capital-intensive, larger-scale enterprises while simultaneously stimulating sectors dominated by smaller enterprises. However, smaller enterprises typically undertake extremely limited formal training. Informal, on-the-job training may suffice, though this may not always be the case. Small-scale enterprises commonly suffer difficulties raising financing, and this may lead to underinvestment in specific training by such firms. If so, the appropriate response is presumably to make funds more readily available to the small-scale sector, even if use of these funds proves fungible as to use in training or other forms of investment. However, as with individual persons, such a strategy is made more costly through the very high default rate typical of loans to small enterprises.

Larger enterprises normally raise funds with greater ease, and indeed this may be partially why they undertake more formal training. Yet the larger enterprises may underinvest in training, relative to the socially desirable rate, especially if the financial sector imposes a high discount rate on borrowers, encouraging an excessively myopic view with respect to investments in training in newly-emerging fields.

Information available, to individual workers and to employers contemplating training, about future skill needs and potential returns is never perfect.

The difficulties of anticipating these needs are exacerbated during the flux of a major structural adjustment. Formulation of expectations with respect to future skills and occupational demands may well be less than fully rational, and any inherent biases in this formulation will lead to inappropriate decisions with respect to investments in training. Yet whether any corrective policy action will improve or worsen this situation is obviously dependent on more complete, or at least less biased, information being possessed by policy makers. To the extent that government sets the overall policy framework, the environment for future skill demands may be better understood by policy makers. On the other hand, it is far less likely that anyone in government will possess a better understanding of the future of a particular industry than do entrepreneurs already in that industry. This naturally suggests a partnership between employers and policy strategists in the design of a training policy, which is dealt with more fully in a later section. Meanwhile, let us merely note that if government is in possession of better information, then the appropriate response is presumably one of circulating that information.

This last point touches upon a complex issue of credibility of such information and ultimately upon the viability of the structural adjustment process. In the face of less than complete information, training decisions – by the private or public sectors – are inherently risky. Insufficient training may result during an episode of structural adjustment because workers' and even employers' perceptions of the associated risks may be inappropriate or because they are excessively risk averse. A major element in formulating attitudes to risk is whether the announced goal of structural adjustment is perceived as credible. Certainly the majority of trade liberalization episodes are reversed within a fairly short time interval, establishing an international record warranting scepticism about permanence of change. Whether the adjustment programme is sustained depends, to a significant extent, upon whether retraining is pursued. In the absence of sufficient training, the transition into new jobs will be delayed, unemployment will be exacerbated, newly-competitive exports fail to expand resulting in foreign-exchange shortages, and pressures to reverse initial announcements consequently mount. Perhaps one important element in reassuring both workers and employers as to government commitment to continued adjustment may then be signalling commitment to retraining itself.

Another aspect of information failures in relation to training is the asymmetry of information available. At least three examples may be cited. First the selection of the most appropriate trainees is rendered more difficult when incomplete information about applicants is provided. This may well result in an unwillingness to provide sufficient training, perhaps warranting policy encouragement to make less than fully-informed selections. Alternatively, when the rewards to training are substantial for workers, there is a strong incentive to invest resources in signalling one's strengths to those making selections. To the extent that such signalling actually improves the matching process it can be productive, but otherwise excessive signalling is wasteful and needs to be discouraged.

A second illustration of asymmetric information in training arises in choosing among training programmes. Privately-offered training, and perhaps even some public programmes, may have an incentive to overstate the content and potential returns to selecting their particular scheme. To the extent that government is better placed to evaluate private programmes than is the individual trainee, a process of certification of programme content and quality can aid meaningful selections. Often this takes the form of certification that the programme meets minimum standards, though a well-informed public agency could presumably go much further in providing more reliable information about the specifics of content.

The third illustration of the difficulties arising from asymmetric information is a very important one. In many contexts, on-the-job training proves more cost-effective than off-site programmes. Yet, since it is extremely difficult for any public agency to monitor how much on-the-job training is really taking place, offering incentives to employers for on-the-job training would incur high levels of potential waste. Training subsidies to employers are consequently often confined to off-site training even though this may ultimately be less cost-effective.

The foregoing discussion of various market failures in the direct provision of training, and some possible corrective strategies, has focused upon failures inherent to the provision of training. Besides these complications, additional problems may stem from existing policy interventions which either were already inappropriate before the structural adjustment commenced or have subsequently been rendered inadequate. Existing publicly-provided training programmes, and even the educational system which provides a background to more specific training, are obvious examples of strategies likely to demand urgent attention in the midst of structural adjustment, especially to the extent that such training and education is geared to generation of skills no longer in demand.

Labour Markets

During a structural adjustment, the flexibility of labour markets has a major impact upon the extent, nature and context of training undertaken. The extent to which employees are made redundant from their existing activities is shaped by how flexible employers in potentially declining activities prove to be. Conversely, the rate of absorption into new posts is affected by the capacity of the newly-competitive activities to generate jobs quickly. In the balance, whether training of unemployed persons or of current employees is called for, the nature of wage signalling of skill shortages to potential trainees and policy makers alike, and indeed the survival of demand for existing specific skills, are all at issue. In the interests of both employment generation and of training impacts during structural adjustment, careful consideration needs to be given to a number of policy options and reforms, though the nature of these alternatives naturally depends upon the specific context.

Consider first some issues in terms of redundancy. Loss in competitiveness of industries, at existing cost levels, reduces the demand for labour in these activities. The extent to which this demand reduction results in job loss depends, in part, on the downward flexibility in wages combined with the elasticity of demand for labour as wages decline. Minimum wage regulations, collective bargaining agreements, explicit or implicit contractual arrangements with individual workers, may each limit any downward adjustments otherwise to be expected as the demand for labour declines in specific spheres. In the presence of greater wage flexibility, continued competitiveness of a given activity may be permitted, despite structural price changes, obviating the need for such extensive retraining.

Minimum wage regulations are unlikely to set a floor on skilled workers' wages, prior to structural adjustment, but could well do so as specific skills otherwise become redundant. Moreover, even if minimum wage regulations only set a floor to unskilled workers' pay, the consequences for training may none the less prove real, since entry into the newly-competitive spheres may demand training of previously unskilled workers. Revision to existing minimum wage regulations may thus warrant careful review in terms of both job creation and training needs, even if the existing regulations were not binding on skilled workers prior to the structural adjustment programme.

An episode of major structural adjustment may also represent an appropriate opportunity to review the legal framework of collective bargaining: enhancing flexibility in collective agreements may, for instance, prove critical to prevention of major bankruptcies and consequent sudden job loss with commensurate pressures for massive and speedy retraining.

Inflexibility in wages, for whatever reason, can readily imply excessive rates of redundancy and pressures to retrain during structural adjustment. However, various elements in job security provisions may also act in the opposite direction, resulting in too little training. Legislated minimum periods of notice in the event of layoff or plant closure, minimum severance pay formulae, and perhaps especially requirements in some less-developed countries (LDCs) that government approval be obtained prior to any reductions, can all limit the ability of employers in declining activities to release workers for retraining in newly-competitive spheres.

Public-sector demands for labour and attitudes to job security are also likely to differ substantially from those of private-sector employers, though in fact the reactions of the public sector will depend very much upon the form of the structural adjustment programme. In the face of trade liberalization, or other forms of price reform, the public-sector demand for labour is likely to prove less elastic than would private-sector employment in similar activities. The public sector also typically offers a greater degree of job security, and thus will be slower to make any adjustments. To this extent, when public-sector employment is substantial, the pressures to retrain, during any given set of price adjustments, are likely to be less (though ultimately this may not be in the best national interests). Yet, in practice, structural adjustment rarely involves price restructuring alone. More commonly, even trade liberalization follows a macroeconomic crisis and is accompanied by pressures or a resolve to improve the budgetary position. Increased public enterprise losses may not only be unacceptable in such a context, but indeed there may well exist concerns to enhance existing public enterprise financial contributions. If so, it is quite conceivable that a substantial, previously overstaffed public enterprise sector may shed more labour than would private employers, considerably expanding the demands on the training system in the process of structural adjustment.

Turn now from job exit to issues of entry into new jobs and the consequential impact on training. Some barriers to job entry can readily be in the general social interest: for instance, certification of professionals and craftsmen can serve to prevent fraudulent claims to competence. Yet such barriers can also become excessive, representing protection of monopoly interests of existing members of an occupation. Similarly, excessive requirements in terms of subsequent dismissal can deter employers from initial hiring. Inability to migrate to the location of newly-emerging jobs (a problem in some of the transition economies, for instance, where an effective housing market does not yet exist), can also act as a barrier to applying for jobs. No matter what the source of the barrier to entry, the outcome is too little training in the newly-demanded skills as structural adjustment proceeds. However, the most appropriate policy response is to address the ultimate source of job entry restriction, rather than to promote additional related training directly. Indeed, if any barriers to entry are not corrected, then training for such jobs may well simply go to waste.

Even in the absence of barriers to entry, the demand for new skills is likely to prove less responsive to wage costs in the short run. In the longer run, production processes can be adjusted to allow for availability of skilled personnel. Combined with an inevitable lag in training, wages for occupations in high demand following the structural adjustment are therefore likely to overshoot their long-run level. In the transition, this means those initially possessing the newly-demanded skills receive a substantial rent. More importantly, the sharp initial rise in wages will tempt many to contemplate training for these spheres – a temptation which may be excessive if trainees fail to recognize that returns on these skills will decline as demand adjusts and supply increases.

Finally, in discussing flexibility of the labour market, the combined outcome of exit and entry must be addressed. Where wages in labour markets subject to declining demand prove inflexible downwards and barriers to entry prevent new hiring, the outcome is open unemployment. This has profound consequences for the nature of any training programmes. An argument can be made for training of unemployed persons simply to occupy their time and to limit the sense of alienation from the job market. Such a position has been advocated for the long-term unemployed even in contexts other than structural adjustment. However, given that training is normally fairly expensive, in the end one must hope that training of the unemployed proves constructive in their eventual post. This presents a major problem of anticipating the type of job an unemployed person will enter, and hence the relevant form of training. This presumably speaks for less specific training of the unemployed, aiming at more general sets of skills which can be applied to a range of jobs. Yet discerning the future applicability even of more general skills may have critical consequences for the design and implementation of training programmes, as discussed in a later section. Meanwhile, it should be noted that the mere offer of support for the unemployed while training may induce willingness to quit existing posts and hence exacerbate the unemployment effects of structural adjustment. Even if unemployed trainees receive no greater cash support than other unemployed persons, subsidizing direct costs of training may make the prospect of being temporarily unemployed sufficiently less onerous as to tempt marginal workers to quit jobs which they believe to be in decline as a result of the structural adjustment.

ADJUSTMENT PROBLEMS IN CLOSELY-RELATED SPHERES

So far, attention has been focused upon the role of policy in framing training decisions and outcomes, during structural adjustment, when idiosyncracies in training decisions themselves or in the labour market would otherwise result in an inadequate training programme. However, important decisions in spheres other than training and labour themselves frequently lead to inappropriate training strategies during structural adjustment. Since it is critical to recognize the ultimate cause of inadequate training before designing corrective policies, some thought needs to be given here to this set of issues.

Perhaps the most obvious set of issues arises with respect to investments in physical capital. There is no point in training workers on the presumption that new activities will become competitive if investments in fixed capital for those activities are not realized. There is no point in training workers to use the latest technologies if no upgrading of outdated equipment occurs.

The latest equipment is, of course, not always appropriate, nor is large capital expansion necessarily called for in newly competitive industries (especially when excess capacity already exists in these). None the less, in many contexts private investments may not suffice without some policy correction. In broad terms, a distinction should be made here between the need for additional policy initiatives as opposed to removal or reform of existing policies. Among the former, it is commonly maintained that the objectives of the financial markets may diverge from the social interest. In particular, private capital markets may be excessively myopic or risk averse, and consequently fail to fund investments with longer-term payoffs or where risks are relatively high (including the risk of insufficient collateral possessed by potential investors). If this is diagnosed to be the case, then a programme to offer funds on realistic terms to investors may be a critical corollary to training for these expansion areas, though perceiving such warranted action is not easy and many existing programmes simply result in high default rates.

Perhaps even more important is the need to reform various existing capital-market policies. In the absence of financial liberalization, trade liberalization may generate appropriate commodity price signals yet fail to generate commensurate investments. In the transition economies, the need for financial reform is extreme, where no private banking system exists and where many financial institutions, common to the industrialized countries, have no history (such as venture-capital lending). In many developing countries, credit issued by state-owned commercial or industrial development banks continues to be allocated according to planning decisions and private investments (and even use of existing capacity) are occasionally subject to licensing restraints. To the extent that these existing policies prevent expansion of the newly competitive activities, during structural reform, training for these new industries may prove to be a complete waste. There is a clear need to coordinate training programme decisions with financial reforms and the resultant patterns of physical investments.

A second sphere where coordination may be warranted is between commercial policy and training. Even when structural adjustment is a result of trade liberalization, removal of the protection structure is never complete. Remaining ambiguities in the permanence of tariffs and quantitative restrictions can raise considerable uncertainty with respect to training decisions, both on behalf of those in government responsible for training policy and on behalf of employers and workers. To send consistent messages with respect to training decisions, it can therefore be critical to establish a long-term import–export policy.

One specific aspect of such a longer-term strategy worth separate mention is the adoption of infant industry (or industrial policy) protection. The experiences of many developing countries with infant industries have been negative; the infants frequently fail to mature. However, it seems that one critical element in the East Asian industrial strategies has been the coordination of industrial policy with commensurate training requirements (World Bank 1993). Where the skill requirements of the infants are unlikely to prove firm specific, individual employers naturally prove reluctant to finance the training necessary for ultimate success of the infant. Most typically, for success in these contexts, employers' associations need to work with government and employees in the design of both the industrial and training policies.

In the developing countries, structural adjustment frequently follows a balance-of-payments crisis, often associated with a substantial budget deficit. The structural adjustment package then comprises both relative price restructuring – through removal of trade protection, devaluation, removal of price controls and perhaps tax reform – and elements of aggregate demand management. Additional tax effort and government spending restraints, combined with limited credit creation, thus commonly engender serious contraction at the same time that relative price shifts are meant to lead to industrial restructuring. The important implication, from the point of view of training decisions, is that displaced workers and new job market entrants probably face significant periods of unemployment prior to entering one of the newly competitive fields. This makes problems of coordinating with future employers, and in particular anticipating more specific skill needs, considerably more difficult. Expanding training initiatives while simultaneously engineering a recession may prove counterproductive, and this needs to be borne in mind (both by government and the international agencies) when weighing the costs of extending and deepening a recession.

DATA COLLECTION FOR POLICY FORMULATION

A wide range of potential policy initiatives have been identified in the previous two sections on market maladjustments in training, employment and a number of closely-related spheres. Corrective policy actions require appropriate information. The nature of these requirements depends to a significant extent on the form of the policy initiatives envisaged. For instance, lending to individual workers undertaking training, or tax relief for firms offering additional workplace training, irrespective of field of skill generation, requires monitoring and perhaps some follow-up evaluation. On the other hand, publicly-provided training and incentives for training in specific areas require decisions by policy makers with respect to appropriate areas for training. The latter is obviously more difficult.

The most traditional method of projecting training requirements is manpower planning. Although still in common use, manpower planning is now understood to exhibit several serious weaknesses and to perform poorly. Briefly, manpower planning relies on a more or less detailed projection of the sectoral pattern of output in the medium-term future. The skill requirements of each sector are estimated, usually based upon a given assumed occupational structure for each sector. The differences between these forecast skill requirements and the existing skill profile thus become the additional training requirements. The weakest links in this approach reside in the difficulty of projecting detailed sectoral outputs in a rapidly changing world, in the strong assumption of fixed skill requirements for each sector irrespective of technological change and of shifting skill costs, and in defining training 'needs' irrespective of training costs. In essence, manpower planning typically relies exclusively on quantitative projections without regard to costs and prices.

A major alternative, where specific skill demands are required for adequate policy formulation, would be to rely completely on price signals. In particular, occupations or skills commanding rapidly rising wages may be assumed to have sharply rising demand relative to supply. If these returns, in the form of higher wages, justify the expense of the particular training, then this may represent a sphere where additional training is warranted. Collection of wage data by occupation, through stratified, enterprise sample surveys, can be achieved relatively quickly and inexpensively. The speed of information feedback may, indeed, be critical, especially if major training initiatives are envisaged during an episode of speedy structural adjustment. However, this approach also has some very serious weaknesses.

First, some care is required in interpreting the enterprise-based data. Typically, smaller enterprises are excluded from quick surveys, and their skill requirements may be quite different from those of medium to large units. Moreover changes in average pay in an occupation are not necessarily reflective of rising wages; indeed, it is quite plausible that average pay may rise while laying off employees (rather than reflecting rising demand), especially if the most experienced or best performers are retained. Second, even if a representative sample is established and rising pay of individual workers in certain occupations is determined, translating this into training requirements presents difficulties. As already mentioned, pay in an occupation may well overshoot its longer-term trend during a structural adjustment; high returns on specific skills may prove transitory and training investment decisions based on these transitory returns alone would be inappropriate. Even the long-term changes in relative pay can prove misleading, for there is no necessary association between the extent of wage increment and the quantity of extra trainees which would reestablish the previous pay level. Where demands for a particular skill are very insensitive to wages, a large pay increase may reflect only a small increase in the number of workers demanded. Since these sensitivities vary across occupations/skills, the relative extent of pay increase will not reflect quantitative requirements. However, the (long-term) pay increase in a skill will reflect the (long-term) returns from additional expenditure on training in a specific field, provided that no further changes in departures from competitive market conditions occur.

Both manpower planning and monitoring the wage returns on skills are subject to a number of caveats and problems as devices for planning training profiles. It may be tempting to think of manpower planning offering a longer-term approach, especially in conjunction with an (infant) industrial strategy. Yet, even given the sectoral pattern of output, neglecting relative costs of skills represents a major flaw in the typical manpower planning approach. Conversely, wage monitoring may offer a quick check on areas of rising demand at present. Yet overshooting and variations in wage sensitivity remain critical problems. In principle it is possible to imagine merging the two approaches, modifying the fixed occupational requirements of manpower planning to allow for rising wage costs (perhaps using a computable general equilibrium model). Yet the information required to construct such models in a meaningful manner is rarely available in great detail or in a timely fashion.

In the end, it is extraordinarily difficult for a policy-making unit to project detailed training requirements sensibly, irrespective of the method adopted. This lacuna should have a major influence on the choice of a policy strategy. There is a spectrum of policy possibilities, ranging from very detailed public choice with respect to fields of training through to policy incentives irrespective of field. The less able is a policy unit to undertake realistic projections of the cost-effectiveness of specific areas of training, the more should the policy strategy lean towards the latter end of the spectrum. A compromise might rely on very broad projections – that more or less engineering training is likely to prove useful without predetermining the specific form of engineering.

As noted at the beginning of this section, no matter where the policy choice falls in the spectrum of specificity of training, some monitoring of the actual performance of training initiatives is probably desirable provided that costs of monitoring are not excessive. A common and very useful device for such monitoring is a tracer study.

Tracer studies follow individuals who have entered a training programme, to discover how useful the training subsequently proves. One criteria of success often adopted in such studies is the frequency with which graduates continue in the specific line for which they are trained. However, this may not always be the decisive factor in determining the usefulness of training. Skills learned while training for one profession may be transferable, to a greater or lesser extent, to alternative careers. At least the private rewards to the training programme are therefore better measured by the wage gain resulting from the training. In measuring such gains some care must be taken in the sample design for the tracer study. One common error is to omit persons currently unemployed, despite completion of the training programme. Obviously such an omission overestimates the usefulness of training. In particular, backward tracing – locating individuals with relevant training at their current place of employment – automatically possesses such a bias. On these grounds it is better to think of a forward tracer – attempting to find persons from a list of graduates. Yet even a forward tracer may exhibit very serious biases if only a small fraction of graduates can be traced and if these persons are untypical of the programme. One method sometimes used to ensure a higher rate of forward tracing is to send annual cards to the last-known address of graduates, promising a small payment if a corrected address card is returned. This may seem prohibitively expensive, but there may be a worthwhile tradeoff in pursuing a smaller sample with a high response rate. The mere fact that graduates do well is no indication that this success is attributable to the programme. The issue is whether graduates fare better than similar persons who did not benefit from the programme. To detect this, a well-designed tracer study must establish the background of persons undertaking training, and also sample from a control group who do not undertake training. The value of a tracer study can be considerably enhanced if information about the establishment of subsequent employment is also collected, to detect which types of employers are ultimately benefiting from the training programme. Unfortunately the latter type of information is rarely collected, and most training studies focus either on characteristics of trainees or on those of the place of employment, but almost never investigate the interlinkages between the two.

THE FORM AND IMPLEMENTATION OF TRAINING PROGRAMMES

As noted in the introduction, training programmes to aid in structural adjustment are, frequently, poorly conceived. However, there are two quite distinct aspects of this. One basic reason why training programmes are often poorly conceived is because such training is undertaken in conjunction with, or in attempt to compensate for, other poorly conceived policies. Several examples are discussed in earlier sections of this chapter: policies generating excessive inflexibility in the labour market, resulting in higher rates of unemployment than might otherwise occur during structural adjustment, are better addressed through removal of barriers to mobility than through attempts to train the unemployed; a failed strategy of infant industry identification can engender a poorly-conceived training effort to match, yet the source of the failure is in the infant industry protection; or macroeconomic management which fails to generate jobs can make training programmes seem weaker than they are. Training must be seen as part of an overall strategy, and failure to design non-training policies appropriately may readily render training itself less effective.

The second basic reason for the poor design of training programmes during structural adjustment resides, however, in the form and implementation of the training strategy itself. This may be true no matter whether other policies are approximately correct or not, and the present section therefore focuses upon this second context.

The role of training during structural adjustment obviously varies with the nature of that adjustment. The extent to which training displaced persons involves training the unemployed or those with job offers, involves training for activities completely unrelated to prior experiences or only demands finer tuning, and involves training predominantly recent school leavers or substantial numbers of mature workers, depends upon the context. No one set of policies will suffice for all occasions. Rather, a menu of alternatives needs to be considered, and indeed even in any given situation it may be advisable to offer a menu of alternatives.

In designing this menu, many of the industrialized countries which have implemented more successful training strategies have drawn upon a high degree of coordination and cooperation among employers, employees and their unions, government and training institutions (see Lynch 1993). When training is publicly provided, it may thus be critical to involve employers (or employers' associations) and employees (or unions) in the design and running of the training centre. When training is offered through private, off-site institutions, government monitoring and feedback from employees and employers (or their direct involvement in management) may be a crucial element. When it is unemployed workers who are being trained, it is the longer-run interests of potential employers that are being served, rather than providing skills to existing employees. In these circumstances, it may be more difficult (yet no less important) to ensure employer involvement. To achieve this, government may need to play a coordinating role, or even to offer some form of incentive for participation.

In the case of both apprenticeships and on-the-job training, employer involvement may be taken largely for granted. These forms of training have a high chance of being utilized directly by the trainee. Moreover, on-site training, integrated with normal production, probably represents a very effective learning environment. In these senses, such formats are highly desirable. On the other hand, on-the-job training does exhibit some limitations. First, as already noted, offering effective incentives to promote on-site training is difficult at best, since it is almost impossible to monitor the extent of (additional) training actually undertaken. Second, it may be difficult to promote more general training through on-site mechanisms (unless workers are able to finance a cut in pay during such episodes). In Japan, much of the training in larger firms is precisely of a form which is integrated with the production process and even more general training has been provided through these mechanisms, because of the very low turnover rate in jobs (see Hashimoto 1994). Yet in other countries which have tried to legislate greater job security, the result has been to diminish training with greater use of casual labour to bypass the regulations (see Fallon and Lucas 1991). A third limitation of enterprise-based, on-the-job training, and perhaps the most telling limitation for structural adjustment, is that it cannot reach the unemployed.

Given these limitations, enterprise-based training and apprenticeships need to be supplemented by additional training mechanisms during structural adjustment. Germany has a very successful vocational education system, which comprises both plant-based practical training and school-based technical preparation (see Lane 1991). However, in considering emulation of the German system, it should be remembered that coinvestment in training, codetermination of the content of the training programme, and certification of skills upon completion are key features of this programme, in addition to the dual components. Moreover, there is an obvious difficulty in promoting the plant-based portion of such vocational training (even in the form of payless internships) during the exacerbated unemployment associated with structural adjustment.

What emerges is that – desirable as on-the-job, enterprise-based training may be, whether in the context of vocational education, apprenticeships or less formal production-based training – it is unlikely to suffice in reaching the unemployed during structural adjustment. To train the unemployed may therefore require either public training institutions or some form of subsidy to privately-provided institutional training. The relative merits of public versus private provision in this context may well vary from country to country. Much depends upon the competence of the public sector in organizing such activities and indeed on the competence of the private sector, especially in the transition economies with so little private-sector experience in training or otherwise. Private-sector provision may suffer from the additional limitation, mentioned already, of possessing an incentive to cut costs and hide an inferior quality training. No matter whether the training of the unemployed is provided by the public or private sector, there is a strong case to be made for keeping this training from becoming too skill-specific, given the extreme difficulties of reliably forecasting skill demands.

Apprenticeships, internships during vocational education, and institution-based training, each typically call for at least part of the cost to be borne by the trainee. Given the usual severe limitation on private financing available to trainees (and especially to poorer workers) government assistance may well be warranted. This assistance is often in the form of grants to cover some portion of tuition costs, forgone earnings or a stipend. However, a programme of subsidized loans may be far more cost-effective than grants. Successful trainees will presumably command future incomes, leaving them capable of repaying the principal plus some interest. If the risk of no returns to the training is to be borne by the state, this can be handled by tying the rate of repayment to actual future earnings. Any repayment should permit establishment of a revolving fund, allowing loans to the next generation of trainees. Moreover, a loan, by imposing some future cost on trainees, may enhance trainee commitment to extracting the maximum from their experience.

Direct costs of training are also frequently subsidized, and this is often a source of serious error. The evidence from education clearly indicates that the quality of teachers dominates having expensive school buildings in providing a first-class education. All too frequently, governments and the international agencies subsidize the building or renovation of training facilities without adequate provision for recurrent costs, and for the costs of high-quality trainers in particular. Indeed, in the context of a substantial structural adjustment, the availability of appropriate trainers can be a major issue, since there may be little national experience in the newly-competitive fields. When this is true, one resolution may be to allow the immigration of high-level trainers, at least for a transition period, even though this may be very expensive.

In the longer run, coordination of the educational system and post-school training is vital. Post-school training must build on the prior foundation to imbue more job-specific skills. In any rapidly changing society, including ones undergoing structural adjustment, formal schooling must also serve as the basis for subsequent retraining. Consequently, an appropriate base for training and retraining needs to be established during formal schooling. In turn this should have a major influence on the structure and content of the educational system, on which governments in most countries have a significant voice. Naturally, formal schooling plays many roles in society, of which skill provision for work is only one. Ethical training, socialization, and even promotion of national unity are frequently goals of the educational system. None the less, that component of schooling dedicated more to productivity enhancement must be designed with ultimate training and retraining in mind.

In the context of a rapid structural adjustment, the potential impact of altering the schooling system is limited. It can take many years for graduates of the revised system to form the majority of the labour force. Yet the context of a structural adjustment may be a good time to review the need for educational reform if only because continuing adjustments are likely to be essential in a dynamic economy. Moreover, to the extent that the schooling system in the past has failed to provide the basic inputs needed for retraining during a structural adjustment, current retraining may require a higher academic content. This could be achieved through a dual structure as in Germany (though with some form of adult education) or through incorporating relevant components of a basic education alongside more practical skill acquisition.

Technologies are changing rapidly, and so is the nature of work relationships. Employee feedback on production modes and even involvement in management decisions have assumed greater importance in the industrialized countries in recent years. Some of the skills required for these new technologies and production modes are cognitive (including computer facility, maths and language skills). These skills ought to derive from the schooling system, but where they do not (or did not) an adult education component of training during structural adjustment must compensate for these omissions. Other skills required by the new production modes are, perhaps, more behavioural: the ability to work in teams, to take decisions and to share information. Indeed, it is not only workers but also management which often requires major adjustments in behavioural patterns as a result of the alternative modes. Teaching such behaviour through institutionalized training may not be easy. Perhaps there is no substitute for employment-based experience in these contexts. If so, then the relevant skills will only be derived if the structural adjustment is engineered to generate appropriate jobs, through which these capabilities may be learned, rapidly.

SUMMING UP

The central difficulty encountered in training during substantial structural adjustment is that much of the training is of unemployed persons. No good mechanisms exist for reliably predicting newly-emerging spheres of productive activity or the skills which these will demand. Neither manpower planning nor devices for tracking wages as signals of skill 'shortages' suffices for predicting areas where training may be demanded, though both can help to a limited extent.

Training may help in diminishing the rate of unemployment by speeding new job entry, yet even this may be untrue since subsidized training could induce a higher rate of quits. At best, training represents a partial solution to the unemployment typically generated by structural adjustment. Other policies are far more potent in their capacity to diminish the impact of unemployment. The latter include removing obstacles to labour-market flexibility, maintaining an appropriate cost of capital to discourage excessive capital intensity while permitting investments for job creation in the newly-competitive spheres, recognizing the economic and social costs of unemployment when designing exchange-rate and fiscal strategies, and design of a commercial policy in line with comparative advantage as dictated, in part, by the skill structure of the labour force.

Evaluation of training programmes during structural adjustment must be seen in this light. To blame a training programme for not offering a substantial reduction in unemployment may well miss the point. This is not to imply that continuing evaluation of subsidized training efforts is unimportant. Tracer studies, if well designed, can provide critical feedback on the performance of more formal training efforts. On the other hand, training which is integrated with ongoing production is more difficult to identify and hence to evaluate even through tracer studies.

There are several reasons why the extent of training of the unemployed and of others is likely to prove insufficient, both in the sense of being too little to be efficient and in providing inadequate training for able but poorer persons in particular. No one mechanism will normally suffice to deal with these inadequacies. A menu of alternatives needs to be considered and even to be made available. A system of loans to trainees may generally prove preferable to direct grants. In addition, some incentives in the form of cost subsidies or tax relief to employers may be warranted both to lower the cost of labour and hence accelerate job creation and to encourage the provision of more general training.

Enterprise-based training is frequently the most effective in providing (relevant) skills. Unfortunately, this option is difficult for government to monitor and hence to encourage effectively, and is not an option usually accessible for the unemployed during structural adjustment (though internships warrant serious consideration). None the less, in training the unemployed it is important to involve potential employers in the design and management of the programme, thus retaining a critical feature of enterprise-based training. Such involvement can be difficult to promote and may require some incentives, either for individual employers or for their associations.

A common element in the menu of training options is publicly-operated training facilities. Performance of such centres, relative to private-sector alternatives, obviously varies considerably from context to context. Tracer studies can help in these comparisons. Meanwhile, it should be remembered that private training facilities can suffer from a tendency to cut costs and overstate the efficacy of their programme to less than fully-informed trainees. More generally this points to the importance of national certification both of training centres and of trainees, which has been an important element in some of the European economies.

No matter whether training is offered through public facilities or subsidized private-sector programmes, financing capital costs of building new training centres frequently misses the point. More typically it is the running costs, both of appropriate materials and especially of high-level trainers, which determines the quality of skill generation. In turn, to ensure the availability of high-quality trainers, temporary relaxation of select immigration controls may be needed.

If the education system has left workers with an inadequate set of basic skills as a foundation for retraining, this omission may need to be addressed simultaneously with more specific skill production. A dual system, similar to the German vocational training scheme, may be warranted, though incorporating a major component of adult education. In the longer run, an overhaul of the education system needs to be coordinated with a view to the demands of future training and retraining in a dynamic economy. As the economy emerges from the higher levels of unemployment suffered during the structural adjustment, the menu of options offered will need to be revised, probably phasing out some of the existing programmes intended for the unemployed in favour of more enterprise-based apprenticeships and on-the-job training.

Meanwhile, given the severe difficulties of predicting the specific tasks to be performed by those now unemployed, training of these displaced workers and new job market entrants should presumably be kept fairly general, offering skills which will enhance productivity over a wide range of activities no matter which of these the trainee takes up.

NOTE

* An earlier version of this chapter was published in the *International Labour Review*, **13** (5–6), 1994.

REFERENCES

Fallon, Peter and Robert E.B. Lucas (1991), 'The Impact of Changes in Job Security Regulations in India and Zimbabwe', *World Bank Economic Review*, **5** (3) September, 395–413.

Hashimoto, Masanori (1994), 'Employment-based Training in Japanese Firms in Japan and in the United States: Experiences of Automobile Manufacturers', in L. Lynch (ed.), *Training and the Private Sector: International Comparisons*, Chicago: University of Chicago Press, pp. 109–48.

Lane, Christel (1991), 'Vocational Training and New Production Concepts in Germany: Some Lessons for Britain', *Industrial Relations Journal*, **29**, 247–59.

Lynch, Lisa M. (1993), *Strategies for Workplace Training: Lessons from Abroad*, Washington, DC: Economic Policy Institute.

World Bank (1993), *The East Asian Miracle: Economic Growth and Public Policy*, Washington, DC: Oxford University Press.

8. Human resources and structural adjustment: evidence from Costa Rica

Lucy P. Nichols

INTRODUCTION

Structural adjustment was implemented in many developing countries in the 1980s with less than hoped-for success. Many African countries and a few in Latin America still have not restored stable growth and development. Success may have been limited because similar adjustment programmes have been recommended to disparate economies, without sufficient reference to their underlying capacity to adjust.

The hypothesis tested here is that a good human resource base makes an economy more flexible, especially in its labour market, and gives a country a higher capacity to adjust to internal and external economic shocks. In other words, countries with good human resources have higher supply elasticities than countries with less-good human resources.

Also, thinking dynamically, such countries can reassign their workers at shorter intervals because of their workers' greater ability to learn new tasks and to innovate. This continuous change or flexibility becomes these countries' main asset, making the specific products exported less important than the diversified package of skills that can be redeployed to chase changing market opportunities. This flexibility is part of the newly industrialized Asian countries' manufacturing success.

The benefit of flexibility is not confined to manufacturing. Countries can also pursue market niches for agricultural products – office plants, cut flowers, out-of-season strawberries, boutique fruits and vegetables, macadamia nuts. Perhaps it is widespread rural literacy that makes this sort of agricultural re-tooling possible. The export of ever-changing agricultural products also requires, among other things, proximity to a market, adequate rural finance, transport infrastructure and skills, and that total exports remain small enough to avoid triggering protectionism in the importing country. Human-resource-based flexibility may also play a role in the export of services, particularly tourism.

Structural adjustment is conceptualized as changes in the real economy, rather than as improvements in financial indicators, or as adoption/implementation of policy packages or structural adjustment programmes. Adjustment is understood to mean shifts in the production of tradables relative to non-tradables induced by real devaluation; shifts in the production of exportables relative to import substitutes caused by trade liberalization; and shifts in the production of non-traditional exports relative to traditional exports, also induced by trade liberalization.

'Workers with a good basic education' serves as a proxy for the broader notion of 'a good human resource base'. The *World Development Report* (World Bank 1987: 63) argues that basic education imparts literacy, numeracy, greater ability to think adaptably, and time-based discipline. The list could also include a higher degree of personal efficacy and ability to innovate. Industry is thought to require workers with at least a primary education.[1] In principle, a similar case could be made for other aspects of 'good human resource base', such as widespread good health.

The general hypothesis that good human resources give an economy flexibility and a higher capacity to adjust is tested using data from Costa Rica, a country with superb human resources compared with other middle-income countries and a record of equitable and effective structural adjustment in the 1980s.[2] This proposition could have been tested in many ways, including using cross-section and case-study methods. This study, however, works at the micro-sectoral level, looking for evidence that sectors with more people with a basic education tend to expand more during adjustment than sectors with fewer people with a basic education. This would be consistent with schooling facilitating adjustment or giving Costa Rica a higher capacity to adjust.

However, because Costa Rica has an abundant supply of basic-educated labour, it could also be argued that sectors with more people with a basic education expanded more during adjustment than other sectors because trade liberalization helped Costa Rica better realize its comparative advantage in basic-education-intensive products. Working within one country, it is not possible to disentangle the two effects.

THE MODEL

The model examines three explanations of the capacity to adjust, testing the relationship between the adjustment of sectors and their human capital, wage levels and trade status. The model is estimated using ordinary least squares for individual employees in the Costa Rican workforce in 1989, using a large, 10,000–12,000-person sample.[3]

The equation is:

$$SA = b_0 + b_1ME + b_2FE + b_3MA + b_4FA + b_5MA^2 + b_6FA^2 + b_7G \\ + b_8D_1 + b_9D_2 + b_{10}\ln W + u_i \qquad (8.1)$$

where:

SA, the structural adjustment variable, is the change in share of total employment of each individual's sector of employment between 1980 and 1989, measured in percentage points;

ME and FE are the number of years of schooling completed by males and females;

MA, FA, MA^2, FA^2 are the age and age-squared of males and females over 12;

G is a dummy variable representing gender which takes the value 1 if male and 0 if female;

$\ln W$ is the natural log of the hourly wage of each individual in current colones;

D_1 and D_2 are dummy variables that distinguish sectors by trade status. First, following Krueger (1981), D_1 represents sectors comprising mainly exportables, and D_2 sectors comprising mainly non-tradables; the intercept refers to importable sectors. This conventional distinction between exportable (X) and importable (M) sectors fails to capture the shifts in production (and employment) that occurred under adjustment because Costa Rica diversified out of traded goods with poor prices and markets (traditional agricultural exports and exports to the Central American Common Market) into traded goods with better prices and markets (non-traditional exports to third markets). Thus, an alternative classification scheme is also tested where D_1 represents sectors comprising mainly non-traditional exports (NTX) and D_2 mainly non-traded goods; the intercept refers to traditional export sectors (TRX) in this case.

The next four sections of the chapter consider the strengths and limitations of the model, examining the dependent, human capital, wage and trade status variables, respectively. The subsequent section presents results, and the last section offers conclusions.

SECTORAL ADJUSTMENT IN COSTA RICA IN THE 1980s

Adjustment is measured by the change in the share of total employment of each individual's sector of employment between 1980 and 1989, years that span a decade of stabilization and adjustment in Costa Rica. The year 1980 was chosen because it is the approximate onset of the external shocks that made adjustment unavoidable. The end year 1989 was chosen because it was the last year available at the time the empirical work was done. The 10-year period is sufficient to see real, supply-side changes in the economy, although the process of adjustment continued after 1989.

Output or trade data could have been used instead of employment data to rank sectors by adjustment consistent with a definition of adjustment as changes in the real economy. Such data were not available for all sectors at the International Standard Industrial Classification (ISIC), two-digit level. Employment data, on the other hand, were complete and available annually from Costa Rica's *Direccion General de Estadistica y Censos* (DGEC).[4]

An ideal measure of adjustment would have distinguished between the effects of initial external shocks, adjustment policies, and adjustment that might well have occurred in response to shocks but apart from adjustment policies. Unfortunately, it is impossible to make these distinctions using the available data.

During adjustment, some sectors will expand and others contract, in accordance with changing price incentives. The words expand and contract will be used to describe sectoral employment changes when the direction is known, reserving the word adjustment to refer to movement in either direction.

Thus, adjustment is measured as sector i's share of total workforce employment in 1989 less its share in 1980, as expressed in equation (8.2), below.

$$SA_i = \frac{l_{i89}}{L_{89}} - \frac{l_{i80}}{L_{80}} \qquad (8.2)$$

where:

l = number employed in sector i;
L = total workforce employment.

Large changes in a sector's share of total employment indicate large changes in the numbers of people employed, which in turn indicate large shifts in the distribution of production across sectors and therefore broader and more effective adjustment.[5]

Table 8.1 ranks the 35, two-digit ISIC sectors in Costa Rica from those that expanded most between 1980 and 1989 to those that contracted most according to variable *SA*. The rankings in Table 8.1 correspond to the pattern of adjustment observed in Costa Rica in the 1980s. The textile and garment sector increased its share of employment by 2.5 percentage points, a far greater change than any other sector. Much of the increased employment is in

Table 8.1 Sectoral ranking by change in employment share (SA)

Rank SA	Sector number	Name	Change share employ	Rank SA	Sector number	Name	Annual growth rate
1	32	Textiles	2.53	19	96	International organization	0.03
2	95	Personal services	0.73	20	82	Insurance	0.01
3	91	Public administration	0.73	21	94	Entertainment	-0.01
4	12	Forestry	0.32	22	72	Communications	-0.04
5	13	Fishing	0.26	23	92	Sanitation	-0.05
6	83	Business services	0.26	24	11*	Agricultural services	-0.05
7	39	Other manufacturing	0.25	25	42	Water	-0.06
8	62	Retail trade	0.22	26	29*	Mining[a]	-0.19
9	19	Other agricultural products	0.20	27	36*	M/NM[b]	-0.28
10	33	Wood, furniture	0.18	28	38	Machines	-0.28
11	61	Wholesale trade	0.17	29	41*	Utilities	-0.41
12	15	Cattle producer	0.17	30	14	Bananas	-0.44
13	35	Chems, plastic	0.15	31	10	Coffee	-0.52
14	34	Paper products	0.13	32	16*	Coffee, sugar	-0.53
15	31	Food, drink, tobacco	0.11	33	93	Social services	-0.94
16	81	Financial firms	0.09	34	71*	Transport	-1.27
17	63	Restaurants, hotels	0.06	35	50	Construction	-1.59
18	18	Basic grains	0.04				

Notes:
a. Mining aggregates ISIC sectors 21 through 29.
b. includes non-metal manufacturing (36) and metal manufacturing (37).
* Star indicates sectors that decreased in absolute as well as relative terms.

Source: DGEC, *National Survey of Employment*, 1980 and 1989.

227

maquila industries, set up in response to drawback incentives and export-promotion policies. The employment share of two sectors, construction (50) and transport and storage (72), significantly declined. Construction was booming in 1980, which may exaggerate its decline. Transport may have fallen with the decrease in trade within the Central American Common Market (CACM), which moved largely by truck.

Table 8.1 also shows clearly Costa Rica's success with non-traditional exports and the decline in traditional exports and some import substitutes. The fastest-growing sector is textiles. Also at the top are forestry, fishing, other manufacturing, and other agricultural products, all sectors with non-traditional products. The only non-traditional 'export' not highly ranked is tourism, perhaps because much of the growth in this industry has occurred since 1989. Also, most of the traditional exports – coffee, coffee and sugar, bananas, and three import-substituting, manufacturing sectors, non-metal manufacturing (36), metal manufacturing (37) and machines manufacturing (38) – contracted.[6]

HUMAN CAPITAL VARIABLES

Years of schooling is a proxy for the underlying basket of qualities bestowed by education – workplace discipline, personal efficacy, ability to think, learn, retain information and innovate. Regression analysis assumes that each year of school gives each individual a uniform incremental amount of the qualities that matter to adjustment. This may not be the case, because in primary school the student may learn one set of skills useful during adjustment (for example, discipline, basic literacy) and another group in secondary school (for example, personal efficacy, problem solving). The gifts bestowed in the early years may be different from the gifts bestowed later, in kind and magnitude. If they are different baskets of gifts, they are unlikely to be of uniform size. However, years of schooling is the only variable available. More research could be done to identify which skills imparted in school matter to economic flexibility and adjustment.

The relationship between *SA* and schooling is a gently sloping convex curve. The extraordinary increase in the share of total employment of the textiles and garments sector, sector 32 (2.5 points) is more than three times the increase of the next-fastest expanding sector, personal services (0.73 points). The textiles sector is also a large sector. Thus, textiles exerts significant leverage over the slope of the relationship between *SA* and schooling; that is, it is a strong outlier. When this sector is excluded from the sample, the relationship between *SA* and schooling is approximately linear (and positive), and it is in this form, for simplicity, that schooling is entered into the model (adding ME^2 and FE^2 does not alter the results). When the relationship between SA and years of schooling is modelled as linear, tertiary education lies well off the regression line, so the sample is limited to employees with 12 or fewer years of school. Since the model aims to test the influence of basic education on SA, this could be done on theoretical as well as on practical grounds.

The relationship between SA and age appears to be U-shaped, so age is entered into equation (8.1) in quadratic form. The gender dummy variable allows the intercept in equation (8.1) to differ for men and women. Separating age and schooling by gender allows the slope of the relationship to differ for the two sexes. If the gender dummy alone had been included, the model would have assumed that age and education, together, have the same influence on adjustment for men and women.

The hypothesis was that during adjustment sectors with more people with a basic education would tend to expand more than sectors with fewer people with a basic education; that is, the signs on the education variables (ME, FE) were expected to be positive. The shape of the age curve suggests that sectors with more young and old workers would expand more than sectors with relatively more prime-age workers.

Sectors which employ more women were expected to expand more during adjustment than sectors which employ fewer women if manufactured exports were important expanding sectors and/or if sex segregation clustered women into sectors which grew strongly for other reasons. Thus, the sign on the dummy variable representing gender (G) was expected to be negative. Recall that G takes the value 1 for men and zero for women.

WAGES

Theory

Krueger (1981) and others[7] suggest that a sector will expand less under adjustment if wages in that sector are 'artificially high' because of minimum wage laws or union power, among other things. This is because high wages raise costs and reduce international competitiveness.

If the Krueger thesis is correct, sectors employing more individuals with 'artificially high income' will expand less than sectors with fewer such individuals. 'Artificially high income' refers to a bonus unrelated to personal characteristics (that is, after controlling for schooling, age, and gender). The sign on the wage variable would be expected to be negative.

Alternatively, 'artificial' or 'unexplained' income may capture unobservable human capital characteristics that reflect higher productivity.[8] Gender, age and education are known to be sound proxies, but variation around group averages occurs. For example, two people who completed the same number of years of school are not likely to embody the same amounts of the 'gifts' of education, because of differences in innate ability or the quality of their education. Or, firms (or sectors) may pay higher wages to keep more productive people.[9] If the income variable captures unmeasured human capital characteristics, then the sign on wages would be expected to be positive. If the data were available, the model could also usefully include direct measures of productivity.

This study can only measure the net effect of contending forces, although the sign of the estimated coefficient on the wage variable will suggest which force is stronger.[10]

Evidence of Intersectoral Wage Differences

Prior research shows that incomes differ across sectors for equally qualified people in Costa Rica. Trejos (1989: 13, Table 1) summarizes 25 studies of segmentation in the Costa Rican labour market between 1983 and 1988. These studies test wage differences between formal/informal and public/ private sectors rather than between sectors grouped by industrial activity (ISIC) or trade orientation. Three control for education level, including Uthoff and Pollack (1985), and Gindling (1986 and 1991). Gindling and Berry (1992: 43–4) summarize the findings:

> Tests by Gindling (1989b) and by Pollack and Uthoff (1986a) found wage differentials of 20–30% between private-formal and the informal sector and 10–20% between the public formal and private formal sectors, after controlling for human capital characteristics and selectivity bias. Differential enforcement of minimum wage laws in the private sector and public sector hiring and wage policies presumably contribute to the gaps.

Gindling and Berry (1992: Table 19) also present data on real earnings in 1980, 1983 and 1988 in the exportable, importable, non-traded and public sectors, adjusted for education, experience and health of workers. They find that the exportable sector is unambiguously the lowest-wage sector and the public sector is the highest-wage sector in most cases in 1980 and 1983, although the public sector loses its privileged position by 1988.

Thus, previous research has shown that workers in some sectors tend to earn a bonus unrelated to personal characteristics. Gindling and Berry (1992: 50) suggest that the main intersectoral wage gap will be between the less-protected exportables sector (agriculture/rural) and the other three sectors (urban/manufacturing/services).

Gindling and Berry's findings were confirmed in the course of the present research by a direct test of intersectoral differences of income between ISIC, two-digit sectors undertaken using the National Survey of Employment.[11] Significant wage differences exist between two-digit, ISIC sectors that are not due to measurable personal characteristics.

Definitions

The ideal measure of income would be the gross payroll cost to employers per person-hour (how much the employer pays), including non-wage payments to workers. Unfortunately, payroll data are not available for all two-digit ISIC sectors in Costa Rica. Thus, the wage variable used here approximates how much income an employee receives, using data from the DGEC's 1989 National Survey of Employment.

However, workers' wages underestimate the ideal income measure, gross payroll per worker, because income-in-kind and non-wage costs to employers are not counted, including large contributions to social security.[12] This discrepancy could lead the model to underestimate the effect of W on SA, if evasion of non-wage costs differs systematically between exportable, importable and non-traded sectors (or indeed, traditional, non-traditional and non-traded sectors). That is, evasion would cause total employment costs to differ by sector for reasons unrelated to the personal characteristics of workers. To my knowledge, no data exist on the evasion of non-wage employment costs by sector in Costa Rica. But given that agricultural workers in Costa Rica are frequently employees and enforcement is known to be poor in agriculture, then bias could be present depending on how agricultural employees are distributed between exportable (non-traditional) and importable (traditional) sectors.

The wage variable was income-per-hour-worked calculated from monthly income in current *colones* from a worker's main job divided by the number of hours worked in that job per month.[13] Standardizing by number of hours worked removed one source of wage difference between individuals that was extraneous to the argument. Wages from additional jobs were excluded. The model attempts to explain the adjustment of each sector; people with second jobs would have been classified in two sectors. Their major influence on sectoral adjustment was assumed to be in the sector where they work the most hours, that is, their main job.[14]

The natural log was used because proportional differences in wages between sectors unrelated to personal characteristics were more important than absolute differences. For example, a 10 per cent difference in wages was significant, whereas a $10 difference was not, because whether $10 was important depends on whether it was a high- or a low-wage sector. The logarithmic form also implied that a $1 increase in artificially high wages at the top of the distribution did not make as great a difference to sectoral adjustment as a $1 increase at the bottom.

SECTORAL TRADE STATUS

The model includes dummy variables representing the trade status of sectors for two reasons. First, the incentive to expand will be greater for sectors producing more exportables, hence trade status may explain significant amounts of sectoral adjustment on its own. Second, the relationship between sectoral adjustment and wages may differ for sectors grouped by trade status.

The 35 two-digit ISIC sectors are disaggregated into exportable, importable and non-traded sectors using the methodology set out by Krueger (1981: 14–16). The sectors are also *separately* disaggregated into non-traditional and traditional export sectors and non-traded sectors, by first classifying each sector's exports as traditional and non-traditional.[15] This alternative scheme recognizes that almost all sectors in Costa Rica export, even import-substituting sectors, and assumes that movement towards new exports or new markets is what defines a non-traditional sector, not necessarily that non-traditional exports are a large proportion of sectoral exports, production or consumption.

Two practical difficulties exist. First, what constitutes a non-traditional export? And second, how many non-traditional exports are enough to classify the whole sector as non-traditional?

Non-traditional exports are defined many ways in Costa Rica. The DGEC defines non-traditional exports as all exports except those named by law as traditional.[16] However, this definition makes no reference to the destination market of the goods and/or whether they are in some sense 'new' under adjustment. For example, classic import substitutes, such as industrial goods exports to the CACM, would be considered non-traditional, even though one of the main aims of adjustment is to make them internationally competitive and divert them to world markets.

Thus, a narrower definition of non-traditional export will be adopted here. As in the DGEC figures, it is necessary that a product be defined by law as non-traditional, but one or more of the following criteria must also be met:

1. that it was newly exported between 1980 and 1987, regardless of market;[17] or
2. that it was an existing export, but more than half was sold outside of Costa Rica and the CACM in 1986; or
3. that it was an existing export sold mainly to the CACM, but found a new market outside the CACM between 1980 and 1987.

The Ministry of Planning (MIDEPLAN 1988) provided the data, the value in thousands of US dollars of exports (classified at the Standard International Trade Classification (SITC) four-digit level) defined by law as non-traditional in each year from 1980 through the first half of 1987, broken down by destination market.

The second step was to classify sectors as traditional and non-traditional by calculating U, the share of non-traditional exports in total sector exports. U is given by:

$$U = \frac{\text{value of non-traditional exports of sector } i \text{ in 1986}}{\text{the value of total exports of sector } i \text{ in 1986}} \tag{8.3}$$

The cutoff line is arbitrary. An ISIC, two-digit sector is non-traditional if the value of non-traditional exports of its constituent four-digit sectors is greater

Table 8.2   ISIC sectors grouped by trade status

Classification 1			Classification 2		
X	M	NT	TRX	NTX	NT
10	29	11	10	12	11
12	37	41	14	13	18
13	38	42	15	19	29
14	18	50	16	31	41
15	34	61	36	32	42
16	35	62	37	33	50
19	36	71		34	61
31	39	72		35	62
32		81		38	71
33		82		39	72
63		83		63	81
		91			82
		92			83
		93			91
		94			92
		95			93
		96			94
					95
					96

Notes: X refers to exportables, M to importables and NT to non-tradables, TRX to traditional exports and NTX to non-traditional exports. The corresponding names of these ISIC, two-digit sectors appear in Table 8.1. The non-tradables groups differ slightly because sectors 18 and 29 are importables under Krueger's definition, but do not export and are non-tradable by default in the alternative classification.

than the value of the traditional exports of its constituent four-digit sectors in 1986; thus, a sector is non-traditional if U is greater than 0.5.

Table 8.2 presents the two trade classifications.[18] During adjustment, output in traded sectors is expected to expand relative to non-traded sectors and output of exportables to expand relative to importables. Thus, using the X/M trade-status variables, the sign on D_1, which represents exportable sectors, is expected to be positive and the sign on D_2 representing non-traded sectors, to be negative, because the control group is importables.

For the TRX/NTX grouping, theory is less clear. Given Costa Rica's stimulus to non-traditional exports, sectors dominated by non-traditional exports should have expanded faster than sectors producing mainly traditional exports, yielding a positive coefficient on D_1. Theory does not predict whether traditional export or non-traded sectors should expand faster under adjustment.

THE RESULTS

This section will present and analyse the results of the regression of *SA* on personal characteristics, wages and trade orientation of sector of employment expressed as equation (8.1), for all sectors and for private sectors only.

The results are presented with and without sector 32, the textiles and garments sector, which is a strong outlier that may distort the measured slope of the regression line and therefore the signs of the estimated coefficients. The without-32 results are presented as a check on the with-32 case, and reported when they differ. Without 32, the residuals are well-behaved.

The results are also presented separately using the two schemes for distinguishing sectors by trade status – exportables, importables and non-traded goods (X/M) and traditional exports, non-traditional exports, and non-traded goods (TRX/NTX).

The Results for All Sectors

Table 8.3 presents the results of equation (8.1) for all sectors. The model explained about 20–30 per cent of the variation in *SA* for all sectors taken together when sector 32 was included and 10–15 per cent when it was not. The R^2 coefficients are low, but this was to be expected given the complexity of the underlying economic relationships. By singling out three types of variables – personal characteristics, wages and trade orientation of sectors – a large number of variables were left out of the equation. That these three factors explained a third of the variation in the change in employment of share of sectors between 1980 and 1989 is remarkable. And since the model aimed not to predict, but to explain the forces at play, a low R^2 is acceptable.

Table 8.3   Results for all sectors

Variable	X/M	TRX/NTX	X/M	TRX/NTX
	With sector 32		Without sector 32	
b_0	1.48	0.96	0.86	0.51
	(76.64)	(51.99)	(54.50)	(33.22)
ME	0.06	0.03	0.03	0.02
	(110.21)	(67.64)	(76.90)	(58.93)
FE	−0.03	−0.03	−0.04	−0.04
	(−38.29)	(−38.85)	(−55.82)	(−54.47)
G	−1.90	−1.55	−1.31	−1.19
	(−101.56)	−86.11)	−86.55)	−79.82)
MA	−0.01	−0.01	−0.01	−0.01
	(−21.76)	(−20.93)	(−15.63)	(−16.16)
FA	−0.04	−0.03	−0.03	−0.03
	(−34.85)	(−33.35)	(−31.35)	(−31.93)
MA^2	0.00	0.00	0.00	0.00
	(24.26)	(22.97)	(21.63)	(21.61)
FA^2	0.00	0.00	0.00	0.00
	(18.17)	(18.84)	(20.67)	(22.01)
lnW	−0.04	−0.09	−0.10	−0.11
	(−17.27)	(−42.30)	(−57.57)	(−67.67)
D_1	0.36	0.77	−0.04	0.35
	(79.80)	(223.56)	(−11.42)	(122.91)
D_2	−0.29	−0.05	−0.23	0.04
	(−63.35)	(−14.07)	(−64.97)	(15.48)
R^2	0.23	0.29	0.11	0.14
F	14,358.53	19,557.39	5,719.48	7,210.94

The *F*-test and *t*-statistics were significant at virtually the 100 per cent level; even weak relationships were found to be significant with the very large sample used. Also, the results were remarkably consistent in sign and under both groupings of sectors by trade status.[19]

The human capital variables performed almost as expected, similar both in sign and in approximate magnitude under both trade schemes. The estimated coefficient on male education was positive. For example, in the X/M (with-32) case, the estimated coefficient on *ME* was 0.06. Thus, sectors that expanded more tended to have a greater proportion of males with more schooling than sectors that contracted or expanded less. That is, a sector in which

males had on average one more year of schooling expanded their employment share by 0.06 percentage points, other things being equal.

The coefficient on FE was negative, the only unexpected result. This is
because women are clustered into four sectors, one of which (social services)
is characterized by high education and declines under adjustment and another
(personal services) is characterized by low education and expansion.[20] These
two large, non-traded sectors determined the slope of the relationship between FE and SA. Without the four, female-intensive sectors, the estimated
coefficient on FE became positive and stronger than that for men.

The education coefficients retained their signs and magnitudes when trade-
status variables were included, suggesting that the trade-status dummies are
not primarily measuring the influence of education on SA. This was confirmed by the simple correlation coefficients between the dummy variables
and ME and FE, which show the variables were not collinear.

The negative coefficient on G, the gender dummy, suggests that sectors
that grew faster under adjustment have higher shares of women employees
than sectors that grew less fast or contracted. This is true under both trade-
orientation schemes, although the influence of G was smaller without the
textiles and garments sector, where female employment is high.[21]

The positive association between women and sectoral expansion during
adjustment was partly demand-led, due to the growth of manufactured exports which employ disproportionately large numbers of women. This association was also partly supply-led, the result of an increase in the female
workforce participation rate (FWFPR) which inflated employment in sectors
where women are traditionally clustered; two of these strongly expanded
during adjustment.[22] That the estimated coefficients on education and age
remained significant even with wages included in the equation suggests that
education and age genuinely affect SA. Income often varies systematically
with both education and age.

If the Krueger thesis is correct, that sectors with 'artificially high wages'
are less internationally competitive and therefore expand less under adjustment than other sectors, then the wage variable would be negatively correlated to SA. On the other hand, if the wage variable essentially captures
unmeasured human capital characteristics, then the estimated coefficient would
be expected to be positive.

The estimated coefficient on $\ln W$ was negative, with and without sector 32
and for both trade schemes. That the estimated coefficients on $\ln W$ were
significant suggests that wages differ between sectors after controlling for
personal characteristics, which confirms previous findings. That the coefficient was negative suggests that sectors that have grown faster under adjustment have a lower share of individuals earning 'artificially high wages' than
sectors that grew less fast or contracted, as Krueger would suggest.

Thus, in the X/M (with-32) case, the estimated coefficient on ln$W$ was −0.04. So, an increase in ln$W$ by one unit (a 2.7-fold or 171 per cent increase) would be associated with a 0.04 percentage point decrease in SA, other things being equal.

The signs of the estimated coefficients on the trade-status dummies were largely as theory would predict.

Using the X/M classifications (with-32), the estimated coefficient on D_1 was 0.36. This suggests that exportables sectors grew on average 0.36 percentage points more than importables sectors, holding other variables constant. However, in the without-32 case, the sign on D_1 was negative, suggesting that exportables sectors grew less than importables sectors, everything else being equal. Since the without-32 results were a check on the with-32 case, the result must be regarded as inconclusive. Exportables and importables may not have adequately captured the shifts that occurred in Costa Rica in the 1980s, such that the expected relationship was not present when the outlying exportables sector, textiles and garments, was eliminated. Hence, the model was also estimated using traditional and non-traditional export sectors.

However, the estimated coefficient on D_2, non-tradables, was as predicted, with and without sector 32; non-tradables were expected to be negatively associated with SA relative to importables. In the X/M (with-32) case, the estimated coefficient on D_2 was −0.29 which means that employment share in non-traded sectors declined on average by 0.29 percentage points relative to importables sectors, other things being equal.

The TRX/NTX groupings also produced the expected results. With sector 32, the positive coefficient on D_1 shows that non-traditional sectors grew on average 0.77 percentage points more than traditional sectors, other things being equal. Without sector 32, the coefficient remained positive, but about halved in size.

The sign on the dummy variable representing non-traded sectors, D_2, was negative when sector 32 was included and positive when sector 32 was excluded. Thus, non-traded sectors declined on average by 0.05 percentage points relative to traditional sectors with sector 32, and increased by 0.04 percentage points relative to traditional sectors, without sector 32. As in the X/M case, the evidence on the relationship between non-traded sectors relative to traditional sectors must be considered inconclusive, because the with-32 and without-32 results conflicted.

Results for Private Sectors Only

Table 8.4 presents the estimated coefficients from equation (8.1) for private sectors only, with and without sector 32 and using both trade-status groupings.

Table 8.4 Results for private sectors only

Variable	X/M	TRX/NTX	X/M	TRX/NTX
	With sector 32		Without sector 32	
b_0	1.00	0.54	0.48	0.14
	(49.56)	(27.81)	(30.63)	(9.39)
ME	0.06	0.03	0.03	0.02
	(99.38)	(54.98)	(69.12)	(49.20)
FE	0.01	0.01	−0.01	−0.01
	(15.11)	(9.38)	(−10.39)	(−11.36)
G	−1.24	−0.96	−0.85	−0.74
	(−62.98)	(−50.56)	(−56.17)	(−49.98)
MA	−0.02	−0.02	−0.02	−0.01
	(−41.94)	(−21.72)	(−37.34)	(−37.52)
FA	−0.02	−0.02	−0.02	−0.02
	(−22.18)	(−21.72)	(−20.48)	(−21.44)
MA^2	0.00	0.00	0.00	0.00
	(38.04)	(36.10)	(37.20)	(36.95)
FA^2	0.00	0.00	0.00	0.00
	(16.12)	(17.26)	(21.02)	(22.54)
$\ln W$	−0.05	−0.11	−0.13	−0.15
	(−22.06)	(−50.20)	(−76.32)	(−88.52)
D_1	0.35	0.73	−0.05	0.33
	(77.73)	(213.03)	(−15.02)	(125.76)
D_2	−0.36	−0.14	−0.31	−0.04
	(−78.88)	(−39.93)	(−95.13)	(−17.38)
R_2	0.31	0.36	0.22	0.24
F	17,925.42	22,869.02	10,484.11	12,868.78

The results were very similar to those for all sectors, although by increasing the homogeneity of sectors, the explanatory power improved; R^2 ranged from 31 to 36 per cent with sector 32 and from 22 to 24 per cent without sector 32. The *F*-statistic also rose in all cases. Since the public sector sometimes resists or is less affected by some of the incentives changed by adjustment, removing it should have increased the significance of the measured relationships.

The estimated coefficients on male education (*ME*), gender (*G*), the age variables, wages ($\ln W$) and the trade-status dummy (D_1) had signs and magnitudes similar to the all-sector case. Only the coefficients on female education (*FE*) and D_2 changed as follows.

First, the estimated coefficient on *FE* (with-32) turned from negative to positive for both trade groupings, probably because social services were removed. However, once the textiles and garments sector was also removed, the sign reverted to negative. The results were inconclusive.

Second, the coefficient on D_2 using the TRX/NTX trade-status classification became more strongly negative with- and without-32 compared to the all-sector case, turning from positive to negative when sector 32 was removed. It appears that non-traded sectors declined more relative to traditional sectors, once the public sector was removed. That is, private non-traded sectors contracted more than public non-traded sectors.

The estimated coefficient on wages remained negative in all cases, as the Krueger hypothesis predicts, but became stronger once the public sector was removed; since the public sector does not respond as directly as the private sector to changing relative prices, 'artificially high' wages are less likely to explain its employment changes.

CONCLUSIONS

The model presented here confirms that sectors which expanded during adjustment had higher proportions of people with more basic education than sectors which contracted or expanded less, which is consistent with the argument that better human resources facilitates economic flexibility and adjustment. Such sectors would also have expanded if trade liberalization allowed Costa Rica to take better advantage of its comparative advantage in products requiring large numbers of workers with a basic education. It is not possible to distinguish the presence or magnitude of the two effects within a one-country study.

Male education was found to be positively associated with *SA* under both trade-status schemes for all sectors and for private sectors only. This was true even after the influence of wages and trade status of sectors was controlled. Female education was found to be negatively associated with *SA* under both trade-status schemes. This was an unexpected result given that basic education is thought to be essential to employment in the garments and textiles sector and that this sector flourished during adjustment in Costa Rica. It appears that two large sectors, one characterized by high education and decline under adjustment and another characterized by low education and expansion, dominated the slope of the relationship between *FE* and *SA*. Without the female-intensive sectors, female schooling was positively associated with *SA*, as it was for men.

It seems equally true that sectors that expanded during adjustment had lower proportions of people earning 'artificially high' wages than sectors that contracted or expanded less; that is, after controlling for personal characteristics of workers, wages were negatively associated with *SA* in all cases. The consistent negative sign on wages suggests that it was predominantly picking up institutional rigidities in the labour market, as Krueger predicts, rather than unmeasured human capital characteristics.

Gender influenced the results strongly. The relationship between *SA* and schooling was different for men and women. The significance of the gender dummy variable suggests that the relationship between *SA* and the other variables had different intercepts for men and women. It is likely that the positive association between sectoral expansion and female employment during adjustment was a product of both changing incentives under adjustment and the increase in female workforce participation.

Trade status explained a significant portion of the variation in relative sectoral adjustment in its own right. The trade-status dummy variables performed as expected. Exportables sectors expanded relative to importables sectors, although this result was not confirmed by the without-32 case. Non-tradables sectors contracted relative to importables sectors.

Likewise, non-traditional sectors expanded relative to traditional sectors, even when the textiles and garments sector was removed. Non-traded sectors contracted relative to traditional sectors, with one exception (the all-sector, without-32 case).

These results are presented in the spirit of explaining what happened, rather than constructing a model capable of prediction. The model at best explains about a third of the variation in *SA*; many other things are going on here in addition to the variables included in the equation.

The virtue of the exercise is to have captured small associations that some suspected were present, but had not previously been measured. The influence of schooling on the adjustment of sectors was found to be weak and diffuse: but it was there, and was not noticeably less important than the influence of wages, which have been the subject of most of the debate thus far.

NOTES

1. Although the evidence is thin, this idea is not contested. Lim (1980) and Ramanayake (1984) argue that workers in export-processing zones generally have at least some secondary schooling.
2. For details of Costa Rica's record of structural adjustment, see Nichols (1993).
3. The workforce includes employed people only, because the earnings of the unemployed and inactives do not accurately reflect wages in the sectors to which they are assigned. The sample is further narrowed to employees (wage-earners) because the income data are more accurate, although the relationships were also explored for employers, the self-employed, and unpaid family workers. See Nichols (1993). The workforce excludes workers with unknown values for sector of employment and schooling.

4. Data on employment by sectors are available after 1986 at the four-digit level. But because this study required a measure of employment change between 1980 and 1989, it was forced to work at the two-digit level.

5. The ranking was also done using a second adjustment measure, the average annual growth rate of sectoral employment between 1980 and 1989. This measure did not capture the broad-based shifts in employment that accompanied adjustment as well as *SA*, the change in the sectoral share of total employment, because a few small sectors that grew quickly from a small base dominated the expanding sectors. The results are available in Nichols (1993).

6. The only traditional export not contracting is cattle, where employment change was estimated arbitrarily, because of incomparability between the 1980 and 1989 surveys.

7. Works in this vein include Edwards and van Wijnbergen (1989), Lal (1984), Lopez and Riveros (1989), Riveros (1988), Demery and Addison (1988), Paldam and Riveros (1987), Fallon and Riveros (1989) and Fields (1983).

8. See article by Juhn, Murphy and Pierce (1993).

9. See Stiglitz (1974) on the efficiency wage hypothesis.

10. A test of the competing hypotheses would require disaggregating the ISIC sectors to the four-digit level where industries would be more homogeneous with respect to type of workers, working conditions, production and changes brought about by adjustment, union power and enforcement of regulations.

11. The equation tested was $\ln W = b_0 + b_1 ME + b_2 FE + b_3 MA + b_4 FA + b_5 MA2 + b_6 FA2 + b_7 G + b_8 D1 + b_9 D2 + u_i$, where all the variables are defined as in equation (8.1). See Nichols (1993) for tests and results.

12. According to Gindling and Berry (1990: Table 9), employers paid payroll taxes worth 21.25 per cent of base wages in 1978–82, 23.75 per cent in 1983–84 and 24.75 per cent in 1985–87. Employees paid another 7.5 per cent of base wages from 1978 to 1982 and 9 per cent thereafter. Other non-wage costs included vacations (3.8 per cent), holidays (2.1 per cent), loans (8.3 per cent) and Christmas bonus (8.3 per cent). Gindling and Berry (1990: Table 9).

13. Earnings for employees include wages, salaries, commissions, overtime, regular bonuses, plus all obligatory employee payroll deductions for social security, the Workers' Bank, savings and pension systems and non-obligatory deductions for personal loans or credits.

14. The number of people with part-time jobs is small in any case.

15. Non-traded sectors were those that did not have exports.

16. The 1984 Law for the Financial Equilibrium of the Public Sector defined traditional exports to include coffee, bananas, cocoa, sugar, cotton, tuna, beef and unfinished leather, unfinished wood products, and unprocessed minerals and mining products.

17. Costa Rica changed its custom's nomenclature in 1986, making comparisons of 1980–85 export lists with 1986–89 lists difficult. Products appearing for the first time in 1986 (that is, not obviously matched to a 1985 customs category) are assumed to be an artifact of the customs change and are not counted as new.

18. Statistics used to distinguish between exportable, importable, and non-traded sectors and between non-traditional, traditional and non-traded sectors are available in Nichols (1993).

19. The equations were also estimated using the same dependent variable, *SA*, but independent variables calculated from 1980 data. The results differ little. See Nichols (1993) for details.

20. The other two female-dominated sectors are textiles and garments and retail sales. Together, these four sectors account for two-thirds of total female employment.

21. The expanding female-dominated sectors (textiles and garments, personal services and retail sales) had more influence on the relationship between *G* and *SA* than the one female-dominated sector that contracted; social services declined sharply due to government budget cuts. The three growing sectors comprised nearly half of total female employment while social services accounted for only 19 per cent.

22. The rise in the FWFPR may be mainly the result of long-term changes in schooling and fertility, and thus largely unrelated to changing relative prices under adjustment, or as

Pollack (1985) argues, women may have entered the workforce to bolster family income when real wages fell during stabilization (1982–84).

REFERENCES

Demery, L. and T. Addison (1988), *Adjustment and Income Distribution: The Role of Labour Markets*, Discussion Paper, No. 81, Warwick University, Development Economics Research Centre.

Edwards, S. and S. van Wijnbergen (1989), 'Disequilibrium and Adjustment', Chapter 28 in H. Chenery and T.N. Srinivasan (eds), *Handbook of Development Economics*, Vol. II, New York: Elsevier Science Publishers B.V.

Fallon, P. and L. Riveros (1989), *Adjustment and the Labour Market*, Policy, Planning and Research Working Paper, No. 214, World Bank.

Fields, G. (1983), *Export-led Growth and Labour Markets*, Discussion Paper, No. 32, University of Warwick, Development Economics Research Centre, June.

Gindling, T.H. (1986), *Does Segmentation Exist in Costa Rica's Urban Labour Market?*, Documento de Trabajo, No. 92 Universidad de Costa Rica, Instituto de Investigaciones en Ciencias Economicas, San José.

Gindling, T.H. (1991), 'Labour Market Segmentation and the Determination of Wages in the Public, Private-Formal, and Informal Sectors in San José, Costa Rica', *Economic Development and Cultural Change*, **39** (3), April: 585–606.

Gindling, T.H. and Berry, A. (1990), 'Labour Markets and Adjustment in Costa Rica', Paper presented at the Conference on Labor Markets and Structural Adjustment,' 21–24 May, Warwick, England: mimeo.

Gindling, T.H. and A. Berry (1992), 'The Performance of the Labour Market during Recession and Structural Adjustment: Costa Rica in the 1980s', *World Development*, **20** (11): 1599–616.

Juhn, C., K. Murphy, and G. Pierce (1993), 'Wage Inequality and the Rise in Returns to Skills', *Journal of Political Economy*, **3** (10): 410–42.

Krueger, A. (1978), *Liberalization Attempts and Consequences*, Vol. X of *Foreign Trade Regimes and Economic Development*, Cambridge, MA: Ballinger Publishing Company for National Bureau of Economic Research.

Krueger, A. (1981), 'The Framework of the Country Studies', Chapter 1 in A. Krueger, H. Lary, T. Monson and N. Akrasanee (eds), *Trade and Employment in Developing Countries, Vol. 1, Individual Studies*, Chicago: University of Chicago Press for National Bureau of Economic Research.

Lal, D. (1984), *The Real Effects of Stabilization and Structural Adjustment Policies: An Extension of the Australian Model*, World Bank Staff Working Papers, No. 636.

Lim, L. (1980), *Women in the Redeployment of Manufacturing Industry to Developing Countries*, UNIDO Working Papers on Structural Change, No. 18. UNIDO, Division for International Studies, Global and Conceptual Studies Branch, UNIDO/ID/IS.

Lopez, R. and L. Riveros, (1989), *Macroeconomic Adjustment and the Labour Market in Four Latin American Countries*, Policy, Planning, and Research Working Papers, No. 335, World Bank.

MIDEPLAN (1988), 'The Behaviour of Non-Traditional Exports, 1980–87', *Serie Planidatos*, No. 16, San José.

Nichols, L. (1993), 'Structural Adjustment and Human Resources in Costa Rica', D.Phil. thesis, Institute of Development Studies, University of Sussex, UK.

Paldam, M. and L. Riveros (1987), *The Causal Role of Minimum Wages in Six Latin American Labour Markets*, Discussion Paper No. DRD270, Development Research Department, World Bank.

Pollack, M. (1985), *Household Behaviour and Economic Crisis: Costa Rica 1979– 1982*, Documento de Trabajo, No. 270, ILO, PREALC.

Ramanayake, D. (1984), 'Sri Lanka: The Katunayake Investment Promotion Zone', Chapter 7 in E. Lee (ed.), *Export Processing Zones and Industrial Employment in Asia*, Technical Workshop on Export Processing Zones and Industrialization, Manila: ILO.

Riveros, L. (1988), *Recession, Adjustment and the Role of Urban Labour Markets in Latin America*, Discussion Paper No. 82, Development Economics Research Centre, University of Warwick.

Stiglitz, J. (1974), 'Alternative Theories of Wage Determination and Unemployment in LDCs: The Labour Turnover Model,' *Quarterly Journal of Economics*, **88**: 194– 227.

Trejos, J.D. (1989), Characterization of the Urban Informal Sector in Costa Rica, Documento de Trabajo, No. 125, Universidad de Costa Rica, Instituto de investigaciones en Ciencias Economicas, San José.

Uthoff, A. and M. Pollack (1985), 'Microeconomic Analysis of Adjustment in the Costa Rican Labour Market, 1979–82: Lessons for a Macroeconomic Model', *Revista Ciencias Económicas*, V (1): 57–36.

World Bank (1987), *World Development Report*, Washington, DC: World Bank.

PART V

The View from the Enterprise

9. Training and motivation in the context of new approaches to manufacturing production: evidence from Latin America

John Humphrey

INTRODUCTION

This chapter considers the transformation of training which occurs when firms adopt cellular manufacturing, teamworking and quality at source. It argues that as firms in Latin America adopt new organizational techniques associated with improved quality and productivity, the nature of training and the breadth of training within firms changes. The chapter considers evidence as to whether firms will invest in this training and what types of policy interventions might be required to support training provision.

TECHNOLOGY, SKILL AND TRAINING

Within sociological discussions of the nature of work, the question of training in manufacturing has been closely linked to the issues of technology and skill. Generally speaking, technology is seen to define types of work and the skills needed to carry them out, and technological change is seen as a key factor in changing the nature of work. Touraine's pioneering work in this field, undertaken in the 1950s and 1960s, developed a three-stage model – from craft production, to mass production, to automation (1972: 53). In the transition from craft to mass production, work would be de-skilled, but with the development of automation, direct productive work would be eliminated and work would become more varied and demanding. With automation: 'the worker no longer actively intervenes in the manufacturing process. He superintends, he records, he controls' (Touraine 1972: 56). As a result, the skill content of work, which had declined between the first and second stages, would increase again with automation. The long-term trend towards de-skilling observed in the mass-production stage would be reversed.

Blauner (1964) made use of this three-stage model in his classic analysis of automation, which focused on four industries: printing (corresponding to the craft stage), textiles and automobiles (mass production) and chemicals (automated technology). Blauner argued that automation was eliminating the unskilled factory jobs typical of the mass production stage, and that while such jobs would persist for a very long time, the tendency would be for their relative importance to decline (1964: 169). Industries which did not automate would decline in importance, and automation itself would be applied in an increasing number of industries. Therefore, an upgrading of labour skills would take place, and the process industries of the time were foreshadowing the skill profiles typical of most industry in the future. Workers would require new skills, which would be less practical and more theoretical and conceptual than those in the craft industries. They would receive a combination of extensive formal training and training in-plant, together with the experience of work in teams, which would develop their problem-solving skills.

This approach was subjected to fierce criticism in the 1970s from authors inspired by Braverman and the labour process approach (Braverman 1974; Brighton Labour Process Group 1976), who argued that de-skilling was a tendency inherent in capitalist production, deriving from the antagonism between capital and labour and the need for control to be exercised in the factory. Braverman derided the view that automation would enhance skills – in capitalism, it will serve 'only to deepen the gulf between worker and machine and to subordinate the worker even more decisively to the yoke of the machine' (1974: 231).

In the past decade, the argument that capitalism must degrade labour and skills has been put into question by both theoretical and empirical analyses, centring on the impact of flexible automation, the reemergence of small-scale flexible production and the development of Japanese-inspired organization of work. Instead of the degradation of labour being characterized as an inevitable consequence of capitalist relations of production, it is now increasingly characterized as a consequence of Fordism, which is just one particular approach to capitalist production. It is argued that this approach is being superseded by new paradigms which are more efficient precisely because they seek to mobilize labour's skills and knowledge. However, the different alternatives to mass production have different implications for the way in which work and skills are transformed.

One of the new approaches focuses on the implications of the microelectronics revolution and the spread of flexible automation in industries producing discrete products. The work of Kern and Schumann (1987, 1988) has shown how flexible automation has changed patterns of work in the

German motor industry. Routine, repetitive tasks are increasingly performed by robots and other forms of automated machinery, and the work of the operative becomes that of maintaining equipment, scouting for mistakes and being prepared to deal with unforeseen eventualities. Unskilled workers are being eliminated because the tasks performed by them are being eliminated. The balance of work shifts towards the skilled, technically-trained workers, the *facharbeiter*. As Jürgens (1993: 12–13) points out, these are the skilled, problem solvers who have been through the vocational training and apprenticeship system. In so far as direct production tasks continue to exist, they are carried out by poorly-trained, unskilled workers. Automation increases this skill polarization, and also shifts the numerical balance towards the skilled workers. In the early stages of automation, large numbers of unskilled jobs may be created – the 'pick and place' jobs supplying robots with parts, for example (Jürgens, Dohse and Malsch 1984: 15) – but in the longer term these jobs might be eliminated too, leaving only the more skilled monitoring and repair jobs. Kern and Schumann show how the introduction of flexible automation shifts the balance of work away from repetitive work and towards work involving maintenance or the control of complex machinery (1988: 86–7). The effective use of flexible automation technologies requires a greater input from labour. To make full use of their potential for high-quality, diversified production, and to ensure that operating time is maximized, workers need to be skilled and flexible.[1] This implies high-level technical training so that workers can control and maintain advanced machinery. The model for this training is the German vocational training system, supplemented by continuing high-level training during the worker's time in the plant.

This view of the development of capitalism is not the only one which stresses a break with Fordism. Piore and Sabel (1984) also suggest that a new production paradigm is emerging. While this paradigm does draw on the opportunities opened up by flexible automation, it is independent of it:

> under appropriate conditions of competition, increased efficiency occurs with flexibility at *every* level of technological development. According to this argument what we are now witnessing is not a once-in-a-lifetime burst of improvement in flexible production techniques; rather it is a movement down a development path that we had the potential of taking earlier. (Piore and Sabel 1984: 258–9; stress in original)

The flexible specialization model argues that mass production, or Fordism, was only one possible route for capitalism to take, and that craft alternatives were ignored or suppressed. The non-Fordism option reemerged in the 1970s and 1980s in response to the crisis affecting capitalist economies and the emergence of more fragmented and competitive markets, which put a premium on flexibility. In this view, flexible automation is just one element in a broader institutional and competitive context.

Flexible specialization leads to a radical change in training requirements and locations:

> The extensive division of labour in mass production ... makes it possible to rely on two separate institutions for training employees: the formal education system and the firm itself. The formal education system is well adapted to providing potential employees with an abstract understanding of products and production ... The firm, for its part, is willing to pay for the training of the fraction of the work force that needs skills beyond those acquired by progressing up the job hierarchy.... Flexible specialisation, by contrast, cannot rely on these training mechanisms. Production runs are too short to spend time debugging products designed by inexperienced technicians. Designers must be so broadly qualified that they can envision product and production together; book learning alone does not teach this ability. Production workers must be so broadly skilled that they can shift rapidly from one job to another. (Piore and Sabel 1984: 273)

Piore and Sabel argue that skills are acquired in the community, through the family and through functional equivalents to the family which integrate workers into a community of the skilled. Pride in craft or strong attachments to a firm form the basis for ensuring that skills are acquired, and market mechanisms are of secondary importance (Piore and Sabel 1984: 274–5).

A quite distinct variant of the re-skilling hypothesis has emerged from the discussion of the 'Japanese' model. While Japanese firms have certainly taken a leading position with respect to flexible automation, in some firms, such as Toyota – the archetypal Japanese firm taken as the model for many generalizations about Japan and the future of mass production industries (for example, Womack, Jones and Roos 1990) – emphasis has been placed on reorganization of work. The development of just-in-time (JIT) and total quality management (TQM) has altered the role of labour in mass production industries, quite irrespective of their degree of automation.

As with automation, JIT/TQM requires increased labour involvement and flexibility, but there are two important differences. First, the reorganization of work takes a very different form. It depends more on a re-division of existing tasks than changes in the tasks themselves. It involves (i) the transfer of certain quality checking, machine preparation and routine maintenance tasks to direct production workers, which may be achieved without major changes to machinery and equipment, and (ii) the performance of a wider range of tasks by production workers and the ability to perform different sets of tasks at different times. Automation may play a role in reorganization of tasks, but it is not central.[2] The importance of U-shaped lines devised by Ohno at Toyota and their implications for work are described in some detail by Coriat. The effectiveness of the Ohno strategy lies not in the grouping of machines into cells, but in the linking of machines and product flows in such a way as to enable the number of workers and the range of tasks they perform to be adjusted rapidly (Coriat 1991: 62–3). In this case, flexibility is much more closely linked to the capacity of the worker than the machine, and the range of workers whose skills are raised is much greater than in the automation model.

Second, the JIT/TQM model places greater emphasis on the empirical adaptation of production processes at the point of production. Workers are more involved in the process of improvement. Improvement groups, quality circles, teamworking and *kaizen* are all part of the search for continual improvement on the shop floor.[3] Incremental improvements in production and the use of initiative and problem-solving skills make possible the ceaseless urge for improvement and the economy of time, labour, capital and materials which are so characteristic of the Toyota production system.

The reorganization of work in JIT/TQM has clear consequences for skill and training. The integration of tasks means that production workers must be trained to carry out a wider range of jobs. They will be expected to acquire knowledge through formalized and structured on-the-job training. This involves the planned acquisition of the ability to perform different tasks within a team or work group resulting from the rotation of workers between different jobs. The systematic and continuous acquisition of knowledge through on-the-job learning is one of the most distinctive features of the Japanese system (Hayashi 1992: 145). The integration of functions – the combination of quality, maintenance and production work – implies that production workers must be trained in order to be able to use measuring equipment, carry out statistical process control procedures, adjust equipment, read designs and charts, perform minor maintenance and be capable of alerting specialized staff when they detect problems which they are unable to resolve. Finally, the development of both teamworking and quality circles involves the use of more general abilities such as communication, conflict resolution, negotiation, problem solving and working collectively. In Japan, at least, a system which rewards workers for the acquisition of skill and experience and also penalizes workers who move between firms effectively ensures that workers seek training and the firm gains the returns from it.

There is a clear contrast between these skills and those required by the *facharbeiter* or 'monitor of complex systems' in automation. While both require a broader understanding of the production process than is typically the case in Taylorized production work, the systems monitor will also require considerable training in areas such as hydraulics, pneumatics and electronics. The more complex the machinery and the higher the level of automation, the more training will be required, although there is considerable scope for altering the dividing line between the job of the monitor and the job of the maintenance worker, or abolishing it altogether. In contrast, workers in teams may be involved in either simple or complex processes. The knowledge required need not be extensive, and the shift in work content is as much concerned with attitude and responsibility as with the acquisition of particular skills. A willingness to take initiative and assume responsibility, communication skills, an ability to work with others and a strong commitment to the enterprise are key attributes of the ideal worker. Training may be oriented to the acquisition of these skills and to multitasking and multiskilling.

On the other hand, the Japanese model (or one Western variant seen in some leading French firms) may produce a more profound change, concerning the nature of the relationship between production and training. The usual approach to defining training needs is to specify the production process and its division of labour and to derive from this the skills and competencies of the labour force. By comparing actual and required skills and competencies, training needs can be defined. However, the logic of the empirical adaptation of production processes can lead in a very different direction. One of the distinguishing features of the Japanese approach to production is that the degree of prescription involved in the process is limited. It is accepted that production processes cannot be defined completely in advance and can always be improved through processes of adaptation taking place on the shop floor. This is true for automated processes as well as non-automated ones.[4] If this is the case, then the relationship between work and training may be reversed.

In a factory which is continually changing, because processes are always being improved or because the external environment continually places new demands on it, competitive advantage lies not with a particular production process but with the ability to change it, making both major and incremental improvements. This ability to change and respond (or anticipate) is created by the organization of the firm – typically flat hierarchies, interdepartmental collaboration, teamwork, reward for innovation, and so on – and the abilities of the employees. If all employees, including those on the shop floor, are involved in change, then the training of production workers becomes a determinant of the production process rather than vice versa.[5] The workers' training requirements will be defined by (i) what they need to understand in order to contribute effectively to the transformation of work and (ii) the new skills required by the changes occurring in production. It can be argued that they need the latter in order to be able to think through the former. Without having new skills they cannot imagine a labour process which would require them. Therefore, training requirements are defined by what workers might come to need to know in the future. This perspective on skills is not one emphasized in Japan, but it is emerging in France. The work of Zarifian and Veltz, who are cooperating with leading French firms, is the clearest expression of it (Veltz and Zarifian 1992; Zarifian 1992).[6]

SKILL CHANGES IN DEVELOPING COUNTRIES

The analyses of technical change and skill outlined above have been focused on the experiences of industrially advanced countries (IACs). The impact of such changes on developing economies is not so clear. Three main scenarios for the impact of technical and organizational change can be distinguished in the literature:

1. Marginalization. The changes in IACs cannot be achieved in developing countries, and this widens the gap between them. The latter are left behind.
2. Division of labour. There is a specialization of tasks between IACs and developing countries. The former engage in more complex processes, the latter in simpler ones.
3. Following, catching-up or leap-frogging. New technology and new organization can be implanted in developing countries, and they may provide an opportunity for some leading developing countries to leap ahead of their IAC rivals (Soete 1985: 418).

In the case of new forms of work organization, all three positions have been advanced at various times and with respect to different countries. Marginalization has been suggested by Kaplinsky (1985: 433), who argues that the development of just-in-time production systems will lead to the relocation of suppliers closer to their customers. This would reverse the tendency seen in mass production for simpler parts of production processes to be switched to developing countries. Piore and Sabel (1984: 279) suggest that developing countries might specialize in mass production while the IACs develop flexible specialization. Womack, Jones and Roos (1990: 265–6) predict a specialization of markets, with developing countries increasingly tied into regional rather than world markets.

In spite of these predictions, there is evidence that manufacturing concerns in at least some developing countries are pursuing Japanese-style manufacturing strategies, using at least some elements of just-in-time and total quality management.[7] In response to both increasing competition in domestic markets and the shift towards competition in export markets based not only on price but also on quality, delivery, product range and innovation, companies in developing countries are experimenting with new forms of work organization in order to radically improve their competitiveness. As Bessant (1991) has argued, many of the new techniques can be applied not only to large-batch production processes but also to one-off production, small-batch production and process industries, as well as to parts of the service sector.

To stress the potential importance of Japanese-style work organization in developing countries is not to argue in favour of a wholesale shift in production paradigm from mass production to flexible specialization (or lean production or systemofacture). However, the evidence available does suggest that many firms are experimenting with Japanese-style methods and that this has significant consequences for the nature of skills, and the ways in which they are acquired. In the remainder of this chapter, attention will be focused on Latin America, and particularly on Brazil. The possible consequences of using new forms of work organization and the possible limitations on such developments arising from existing patterns of training and labour relations will be discussed.

MICRO-LEVEL CHANGES IN SKILL AND TRAINING IN LATIN AMERICA

One of the best-known examples of Japanese-style work organization in Latin America is the Ford plant at Hermosillo in northern Mexico. This plant, opened in 1986, was designed to emulate the performance of Japanese plants, which it managed to do in the early years of its operations, providing high-quality output for export to the North American market. Heavy investment in automation was combined with a radical restructuring of work, the pertinent features of which were:

1. teamworking in all areas of the plant;
2. systematic job rotations and multiskilling;
3. the linking of production and maintenance work through a system of temporary secondment of production workers to maintenance crews;
4. recruitment of well-educated workers;
5. initial training followed by experience and training-based promotion criteria to encourage further skill acquisition.[8]

Shaiken's conclusion (1994: 54–6) is that firms can gain good results from using sophisticated technologies even when labour is inexperienced if they recruit carefully, provide extensive initial and ongoing training, and put in seasoned management to oversee the project.

Ford Hermosillo may, however, be an exceptional case, involving an enormous investment in state-of-the-art technology and organizational methods on a greenfield site, rather than the new standard for the rest of Latin America. In fact, other firms in Latin America do appear to be adopting similar strategies with regard to work organization and training, as three examples taken from Brazilian manufacturing will illustrate. They show the potential for changing work organization and its implications for training in more prosaic and commonplace situations which have wider relevance for developing countries. Industry in Brazil has for a long time been characterized by low skill, poor training, high rates of turnover and poor-quality products. In response to changing demands from export customers and liberalization in domestic markets, some firms have been investing heavily in quality and productivity improvement, and this has had clear consequences for skill levels and training activities, as can be seen in the three firms.

Firm One is a subsidiary of a European multinational making motor components. The processes in the plant studied are simple, involving some plastic injection and galvanizing, and stamping, but otherwise mainly involving the assembly of small (less than one cubic foot) items supplied by other plants. The Brazilian subsidiary implemented a quality and productivity programme as part of the company's global strategy. The plant was visited in October 1991 and June 1993. In between visits, production had been completely restructured on a cellular basis. Production was just-in-time, with little or no buffer stocks within or between cells. Within each cell, teamworking was being used, and workers were expected to move between jobs and to switch particular tasks from one work station to another according to the throughput and number of workers in the cell. The members of the cell were also responsible for inspection and routine maintenance. Each cell had three teams (one for each shift) and a team leader – a qualified engineer who reported directly to the plant manager.

In order to develop the cells, the company invested heavily in training in two different ways. First, the firm provided off-the-job training for large groups of workers. For 1993 the training schedule amounted to an average of 68 hours for each of the plant's 292 production workers. All the workers in the plant attended courses given to small groups over a period of six months. These courses included fool-proofing (12 hours), rapid die-change (4 hours), safety (4 hours), basic maths for statistical process control (SPC) (20 hours), level 1 maintenance (6 hours), Crosby (4 hours), zero defects (10 hours) and multiskilling (10 hours). Between 30 and 60 workers were also trained in SPC, use of measuring equipment, welding and galvanizing.[9]

Clearly, courses of this length could do little more than introduce workers to the basic principles of the new production system – operator verification of quality, rapid die-change, SPC, preventive maintenance – and in large part such courses would be motivational – explaining the new system and encouraging workers to participate. However, these off-the-job courses were complemented by systematic on-the-job training within cells. A typical cell would consist of 6–8 workers. Clearly visible in each cell, on the desk used for planning in the meeting area, was a chart outlining skills, as shown in Figure 9.1. For each job in the area and for each of three general skills – SPC, self-

Different jobs to be performed in the cell

	1	2	3	4	5	6	7	8	SPC	Self-checking	Maintenance
Names of workers in team											
1											
2											
3											
4											
5											
6											
7											
8											

(For each job a worker's competence is indicated by means of coloured stickers indicating:
1. Has no understanding of job
2. Partial understanding
3. Full understanding
4. Can teach others
At the bottom of the chart there is a training schedule for the year)

```
                                    Month
Name      Course      Trainer      1 – – – – – – – – – – 12
```

Figure 9.1   Training and ability chart, Firm One

checking and maintenance – coloured stickers are used to indicate the level of competence of each worker in the cell. This is on public display and can provide an immediate visual check on levels of training. Attached to the chart is a second list, outlining the training to be given by workers within the cell to other workers in the cell, month-by-month for the year. In this way, the broadening of competence is institutionalized and established as a priority for the cell. This 'multiskilling' is a broad objective of the company internationally, the plant manager would have to report the levels of training and multiskilling attained in the plant as one of the performance indicators used by head office to monitor plant performance around the world.

One area in which the management at Firm One felt it had not made progress was in changing the occupational and reward structures in the plant to reflect and reinforce the team/cell system and the acquisition of new skills. Firm Two, however, does provide an example of how to make a radical shift in occupational structures. This firm was a Brazilian-owned manufacturer of components for cars and trucks. The component was more complex than that produced at Firm One, and it required a more complex production process involving a lot of heavy machining work. The plant had been restructured into cells. In many cases this involved a group of 3–4 workers operating a set of 6–8 machines arranged in a U-shape.

Traditionally, this type of plant would have an extensive set of job titles, reflecting the many different jobs performed in the plant and the different levels of skill and competence. Firms might have up to 100 job titles such as 'assistant', 'press operator', 'assembler', 'machine operator 1', 'machine operator 2', 'injection moulding worker', 'inspector', 'setter', 'advanced setter' and so on. In order to reflect the development teams and the need for the integration of machine preparation and operation, quality control and minor maintenance, the company had introduced a new occupational structure, as shown in Figure 9.2.[10] The number of occupational categories for production workers was reduced to six. Access to each depended on a mixture of on-the-job training and formal training in the company's training centre. While the initial two days of training was largely motivational and introduced new workers to the concepts of quality control circles, *kanban*, total quality, and so on, the content became increasingly technical. An operator/setter, for example, had to be able to prepare all the machines in the cell and be capable of carrying out routine maintenance on them. This involved courses in basic hydraulics and pneumatics, as well as extensive on-the-job training.

Firm Two had initially adopted an ambitious target – to have all its workers on grade six by 1996 – although this target was not achieved. As can be seen in Figure 9.3, a large number of workers had reached grade four by June 1993, but only three workers had achieved the second level of multiskilling, grade five. The uncertain economic situation in 1992–93 led to a suspension of promotions, even though management had expressed the view that an increased pay bill would be financed from greater productivity. The appreciation of the Brazilian currency following the *Plano Real* stabilization package in 1994 further added to the company's problems. In export markets, it faced a 16 per cent appreciation in the Real, but a declining dollar price from its

Grade One: Operator	
Integration	
Training for QC	
Kanban and cells	Two days
Safety	
Total quality philosophy	
Cleanliness and tidiness	
On-the-job training	6 months

Grade Two: Semi-Skilled Operator			Grade Three: Skilled Worker	
Product knowledge	8 hours		Reading and interpretation of designs	40 hours
Measurement	20 hours		Basic statistics	8 hours
On-the-job training	6 months		Total quality	8 hours
			On-the-job training	12 months

Grade Four (3 options):

Operator Setter		Quality Assurance Worker		Zero Defect Worker	
Machine preparation	8 hrs	Statistical process control	8 hrs	Minor machine maintenance	8 hrs
Lubrication	8 hrs	Graphs and charts	12 hrs	Care of tools	6 hrs
Care of tools	6 hrs	Quality systems	4 hrs	Lubrication	8 hrs
Basic pneumatics	40 hrs			Tool and equip. maintenance	8 hrs
Basic hydraulics	40 hrs			Basic electrics	40 hrs
				Basic hydraulics	40 hrs
				Basic pneumatics	40 hrs
On-the-job training	12 mths	On-the-job training	12 mths	On-the-job training	12 mths

Grade Five:	Grade Six:
Any two of the grade four skills	All three of the grade four skills

Source: Company documents and interviews.

Figure 9.2   Worker development plan, Firm Two

Grade	Occupation	Hours of training required[a]	Average wage[b]	Educational requirement	Employees 1993	Employees 1995
1	Operator	16	100	First grade or night school[c]	110	116
2	Semi-skilled operator	44	121	as above	247	210
3	Skilled operator	100	146	as above	839	476
4	Operator setter	202	177	as above	398	420
	Quality assurance worker	124			49	
	Zero defect worker	250			21	
5	Two level-four skills	226–274	214	First grade	3	8
6	Total quality operator (three level-four skills)	282[d]	285	First grade	0	0

Source: Company documents and interviews.

Notes
a. Cumulative hours of off-the-job training, provided mainly by the company in its own training centre, as shown in Figure 9.2. In addition, on-the-job training is required.
b. This figure represents the mid-point wage (which can vary according to bonuses, merit increments and so on) for each occupation expressed in relation to the mid-point for the operator function.
c. New recruits must have completed first-grade education (8 years). Workers already employed in the plant can only be promoted as far as grade four if they have a completed first-grade education or make a commitment to go to adult education evening classes.
d. Because the training courses for the three grade four occupations overlap, the increase in total hours of training as workers move from grade five to grade six is limited. Extensive on-the-job experience would be necessary, however. Workers would need not only to be competent in all the operations in the production cell in which they mostly work, but also to be capable of working in other cells.

Figure 9.3   Occupational structure at Firm Two, June 1993

main overseas customer. In the internal market, the major customers were using the appreciating currency and declining tariffs on components to force price reductions. In this context, the firm was cutting labour costs by laying off workers, rather than increasing pay. By mid-1995, the number of workers on grade four had fallen in absolute terms because of cuts in the labour force. Similarly, only eight workers had reached grade five, and none had yet reached grade six. In spite of these difficulties, the logic of cellular manufacturing had led the firm in the direction of teamworking and an emphasis on workers being able to perform a range of complex functions in one or more cells. A new occupational structure was then created to provide the structure and incentives needed to make polyvalence work.[11]

In order to provide the training required in-house, the company expanded its Education Centre built in 1983. This was housed in a purpose-built building in the middle of the plant site and provided two sorts of service. First, it helped with adult education. Literacy and numeracy levels of workers are poor among Brazilian labour, even in large firms (see below), and it is very common to find firms providing adult education schemes, or financing the participation of workers in schemes run in the locality. Second, it provided off-the-job training. The aim of the plant was to have more than 100 hours off-the-job training per employee in 1993, and about 80 hours was, in fact, achieved. This compares with levels found in Japanese auto plants (OTA 1992: 15).[12] The Education Centre has a number of tutors, and it also has recourse to the Industrial Training Agency, SENAI, when more advanced courses are provided for skilled workers, but much of the training is carried out by the plant's own staff.[13] An instructor is attached to each manager, and workers are trained to teach other workers.

Firm Three, a Brazilian conglomerate specializing in the production of white goods, has also developed an occupational structure reflecting teamworking. A new factory producing washing machines, dishwashers and tumble dryers was opened on a greenfield site in 1990. Production is based on the *kanban* system of activating production by demand from further along the line, quality-at-source and teamworking. By 1993, the plant demanded completed first-grade education, and it offered adult education to early recruits with less schooling. A clear promotion structure for employees was laid out, based on training courses taken, on-the-job experience and evaluation of performance. Production workers are recruited on the starting grade I A, and can qualify for promotion through grades IB, IC and ID over a period of 36 months, taking courses totalling more than 200 hours, gaining on-the-job experience and showing their ability to work in different jobs. From here, the employee can gain promotion to grade II, and in four more years to grade III. Some of this training will take place inside the plant, other parts will be administered by the levy-financed training agency, SENAI.

Given the newness of the plant, it is not possible to say how the system will work in practice. While all workers could, in principle, move to the top of grade II, further promotion opportunities will be limited. However, the ideology of the system, which is presented clearly to employees in a booklet outlining the scheme, is that workers will be rewarded by increased promotion and increased pay as they accumulate 'points'. These points are awarded according to training courses, job experience and performance evaluation. Workers are given charts to register their progress.[14] To reach the top of grade I, a worker would have to have received training in such areas as: interpersonal relations, accident prevention, *kanban*, preventive maintenance, quality, teamworking, basic mathematics, problem-solving techniques, basic mechanics and basic electrics. As in Firm Two, the aim is to have workers in teams capable of carrying out a full range of production, quality, setting and routine maintenance tasks. Some of these teams would be in cells, others on assembly lines.

TRAINING DEFICIENCIES IN LATIN AMERICA

These three examples show what is possible when firms recognize the training implications of new forms of work organization. These examples also illustrate the extent to which new training needs are extensive rather than intensive – involving large numbers of workers in relatively simple skill acquisition – and centred on the plant rather than on vocational training prior to employment or intensive training located in specialized training centres. However, there is also ample evidence that education and training remain serious problems for firms wishing to restructure their productive structures in Latin America. A study of 185 firms in the metalworking industries of four countries by PREALC provides important information. Some of the results are summarized in Table 9.1. The survey considered the use of techniques which change the work performed by labour – SPC, teamworking, and the integration of inspection and maintenance tasks with production work. It shows, first, that changes to the nature of work are taking place in Latin America, particularly in Brazil and Mexico. Tasks are being integrated. Firms are expecting to move further in this direction. Overall, in all of the countries, a minority of firms were using most of the techniques, even though one would expect larger firms in the metalworking industries to be among the first users of JIT/TQM.

This use of techniques associated with JIT/TQM is, however, combined with considerable doubts about workers' aptitudes, basic educational standards and skills. Most firms complain that workers have difficulties in taking responsibility and initiative. The kinds of abilities which a basic education might be expected to provide, such as the ability to concentrate, a capacity for abstraction, capacity to learn new skills, the ability to read and write and verbal skills, are all deficient. These are signs of failure in the educational system, and overall the level of problems reported by Brazilian firms is worse than in the other countries. The problems are widely known. A study, by Fleury and Humphrey, of 18 firms introducing new productivity and quality programmes, showed that the one area of government policy most regarded as in need of urgent action by company bosses was basic education (1993: 43–4). Table 9.2 shows the extent of the problem. The three firms cited above all saw first-grade education as the basic minimum they required for new employees,[15] but data from the most developed re-

Table 9.1   Indicators of reorganization, metalworking industry, four
countries (percentage of firms responding 'yes')

	Argentina	Brazil	Chile	Mexico
Programmes adopted 1990–92:				
Maintenance tasks transferred	10	42	13	16
Inspection/quality tasks transferred	29	53	50	48
SPC	0	43	0	36
Work teams	19	26	30	38
Programmes planned 1993–95:				
Maintenance tasks transferred	12	43	27	36
Inspection/quality tasks transferred	48	72	57	68
SPC	6	55	20	54
Work teams	23	57	40	44
Workers' aptitudes:				
Difficulties in assuming responsibilities	70	94	83	83
Difficulties in taking initiatives	63	84	79	67
Basic education issues:				
Workers unable to concentrate	66	65	64	63
Lack of capacity for abstraction	54	49	41	54
Cannot learn new skills and abilities	42	69	64	56
Difficulties in reading and writing	33	65	39	51
Limited verbal skills	30	54	45	44
Skill:				
Poor middle management	58	77	70	78
Workers cannot operate new equipment	42	60	53	57
Scarcity of skilled production labour	78	67	79	76
Scarcity of technical and professional staff	33	75	68	69
No. of companies surveyed	52	53	30	50

Source: Abramo (1993).

gion of the country, the metropolitan region of São Paulo, shows clearly
that formal sector manufacturing industry is unable to obtain even young
workers with this level of schooling. Less than half the population aged 18–
24 of the metropolitan region had completed first-grade education in 1987,
and among manual workers in industry, the corresponding figure was only
38.5 per cent. Among metalworkers, very much the elite of the manufacturing labour force, 45.8 per cent of young workers had completed first grade.
For older workers, the figures are much lower. This is why so much emphasis is placed on adult education and basic training in literacy and numeracy
in innovating firms in Brazil.

In the light of the deficiencies in basic education highlighted by the PREALC
study it is perhaps surprising that any training takes place at all, particularly

Table 9.2 *Proportion of selected groups having completed at least first-grade education, São Paulo metropolitan region, 1987, age groups 18–24 and 25–59 (in per cent)*

	Completed first grade	
	18–24 Years	25–59 Years
Whole population	52.4	37.4
Employed in manufacturing	48.6	40.9
Manual workers in industry with formal registration[a]	38.5	25.3
Manual workers in metalworking with formal registration[b]	45.8	29.5

Notes:
a. Manual Occupations are those in the PNAD which correspond to the Brazilian Occupational Classification codes 700–999. Formal registration refers to workers whose work documents have been signed by the employer. This formalizes the employment contract.
b. Metalworking includes the metallurgical, mechanical, electrical/electronic and transport materials industries.

Source: Calculated from Pesquisa Nacional por Amostra de Domicílios (PNAD) data for the São Paulo metropolitan region.

as Latin American firms have in the past tended to underinvest in training. It is possible that firms are complaining too much. Few managers are ever satisfied with their labour supply, even though they may do little to rectify the situation. It is clear that use of JIT/TQM techniques is not necessarily blocked by these labour supply problems. Brazil, which not surprisingly has the worst indicators for basic education, also has the highest use of programmes which extend the activities of production workers. What does this imply for the spread of JIT/TQM?

First, the contrast between poor education and training and widespread adoption of JIT/TQM shows that poor educational standards are not a barrier to the use of JIT/TQM. However, firms may have to invest heavily in education and training to improve labour's skills and capacities. This is evident in Brazil. Firms developing JIT/TQM have often developed adult education programmes for their labour forces, literacy and numeracy programmes, and intensive training programmes, not only in technical skills but also in such basic skills as communication and group discussion.[16] This imposes a cost burden that firms struggling to compete in rapidly liberalizing economies could well do without. It also poses a particular problem for smaller firms, which may lack the infrastructure and resources to invest in education programmes, and which may not be able to pay higher-than-average wages to secure the better-educated labour. The state should take seriously the complaints of entrepreneurs noted above, and consideration might be given to support for firm-based adult education, particularly for small and medium-sized firms, if standards cannot be raised quickly.

Secondly, it seems clear that the quality of labour matters for firms introducing JIT/TQM, and there is a risk that firms which have difficulties in finding or training suitable labour may adapt their work organization to the characteristics of their labour forces. Instead of making heavy investments to make JIT/TQM possible, they will instead opt for production practices which need less input from labour. Firms become locked into cycles of labour capacities and work organization which reinforce each other. Poorly-trained and -educated labour becomes confined to tasks which do not develop capacities. Carvalho (1994) has expressed concerns about work organization and education in the Brazilian petrochemical industry. Firms will either fail in their attempts to adopt JIT/TQM at all or seek variants of JIT/TQM which do not require increased skills and responsibilities compared to more traditional work organization. The dangers in this are highlighted by Posthuma's analysis of firms in Zimbabwe (Posthuma 1995). Her study shows how six firms adopted a JIT approach, working with a team of local consultants. In most cases, a lack of commitment by top management and a failure to either train or motivate labour led to poor results. Initial gains were made but then lost.

TRAINING PROVISION IN BRAZILIAN INDUSTRY

Training of employees within firms or financed by firms should be central to new manufacturing strategies, and it is widely recognized that improvements in productivity over the coming decade will require enormous investments in training. In at least some cases, as shown above, firms are making the required efforts to improve the capacities of their labour forces. Training efforts arise in the context of a radical restructuring of production involving major changes to the content of work, and a major shift in occupational structures designed to facilitate functional flexibility and skill acquisition. Given the problems noted in the previous section, why were the three Brazilian firms studied willing to make big investments in training, and what does this imply for training policy?

Two possible explanatory factors would seem to be ruled out. First, the state has not increased support for training. On the contrary, some tax breaks for training have been removed. Given that they were considered to be largely ineffective, this would not have hampered training provision, but it would not have encouraged it either. It is also noteworthy that many of the increased training efforts of firms do not appear to be financed through the existing levy system. SENAI's major expansion of activities has been in services paid directly by the firms themselves. Secondly, JIT/TQM does not involve highly specific training whose benefits will only accrue to the trainer. While it is true that the implementation of JIT/TQM is firm specific – one firm will use the *kanban* pull system to control production, another might use a variant of materials requirement planning, depending on the nature of the production process; one will look to Deming as a source of inspiration, another to Crosby – much of the training involved is based on general courses, such as the introduction to SPC or the use of measuring equipment or, even more basically, how to work in groups.

Five factors seem to explain why the three firms were willing to invest in training:

1. Firms in Brazil are under considerable pressure to improve their competitive performance following the trade liberalization policies introduced in 1990. Markets are no longer protected to anything like the extent seen since the 1930s. This change alone may encourage investment in training as firms seek to reduce the competitive gap between their past performance and international standards (see Cassen and Mavrotas, Chapter 5 in this book).

2. With JIT/TQM, the gains from training can be immediate and apparent. At the same time, the simple training required for much of JIT/TQM can be applied immediately in production and reinforced by job rotation and on-the-job training.

3. JIT/TQM greatly increases the costs of *not* training. As Oliver and Wilkinson (1992) have argued, JIT systems are vulnerable to disruption. There are few buffers, and the impact and spread of disruption are rapid. Therefore, in so far as JIT is being introduced, extensive training is needed to make it work. This training aims both to increase competence and also to change attitudes. Motivation is central to JIT/TQM, and an important component of training programmes is motivational. For example, the training programmes for TQM at an electronics multinational included in the Fleury and Humphrey study (1993) involved not only elements of customer awareness and the importance of quality as a competitive advantage, but also exercises in identifying internal 'customers' within the plant and establishing their requirements. Once again, this type of training can be reinforced by subsequent practice. Identifying internal clients can be followed by encouraging these clients to complain directly to 'their' suppliers when things are not right.[17]

4. JIT/TQM can often provide substantial short-term benefits – gains in space, stock reduction, defect rates and so on. It is only over a period of time that the need for substantial investments in training becomes evident as firms seek further improvements and the consolidation of the achievements already secured. At this point, firms may well see the need

to make substantial investments in training, but they only emerge once
the company is committed to JIT/TQM. [18]

5.   When JIT/TQM is accompanied by a shift in occupational structures of
the type seen in Firms Two and Three, management may be able to
exercise a higher degree of control over the rewards for training, and this
can reduce turnover and increase motivation. By paying wages well
above the going rate to those workers who reach the higher levels of the
new occupational structures, management may reduce turnover. At the
same time, performance appraisal and appraisal-linked promotion can
encourage workers to translate their increased knowledge into better
performance.

For all these reasons it is not at all uncommon for a commitment to JIT/TQM
to be accompanied by investments in training. Training is essential for JIT/
TQM, and given that both the costs and the benefits of embarking on a new
production strategy are considerable and unpredictable – they are not incremental or marginal, but rather require a leap of faith – firms may 'buy in' to
training as part of a much broader package of change. Their whole attitude to
labour and training is transformed by the shift in production strategy.

Does this mean, then, that training is no longer a problem which needs to
be addressed by the state? Is the key question the adoption of new production
strategies based on just-in-time and total quality, with training following on
as a consequence of this decision? The results of the PREALC study urge a
certain caution in this regard.

THE LIMITS TO TRAINING PROVISION

The apparent evidence of a willingness of firms in Brazil to engage in extensive training as part of a process of restructuring production should not, by
itself, be taken as evidence that no market failures are likely to occur. The
three firms studied were all large enough to have extensive in-house training
and personnel departments, which many firms do not have. They also made
use of the levy-funded training agency, SENAI. Firm Three, for example,
used SENAI for its more advanced courses, and SENAI also provides both
training materials and courses for trainers, which facilitate the efforts of firms
conducting their own training. It is also clear that for more technically-
qualified work associated with the restructuring of production (quality audit,
maintenance of electronics-based machinery, advanced measurement skills
and so on), training will be beyond the capacity of most firms to provide.

It is not impossible that the private sector could provide such courses, were
the demand to be evident. However, in Chile, where training provision has
been given over to the private sector, there is little sign that provision of

specialized, industry-oriented courses is widespread. On the contrary, one of the criticisms of private training provision is that it is mainly concentrated in areas where there is a large demand for standardized courses, such as in language training and computer skills. It is notable that when groups of firms feel the need to develop skills, they seek collective organization to provide them rather than wait for the private sector to supply individual firms. This suggests that coordination of training demands is required. One means of coordinating such demands is through levy-financed agencies such as SENAI. While it is not the only means, it clearly has played an important role in São Paulo, and the firms in the Fleury and Humphrey survey were generally very positive about its role.

The three firms discussed above also differ in one key respect from many other firms, not only in Brazil, but in other countries. They had made a wholesale commitment to the new production system, and they had restructured their layouts, production control systems, occupational structures and managerial hierarchies to make this commitment work. Improvements in training were part of a wider package of changing organization and labour use. However, as Kaplinsky (1995) has argued, it is possible to distinguish between JIT/TQM as system and as technique. Systemic, plant- or company-wide applications are not nearly as common as the adoption of specific techniques. Systemic change is beyond the capabilities of many firms. While in principle this may seem the best option, in practice it requires considerable foresight, risk taking, resources and managerial skills. For many firms, these are in short supply, and significant gains can be made in the short term from limited applications of JIT/TQM techniques. [19]

In this situation, the 'average' firm, as opposed to the leading innovators, might well require some support for training. Without it, firms may become locked in a low-level equilibrium, providing little training or skill and adapting their use of JIT/TQM to the inadequacies of the labour they are employing. In some cases, this may not have serious consequences for quality and productivity. Firms working with simple processes may be able to benefit from relatively straightforward use of pull-systems or production, cells and operator responsibility for quality, which do not involve major enhancement of workers' skills. But when processes become more complex – either because of the precision of the operation or the complexity of product flows, low-skilled labour may be a significant barrier to efficiency. As processes become more complex, and more unpredictable, the ability to understand what is happening and either to intervene or to communicate the problem to others becomes crucial.

Small and medium-sized firms may face particular problems with regard to training. When demand for skilled labour is concentrated on a few toolroom and maintenance workers, small firms can 'poach' ready-trained workers from larger firms. Skills are general, and the firm can pay attractive wages for a small number of workers.[20] If the whole workforce has to be trained, this option is not feasible. Poaching would be difficult, and paying high wages would offset one of the cost advantages of the small firm. Therefore small firms may be placed at a disadvantage.

One key implication of the argument so far is that part of the problem lies in the demand for training. Firms need to perceive the need for training. Therefore, the promotion of training should be closely linked to programmes aimed at improving quality and productivity. If firms reorganize work, they should be able to use better training and take advantage from it, which encourages them to make the efforts to overcome the very real problems involved in training. In other words, the key to training provision lies not only in providing the right type of training at the right cost (although both are important) but in creating the conditions in which the firms can benefit from training. The promotion of training can be linked to broader policies of promoting company performance, of which there are several different types aimed at different types of firms:

1. Training can be linked to reorganization initiatives such as the Brazilian government's Brazilian Programme for Quality and Productivity (PBQP), and the provision of support can be channelled through sectoral associations active in the field. A levy-funded body such as SENAI can be drawn into the promotion campaign. It is reasonable to suppose that government encouragement for JIT/TQM adoption and the fostering of flows of information between firms by means of sectoral associations, as seen in the PBQP, will by themselves encourage some systemic JIT/TQM and the training efforts associated with it, particularly if firms can reduce turnover as a result of providing better promotion opportunities and a better working environment.

2. Training can be put in the context of promoting links between large and small firms. When small firms are linked to larger ones as subcontractors, the resources of the latter may be used to help the former, but this may require outside help. In developing countries, large firms developing JIT/TQM often complain that they cannot focus their production, deverticalizing and contracting out, because they cannot find reliable suppliers. If technical assistance and training support is targeted at potential or actual subcontractors, possibly with some financial contribution from the larger customer, the small and medium enterprises (SMEs) may see the need for change and have the means to make it. In Brazil, SEBRAE, the government-sponsored service for small enterprises, has launched a 'Programme to Upgrade Small Suppliers'. The programme is aimed at the small firms who provide specialized components or services and it seeks to raise their quality and delivery standards. To do so it

hooks into existing supply chains. For example, in the case of footwear, the entry point is the large shoe manufacturer through whom contact is established with the small suppliers. The upgrading work itself includes training for both the contractor and the small suppliers.[21]

3. Small firms can also gain from developing links with each other. In Chile, for example, SERCOTEC has developed *Proyectos de Fomento* as a means of stimulating cooperation between small firms.[22] The aim is to develop a better interface between the firms and their market and institutional contexts, joint action, and improved economies of scale and scope through interfirm divisions of labour. Training can improve, first, because a group of small firms can more easily make its needs felt to institutions and markets. Their size has more of an impact in the market. In the case of training, for example, 20 small firms may have more of an opportunity to buy courses which are tailored to their needs.[23] Second, closer contacts between firms in the same field can help to display the advantages of training. If one firm appears to benefit, others will follow. Third, cooperation may also reduce 'poaching' of workers. Fourth, training is developed as part of a broader package of improvement which arises from the increased division of labour between firms. If firms use the gains made from this division of labour to open up more demanding markets requiring better quality and reliability of delivery, then each firm needs to improve its performance. In this context, training offers benefits because it occurs in a context in which all the firms are trying to improve their performance.

Once the issue of creating a demand for training has been addressed, the issue of how training should be supplied becomes important. Centralized, out-of-plant training is not suitable for the extensive application of limited skills, and the particular courses offered have to be tailored to the needs of the firms concerned.

In a market-oriented model of training provision, as in Chile, the state plays a role, assisting with diagnoses of training needs, establishing contacts between providers and purchasers, assessing the quality of provision, and providing credit or subsidies for purchasers. Much of the rest is left to the private sector, but it seems clear that private bodies seem better able to offer courses which are less technical in content and open to a wider audience. In Chile, the majority of courses offered by private training agencies (OTEs) are in general skills such as computing and languages, which are not in any way industry specific (SENCE 1993). Courses which require greater technical knowledge and input require greater links with the recipients. Sectoral associations and sectoral technical institutes may be able to remedy some of these deficiencies. In the textile industry and in the furniture industry in Chile, sectoral associations are actively seeking to offset skill deficiencies, particularly in the areas of design and technical skills, which are central to market-upgrading strategies. If the state wishes to support training (and even in free-market Chile this has been done through tax credits), encouraging the development of coordinating bodies in the private sector may be an efficient way to proceed, particularly in sectors in which firm size is small. The promotion of sectoral and intermediary bodies and of networks of firms for training would be part of broader packages of promotion outlined above.

Alternatively, training could be provided in part through levy-financed training boards, as in Brazil and Colombia. In Brazil, the training board has shown itself adept at responding to emerging needs and complementing its activities by providing non-levy financial training. Even in the case of large firms, which have the infrastructure to deliver training and human resources departments which can define needs and put on courses, there are unrealized economies of scale in training, particularly in developing materials. In São Paulo, the levy-financed training agency, SENAI, sells course materials to firms, and it has recycled courses developed by leading companies. One of its most popular short courses, Statistical Process Control, was originally developed by GM for use by its suppliers. Increasingly, SENAI's services are being called upon by firms to a level beyond the entitlement arising from the levy, and SENAI is charging firms for its expertise. This again indicates that with the increasing pressures in the economy to improve quality and productivity, the demand for training will emerge. The role of government is to ensure that this demand can be met by bodies which are responsive to the training needs of companies of different sizes and with different problems.

NOTES

1. There is now a large literature on the central role of workers in the automated factory. Far from labour's role being eliminated, automated factories require key inputs from labour if they are to function correctly.
2. This is a crucial difference between Kern and Schumann's analysis and the Japanese model. Kern and Schumann argue that when tasks are automated, production and quality control tasks do tend to be integrated, but their discussion of the transformation of assembly work in the context of matching the Japanese is almost entirely centred on the possibilities for automation (1988: 57–9). From the JIT/TQM perspective, flexible automation may be required to overcome specific production bottlenecks, but it is not a necessary condition for flexible production. Conversely, it is not a sufficient condition. Flexible machinery can be used in inflexible ways. Clearly, Japanese firms make extensive use of automation, but this is driven forward by labour cost considerations. Japanese firms overseas and emulators of Japanese methods may employ them with less automation, particularly in developing countries.
3. Kaplinsky (1994: xviii) defines *kaizen* as 'a process of continuous improvement in production procedures and product characteristics, usually resulting from direct participation by the labour force'. The importance of these improvements for overall productivity is,

however, subject to some dispute. Many suggestions are certainly made by workers, but they may be minor and marginal. Engineers and technical staff may play a much larger role. Nomura (1993: 57) argues that quality circle activities at Toyota are peripheral and designed to motivate workers.

4. For a comparison of French prescription and Japanese continual improvement in the commissioning of automated bottle-making plants, see Freyssenet (1992).

5. This focus on production workers should not obscure the enormous importance of other factors, such as managerial structures, the integration of engineering and production work, accounting systems and so on, which are crucial for flexible response and continuous improvement.

6. The clearest expression of these ideas to be given to the author came from a manager at a French subsidiary in Brazil.

7. See, for example, (ed.) Kaplinsky (1994) and Humphrey (ed.) (1995).

8. These points are taken from Shaiken (1990, 1994).

9. The courses concern techniques and principles of just-in-time and total quality control. SPC is a technique for monitoring process variations using means and variance calculations to determine when a process is going out of its control limits. Crosby refers to Philip Crosby, an American quality guru and author of *Quality is Free*.

10. Toolroom and maintenance workers are not included in this scheme.

11. The importance of the macroeconomic and policy context comes out clearly in the case of Firm Two. First, the instability of recession, sudden expansion, inflation and currency appreciation created many problems for management, particularly with regard to developing good relations with the workforce. Second, the company's profit-sharing scheme was thrown into disarray by new government regulations on profit sharing in December 1994.

12. Because training is so important for promotion in Firm Two, access to it must be transparent. In Firm Two, as in Firm One, the courses already taken by workers and plans for the coming year were on public display in each team's meeting area.

13. SENAI, the National Industrial Apprenticeship Service, is a levy-financed training agency run by the private sector but set up by the state. It offers some free training for levy payers and also a range of courses and course materials which firms can purchase. Its courses vary from traditional apprenticeships to courses on basic mathematics for industry and the principles of SPC.

14. The sting in the tail is that workers showing a poor overall performance will be dismissed, and the teams are under great pressure to perform well, which in turn means intense peer group pressure on individuals in teams.

15. This would be the level that Berge and Wood (Chapter 1 in this book) define as BAS-ED.

16. See Fleury and Humphrey (1993), Gitahy and Rabelo (1991) and Posthuma (1991).

17. For this to work, flows of products and responsibility for them need to be transparent. Low or no-buffer systems linking cells is one means of doing this. In Firm Two, each cell received a day-by-day evaluation of its output from its clients, indicated by the smiling to glum faces – good, okay, bad.

18. In other areas, such as the ISO 9000 certification, the motivation and development of personnel may be a requirement of new working practices. If firms regard ISO 9000 as essential for market access, then training is essential.

19. The viability of such limited applications in the longer term and the likelihood of firms moving from 'technique' to 'system' depend on the assumptions made about competitive pressures, the obstacles to systemic adoption and the extent of the gains available from non-systemic adoption. See Humphrey (1995) for further discussion of this point.

20. Levy-based training systems are one way of forcing small firms to pay for training. The levy, in effect, subsidizes the training activities of the firms from which they poach their skilled workers.

21. For more on these questions, see Schmitz (1994).

22. For more information on *Proyectos de Fomento*, see Henriques (1992) and Dini (1993).

23. So far in Chile, the growth of training consortia has been limited, even though the state has allowed firms to create collective purchasing agencies which pool their tax breaks for training (Espinoza 1994: 21), but since 1994 their scope may have been expanded and

their formation made easier by the new Frei administration. In the case of smaller firms, the initial training effort may need to focus on the owners themselves, who may lack the basic skills required for reorganizing production.

REFERENCES

Abramo, Lais (1993) 'Transformations in the world of work, schooling and skill in a context of technological change', Paper presented to 5th Workshop on Planning Policy and Education Management, Santiago, October.

Bessant, John (1991), *Managing Advanced Manufacturing Technology*, Manchester/Oxford: NCC/Blackwell.

Blauner, Robert (1964), *Alienation and Freedom*, Chicago: Chicago University Press.

Braverman, Harry (1974), *Labour and Monopoly Capital*, New York: Monthly Review.

Carvalho, Ruy de Quadros (1994), 'Limited technological capability and the use of labour in Brazilian industry', *São Paulo em Perspectiva* **8** (1), 133–43.

Coriat, Benjamin (1991), *Thinking the Opposite Way Round*, Paris: Christian Bourgeois.

Dini, Marco (1993), 'Development projects', Santiago, SERCOTEC, mimeo.

Espinoza, Eduardo Martinez (1994), 'Vocational training in Chile: a decentralised and market oriented system', *Training Policy Studies*, **8**, Geneva, ILO: Training Policies and Programme Development Branch.

Fleury, Afonso, and John Humphrey (1993), *Human Resources and the Diffusion and Adaptation of New Quality Methods in Brazilian Manufacturing*, Brighton, IDS, Research Report, No. 24.

Freyssenet, Michel (1992), 'The social aspects of automation: Japanese experiences', in H. Hirata (ed.), *Autour du 'Modèle' Japonais*, Paris: Harmattan, pp. 157–67.

Gitahy, Leda, and Flávio Rabelo (1991), 'Education and technological development: the case of the motor components industry', DPCT/IG/UNICAMP, Textos para Discussão, No. 11.

Hayashi, Etsuko (1992), 'Human resource management in Japan – "Japanese-style" on-the-job learning', in Edward Chen, Russell Lansbury, Ng Sek-Hong and Sally Stewart, *Labour–Management Relations in the Asia–Pacific Region*, Hong Kong: University of Hong Kong, Centre of Asian Studies, pp. 143–60.

Henriques, Lycette (1992), 'Development Projects: a new focus for the modernization and development of SMEs", Santiago, SERCOTEC, mimeo, August.

Humphrey, John (ed.) 'Industrial Organization and Manufacturing Competitiveness in Developing Countries', *World Development*, **23** (1).

Humphrey, John (1995), 'Industrial reorganization in developing countries: from models to trajectories', *World Development*, **23** (1), 149–62.

Jürgens, Ulrich (1993), 'Internationalisation strategies of Japanese and German automobile companies with special emphasis on Volkswagen', in S. Tokunaga, N. Altmann and H. Demes (eds), *New Impacts of Industrial Relations – Internationalisation and Changing Production Strategies*, Munich: Iudicium.

Jürgens, Ulrich, Knuth Dohse, and Thomas Malsch (1984), *New production concepts in West German car plants*, Discussion Paper pre84–223. Berlin: Wissenschaftszentrum, Research Unit Labour Policy.

Kaplinsky, Raphael (1985), 'Electronics-based automation technologies and the onset of systemofacture: implications for Third World industrialisation', *World Development*, **13** (3), 423–39.

Kaplinsky, Raphael (1994), *Easternisation*, London: Frank Cass.

Kaplinsky, Raphael (1995), 'Technique and system: the spread of Japanese management techniques to developing countries', *World Development*, **23** (1), 57–71.

Kern, Horst, and Michael Schumann (1987), 'Limits of the division of labour: new production and employment concepts in West German industry', *Economic and Industrial Democracy*, **8**, 151–70.

Kern, Horst and Michael Schumann (1988), *The End of the Division of Labour*, Madrid: Ministerio de Trabajo y Seguridad Social.

Nomura, Masami (1993), 'Farewell to "Toyotaism"?, in *Des Realités du Toyotisme*, Actes du Gerpisa, No. 6.

Oliver, Nick and Barry Wilkinson (1992), *The Japanisation of British Industry*, 2nd edn, Oxford: Blackwell.

OTA (1992), 'Worker training: competing in the new international economy', Washington, DC: Congress of the United States, Office of Technology Assessment.

Piore, Michael and Charles Sabel (1984), *The Second Industrial Divide*, New York: Basic Books.

Posthuma, Anne (1991), 'Changing production practices and competitive strategies in the Brazilian auto components industry', Unpublished D.Phil. dissertation, University of Sussex.

Posthuma, Anne (1995), 'Japanese techniques in Africa? Human resources and industrial restructuring in Zimbabwe', *World Development*, **23** (1), 103–16.

Schmitz, Hubert (1994), 'Collective efficiency: growth path for small-scale industry', Brighton: Institute of Development Studies, University of Sussex, mimeo.

SENCE (1993), *Boletin Sence*, **5**.

SERCOTEC (1993), 'Principal activities of SERCOTEC in 1992', Resumen Entregado en Conferencia de Prensa, Press Release, 15 January.

Shaiken, Harley (1990), *Mexico in the Global Economy: high technology and work organization in export industries*, Center for US–Mexican Studies, Monograph Series No. 33, University of California, San Diego.

Shaiken, Harley (1994), 'Advanced manufacturing in Mexico: a new international division of labour?, *Latin American Research Review*, **29** (2), 39–71.

Soete, Luc (1985), 'International diffusion of technology, industrial development and technological leapfrogging', *World Development*, **13** (3), 409–22.

Touraine, Alain (1972), 'An historical theory in the evolution of industrial skills', in L. Davis and J. Taylor (eds), *Design of Jobs*, Harmondsworth: Penguin, pp. 52–61.

Veltz, Pierre and Philippe Zarifian (1992), 'The systemic model and flexibility', in Guy de Terssac and Pierre Dubois (eds), *Les Nouvelles Rationalisations de la Production*, Toulouse: Cèpaduès-Editions.

Womack, J., D. Jones, and D. Roos, (1990), *The Machine that Changed the World*, New York: Rawson Macmillan.

Zarifian, Philippe (1992), 'The acquisition and recognition of competencies in a skill-enhancing organization', *Education Permanente*, No. 112, October.

10. Skills and capabilities: Ghana's industrial competitiveness

Sanjaya Lall and Ganeshan Wignaraja

INTRODUCTION

One of the most serious problems facing Ghana today is a weak industrial supply response to structural adjustment, particularly in manufactured export growth and diversification. In the past, before adjustment policies were implemented, the main reasons offered for the stagnation and decline in the Ghanaian industrial sector were external shocks, political uncertainty, macroeconomic mismanagement, hostility to private (domestic and foreign) firms, a grossly inefficient public sector and an inward-looking trade regime.[1] These analyses called for better governance, stabilization, import liberalization, privatization and more openness to foreign direct investments – the staple of adjustment programmes the world over. Most analysts, cast in the neoclassical mould of the World Bank, predicted that the adoption of liberal market-friendly policies would by itself be enough to revitalize industrial growth and export expansion. There was some expectation, not least in the Ghanaian government, that Ghana would become an East-Asian-style 'tiger' in Africa by being the first country to implement comprehensively a full-blown structural adjustment programme.

There is little doubt that the World Bank type of analysis had a lot of validity: external shocks and poor policies did have a negative effect on Ghana's industrial and manufactured export performance. However, these factors do not fully explain the extent of uncompetitiveness and the lack of dynamism in much of Ghanaian manufacturing. Now that adjustment has been in place for nearly a decade, and manufactured export performance remains weak and the base of exports narrow and confined to a few resource-based activities, it is time to look for more fundamental explanations for competitive weaknesses. These explanations are based on an examination of the skills and knowledge needed to set up and efficiently operate modern industry, what is broadly termed 'technological capabilities' (TCs). It is argued that it is the low level of TCs that explains why so much of Ghana's manufacturing remains confined to the lowest end of the technology scale and why it responds so poorly to the incentives that the structural adjustment has provided. To the extent that this is so, policy remedies have to address other issues than those normally considered by analysts and donors.

This chapter attempts to explain Ghana's manufactured export performance after structural adjustment using the technological capabilities approach. Drawing on case studies of 32 manufacturing firms in four industries (textiles and garments, metalworking, woodworking and food processing), this chapter undertakes a qualitative analysis of TCs in Ghana and considers some of the principal influences on technological development (including entrepreneurship, technical manpower and training).[2] Where possible, comparisons are drawn with other developing countries.

APPROACHES TO INDUSTRIAL COMPETITIVENESS

In recent years, there has been increasing recognition among economists that an essential ingredient in the competitive advantage of nations is *the ability of manufacturing firms to become technically efficient in a world of constantly changing technologies.*[3] While there are many theories of comparative advantage that include technology as a major determinant, almost all of them take the micro-level process by which technology is mastered and improved for granted. Their focus on major technological innovation and frontier proprietary technology as a source of comparative advantage ignores the fact that 'minor' technical change may be equally important as a source of competitive advantage. More importantly from the viewpoint of developing countries, it ignores the fact that even to use a given technology efficiently may involve a long, difficult and costly process of learning. This section examines the assumptions on technological capabilities (TCs) that underlie standard theories of comparative advantage. It then introduces the TC approach based on empirical research on firm-level technological development in developing countries.

The Neoclassical Approach

In the standard neoclassical approach all markets are assumed efficient. Product markets give the correct signals for investment in new activities and factor markets respond to these signals without serious lags or friction. At the firm level, given perfect competition, information, foresight and efficient factor markets, the optimum point on the production possibility frontier is chosen according to prevailing factor prices.

All firms are by definition equally efficient: technology is freely available, with full knowledge on techniques available to all firms – most importantly, it is costlessly and instantly absorbed, and any 'learning' process is known, predictable and automatic. Over time, as factor prices change to reflect changing endowments, their activities change accordingly – this represents the optimal pattern of specialization and forms the basis for evolving comparative advantage. With these assumptions, it follows logically that interventions can only be distortionary. There is, however, nothing in neoclassical theory which says that if the assumptions are changed and market imperfections admitted, its welfare and policy conclusions remain the same. The extent to which the initial assumptions apply in practice is an empirical question. It is neoclassical development economists who, generally implicitly, have tended to assume that markets in developing countries are in fact efficient, and that imperfections are of little practical or policy significance.

The Technological Capabilities Approach

It may be useful to describe briefly the micro-level perspective on industrial development.[4] This provides a more realistic and complete framework for the analysis of market failures and the need for interventions than the simple neoclassical model based on a unique static equilibrium. Industrial competitiveness in developing countries depends essentially on how well individual firms manage the process of technological and managerial development. Technology is not perfectly transferable like a physical product: it has many 'tacit' elements that need the buyer to invest in developing new skills and technical and organisational information. Technological development thus does not mean innovating new technologies (though this is clearly one end of a broad spectrum of technological effort) but, at least at the start, efficiently using imported technologies.

The process of gaining technological competence is not instantaneous, costless or automatic, even if the technology is well diffused elsewhere. It is risky and unpredictable, and often itself has to be learned: in developing countries new firms may not even know what their deficiencies are or how to go about remedying them. The development of competitive capabilities may be costly and prolonged, depending on the complexity and scale of the technology. It involves interactions with other firms and institutions: apart from physical inputs, it calls for various new skills from the education system and training institutes, technical information and services, contract research facilities, interactions with equipment suppliers and consultants, standards bodies, and so on. The setting up of this dense network of cooperation needs the development of special skills. This constant and uncertain process of learning differs radically from the standard neoclassical model of firm development, and leads to different policy implications.

Industrial development is not just about starting new activities. As economies progress and mature, it involves *deepening* in any or all of four forms – technological upgrading of products and processes within industries, entry into more complex and demanding new activities, increasing local content, and mastering more complex technological tasks within industries (from those relevant to assembly to those needed for more value-added activity, adaptation, improvement, and finally design, development and innovation). Each involves its own learning costs. These costs differ by activity, rising with the sophistication of the technology, the extent of linkages and the level of technological capabilities aimed at. Progressive deepening is to some extent a natural part of industrial development, but it is not inevitable. Its pattern and incidence differ greatly, *depending on the strategies pursued by the government.*

Industrial progress in developing countries depends *essentially on how well firms manage this complex process of technological development.* The process of capability development may face various market failures. Free markets may not, in other words, give correct signals to resource allocation between simple and difficult activities or between investments in importing technology and internal technological effort. The first is the basis of the classic case for infant industry protection: *in the presence of learning costs, a latecomer to industry necessarily faces a disadvantage compared to those that have undergone the learning process.* This disadvantage may be exacerbated by the lack of appropriability of some forms of investment in learning (externalities in the form of skills and information that leak out to other firms), the technological linkages with other activities that are also undergoing uncertain learning processes and the absence of developed capital markets capable of financing the learning process.

Given these costs, cumulative learning effects, externalities, unpredictabilities and capital-market imperfections, all endemic to developing countries, exposure to full import competition can prevent entry into activities with relatively difficult technologies. Thus, interventions may be necessary to induce the deepening of technologies that may be in the country's longer-term comparative advantage.

However, intervention in the form of protection against competition may itself take away the incentive to invest in learning. Moreover, widespread and open-ended protection of a large range of activities may result in little learning, general inefficiency and a lack of industrial dynamism. Since protection penalizes consumers and downstream industries, it is imperative that this cost be offset by dynamic gains in learning and spillovers to make it economically worthwhile to intervene. Efficient industrial policy requires that protection be *limited* in extent and duration, and that its deleterious effects be *offset* by measures to force firms to invest in developing their technological capabili-

ties, and by containing its effects so that export activities are not handi-
capped.

The most effective way to do this is to combine domestic protection with
strong export orientation, providing a cushion for learning along with incentives to be fully competitive, and letting export activities operate in an effective free-trade regime as far as their access to inputs is concerned. This
particular design of protection to infant industries constitutes the crucial
difference between 'classic' import-substituting regimes, which promoted
some learning but distorted its direction and dynamism, and the aggressively
export-oriented regimes of East Asia, which combined extensive and variable
protection with powerful push to their firms to enter world markets.

The insights yielded by the technological-capability approach to industrial
competitiveness can be applied to structural adjustment. Inefficient interventions result in truncated and distorted learning, and reform is clearly needed
in 'classic' import-substituting regimes. However, rapid exposure to import
competition can kill off activities that are potentially competitive but are not
given the time or the resources to complete their learning process or to
'unlearn' past distorted learning and become competitive. There is a costly
learning process involved in *adjusting* to competition if past interventions
have been excessive and have not created the environment for healthy learning in industry. Reforms have therefore to be gradual, based on relearning
needs and guided by an overall strategy.

Since learning costs differ between activities, interventions and liberalization have to be *selective* rather than uniform. This goes against the basic
neoclassical tenet that protection should never be discriminatory, based on its
simplified view of passive and uniform learning across activities. In simple
activities the need for protection may be minimal, because the learning period is relatively brief, easy to get information on, and predictable. In complex large-scale activities, with advanced information and skill needs, wide
linkages and intricate organizations, by contrast, the learning process could
spread over years, even decades. It may never be undertaken (unless there is a
strong natural resource cost advantage) unless protection is given.

Since the factor needs of technology development, as for new skills and
information, differ by activity, interventions in factor markets have to be
integrated to interventions to protect or promote activities. Factor markets
often fail in developing countries, and such failures are more readily accepted by institutions such as the World Bank. One of the main concessions
to the need for policy is in the field of education, where the World Bank
agrees that markets fail but suggests that interventions are 'market friendly'
because they do not discriminate between activities. While this is true of a
part of education at the basic levels, interventions in higher education and
training can be highly selective if they are geared to the specific needs of

industries being targeted for promotion. For instance, a government setting up an electronics industry has to target the training of electronics engineers and technicians – this is exactly what the NIEs of Asia did – if its overall policy is to succeed. The identification of market-friendly interventions with education and technology is untenable, since such interventions can be highly selective.

SAPS AND INDUSTRIAL COMPETITIVENESS IN GHANA

Structural adjustment programmes (SAPs) as designed and implemented by the World Bank are strongly based on the neoclassical approach outlined above. They thus start from the presumption that markets are essentially efficient in developing countries and government interventions in resource allocation essentially distorting and inefficient. The only exceptions allowed by the World Bank are market failures in the provision of infrastructure and education, where it recommends functional or market-friendly interventions that do not discriminate between activities.[5] Selective interventions, on the other hand, are taken to be 'market unfriendly' and to distort efficient resource allocation. In most such writings no case is admitted for infant industry protection or for other sources of market failure that can call for selective interventions to restore market efficiency. In the few instances that such cases are admitted in theory, it is argued that in practice governments cannot intervene efficiently, and that market failures are invariably less costly than government failures. Since the debate on these issues is well known, it is not necessary to go into them at great length here.[6]

The 'ideal' form of structural adjustment recommended by the World Bank follows logically and forcefully from these assumptions. No empirical evidence is needed, and indeed none is sought, to support the argument. To simplify, this takes the form of five prescriptions:

1. Remove all forms of selective intervention and restore free-market-driven resource allocation (often referred to as 'getting prices right'). In the trade arena, expose industrial activities to international competition, as a precondition to other adjustment measures. Allow free entry to foreign private investment, and exercise as little discretion as possible in intentional investment flows. In the domestic arena, promote liberal entry, exit, ownership and flexible labour markets; privatize public enterprises wherever possible, restructure them where not.
2. Get prices right in all economies in the same manner regardless of the level of development, since by definition all markets are efficient (or more efficient than governments).

3. Carry out reforms quickly and across the board, since there is no economic justification for continuing to differentiate between activities. No 'strategy' is needed to guide the restructuring or upgrading process at the level of industry or firms since markets will give the correct signals.
4. Do not link the pace of reforms to the incentive structure to measures to improve human capital or infrastructure, since this will take much longer and, in any case, factor markets will also respond better if the overall price signals are correct.
5. Finally, having got rid of the legacy of inefficient interventions, do not retain any further scope for selective interventions to promote industrial growth.

This 'ideal' form of adjustment that the World Bank would like to implement is rarely found in practice. SAPs differ greatly over time and between countries in their design, content and implementation, depending on the bargaining power and conviction of the governments concerned, and on exogenous events and political expediency.[7] As a consequence, it is difficult to evaluate empirically the effects of SAPs, especially on a specific sector such as industry. There are, in addition, numerous problems in separating the impact of adjustment from those of other factors. In particular, many analysts tend to include stabilization as part of adjustment – this is suited to certain purposes but cannot reveal the impact of liberalization on industrial performance. Many analyses have been carried out, particularly in Africa, to assess the impact of SAPs. They usually involve quantitative comparisons of adjusting economies with non-adjusting ones, or of adjusting economies before and after adjustment (or sometimes a combination).[8] Needless to say, these comparisons are fraught with a number of methodological, data and analytical problems, and it has proved extremely difficult to establish a clear causal relationship between adjustment measures and economic performance while taking account of all other influences on performance.

It may therefore be more instructive to look in greater detail at the experience of Ghana, the country with the longest history of consistent adjustment in Sub-Saharan Africa. This analysis is not just a mechanistic comparison of 'before and after' figures, but a micro-level analysis within a clear TC framework that allows us to interpret and explain the efficiency and supply response of the industrial sector.

In the World Bank's assessment, Ghana is now the most advanced country in Africa in terms of adjustment, and has come closest to low tariff-based protection and free trade.[9] The reforms undertaken are impressive: a massive depreciation in the exchange rate (from 2.75 cedis to the dollar in 1982 to 920 cedis in early 1994); the removal of all quantitative restrictions on imports and the lowering of tariffs to a relatively uniform 10–25 per cent range (only luxury products are at the high end of this range); a reduction of corporate taxes (to 35 per cent) and in capital gains tax (to 5 per cent); the removal of price controls and subsidies; the abolition of credit ceilings and guidelines; the privatization of state-owned enterprises; the revision of the foreign investment code; and the granting of incentives to exporters and investors in infrastructure.[10] By the start of the 1990s Ghana had a relatively stable, open and liberal economy, and was often referred to as a 'model' adjuster in Africa.

Ghana started its policy reform with an Economic Recovery Programme in 1983. In the initial stages, as far as manufacturing was concerned, this involved freeing up the allocation of foreign exchange for intermediate inputs and spares. There was no direct import competition to Ghanaian industry at this stage. The first World Bank structural adjustment programme started in 1986, and was followed by two others until 1991. It was over these SAPs that the process of liberalization and market orientation was launched. There was a substantial increase in net inflows from foreign sources (mostly in the form of aid), from $196 million in 1985 to an average of $878 million per annum over 1989–92.[11] This allowed the economy to finance imports and to revive domestic demand.

What was the response of the industrial sector? Data in the World Bank study show that the average growth rate of manufacturing, negative in the first half of the 1980s, rose to 4.5 per cent per annum over 1987–91 – the predicted positive response. However, this average is misleading. Manufacturing value added (MVA) did rise rapidly after 1983, when imported inputs were made available to existing industries that were suffering substantial excess capacity. The rate of growth was 12.9 per cent in 1984, 24.3 per cent in 1985, 11.0 per cent in 1986, and 10.0 per cent in 1987. However, as liberalization spread to other imports and excess capacity was used up, the exposure to world competition led to a steady deceleration of industrial growth. Thus, the rate of growth of MVA fell to 5.1 per cent in 1988, 5.6 per cent in 1989, 1.1 per cent in 1990, 2.6 per cent in 1991 and 1.1 per cent in 1992. These growth figures, in the shape of an inverted-U with a long taper in recent years, do not suggest that Ghanaian manufacturing has reached a stage of dynamic takeoff.

It is useful to look at the industrial sector in more detail. Employment in manufacturing fell from a peak of 78,700 in 1987 to 28,000 in 1993.[12] There was a rise in the number of small enterprises, but this was mainly in low-productivity activities aimed at local markets, sheltered from international competition, and not enough to lead to longer-term growth and competitiveness. Foreign investment did not respond to the adjustment, and there was no increase in annual inflows after the SAPs. Moreover, the little that came concentrated on primary activities rather than on manufacturing. Domestic private investment did not pick up sufficiently to lead to a surge of manufacturing growth.

At the same time, large swathes of the manufacturing sector were devastated by import competition. The long period of import-substituting industrialization in Ghana, with the lead taken by state-owned enterprises, left a legacy of inefficiency and technological backwardness. It also has left some technological capabilities, but not at the level that rapid liberalization could stimulate them to reach world levels in a short period and with relatively low investment. The adverse impact of liberalization was strongest in the more modern, large-scale part of the industrial sector, which had the most complex technologies and so suffered most from the lack of technological capabilities. Industrial survivors and new entrants are basically in activities that have 'natural' protection from imports: very small-scale enterprises, making low-income or localized products, and larger enterprises protected by high transport costs or based on processing of local raw materials.[13]

As far as manufactured exports are concerned, the expectation was that they would grow and diversify rapidly under the new incentive regime and absorb resources released from inefficient import-substituting activities. The data show that while manufactured exports *have* grown since 1986, the values are extremely small, coming to a total of $14.7 million in 1991. There was little sign of a broad-based response on the part of Ghanaian manufacturing enterprises, particularly in its main potential area of comparative advantage, cheap labour. There was practically no diversification of manufactured exports: the growth came mainly from wood and aluminium products, both long-established export sectors, and from firms already established in export markets, rather than from new products or producers.[14]

Labour-intensive exports such as garments, footwear, toys or other light consumer goods, which led the initial export thrust of the Asian NIEs, were conspicuous by their absence in Ghana. Such low-technology 'entry-level' activities, where Ghana should be developing a competitive edge, have been unable to survive the import threat. Conventional wisdom suggests that cheap labour should be the main source of comparative advantage in manufacturing for newly-industrializing countries. What this ignores is that even the ability to compete internationally in labour-intensive industries requires a level of productivity and managerial and technical skills that is presently lacking in Ghana. The few relatively well-managed firms that exist are largely foreign owned; among local enterprises the better ones have entrepreneurs that are well educated. The typical local firm, on the other hand, has entrepreneurs with low education, a poorly-skilled workforce and no methods for raising their technological capabilities. Most lack the ability even to perceive and define their technological problems.[15]

The theory underlying SAPs does not offer a satisfactory explanation for this phenomenon, since it ignores the need for technological-capability development in becoming competitive and the need to overcome market failures in this process. A recent study of technological capabilities in Ghana in the adjustment period concludes that the generally low level of the capabilities have meant that rapid liberalization, unaccompanied by supply-side measures to develop skills, capabilities and technical support, have led to significant and costly deindustrialization.[16] The growth of new activities and micro enterprises that is taking place is insufficient to provide a large momentum to growth of production or exports. The expectation that liberalization by itself will transform Ghana into a 'Tiger' along the lines of East Asia appears facile and unfounded.

Exposure to market forces in these conditions may actually be retarding the development of Ghana's comparative advantage. The rapid pace of exposure to world competition is killing off not just inherently uneconomic activities but also some that could be the basis of new manufactured exports. The lack of policies to upgrade skills, technical information and technological support is exacerbating market failures in inputs that are essential for developing competitive capabilities. Ghana's comparative advantage is likely, in this policy framework, to evolve very slowly unless there is a rapid inflow of foreign manufacturing investments. However, the lack of industrial capabilities itself means that foreign investors are not attracted to set up facilities that are immediately exposed to direct import competition.

The experience of Ghana clearly has an important bearing on the general issue of industrial adjustment in Sub-Saharan Africa: an initial favourable response of manufacturing to adjustment may not lead to sustained growth and diversification if all SAPs do is 'get prices right'. The existence of pervasive market failures raises the costs of adjustment to import competition and holds back the creation of new manufacturing activities and exports in response to the new incentives. The design of SAPs, by ignoring the phenomenon of capability development, places too much store by free markets that work rapidly and effectively.

Is Ghana an economically weak 'outlier' whose experience cannot be generalized? It would appear not. Ghana is by African standards a fairly well-endowed and promising economy: it has a relatively good stock of human capital, and its location, resource base and infrastructure would place it in the top quarter of African economies.[17] It has implemented a difficult programme of stabilization and liberalization with admirable consistency. All this suggests that its experience illustrates the response of the industrial sector to adjustment more clearly than any country in the region.

TECHNOLOGY CASE STUDIES IN GHANA

The analysis of technological capabilities (TCs) in Ghana draws on the results of a survey of manufacturing firms undertaken for the World Bank and subsequently published.[18] The survey, undertaken in 1992, consisted of 32 firms in four industries: textiles and garments, woodworking, metalworking and food processing. The purpose of the survey was to analyse the process of acquiring TCs in firms, the technological strengths and weaknesses of different types of firms, and the influences on technological capability acquisition. The study covered a mix of firms from different size classes, ownership forms (foreign, local non-African, local African) and differing performance categories (growing, reviving, stagnant and dead).

The study involved classifying the technological performance of the sample firms into three categories (investment, production and linkage),[19] and making a detailed evaluation of their capabilities in each. This analysis was used to draw up a list of technologically 'competent' firms. The choice was based on a combination of indicators, since much of the data involved were qualitative. Most of the competent firms were easy to identify, by virtue of their clearly superior investment and production engineering capabilities. The list, impressionistic though it is, is similar to industry analyses of industrial competence widely used by international consultants.

Characteristics of Technologically-competent Firms

Of the 32 Ghanaian firms, 13 firms (41 per cent of the sample) were identified as relatively competent. It has to be emphasized that inclusion in this list *does not mean that these firms are technologically capable by world standards.* On the contrary, the evidence suggests that the level of technological mastery by Ghanaian firms of the technologies they use is relatively poor. There is little or no process or product development by even the best sample firms that can be regarded as 'innovative'. The kinds of 'minor innovation' that have been found in many more industrialized developing countries to lead to the raising of machine productivity beyond its design capacity, the use of completely different raw materials, the development of technologically complex new products and so on, are rarely found in the Ghanaian sample. In general, the best that the competent firms do is to use imported technologies relatively well and make some adaptations to local circumstances. Table 10.1 shows the characteristics of the competent and other firms and reports the results of some statistical significance tests.

Let us start with the *general features* of the competent firms. Of the 13, the largest number (five) are in the food processing industry, followed by metalworking (four); textiles and garments and woodworking have two firms each.

Table 10.1 Technologically-competent and other Ghanaian firms

	Employment (nos.)	Age in production in 1992 (years)	Capacity utilization rate (%)	% Non-African/ foreign equity	Average wage (US$)	Entrepreneur's education (years)[a]	Production manager's education (years)	Scientists engineers technicians (% of employment)	Engineers only (% of employment)	Quality control & maintenance manpower (% of employment)
Technologically-competent firms										
Observations	13	13	12	13	13	13	13	13	13	11
Mean	192.3	19.0	66.0	35.4	64.6	17.1	15.5	6.7	1.6	6.5
Standard deviation	176.1	10.7	29.3	38.3	21.4	3.2	2.4	6.2	1.7	3.4
Other firms										
Observations	18	18	13	18	18	18	18	17	18	18
Mean	69.7	22.7	32.0	18.9	43.9	11.7	8.9	2.8	0.9	1.8
Standard deviation	81.0	14.9	16.9	34.5	15.9	3.4	6.5	2.7	2.3	3.5
t-statistic[b]	2.6*	-0.76	3.6*	1.26	3.09*	4.50*	3.47*	2.25*	0.93	3.15*

Notes:

a. The number of years of education were computed as follows: middle school (8 years), secondary school (12 years), diploma (14 years), B.Sc. (17 years), M.Sc. (20 years), Ph.D. (22 years).

b. * denotes statistical significance at the 5 per cent level.

Source: Lall et al. (1994).

While one should not read too much into the industrial distribution of such a small sample of firms, it is worth remarking on the fact that the two activities in which Ghana may be expected on *a priori* grounds, and on the basis of the experience of other developing regions, to have a comparative advantage are garments (which is low technology and labour-intensive) and furniture (which is local resource-based and labour-intensive). Yet these activities seem generally to register low levels of TC, not just in the sample but also in the industry more generally.

The food-processing and metalworking industries, with relatively more competent firms, are essentially oriented to the domestic market. In addition, many of the competent firms in metalworking, normally an engine of technological development, are in relatively simple technologies. There is little sign that more advanced engineering activities are emerging in Ghana. The implications of these trends for future growth and export dynamism are not very promising.

The statistical findings are as follows:

1. *Technologically-competent firms are larger than other firms.* There is a statistically significant difference between the average *employment size* of the two groups, with the mean for the competent firms coming to 192 employees and for the other firms 70 employees. Of the 13 firms in the table, eight are large (more than 100 employees), three are medium sized (30–99) and only two are small (less than 30). The correlation between size and competence may indicate one or more of three things. First, it may indicate that firms have reached large size *because* they were competent, that is, they earlier invested in TC development to a greater extent, or more effectively, than other firms. Second, it may be due to the distribution of activities and technologies in the sample, that is, in many of the technologies covered there were economies of specialization and size that meant that only large firms could reach efficient levels of TCs. Third, it may reflect the existence of market segmentation, that is, only firms above a certain size were able to gain access to the skills, information and credit needed to be competent.

    It is not possible to say firmly which of these explanations has most validity, and there is probably some validity in each. The distribution of the firms in the case studies may in some cases have led to the association between size and competence, particularly (given the scale-intensive processes used in modern food processing) in the sample food-processing firms. Even in these technologies, however, the fact that certain firms were competent could be traced to their TC efforts rather than to size *per se*. In the case of garment, woodworking or most metalworking technologies, where the size threshold for competence was relatively low, there were still large differences in competence between firms of similar sizes. This suggests again that technical competence was directly traceable to deliberate investments in TC development.[20]

2. *There is no significant difference between the age in production* of the two groups. The technological learning process is not a simple function of years of experience, but more the result of a deliberate investment in creating skills and information. The ability to undertake this investment is dependent on several factors apart from age. It is interesting to note, however, that only three of the competent firms were formed after the start of the economic recovery programme of 1983 which started the liberalization process.

3. *Performance indicators* such as growth and capacity utilization in capable firms are significantly better for technologically capable than other firms. This is not unexpected, but it is encouraging that the technological-capability measures, which were not based on performance measures but on direct observation of technological functions, are related to it.

4. *Ownership does not matter.* Four of the firms are foreign controlled (two being part of large MNCs); three are owned by non-African settlers, and the remaining six by local Africans. The division of the sample firms into African and other (foreign or local non-African) fails to show statistical significance. Though the mean for non-African ownership is higher in capable firms, the *t*-statistic fails to reach acceptable levels. This seems surprising at first sight, since there is a general presumption that MNCs would have greater TCs than local firms in a less-industrialized country such as Ghana. The reason is probably the small size and purposive nature of the sample, but it may also lie in the fact that existing levels of technological capabilities reflect the legacy of decades of relative isolation and hardship. Even MNCs have to make do with the base of skills that is generally available: thus, in the longer term they may well develop better capabilities than local competitors but these capabilities may not match those of their affiliates in countries with higher levels of education, training and management experience.

5. *The average wage is significantly higher* in capable firms than in other firms (the means are $65 and $44 per month, respectively). This may be due to a number of factors, such as differences in size, capital intensity, labour-market distortions or location between the firms. It may, however, also indicate that capable firms employ workers with higher skill levels, give more training and then offer higher wages to retain workers, or are more productive for given skill levels for other reasons. The data do not allow these different hypotheses to be tested properly, but there is some evidence (see below) that the more competent firms do have higher skill levels that are related to their investments in TCs.

6. *Competent firms have much higher levels of education for the entrepreneur*[21] than other firms. The mean comes to 17.1 years of education in the former and 11.7 in the latter, and the difference is highly significant statistically. This suggests that education adds to the competence, 'vision' and organizational abilities of entrepreneurs, and is explored further below.
7. *Competent firms also have much better educated production managers.* This difference is also highly significant, with the mean being 15.5 years of education for competent firms and 8.9 years for other firms. This indicates that it is not just the 'vision' of the entrepreneur that matters, but that a technically-competent production manager is also needed to catalyse the learning process (the role of the technological catalyst is discussed in the next section).
8. *Competent firms employ more technical manpower.* They have a significantly higher proportion of engineers and technicians in their workforces than other firms (6.7 per cent of total employment compared to 2.8 per cent). They also have larger proportions of employees in QC and maintenance (6.5 per cent and 1.8 per cent) than other firms. This shows the importance of having adequate numbers of technically qualified personnel who can absorb new technologies and of paying adequate attention to certain vital process functions. However, the employment of engineers by itself does not show any statistically significant difference.

Technological Competence and Human Capital

The relevance of 'human capital' to technological competence and development is universally accepted in the literature. However, human capital may have many ramifications, each of which should be considered separately. A firm has a stock of skills given by the background and training of the entrepreneur or business leader, the production manager (who is generally the most important person, after the entrepreneur, in deciding the technical strategy and progress of a firm), and other technically-qualified personnel hired from the labour market (locally or abroad). In addition, it has workers of different levels of quality and education. Over time, it adds to this stock by investing in training its employees, in-house or externally (locally or abroad); it also loses skills as employees leave the firm to set up on their own or join other firms. These broad components of human capital are considered separately below.

Entrepreneurs and production managers

As noted above, the level of education of entrepreneurs and production managers of the technologically-capable firms is significantly higher than in other firms. Here we explore in greater detail the characteristics of the sample entrepreneurs and the production managers, starting with a brief description by industry.

In the *garments* industry, the average age of the entrepreneur is 62, and none has university education. Most are secondary school graduates, while two have had vocational training in dressmaking. It has served as the entry into manufacturing for some of the local non-Africans who were required to invest in industry under the old regime. This rather simple educational background is in keeping with the nature of the technology involved, especially for garment making. Nevertheless, a comparison with Sri Lanka suggests that garment entrepreneurs in Ghana have relatively low levels of formal education. Table 10.4, with the educational background of nine Sri Lankan entrepreneurs, shows that two have MBAs from abroad and three are chartered accountants. The low levels of Ghanaian entrepreneurs may have contributed to the weak supply response of this industry. It is, however, difficult to relate technological performance in this subsector to anything because of the generally declining state of all the firms.

In *food processing*, where the technology is far more demanding and the sample firms larger, the background of the entrepreneurs/CEOs tends to be much more impressive in educational terms. Five have university degrees, of which three are in chemistry or food technology from developed-country universities. Two are secondary school graduates, and have worked their way up in their firms. The best firms in the sample all have highly-trained leaders.

In *woodworking*, of the seven firms on which this information is available, the average age of the entrepreneur (46 years) is much lower than in textiles and garments, but the general level of education is higher, though not as high as in food processing. There are only two entrepreneurs with university degrees – these are the heads of the two firms classified as technologically capable. The others are primary, middle or secondary school graduates. Of these, two started as traditional carpenters.

In *metalworking*, the average age of the entrepreneur (46 years) is the same as in woodworking, and the level of entrepreneurial education is somewhat higher. Of the eight entrepreneurs on whom information is available, five are university graduates, all trained abroad. Four of these have engineering degrees, one has a management degree.

It is interesting to look specifically at the characteristics of the entrepreneurs of the six capable *African-owned firms*, two in food processing, one in furniture and three in metalworking. Of these, the flour mill shows the capability to manage well the transfer and absorption of technology, while the fruit-processing firm shows more innovative capabilities based on the application of scientific knowledge by the entrepreneur. The furniture firm Peewood shows good management skills and is able to buy technology from abroad.

The metalworking firms Domod and Alugan show good mastery of their process technologies and the ability to find economical sources of equipment. SIS Engineering shows good capabilities in all these activities as well as some product design ability, though not at an advanced level that would require formal R&D.

Table 10.2 shows the age, educational and work experience of these African entrepreneurs. It is clear that these entrepreneurs are *relatively young and highly educated*. Technical education *per se* is not a distinguishing feature, though in the case where it does exist it is a valuable asset to the firm. Most of the entrepreneurs are from a business studies background, and nearly all have some experience of working in a business, of which three have experience overseas (generally the same line of business as their present one).

These characteristics have interesting, and potentially important, implications for TC development. Entrepreneurial success among Ghanaians is clearly associated with high levels of education. This may simply reflect that better-educated entrepreneurs have better access to segmented factor markets and official favours. It may, on the other hand, imply that education is associated with qualities that conduce to technological acumen: like analytical and organizational skills, an appreciation of technological factors, the ability to seek out necessary information and the relevant professionals, and a willingness to try new methods and technologies. There is evidence of market segmentation, but on the whole we find support for the hypothesis that education provides real benefit to technological effort (aided in some cases by relative youth).

Work experience in general has obvious benefits for the accumulation of technical know-how and institutional and marketing skills. Work experience overseas probably gives exposure to a broader range of experience and techniques. These associations are not at all surprising, but it is interesting to have them show up so clearly in this sample.

The implication is clearly not that all African entrepreneurs have to be modern, well-educated, young people with work experience. There are always exceptional entrepreneurs who are 'born and not made', and rise above the constraints of low educational status to use the skills of others in building up successful businesses. However, it is still likely to be true that success in modern industry is facilitated by the cognitive, social, technical and other skills imparted by education.

The background of the *production managers* is directly relevant for explaining the ability of firms to develop technologically. In *garments*, the two most capable firms, Nitra and Overseas Knitwear, have production managers – an expatriate (German) textile engineer in the former and the owner's second son in the latter. Nearly all the technological capabilities that exist in both firms are directly traceable to these production managers (they are the

Table 10.2 Characteristics of entrepreneurs of technologically-capable African firms

Firm	Age of entrepreneur	Highest educational qualification	Subject of qualification	Previous work experience
Golden Spoon	n.a.[a]	Chartered Act. (L)	Accountancy	In other flour mill (L)
Astek	n.a.[b]	Ph.D (F)	Chemistry	Standards Board (L)
Peewood	42	BA (F)	Management	Furniture firm (F)
Domod	46	BA (L)	Business Act.	Aluminium marketing (F)
Alugan	35	M.Sc. (F)	Management	Employed (F, L)[c]
SIS Engineering	46	B.Sc. (F)	Plant Engineering	University lecturer[d]

Notes:

a. Relatively young, probably in 40s. The firm was started by a group of similar young people.
b. Probably in his 50s.
c. The present entrepreneur was educated and worked in the US before taking over father's business.
d. The entrepreneur was a lecturer in the University of Science and Technology, and was educated in the UK, where he also worked for some time. F = Foreign, L = Local.

Source: Lall et al. (1994).

technological 'catalysts' discussed later). The German has also introduced the CAD system to Nitra, which is used by a Ghanaian trained by him and has proved a competitive advantage to the firm.

In the *food-processing* industry, each production manager is university trained, one with postgraduate education in food science. Three are mechanical engineers. There are two expatriates in MNCs, while the third operates with a local biochemist. One firm has a local non-African; the others are all Ghanaian Africans. The noteworthy one is the production manager of Picadilly, who used his mechanical engineering skills to transform the obsolete machinery into a well-functioning plant.

In the *woodworking* industry the general level of education of production managers is not very high. The two smallest firms do not have a production manager at all. One has a production manager with only primary education. Another has a secondary graduate with no training in woodworking. According to the available information, only the two technologically-capable firms have production managers with diplomas in joinery and woodworking.

In *metalworking*, two firms (both in structurals) have no production managers. Of the others, only an Indian-owned steel mill has a production manager with a graduate engineering degree in metallurgical engineering, probably necessary in such a complex technology. The others all have diploma holders in mechanical engineering, except for one which had a secondary school graduate with previous experience in the industry (it had an engineer in charge of maintenance and QC). This is generally in conformity with the relatively simple nature of the technologies employed by these firms.

It may be relevant at this point to discuss the role of the *technological catalyst* in the relatively small and low-technology firms that populate the Ghanaian industrial sector. The 'catalyst' is an individual whose efforts and knowledge are critical to the technological upgrading of the enterprise. In most of the competent sample firms there was usually someone who played this role, generally the production manager or equivalent who worked closely with the entrepreneur or else was given a free hand to upgrade the technology of the enterprise. In small, newer, less mature enterprises, the existence of a catalyst seems to be essential to technological development.[22] In some cases it is the entrepreneur himself, setting up in business to exploit his skills or innovations. In others, it is someone selected by the entrepreneur to take the technological lead: in this sense, it is a reflection of the entrepreneur's education and vision.

Technical manpower
Table 10.3 shows the breakdown of employment by various technical qualifications, *including* the entrepreneur and the production manager. The categories used are scientists, engineers and technicians (together and separately).

The employment of *scientists, engineers and technicians* was found in the previous section to be significantly larger in technologically capable than in other firms. The firm-level figures are now considered by industry, and comparisons are drawn with other developing countries wherever possible.

In *textiles and garments*, each of the firms had one technical person, with the exception of the dead firm and a small firm. Not surprisingly none had a science degree, since this activity has no need for such training. However, only two firms have an employee each with an engineering degree – and these are the best firms in the sample. The others have non-degree-level technicians, essentially to service the sewing machines. The total level of technical employment is low, even by the standards of this simple industry.

A comparison with Sri Lanka, a relative newcomer to the industry and not as advanced in garment quality or technology as the East Asian NIEs, can illustrate this point. Table 10.4 shows the employment of engineers and technicians in a sample of Sri Lankan firms.[23] Each of the ten garment firms (large operations with 330 to 1,900 employees each) has at least 10 technical personnel, six firms have more than 20 technical personnel and two firms have more than 40 technical personnel. In more sophisticated operations, say, in Hong Kong and Taiwan, this figure is likely to be higher. The technical level of the Ghanaian garment industry, as measured by its use of engineering and technical personnel, is very low.

In *food processing*, the picture is different. Nestlé claims to have 20 per cent of its employees technically qualified, the absolute number exceeding the rest of the sample put together. The dairy products affiliate comes next, with nearly 9 per cent of its employees with technical qualifications. Cadbury is relatively low considering the nature of its technology (which is very similar to Nestlé's). The lowest is the biscuit maker (Picadilly), because of the simpler nature of its product.

In general, these data correspond with the relative performance of the firms within their respective technological segments. Nestlé, for instance, is distinctly a better performer in the market than Cadbury, and the two multinationals show very different propensities to invest in human capital. Picadilly does not really need any highly qualified technicians, but its access to an engineer (the production manager) allows it to perform very well.

In the *woodworking* industry, none of the firms has any scientists, and only two have any engineers. Technicians are found in four firms; the three smallest firms do not have a single technically-qualified person (including the entrepreneur). In the absence of data on other countries, it is difficult to assess how Ghanaian firms fare in relative terms.

In *metalworking*, there are no scientists, and relatively few engineers. Of the seven engineers in the industry, three are in Tema Steel, all recently imported from India. The others are distributed over four firms, including

Table 10.3   Technical manpower indicators and training in Ghanaian firms

Firm	Engineers and technicians[a]		Engineers only[b]		QC Personnel	External training[c]
	No.	% of employees	No.	% of employees	% of employees	% of employees
Textiles and garments						
Nitra	1	1.1	1	1.1	3.3	0.0
Adas	1	1.4	0	0.0	0.0	0.0
Awura Abena	1	2.4	0	0.0	0.0	0.0
Terrycott	1	3.3	0	0.0	3.3	0.0
Overseas Knitwear	1	4.2	1	4.2	0.0	0.0
Thadani	0	0.0	0	0.0	0.0	0.0
Wiredu	1	7.7	0	0.0	0.0	0.0
Mutual Union[c]	0	0.0	0	0.0	0.0	0.0
Food processing						
Nestlé	130	20.0	n.a.	n.a.	2.0	1.2
Cadbury	10	4.1	1	0.4	2.8	2.4
Gihoc Cannery	8	3.5	1	0.4	1.8	3.5
Picadilly	2	0.9	1	0.5	0.9	0.0
Golden Spoon	11	5.5	1	0.5	2.0	0.0
Fan Milk	15	8.7	3	1.7	2.9	0.6
Astek	4	5.0	1	1.3	5.0	5.0

Woodworking						
Furnart	7	2.6	2	0.7	n.a	0.0
TMG	2	0.9	2	0.9	0.0	0.0
Peewood	3	2.0	0	0.0	0.7	0.0
Ashanti Furniture	2	1.5	0	0.0	0.0	1.5
Barhat	3	4.6	0	0.0	0.0	0.0
Kyere	0	0.0	0	0.0	0.0	0.0
Progressive	0	0.0	0	0.0	0.0	0.0
Amoo	0	0.0	0	0.0	0.0	0.0
Metalworking						
Tema Steel	17	4.0	3	0.7	n.a	0.0
Domod	5	3.3	1	0.7	0.0	0.0
Alugan	10	14.1	0	0.0	1.4	4.2
UTC	1	3.3	0	0.0	3.3	3.3
Agbemskod	2	7.1	0	0.0	0.0	7.1
Addoh	0	0.0	0	0.0	0.0	0.0
SIS Engineering	3	15.8	1	5.3	0.0	0.0
Suame Foundry	3	18.8	1	6.3	0.0	0.0
Halaby	1	7.7	1	7.7	0.0	0.0

Notes:

a. All degree and diploma holders.

b. B.Sc degrees in different types of engineering.

c. External training refers to numbers of employees sent on courses in Ghana and abroad in 1990–91.

Source: Lall et al. (1994).

Table 10.4 Entrepreneurship, technical manpower and training in Sri Lankan firms

Firm	Entrepreneur's highest level of education	Entrepreneur's educational specialization at tertiary level	Engineers and technicians		Engineers only		Quality Control manpower	% Trained externally
			No.	% of emp.	No.	% of emp.	(% of emp.)	(% of emp)
Garments								
Alliance	Secondary	None	17	5.2	0	0	4.6	1.5
Cadillac	Chartered act.	Act.	27	2.7	1	0.1	9.5	3.4
Colmans	Secondary	None	12	1.8	0	0	2.8	3.8
Dial	Chartered act.	Act.	36	2.4	11	0.7	5.9	1.0
Eskimo	MBA (abroad)	Busin. studies	56	6.2	2	0.2	4.5	2.2
Gartex	n.a.	n.a.	11	1.8	1	0.2	3.1	2.0
Hirdaramani	Secondary	None	20	2.3	0	0	3.5	0.7
Kundanmal	Chartered act.	Act.	25	2.5	5	0.5	8.4	1.7
Smart	MBA (abroad)	Busin. studies	43	2.3	7	0.4	3.2	1.0
Translanka	Secondary	None	15	1.7	3	0.3	3.3	0.2
Average			26	2.9	3	0.2	4.9	1.8

Light engineering

Agro	Secondary	None	5	6.7	1	1.3	4.0	1.3
Browns	Secondary	None	53	4.4	40	3.3	0.3	0.6
Commercials	Chartered act.	Act.	37	2.6	7	0.5	0.1	0.3
Premier	Secondary	None	15	3.6	3	0.7	0.5	1.0
Walkers	Secondary	None	38	3.2	13	1.1	0.1	0.0
Acme	B.Sc.	Mechan. eng.	12	6.8	5	2.8	5.6	7.9
Alpha	Secondary	None	6	3.0	2	1	2.0	0.5
Elsteel	B.Sc.	Mechan. eng.	8	5.3	4	2.7	5.4	5.3
Metalix	B.Sc.	Electri. eng.	7	4.4	4	2.5	3.1	0.0
Swedelanka	n.a.	n.a.	3	7.5	1	2.5	3.6	4.0
Average			18	4.7	8	1.8	2.5	2.1

Source: Wignaraja (forthcoming).

Table 10.5   *Share of engineers in employment in other developing countries*

Country	Firm	Year	Ownership	Employment	Engineers as % Employment[a]
Korea	Daewoo Heavy Industries, Diesel Engine Branch	1978	Local	1,181	14.0
	Kolon	1984	Local	4,132	5.6
	Daesung Electric Industries Co.	1993	Local	946	6.6
	Iljin Industries Co.	1993	Local	422	14.2
	Dong A Corporation	1993	Local	283	11.3
	Sangshin Brake Industry Co.	1993	Local	537	7.4
	Poonsung Precision Co.	1993	Local	857	3.5
Malaysia	Eng Group	1993	Local	230	4.3
	Inventec	1993	Foreign	2,300	5.2
	Panasonic	1993	Foreign	996	8.0
	Motorola	1993	Foreign	5,000	4.4
	Sony	1993	Foreign	4,900	12.7
India	Associated Babcock	1982	Local	5,000	10.0
	Hindustan Machine Tools	1981	Local	25,000	5.1
	TELCO	1982	Local	39,500	4.3

Note: a. The averages of engineers to total employment in the three countries are: Korea 8.9 per cent, Malaysia 7.6 per cent and India 6.5 per cent.

Sources: Korea from Enos (1992) and Yun (1994), Malaysia from Lall et al. (1994) and India from Lall (1987).

298

'capable' firms such as Domod and SIS Engineering. In the very small firms, the figures are difficult to interpret, because the presence of one person shows up as a large percentage. If these are ignored, the employment of *engineers* in the Ghanaian metalworking firms is less than *1 per cent of total employment.* This may be compared to some figures for the employment of engineers by large firms in engineering products in Korea, Malaysia, India and Sri Lanka (Tables 10.4 and 10.5). The average percentages of engineers in total employment in the other countries are: Korea 8.9 per cent, Malaysia 7.6 per cent, India 6.5 per cent and Sri Lanka 1.8 per cent.

These figures should not be taken as direct indications of skill gaps in Ghanaian firms, since the technological level of the firms in the other countries is far higher than those of the Ghanaian sample. However, this is less true of Sri Lankan firms, which are relatively small and in simple technologies, and so more comparable to the Ghanaian sample. This comparison is particularly revealing, since it is difficult otherwise to establish if Ghanaian firms have adequate technical manpower to achieve efficiency. Moreover, even the data on India, Korea and Malaysia are useful to illustrate the kind of skill upgrading that may be needed by Ghanaian industry if it is to enter more complex engineering activities.

Training

The level of employee skills of any firm is affected by its training strategies and by turnover of its employees. Training can take three main forms: (1) apprenticeship, which generally refers to training given to a young entrant who knows little about the skill in question, and who learns by working alongside an experienced worker; (2) on-the-job training, which generally refers to further hands-on skills imparted to a person who already has some theoretical knowledge of the work; and (3) formal employee training, where experienced employees are given formal training to refresh, increase or alter their skills.

It was possible to collect information on the numbers of employees sent by firms for external training, in Ghana and overseas. Table 10.3, above, showed these numbers for 1991, as a percentage of total employment. External training is undertaken by very few firms (nine in total), and seems to be very low in relation to the skill needs of the activities undertaken. Again, a comparison with Sri Lanka shows that there was considerably less sustained external training by garment and metalworking firms in Ghana (Table 10.4 above). By Korean standards, the extent of external training in the Ghanaian metalworking firms is also extremely low: Yun (1994) reports that the average percentage of employees sent on external training in total employment in five Korean-owned metalworking firms was as high as 29.2 per cent in 1993. Of the training offered by Ghanaian firms, most seems to be in management rather than technical skills, and is sporadic rather than sustained. There are few institutions available in the country to provide industry-specific training in activities such as garments and textiles, or furniture making.[24] It is therefore difficult to judge the contribution of the external training that does take place in the sample. There are no data available on training conducted internally by the sample firms. Few of the firms have separate training departments with separate budgets. However, it is possible to review qualitatively the internal training provided. These findings are reviewed by industry.

The *garment* end of the textile and garment industry in most developing countries does not require high levels of education among its shopfloor employees. It does, however, have to invest in training its workforce, especially where export markets, with very demanding standards, are served.[25] Only two firms have training programmes in this group: Nitra and Overseas Knitwear, the two technologically-capable firms. In Nitra, training was under the close supervision of the German production manager, by senior employees. New recruits get 3–4 weeks of training. All staff get occasional half-day courses by the production manager on quality control, clearly an important input into the quality edge that the firm enjoys over local competitors. This sort of personal and systematic attention to training is lacking in other firms.

All the *food-processing* firms provide on-the-job training for employees. Nestlé has the best formal training programme (probably the best of all the sample firms). Apart from the programmes for new recruits, Nestlé has annual training for all employees coordinated by an expatriate training officer. Technical training is conducted on the job by expatriate trainers. Upper management is sent to Nestlé's training centre in the parent's home country for courses in management and marketing. In general, the level of investment in human-capital development in the other food-processing firms seems to be geared to meeting basic production needs rather than to upgrade the stock for coping with technical change and competitiveness.

In *woodworking*, Furnart sets the highest standards of training. It does not take apprentices, but has an extended in-house training programme for production skills that runs over three years and foreign consultants will provide QC training periodically. By contrast, most other firms take recruits with minimal levels of schooling and give them apprenticeship training. The training period varies between two and six years. These firms also try to hire apprentices trained by other firms. They expressed no dissatisfaction with this system of recruitment and training, perhaps reflecting the low levels of skills that had to be imparted.

In *metalworking*, Tema Steel (too complex an activity to rely on apprentices) provides considerable on-the-job training. The new owners hired new recruits from middle schools, and provided intensive on-the-job training by the expatriate personnel. The level of skills was found to be well below that in India and it is felt that more formal on-the-job training systems need to be installed after the task of refurbishing the plant is completed.

Most other firms recruit from primary schools and give apprenticeship training along traditional lines as in woodworking (see above). Interestingly, they did not want technical school graduates for higher-level skills; their owners were suspicious of technical school graduates, and found their training 'too theoretical' and their wages too high. This may be a reflection of their lack of formal training and traditional craft background.

To sum up, there are ten firms in the sample (six in woodworking and four in metalworking) that use apprenticeships for training their workforces. Only two of these, Peewood and SIS Engineering, have been classified as technologically competent. Both have made adaptations to the traditional system to enhance its training potential. SIS Engineering recruits some workers with technical training for supervisory work along with primary school leavers for the shopfloor; it supplements apprenticeship with follow-up on-the-job training.

In general, the apprenticeship system seems well suited to the transmission of fairly simple manufacturing skills to workers with minimal formal education, with little change over the generations. It is less suited to training for the skills needed for modern manufacturing, where completely different types of skills from those possessed by traditional craftsmen may be required, and where a considerably higher level of education is necessary to operations. Even in activities where there is a role for traditional skills like metal- and woodworking, an upgrading of the apprenticeship system to encompass more formal education is called for.

POLICY IMPLICATIONS

The evidence suggests that Ghanaian industry operates with relatively low levels of human capital and invests little in upgrading that capital. There are differences between firms, and education and training show up as important determinants of technological competence. While this confirms expectations as well as the received wisdom from other countries, it is important to go beyond this. The most striking feature of the findings on Ghana is *how low overall levels of skill and competence in manufacturing industry* are. This means that technological and managerial capabilities remain well below the levels needed for Ghana to develop a dynamic industrial sector and to mount a sustained export drive based on new manufactured products (including higher-value-added processing of local natural resources). This has important implications for the theme we started with: the weak supply response of Ghana (and Africa as a whole) to policy reforms and import liberalization.

Let us look at the implications of this, not from the viewpoint of education policies but from that of *industrial development and industrialization strategy*. To some extent, Ghana's lagging competitiveness and dynamism clearly reflects the weak base of technical, managerial and workforce skills. This is not, of course, a uniquely Ghanaian problem. The whole of Sub-Saharan Africa faces severe shortages of skills, especially of technical skills relevant to modern industry.[26] For instance, in 1990 Korea alone had 411 thousand university students enrolled in technical subjects, compared to 111 thousand for Sub-Saharan Africa as a whole. And this does not take into account the quality of the technical training in Africa, which is likely to lag well behind the NIEs. Yet Korea was at roughly the same level of income as Ghana some three decades ago when the industrialization process started.

The importance of skills to industrial competitiveness is, of course, now widely recognized, and there is considerable effort to build and improve education and training structures in developed countries as well as in developing ones. In Sub-Saharan Africa, however, this problem is surprisingly absent in the policy discussion in the context of policy reform and SAPs. This is despite the attention paid to 'capability building' in Africa in many pronouncements by multilateral institutions.

Liberalization does not address any of the skill shortages that may be affecting the efficiency of African industry, yet many existing industries may become competitive if their human resources were improved. It is important to note that a certain amount of capability development has already taken place in many industrial activities; this is a valuable resource that should be conserved and built upon rather than dissipated by a shock therapy that leads to massive deindustrialization. Technological capabilities reside in *groups* of skilled and experienced persons rather than in individuals, and the destruction of enterprises means that the stock of accumulated knowledge is effectively destroyed even if the individuals concerned stay in the country. The design of SAPs should therefore include education and training as an *integral* part of the reform and restructuring process.

The provision of *specialized training* to industry is an important area of supply-side support in the process of structural adjustment.[27] These services are weak in much of Africa, and enterprises themselves (apart from the major multinationals) invest little in training their employees in modern technologies. In Africa there is a great shortage of experienced trainers to staff and manage industrial training systems, and this is the first bottleneck that governments should address in the context of adjustment. SAPs should pay explicit attention to the need for foreign trainers to teach local trainers in the most pressing skill needs of industry, and to the need to set up viable local training systems in the longer term. The problem is once more of the shortage of human resources, and has to be tackled at source.

The levels of skills and capabilities needed by industry also need to be enhanced by providing *technical extension services* to industry, especially to small and medium enterprises (SMEs). Those technical extension services that exist in much of Africa are largely ineffective in providing the kind of inputs that enterprises need to upgrade to competitive levels. The Ghana study showed clearly how the numerous institutions that had been set up to help industrial technology contributed practically nothing to enterprises (see Lall et al. 1994). At the same time, the experience of East Asia shows that the governments there played a much larger role in upgrading the technologies used by their enterprises than interventionist governments in Africa, and that many of these services were extremely demanding in resources.[28] It is also clear that such services should have formed intrinsic parts of SAPs if they were to have any long-term effect on industrial upgrading.

So much for supply-side support to improve industrial skills and capabilities. Let us conclude with the implications for reform to the *incentive system*. The analysis of Ghanaian capability development suggests that a gradual and controlled process of opening up, accompanied by a *strategy* of industrial restructuring and upgrading, is to be preferred to a rapid and sweeping exposure to market forces envisaged by the 'ideal' SAP. The speed of liberalization should be based on a realistic assessment of which activities are viable in the medium term, with the process geared to the learning and 'relearning' needs of various activities. The strategy should be developed in collaboration with the industrial sector, and should be pre-announced so that enterprises have time to adjust.[29] Once announced, however, it is imperative to stick to the programme so that there is no chance of backsliding and allowing inefficient performers to survive indefinitely.

In this entire process the government should retain powers to guide resource allocation, but in a clear and transparent manner, and with strict requirements of capability development. Unlike earlier strategies of import substitution where governments offered protection with little discrimination between activities, no time limit and no requirements of international competitiveness, this model of adjustment, based on strategies pursued in East Asia, places strong pressures on industries to invest in building up new capabilities to face the import and export competition within a limited period. It is designed to overcome market failures, not to ignore them. It involves close monitoring of the progress of liberalization, and it requires that the government is able to address the supply-side needs of industries (see below) along with allowing a phased process of liberalization. The 'ideal' SAP can, by contrast, be extremely wasteful by dispersing and destroying the capabilities already built up and can retard the future development of new and diverse capabilities in industry by ignoring the market failures that exist in this process.

To recommend a more gradual and nuanced strategy of liberalization is *not* to suggest that African countries should simply slow down the adjustment process. They should instead *actively prepare* for it in the grace period provided. There is, however, a strong risk of *government failure*. Most African governments do not at this time have the capabilities to mount effective interventions in support of industrialization. The launching pad of any reform must be improvements in government capabilities themselves. Evidence suggests that these can be improved by training, reorganization of the civil service, better performance incentives and monitoring, and greater insulation from the political process.[30] Without such capability development, *even the market-friendly strategies recommended by the World Bank have little chance of success*. At the same time, it is not recommended that African governments attempt the kind of detailed and pervasive interventions practised in a country such as Korea; this does impose tremendous demands on the government and runs very high risks of hijacking and abuse. The correct form and level of selectivity that can be managed by particular governments at particular times is itself a subject that deserves close study, but is ignored by donors who insist that all selectivity is undesirable.

To conclude, therefore, there is no controversy on the need for 'reform' to get African industry moving. Past strategies clearly have not worked and new strategies are needed: the debate is really on what form these should take. This depends, in turn, on how efficient markets are, and what role governments should play in improving them. On the arguments advanced here, market failures are rife and structural adjustment must be pursued more gradually, with greater control, strategy and involvement by the government. Clearly, many African governments presently lack the capability to mount effective strategies. However, given the need to remedy market deficiencies to achieve sustainable industrial development, the first step in adjustment should be to improve their intervention capabilities. The evidence on the benefits of past SAPs for industrial growth and diversification does not provide much support for the present World Bank 'line'. It is therefore regrettable that the world's premier development institution considers it necessary to pursue such a line. Perhaps the design of adjustment should start with a serious reconsideration of its own conceptual apparatus and beliefs.

NOTES

1. See Fontaine (1992), Steel and Webster (1992), Leechor (1994) and World Bank (1994).
2. For a further analysis of the approach and the sample, see Lall et al. (1994).
3. See, for instance, Fagerberg (1988) and Lazonick (1993).
4. See Katz (ed.) (1987), Lall (1987, 1992b, 1993a and b), Enos (1992). Bell and Pavitt (1993) and Wignaraja (forthcoming).

5. See, for instance, World Bank (1991) and (1993).
6. The underlying arguments are analysed in Lall (1994).
7. See Mosley et al. (1991) and Stein (ed.) (1995).
8. For a recent attempt by the World Bank on Africa see its 1994 study on *Adjustment in Africa*.
9. World Bank (1994: 67), and Leechor (1994).
10. African Development Bank (1994: 57-62).
11. Ibid.: Table 27.
12. Ibid.: 61.
13. Apart from the enclave operation of aluminium processing or protected activities like government-owned petroleum refining, these include some food processing, furniture, cement, simple metal products, and uniforms for the army or schools.
14. The values of the main non-traditional manufactured exports in 1991 were: aluminium $5.5m., wood products $6.2m. (of which furniture accounted for $3.6m. and other wood products for $2.6m.), canned foods $0.3m., tobacco $0.4m., soaps $0.6m., machetes and iron rods $0.8m., and others $1.3m.
15. Lall et al. (1994).
16. Ibid.
17. See Lall (1992a) on levels of technological capability and human capital in Africa in general.
18. For a detailed analysis of different forms of technological capabilities in Ghanaian firms, see Lall et al.
19. See Lall (1992b) for an explanation of what these categories comprise.
20. Market segmentation may well exist in Ghana (as in all developing countries, formal credit markets tend to be biased against small firms). The analysis of the panel data in Lall et al. (1994) suggests that such segmentation exists, but that it does not account for the whole difference in performance between firms of similar sizes. The other factors that show up as important determinants of competence in the next section suggest that segmented factor markets play a relatively minor role.
21. In the case of large professionally managed firms (in this sample mainly multinationals) the entrepreneur is taken to be the chief executive officer of the firm.
22. Enterprises of larger size and with more mature organizational structures do not need to rely on the (partly random) presence of a technologically-gifted person to catalyse the firm. They would tend to have institutional mechanisms to identify, recruit and assign due responsibility to such persons. This is one of the advantages of large size and functionally specialized organizations that was mentioned in the analytical framework.
23. For a fuller analysis of the acquisition of technological capabilities in the sample, see Wignaraja (forthcoming).
24. The Kumasi Technical Institute trains young people in woodworking, but does not seem to provide more advanced employee training.
25. See Lall and Wignaraja (1994).
26. Lall (1992a).
27. See Lucas (1994).
28. See Stein (ed.) (1995) for description of industrial policy in various NIEs and Japan. The NIEs and Japan provided substantial technical extension services to industry in the areas of quality control and metrology, research and development, information on sources of technology and assistance in the purchase of foreign technology.
29. See Lall (1993b).
30. The World Bank's (1993) *Miracle* study provides many useful insights into how Asian governments improved their intervention capabilities.

REFERENCES

African Development Bank (1994), *African Development Report*, Abijan.

Bell, M. and K. Pavitt (1993), 'Technological Accumulation and Industrial Growth: Contrasts Between Developed and Developing Countries', *Industrial and Corporate Change*, **2** (2), 157–210.

Enos, J. (1992), *The Creation of Technological Capabilities in Developing Countries*, London: Pinter.

Fagerberg, J. (1988), 'International Competitiveness', *Economic Journal*, **2**, 355–74.

Fontaine, J.M. (1992), 'Bias Overkill: Removal of Anti-Export Bias and Manufacturing Investment: Ghana 1983–89', in R. Adhikari, C. Kirkpatrick and J. Weiss (eds), *Industrial and Trade Policy Reform in Developing Countries*, Manchester: Manchester University Press, pp. 120–134.

Hussain, I. and R. Faruqee (eds) (1994), *Adjustment in Africa: Lessons from the Country Studies*, Washington, DC: World Bank.

Katz, J.M. (ed.) (1987), *Technology Generation in Latin American Manufacturing Industries*, London: Macmillan.

Lall, S. (1987), *Learning to Industrialize*, London: Macmillan.

Lall, S. (1992a), 'Structural Problems of African Industry', in F. Stewart, S. Lall and S. Wangwe (eds), *Alternative Development Strategies in Sub-Saharan Africa*, London: Macmillan, pp. 103–44.

Lall, S. (1992b), 'Technological Capabilities and Industrialization', *World Development*, **20** (2), 165–86.

Lall, S. (1993a), 'Understanding Technology Development', *Development and Change*, **24** (4), 719–53.

Lall, S. (1993b), 'Trade Policies for Development: a Policy Prescription for Africa', *Development Policy Review*, **11** (1), 47–65.

Lall, S. (1994), 'Industrial Policy: The Role of Government in Promoting Industrial and Technological Development', *UNCTAD Review*, 65–89.

Lall, S., G.B. Navaretti, S. Teitel and G. Wignaraja (1994), *Technology and Enterprise Development: Ghana Under Structural Adjustment*, London: Macmillan.

Lall, S. and G. Wignaraja (1994), 'Foreign Involvement by European Firms and Garment Exports by Developing Countries', *Asia-Pacific Development Journal*, 1 (2), 21–48.

Lazonick, W. (1993), 'Learning and the Dynamics of International Competitive Advantage', in R. Thomson (ed.), *Learning and Technological Change*, London: Macmillan, pp. 172–92.

Leechor, C. (1994), 'Ghana: Forerunner in Adjustment', in Hussain and Faruqee (eds), pp. 153–92.

Lucas, R.E.B. (1994), 'Impact of Structural Adjustment on Training Needs', *International Labour Review*, **133** (5–6), 677–94.

Mosley, P., J. Harrigan and J. Toye (1991), *Aid and Power: The World Bank and Policy-Based Lending*, London: Routledge.

Steel, W.F. and L. Webster (1992), 'How Small Enterprises in Ghana have Responded to Adjustment', *World Bank Economic Review*, **6** (3), 423–38.

Stein, H. (ed.) (1995), *Asian Industrialization and Africa: Studies in Policy Alternatives to Structural Adjustment*, London: Macmillan.

Wignaraja, G. (forthcoming), *Trade Policy, Technology and Export Performance: Sri Lanka's Liberalization Experience*, London: Macmillan.

World Bank (1991), *World Development Report 1991*, New York, Oxford University Press.

World Bank (1993), *The East Asian Miracle–Economic Growth and Public Policy*, New York: Oxford University Press.

World Bank (1994), *Adjustment in Africa: Reforms, Results, and the Road Ahead*, New York: Oxford University Press.

Yun, M. (1994), 'Effects of Sub-Contracting Relationship on Technological Capability of Korean Automotive Suppliers', Doctoral thesis in progress, Oxford University.

Index